Dear Laura,

Published and distributed by Merack Publishing
Jackson, USA
www.merackpublishing.com

Library of Congress Control Number: 2025909393

Elliott Alexandra, Laura
Dear Laura, A Lost Chapter of WWII: A Father-Daughter Adventure of Courage, Faith & Freedom

ISBN
Paperback 978-1-964421-09-4
Hardcover 978-1-964421-15-5
eBook 978-1-964421-10-0

A LOST CHAPTER OF WWII

A Father-Daughter Adventure
of Courage, Faith & Freedom

Laura Alexandra Elliott

THE DUTCH EAST INDIES & SOUTH PACIFIC 1941

MONGOLIA

MANCHURIA

KOREA

CHINA

PORT OF MOJI (KYUSHU)

NAGASAKI

OKINAWA

INDIA

BURMA

HONG KONG

FORMOSA (TAIWAN)

PHILIPPINES

SIAM

FRENCH INDO-CHINA

MANILA

SINGAPORE

SUMATRA

BORNEO

ULU SIAU

CELEBES

DUTCH EAST INDIES

JAVA

BALI

AUSTRALIA

USSR

JAPAN

TOKYO

NAGOYA

BATAVIA (JAKARTA) JAVA

BANDUNG

PANGANDARAN

YOGYAKARTA

MT BROMO

BALI

UBUD

WAKE IS.

IWO JIMA

MARIANA ISLANDS

GUAM

MARSHALL ISLANDS

PALAU
ISLAND

CAROLINE ISLANDS

GILBERT ISLANDS

NEW GUINEA

SOLOMON ISLANDS

GUADALCANAL

Japanese Occupation of The Dutch East Indies & South Pacific, February 1942

MONGOLIA

MANCHURIA

KOREA

CHINA

PORT OF MOJI (KYUSHU)

NAGASAKI

INDIA

BURMA

OKINAWA

FORMOSA (TAIWAN)

HONG KONG

PHILIPPINES

SIAM

FRENCH INDO-CHINA

MANILA

"TEIA MARU" (HELL SHIP)

SINGAPORE

ULU SIAU

SUMATRA

BORNEO

CELEBES

DUTCH EAST INDIES

JAVA

BALI

AUSTRALIA

USSR

JAPAN
TOKYO
NAGOYA

BATAVIA (JAKARTA)   JAVA
BANDUNG
PANGANDARAN   MT BROMO   BALI
YOGYAKARTA
UBUD

WAKE IS.

IWO JIMA

MARIANA ISLANDS

GUAM

MARSHALL ISLANDS

PALAU
SLAND

CAROLINE ISLANDS

GILBERT ISLANDS

NEW GUINEA

SOLOMON ISLANDS

GUADALCANAL

To God from whom all blessings flow and will flow

To Mom & Dad,
Your joy and abiding faith
are a constant inspiration

To the captain and crew of the U.S. Navy Destroyer USS Lardner who
saved my family

To Candice, Margaux, and my grandchildren

To my husband Jerry & Lucy, my muse

To Reinier and the memory of Grandpa, Grandma, and Aletta

To Suzy, Mike, and Mark

To the Truth

CONTENTS

The Family

(Grandpa) Alexander Augustus Vilhelmus Josefus Hasenstab, born Cernica, Yugoslavia, 1892

(Grandma) Irene Alwine Elizabeth Émilie Hasenstab-Kelling, born Ulu Siau, a small island in the Sangihe island group north of the Celebes, 1899

(Great Aunt) Fredike ("Freida") Kelling, born Driebergen, Netherlands, 1890

(Aunt) Aletta Paula Hasenstab, born Batavia (Jakarta), Java, 1921

(Dad) Hans Helmut Hasenstab, born Bandung, Java, 1924

(Uncle) Reinier Gottfried Hasenstab, born Hilversum, Netherlands, 1935

(Mom) June Catherine Hasen, born 1928

Laura Alexandra Elliott, born 1963

(Daughter) Candice Lauren Elliott, born Los Angeles, CA 1986

(Daughter) Margaux Jo Elliott, born Los Angeles, CA 1989

(Grandson) Algernon Elliott Pedley, born Santa Cruz, CA 2021

(Grandson) Reinier Joseph Pedley, born Santa Cruz, CA 2023

Our Happy Birthday Song

Alle Vögel sind schon da,
alle Vögel, alle!
Welch ein Singen, Musiziern,
Pfeifen, Zwitschern, Tireliern!
Frühling will nun einmarschiern,
kommt mit Sang und Schalle.

Wie sie alle lustig sind,
flink und froh sich regen!
Amsel, Drossel, Fink und Star
und die ganze Vogelschar
wünschen dir ein frohes Jahr,
lauter Heil und Segen.

Was sie uns verkünden nun,
nehmen wir zu Herzen:
Wir auch wollen lustig sein,
lustig wie die Vögelein,
hier und dort, feldaus, feldein,
singen, springen, scherzen.

All the birds are already here,
All the birds, all!
What singing, music-playing,
Whistling, chirping, trilling!
Spring wants to come now,
It comes with songs and sounds.

How cheerful they all are,
They move, nimble and gay!
Blackbirds, thrushes, finches and starlings,
And the whole flock of birds
Wishes you a happy new year,
Greater well-being and abundance.

What they declare to us now
Goes straight to our hearts:
We want to be happy too,
Happy like the little birds,
Here and there, in the fields and out,
Singing, jumping, joking around.

AUTHOR'S NOTE

Dad had an uncanny capacity for joy. People often said he flashed a Jimmy Carter smile and even looked like him, too. He loved Mom, birthdays, his garden, and the best of everything—including coveted tables at five-star restaurants (away from drafts), Godiva chocolate, silk smoking jackets (he rarely drank and didn't smoke), and capturing the world's most breathtaking sites in photographs and sketchbooks while traveling as an itinerant hydroelectric engineer and lover of the exotic, often traveling with Mom.

His joie de vivre filled everything our family did, especially birthday celebrations. The tradition was the same for all of us. On my birthdays, just before dawn in the kitchen of our home in suburban Chicago, Mom lovingly lit every candle on her freshly baked German log roll birthday cake with chocolate buttercream frosting (a la Antoinette Pope). Aglow in candlelight, she carried the cake on a silver tray with my dad, brothers, and sister close behind, parading in their pajamas up the stairs and down the hall singing birthday songs in German and English. As they sang, candlelight flooded my dark room when they entered. I sleepily scooched over so they could sit on my bed.

After their serenade, I closed my eyes and made my birthday wish. The dreaminess of those groggy candlelit moments cast a kind of spell making me believe that my wish could come true. Taking a deep breath, I opened my eyes and blew out the candles—always with one to grow on. Opening mostly handmade cards and a few small gifts displayed on another silver tray made me feel even more special, and often included ones from my Aunts Aletta and Dora in England, and from Grandpa and Aunt Freida in Holland. On my sixteenth birthday, my parents gave me my first bottle of perfume, *Miss Dior* by Oscar De La Renta. I'll never forget how special the small bottle with its signature black-and-white checked label made me feel.

Back then, I didn't know why Mom always baked the same birthday cakes with a candle to grow on. I didn't know why the cake and cards were carried on silver trays; or why we sang birthday songs in German and English. I didn't know why Dad never settled for anything but the best. I never knew why he loved pancakes with pure Canadian maple syrup so much, and ate them and chocolate like a man with a hollow leg, or why he was such a food and movie connoisseur. I didn't know why he loved his garden and the Lord so dearly. Why do parents do the things they do? But I know now. The smallest of the things that Dad loved and did, especially his beloved traditions, had unimaginable backstories.

Between a few important birthday celebrations, Dad and I uncovered the truth about his haunting past as a WWII Japanese POW and our family's mysterious fate during the war. Our journey began during my oldest daughter's first birthday (she's now a mother herself) and culminated on Dad's 92nd birthday, which would be his last. Since the Internet or email didn't exist in the mid-1980s, we corresponded through snail mail. I wrote my questions longhand and he sent his replies the same way.

Uncovering his story began with a single question that led to hundreds more like: What was the experience of having the horrors of Pearl Harbor occur in your part of the world, causing a deep-seated fear that the war might come to you next? When it did, how did our family survive captivity?

Our letters continued throughout the years from wherever I made my home, which changed dramatically. I started my correspondence as a young married woman and mother from three different family homes in Los Angeles, then I wrote from Big Sur, Pacific Grove, and Carmel Valley, California as an empty nester. After my divorce, I traveled the world to discover the answers Dad couldn't provide. In doing so, I also answered the many questions I had about life and love. During my travels I sent dispatches to Mom and Dad from far-flung locales including some of the settings of Dad's story in Indonesia and Australia.

Dad once wrote that it's much harder to ask a question then find its answer. My most perplexing and disconcerting questions took decades to formulate—*Why would the Empire of Japan imprison our family and four other radio engineers and their families, 22 people in all, in Indonesia then move them to Japan? And why would one of them die?* When we began our search for answers together I had no idea that the quest would take most of my life and send me on a few around-the-world adventures. Dad was one of my biggest supporters. I felt his presence and encouragement with me in extravagant, playful ways as I continued to seek out the answers on my own after he died.

Dad never returned to Java after the war, although he lived there in his heart for the rest of his life through his cooking, stories, and artwork. As Dad became frail, he once said, "You are my eyes and ears in the world now."

I melted upon hearing those words. He and Mom had brought the world home to me as a child, and I delighted in doing the same for them. While growing up, I learned about the world on exotic trips I took with Mom and Dad as well as from the award-winning, stunning photos Dad snapped while working in remote locations and during his world travels with Mom.

American Society of Civil Engineers, Photo First Prize, awarded to Dad in 1985. Guri Spillway, Venezuela.

And also from his slideshows. In Dad's study, I remember laying on my stomach next to my brothers and sister, head in my hands, waiting for the show to begin. Dad rolled the projector screen from its metal base to secure it to the top of a metal pole. The musty smell of vinyl scented the air. Then he'd turn on the slide projector in the dark room and a beam of light illuminated every speck of dust as an image filled the large, white screen. I can still hear the click, click, click of the loaded slide cassette atop the projector as he cycled through his images. Sometimes we laid on the floor with our cousins, sometimes with friends and neighbors, sometimes with visitors from foreign lands, and later with our own kids.

In an instant, Dad brought the world home to us—the pristine beauty of his new bride at the Taj Mahal, a helicopter journey into the heart of the Venezuelan jungle hovering above the 3200-foot drop of Angel Falls, the world's tallest uninterrupted waterfall; a walk through the streets of El Salvador with steel drummers smiling; traveling along the shores of the Dominican Republic; into China's forbidden city; and surrounded by an erupting Icelandic volcano with Dad dressed in what looked like a spacesuit, nearly singed by a lava flow.

As he clicked through the slides, Dad told us lots of stories. He was a master storyteller and relished taking center stage. One of his most memorable tales was set back in the 1960s and featured a 3 a.m. road trip to Búrfell, a hydroelectric power station[1], with Russian hydroelectric engineer coworkers on an unpaved road in the Icelandic countryside. Suddenly, in the middle of nowhere, the Russians insisted that the driver stop the car. When Dad asked why, they simply said in their very limited English, "It is finished." They quickly pulled marinated lamb out of the trunk and had a spontaneous roadside BBQ. The meal, called shashlik, a kind of shish-k-bab, tasted so good that Dad got the recipe and shashlik became a part of our family's Fourth of July celebrations during the heart of the Cold War.

---

1   https://www.landsvirkjun.com/powerstations/burfell

Dad's study was a place full of treasures, adventure, and wonder—a kind of museum where he had curated items from his travels. A yellow sign with black letters on his study door read: *Inn á eigin ábyrgð*, "Enter at your own risk" in Icelandic. Inside, on one wall hung a beautiful Japanese scroll, a few Javanese Wayang shadow puppets[2], wood carvings (some he carved himself), awards, degrees, small statues, and his photos. This collection of artwork was part of the backdrop of our lives.

A variety of award-winning pictures of orchids, hibiscus, and waterfalls hung on the wall. One photo featured the stunning cascade of Angel Falls; another a rainbow-laced shot of the Cataratas do Iguaçu, the world's largest broken waterfalls, some 275 of them, dotting the border between Brazil and Argentina. Other photos captured his own hydroelectric designs—including the spillways of Guri dam, also known as Raúl Leoni Hydroelectric Plant in Venezuela.

Dad was proud of the giant steel posts he placed beside the electrical power plant at Guri in the shape of his initials, H. H. They would be his legacy, he said. When I was a little girl in the late 60s, Guri was the world's largest hydroelectric project with 10,000 megawatts of installed capacity. The dam Dad designed harnessed the previously unbridled power of the Caroní River "just before it poured into the mythical Orinoco."[3]

"Jules Verne called it "The Mighty Orinoco" in a novel published in 1898, and it was the symbolic prison of Daniel Defoe's illustrious *Robinson Crusoe.* The most famous castaway in history spent 28 years in solitude on an island near the mouth of the river. If only he'd had a strong enough boat, he could have reached the shore and discovered the

---

2 "*Wayang Kulit,* an Indonesian form of shadow puppetry, holds the audience's attention with riveting storylines executed masterfully by the *dhalang,* or puppeteer." https://asiasociety.org/new-york/wayang-kulit-indonesias-extraordinary-shadow-puppetry-tradition

3 https://dialogochino.net/en/climate-energy/32577-venezuelas-electricity-emergency-swallows-up-tens-of-millions-of-dollars/

celebrated Orinoco Delta where he may have met the Warao Indians, the traditional inhabitants of this astounding 25,000 square kilometer labyrinth of 300 channels, whose population is now estimated at around 30,000 people."[4]

I believe a hidden message lay in all of Dad's photos. Beauty found in surrender. The power of breathtaking, jaw-dropping, heart-pounding awe. They relayed an important message to me as I grew up—"impossible" beauty, "impossible" hope, and "impossible" joy are possible. Dad harnessed the power of the "impossible" to create a better world at a time when the world felt like it was falling apart. When my brothers, sister, and I were required to practice "duck-and-cover" drills at school in case of a nuclear attack.

Dad took the time to break down barriers between people and foster peace through the common language of energy[5]. Over the years many decorations and medals joined the photos and carvings. In 1985, he was decorated by the Venezuelan government with a medal for Excellence in Work for the Guri Project. The Icelandic government honored Dad's work on the Burfell Project by awarding him the Knighthood of the Blue Falcon of Iceland.[6]

Mementos of Dad's years of civic service in the villages where he lived and where he attended church also found their way to the wall. The photos, awards, and mementos only slightly pared down over the years as he and Mom downsized and his study found a home in

---

4   https://escales.ponant.com/en/warao-orinoco/

5   His hydroelectric projects in chronological order: Junior Designer, Snowy Mountains Hydroelectric Authority, Australia, 1950-51: Harza Engineering Co., Chicago, 1951-1999: Junior Designer, 1951-54, Gavins Point Powerhouse, Missouri River; Box Canyon Dam, Pend Oreille River. Section Head, 1954-60; Priest Rapids and Wanapum Dams on the Columbia River, Derbendi Khan, Diyala River, Iraq. Department Head, 1960-75; Guri Dam Initial Stage, Caroni River, Venezuela; Burfell Project, Thjorsa River, Iceland; Cerron Grande and San Lorenzo Dams, Rio Lempa River, El Salvador; Bao and Lopez Angostura Projects on the Yaque del Norte River, Dominican Republic. Vice President, 1975-91: Guri Dam Final Stage, Caroni River, Venezuela.

6   https://www.icelandicroots.com/post/2017/09/18/the-icelandic-order-of-the-falcon

smaller spaces. He would go on to author books and articles, including *Davis' Handbook of Applied Hydraulics* and articles about the projects he worked on, including one about the Lopez Angostura Power Tunnel in the Dominican Republic.

But as a little girl, I thought his biggest achievement was the community swimming pool he helped to construct for the village of LaGrange Park, Illinois. My brothers, sister, and I swam there most days between Memorial Day and Labor Day in suburban Chicago where we grew up. I remember the smell of Dial soap as we sudsed up in the showers before taking a swim, Coppertone-scented air of the pool deck, and the smoky grill where we ate yummy hamburgers and BBQ potato chips at the snack bar, a rare treat on a lazy summer day. Our family was given an honorary life-long membership at the Village Field Club,[7] which is still going strong.

Inspired by Dad, I've dedicated my life to building my own "impossible" beauty, hope, and joy by telling inspiring stories that bring understanding and healing to a world thirsty for peace.

A few years before Dad died and about three decades into my search for answers about what happened to our family, I decided to take my first research trip to Australia and Indonesia. The night before I departed, I attended a dear friend's birthday party at a winery in Los Angeles. Even though I didn't know many people, I had fun. As I headed out the door at the end of the evening, an older lady I'd never met before (or seen since) walked up to me with a smile.

"I wanted to meet you all evening, but didn't get the chance," she said. "If you don't mind, I'd like to share a powerful prayer with you before you go; it's changed my life. I feel you are going to need it."

---

7   https://www.villagefieldclub.com/

"Sure," I said with some hesitation. Maybe she'd had a little too much wine? *This should be interesting*, I thought.

"The prayer is simple but powerful . . . God, please bring me the people I need, and bring me to the people who need me."

The look in my eye caused her to take my hands in hers.

"Let's pray it together," she said. So we did.

After our Amens, she added, "Pray it when you need encouragement."

I believe that single prayer changed my life too, for I began to pray it daily. Without her prayer, I wouldn't have been able to write this story. God brought me to the people and places I needed to see. He also brought me to many people who needed me.

From 2014 to 2023 I followed my dreams and began to journey to the center of my own heart as I researched and wrote this story from many exotic locations—Jakarta, Bandung, Yogyakarta, Ubud, Kathmandu, Paris, Prague, and from the shores of The Bali Sea to Finisterre, Spain, to name a few. Then finally writing in Santa Cruz, California; Ketchum, Idaho; and on a yacht named *Blue Moon* on the Salish Sea in the San Juan Islands, Washington. In humble settings and sometimes extravagant ones; always with a cast of caring people, and a few angels, who not only lifted my spirits but also fed my creativity and soul by helping me explore worlds I might never have seen without them. And answering questions I wouldn't have even known to ask.

I believe the lady I met that night in the City of Angels was an angel. We all have them, don't we? People who show up where we are and say (or whisper) the exact thing we need to hear to do the impossible.

I didn't know it at the time, but I would need lots of encouragement since my quest met so much resistance. It ranged from my own doubts in my ability to tell the story to well-meaning people who questioned where my research led. Some thought my findings weren't plausible, let alone possible. In the wake of such crushing pushback, I had a choice—abandon the project or write unabashedly. What started as an attempt to solve a family mystery revealed a lost chapter of WWII. I am certain that more chapters will undoubtedly be written by people who can illuminate this intrigue further.

When Dad and I began our quest nearly four decades ago, I knew only two facts about his WWII experience—the dramatic story of how he came to be born in Bandung, Java in 1924; and the fact that he stood six-foot-two inches tall and weighed eighty-five pounds when the U.S. Marines rescued him and most of our family off a beach at Hamamatsu, Japan, in September 1945. He had spent three-and-a-half years as a Japanese POW, captured in Indonesia and rescued in Japan. I wanted to know what happened in between.

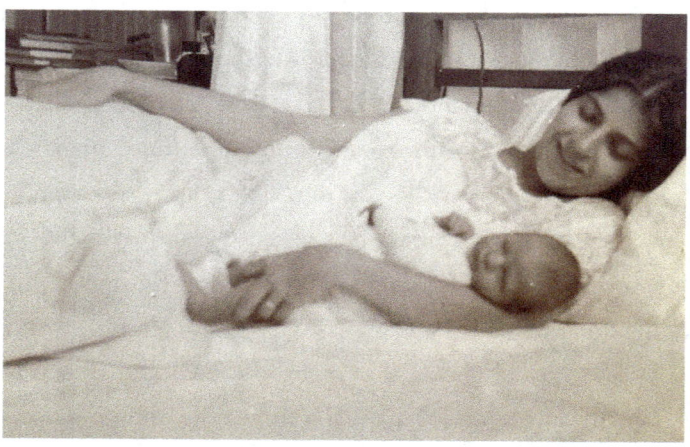

Grandma Irene (Reni) and Dad in 1924, Bandung, Java, Indonesia.

Dad was brave to let me into his secret world. During our quest for answers, I needed to show him the patience he'd shown me while growing up—like when he helped me solve math problems that brought me to tears as a little girl; or when I'd release the clutch too fast while learning to drive a stick. I thought of the times he helped me navigate the ups and downs of serious boyfriends; gave me away in marriage; eased my move across the country to Los Angeles; supported me on the journey of motherhood; and then helped me get over the agony of divorce.

While he was alive, we found our answers talking, laughing, strolling around ponds, walking the beach, watching movies, playing a little chess, and drinking lots of tea while eating Mom's chocolate chip cookies. After he died, he communicated in other powerful ways. The developing narrative evolved into something more than a loving Q & A. When I realized that I just might be writing history, the weight of the task overwhelmed me. *What if I got it wrong? Was I qualified to write such a story?* In order to finish, I needed to silence self-doubt, surrender to the story, and let it take me where it would.

The book came together from the primary research offered by my dad; his brother, my Uncle Reinier; and his sister, my Aunt Aletta, and through the letters of Dad's mom and dad, my grandma and grandpa, who I only met through their letters and diaries.

While the information was valid from a research perspective, I couldn't simply follow those breadcrumbs unquestioningly. I had to use the skills I'd developed while working for the digital arm of the newsroom at the *Los Angeles Times* in order to independently verify their stories. I easily corroborated some while others needed a pickaxe and goggles. For decades, I thought that the most mysterious stories had died with Grandpa. But they were eventually uncovered when miracles led me to the right place at the right time in the right part of the world.

Dad and I pieced his story together within our letters and also over stolen moments during vacations spent together in Illinois, Florida, and California. He wouldn't let us part until he brought out his 18-month calendar and asked me to circle the dates when I would see him again. Up until this point in my life, I had never understood his fascination (some might call obsession) with mastering time. As a child, this inclination drove me crazy. He had itineraries for family vacations worked out down to the minute.

As I wrote, I better understood Dad's fascination with time and history, particularly WWII. For what would be more precious to a man who'd lost over three years of his life as a Japanese POW than the history of the war and living every minute to the full? Time meant more when it was taken away. In business, he was, somewhat surprisingly, a student of the Japanese theory of Time Management.

Over the years, he'd send me large manila envelopes filled with the latest research on how to be more efficient with my time (and included other topics, most concerning how to avoid the impending doom of the latest worrying headlines). I'd like to say that receiving Dad's letters was like receiving little treasures, but that wouldn't be entirely true. Part of his trauma was to do everything he could to protect himself and his family from experiencing danger ever again—any kind of danger. So along with the answers to my questions, he sent what I fondly called *packages of fear*, large envelopes filled with articles, books, and documentation about the things I'd need to be most afraid of—the coming BIG LA earthquake, financial crises, water shortages, possible dam failures, pandemics, you get the idea.

My fear around the envelopes became so palpable, that after a few years, I asked my then-husband to open them and let me know what he discovered inside. Tucked away within the packages, among the fear, treasures usually awaited my discovery and exploration. Some begged to see the light of day even when I didn't feel I had the ability to take them in.

The packages were a metaphor for Dad—fear-filled and joy-filled. Together he and I opened his internal package of fear and brought its contents into the light. Our exploration unlocked mysteries that had been sealed tight in his memory, almost completely destroyed by trauma and the fog of war. I found myself using truth to confront the problem of conquering confusion brought on by trauma.

One packet of fear included an article about how to distinguish important tasks from crucial ones and how the crucial must be prioritized before the important. I didn't really get it as I was a busy working mother too much in the weeds of life to have such an academic, albeit important, barometer of time. I'd seen writing this story as important. Completing this book became crucial the day Mom joined Dad for their first ballroom dance in heaven a handful of years ago.

But I didn't know how. My journey naively began with a search for answers to my questions. However, the real job was to answer Dad's. And as I did, many more stories came to light. Tangents I eventually realized would be best served in books or screenplays of their own. I finally decided that the most authentic way to tell the tale would be as it was revealed to me—in little snippets, because that's how we tell each other stories. We sit around a campfire and talk to each other. We discuss one fact which leads to another, and we put the pieces together.

So, if you will, imagine us sitting around a campfire. Through the crackling flames, we hear voices of the past. Those voices enlighten our present and future. They whisper about how quickly fortunes can change. How, in the blink of an eye, the oppressed can become the oppressor, and vice versa. How discrimination and exploitation can take on many varied, insidious forms.

The book acquired new significance as I wrote during the Corona Era, in the post-Cold War world threatened by a possible WWIII, with authoritarian rule on the rise once again. History has lessons for people who believe lies and perpetuate them. The vainglorious entitled elite blind to the suffering of others as peril swells in plain sight. And yet, a blanket of the ordinary cloaks our day-to-day activities, however nefarious, giving them the feeling of normalcy even if they are part of a sea change, in Dad's case, a tsunami.

I found the NIOD, Netherlands Institute for war, holocaust, and genocide studies[8], in Amsterdam to be a tremendous resource. When I first started researching, all the WWII documents archived were in Dutch, a language I don't speak and found impossible to try to learn. So, while there was an online database, there was a very long, tedious period of time where I needed to translate everything I wanted to explore. But over the years, during the many starts-and-stops of writing this story, the NIOD had coincidentally translated the online database documents into English.

This breakthrough along with many I made with acquaintances on my world-wide travels helped me put together pieces of Dad's story that he either couldn't know, or was unwilling or unable to share during our time together. To this end, the English translation of Ineke Van Der Wal's book, *The Temple with the Chrysanthemums: Dutch Prisoners of War in Tokyo*, has been a wealth of information about Dad's time in Japan. What follows is my memoir along with reimaginings of Dad's story based on true events. Some names have been changed. Some of

---

8   "Almost none of the Japanese archives in the Dutch East Indies were recovered. Most of the documents on the Japanese and their rule come from post-war institutions that dealt with the trial of Japanese war criminals." https://www.niod.nl/en/frequently-asked-questions/does-niod-have-material-japanese-camps-and-prisons

the language used in the letters and accounts are considered offensive today, but they have been unedited to stay true to the point of view of the time, while also honoring how language gives us historical and cultural context.

"Time does not heal all wounds;
it buries them in very shallow graves."

— Anonymous

THE BEST DAYS OF YOUR LIFE

"But a stranger in a strange land, he is no one:
men know him not —
and to know not is to care not for."

—Jonathan Swift

In July 1987, at my home nestled in the hills of Echo Park in downtown Los Angeles, my brother Mike joined me and my then-husband in the celebration of our daughter's first birthday. I stood behind Candice and held her hands in mine, helping her walk barefoot on the expansive redwood deck just outside the French doors of our dining room.

We basically lived in a tree house. Most of our square footage was made up of that outdoor deck, protected by a march of Cypress trees that descended either side of one hundred stairs, terraced every ten steps. The deck was our living room. We loved the house and so did Dad. In my kitchen later that year, he held my huge stuffed Mickey Mouse, the one that he'd bought for me when I was a little girl during our first trip to Disney World. He played with Candice who was sitting in her bouncy chair, giggling, as Mickey gave her kisses.

Then, Dad pulled me aside and said, "These are the best days of your life."

I have to admit his words shocked me. As a young, twenty-three-year-old woman, the idea of already living the best part of my life troubled me. *Was he right?* I wondered.

Back at the birthday party, Candice and I continued to toddle along, eventually walking from the redwood deck into the dining room. She giggled at the sight of her birthday cake. The German log roll cake with chocolate buttercream frosting and two pink candles on top continued our family tradition. Candice pushed my hands away and used a little wooden bench to steady herself.

I smiled at her, one proud mama. Making wooden benches with Dad was another family tradition. Only a few months before, he and Candice had made the bench together. My brothers, sister, and I had all made them with Dad as kids. They had a simple construction made out of five pieces of wood: a large piece for the seat, two smaller ones for the legs, and a few narrow diagonal supports. We used the benches to make us more comfortable while doing chores like weeding flower beds and tending Dad's large garden. They also helped us put whatever we needed within our reach.

Just before I lifted Candice into her highchair and lit her candles to sing our family birthday songs, Mike glanced at the bench and off-handedly whispered, "Concentration camp bench."

"What are you talking about?" I hushed my words as if such a thing could shield my baby from their association with a great evil.

"Ask Dad," my brother said.

I'm not altogether sure why on that happy occasion Mike decided to share this part of Dad's story with me. Maybe his knowledge of the bench was recent, or had burdened or weighed on him so much that just blurting it out made him feel better. Or perhaps, his was a detached observance possibly after coming to terms with what he knew of Dad's story over time. In any event, before my brother whispered those words, no one in the family had spoken of Dad's WWII experience with me. I don't remember when I learned that Dad had been a Japanese POW. I seemed to have been born knowing. The fact was as much a part of me as my skin or hair.

After the birthday party and some soul-searching, I wrote Dad a letter asking him to tell me the story of the very first wooden bench he built. His reply began our decades-long adventure of finding answers together. The quest to uncover the truth would result in discoveries that put long-since forgotten pieces of Dad's life, as well as my own, back together again. We did what he'd spent a lifetime trying not to do—we remembered.

A Need for Six Nails

Within weeks Dad's reply arrived in my mailbox in his signature white business envelope with a no-nonsense black, rubber-stamped return address in the left-hand corner. A handwritten note on his usual blue-lined, wide-ruled notebook paper was tucked inside. Since he had never spoken about his past, reading his answer felt like a portal opening to another world. Over the years we would exchange hundreds of letters. But, something deeper had transpired between us, other than being mere pen pals. We discovered the length and breadth and depth of God's love, each other's hearts, Dad's iron will to live, and his deep longing to share his story.

I wasn't a good student of history before Dad and I began our correspondence, mostly because timelines and the personalities of major world events often felt far away and dusty. As a schoolgirl, teachers required me to outline and memorize my way through world history, leaving me with only an academic understanding, at best. But Dad's incredible storytelling revealed what felt more like a mystery, and made important world events come alive in ways I never knew possible. Our letters and precious time together allowed me to not only better understand history, but also better understand myself.

Dear Laura,

When I was eighteen, three days after the attack on Pearl Harbor, the Imperial Japanese Navy sailed down into the South China Sea.

Suicide dive bombers flew down the stacks of two British battleships, the Prince of Wales and the Repulse, and sank them both. This destroyed the Allied Navy in the South Pacific.

Singapore surrendered and the Dutch East Indies followed. The Japanese landed on the island of Java where I lived with my family. I would celebrate my nineteenth birthday in a Japanese prison camp. A men's camp. I was a boy.

Our quarters were made of bamboo and thatched palm fronds. In normal Indonesian fashion, the floor was raised over the ground, and we slept on mats on this floor. The benches became our chairs.

By the time I turned 20, I'd learned to adapt. I found an opportunity to work in the kitchen. The rule was that the kitchen help could eat in the kitchen but not take food out of the kitchen. This way, I was not hungry.

My job was to keep the fires under the drums going with firewood provided. We were given a small ax to split the wood. Between meals, I had free time and was able to split certain firewood logs into planks. It took a lot of work, and the planks were uneven. The legs were two shorter planks braced by sticks.

The real important part of the bench was the need for six nails. Nails were impossible to get. But the prison camp was surrounded by a six-foot barbed wire fence. The posts were made of bamboo and the barbed wire was nailed into the bamboo post. At times, when the guards were not there, I crept to the fence and pulled *nails out, being careful to only pull out nails which did not cause the wire to droop. By my 21st birthday, I had a little side business making benches. Of course, my market soon dried up because of a lack of planks and lack of trade goods.*

Love, Daddy

Prisoners had no place to sit. A simple torture. I had never considered sitting a luxury. In the writing of this story, I would discover many such luxuries I've taken for granted.

After reading Dad's letter, our wooden benches were more than something to sit upon and make us comfortable. Each bench was a miracle, perseverance and resilience personified. Over the years, I would learn that many things Dad taught us were not only a result of his almost supernatural joie de vivre, but also a direct result of his art of survival. I have the last remaining wooden bench we made together at my home in Santa Cruz. I still use it to weed and help me grasp things that are out of my reach.

The last bench I made with Dad.

Somewhere along the way I got curious about his "little side business." How was his enterprise able to exist without causing him severe punishment? He wrote about his bench business in different letters. In one, he spoke a little bit about a kind of prison economy where prisoners traded things to help them survive.

> Dear Laura,
>
> After many months, I also started to split firewood for the kitchen fires and started to shape some pieces to be flat enough to use in my bench-making business. Sitting on the floor became tiresome and benches were in high demand. I could trade benches for clothes, possessions, or extra food packages prisoners sometimes smuggled into the camp from home. Eventually I ended up with a mattress to sleep on.
>
> Love, Daddy

It wasn't clear to me how the prison economy worked. Dad couldn't quite recall and I didn't press him on it. My research is filled with examples of prisoners who bartered certain commodities within the camps. Prisoners used their ingenuity to provide and pay for objects and services they needed to survive along with supplying basic necessities. These were perilous endeavors, to be sure.

My guess is that Dad paid the guards a percentage of his proceeds from his bench business to keep it going. However, he told me that if he'd been caught securing the precious nails and using the firewood, he would have been killed. It was a delicate, dangerous dance. And yet prisoners didn't mind risking death. It seemed they would forever be captives. If their lives would be filled with suffering, why not take some risk to alleviate the constant pain of an existence full of starvation and sickness?

"As the men became more and more hungry, every article in the camp gained a market value, and when a man had sold all of his own possessions he often turned his attention to the property of his neighbour . . . A large and highly organised black market was established in the camp during the early period of captivity, in part as a result of theft. Anything, from clothes to watches to gold teeth fillings, could be traded on the black market for food. The prices for food on the black market were exorbitantly high, but the black market operators argued that the risks they took to smuggle in the food warranted such high profits. In any case, the smugglers had the food and could charge whatever they liked for it, and there was always a buyer. The black market allowed the prisoners of war to trade among themselves, but it also allowed them to trade with the various Japanese, Korean and Indian camp guards.[9]

---

9   "Discipline at Changi: Crime, punishment and keeping order inside the prison camp" by
     Lucy Robertson. 2013. https://www.awm.gov.au/sites/default/files/2013_edited_-_lucy_
     robertsons_paper_0.pdf

TEA TIME

"Liberty is something you can't understand until it's taken away.
You become a different person.
You become a prisoner.
You learn what it is to survive.
You avert punishment by following the rules.
You have no liberty."

– Hans Hasen, former Japanese WWII POW, March 10, 2010,
the 65th Anniversary of the Fire-Bombing of Tokyo

In 1921, three years before Dad was born, the KNIL (Royal Dutch Indies Army) moved to Bandung in the interest of defending the colony. Many industries followed, including manufacturing, construction, canning, ammunition, as well as a Goodyear tire plant, a quinine factory, and a dairy. The Department of Civil Public Works also moved to Bandung from what was then known as Batavia (now named Jakarta) as did the Department of Agriculture and the Department of Industry and Trade, which created various laboratories. Then came the financial industries of banking, trade, pensions, and the establishment of schools. The Andir airfield (now known as Husein Sastranegara Airport) also opened, offering the first direct flights to Batavia.

Java was important to the Japanese because of its considerable oil deposits; it also had several important refineries. The island was the administrative, industrial, and vital working center for the 3000-mile-long island chain of the Dutch East Indies. It was the heart of the Dutch possessions in the South Seas and found itself in the crosshairs of The Empire of Japan almost six months to the day after the attack on Pearl Harbor, December 7, 1941.

> *"Yesterday, December 7, 1941 — a date which will live in infamy. The United States of America was suddenly and deliberately attacked by the naval and air forces of the Empire of Japan. Last night Japanese forces attacked Hong Kong. Last night Japanese forces attacked Guam. Last night Japanese forces attacked the Philippine Island. Last night the Japanese attacked Wake Island . . . "*

—President Franklin D. Roosevelt, December 8, 1941

The Empire of Japan would capture a sixth of the world in six months[10] and the mighty fell—Hong Kong, Malaysia, Singapore. Close to thirty percent of Japanese POWs died, a higher percentage than German POWs, due to the conditions in the tropics where the smallest cut could turn septic and kill a person in a matter of hours.[11]

---

10 *Japan's Territorial Expansion 1931-1942* https://worldview.stratfor.com/article/japans-territorial-expansion-1931-1942

11 Daws, Gavin. *Prisoners of the Japanese: POWs of WWII in the Pacific.* Print. William Morrow Paperbacks (January, 1996).

But these were just historical facts. I wanted to know about the human experience and what it was like for my dad. I wanted a story I could hold onto, not just generic events, dates, and information that I could uncover through independent research about the Pacific Theater of WWII. I needed to sort out what had happened to my family. The how, what, when and mostly why of it all.

After Dad and I had been writing to each other for five months, it was Christmastime. The year had been a big one for me. I'd married, bought my first house, given birth to my first child, moved across the country, and had been accepted to the school of Industrial Design at the Art Center College of Design in Pasadena, not far from our home in Echo Park. That Christmas, it felt so good to come home to the western suburbs of Chicago and bring my little girl to the house where I'd grown up. I liked L.A. But, I missed my friends and family.

The plane ride home had been full of surprises. I'd been so very careful to do my research to make this first flight with little Candice successful and comfortable. I'd requested the bulkhead seats because all the mommy magazines mentioned that the additional room they would provide was important when playing with and changing a baby. I had the bottles ready so Candice could keep her tiny ear canals open as she fed, which would help to equalize the pressure on her eardrums during the descent into Chicago.

I had packed away a teething ring for her, her favorite blanket and the portable changing pad, diapers, pacifiers, toys, and baby wipes—everything we would need for the four-hour flight including extra clothes for her (and myself just in case she had a blow out, something I had no idea could really happen as a new mom). I made sure we had all the convenient supplies within reach in the diaper bag in the overhead compartment.

I'll never forget the sense of peace I felt when my then-husband and I took our seats at the bulkhead, both exhausted from just getting to and through the airport. We settled in our seats and smiled, happy that we'd taken the steps we could to care for Candice and have a comfortable flight. I let the rushing of that morning drift away. As my queasy belly settled, a stewardess walked up to us and said, "Excuse me, but we need one of you to move because a man with a seeing-eye dog needs to sit here."

Whaaaat??

"Can't someone else move? We have a baby," I said indignantly.

I'm a bit ashamed to say that I didn't have very much grace. I can't remember the reason why one of us had to move. I almost cried, if you can believe it, when my then-husband took his seat twenty rows behind us. The separation felt so very strange. I didn't know if I could fly with Candice all alone without any help.

A large man holding the leash of his seeing-eye dog, a large German Shepherd, took the middle seat next to me. The dog curled up and slept at my feet for the entire flight. He was the perfect distraction for Candice, who loved the dog. Her sweet curiosity wore her out, and she even slept for a while. My flying companion and I joked about our situations and how life can throw us curve balls sometimes. As difficult a time as I thought I'd had that morning, I thought about the man at my side and what it must be like to navigate life without being able to see. God has so many ways to show us the bigger picture if we just open our hearts to things like changes in plans and unexpected friendships.

That afternoon, I brought my baby home to the house where I grew up, a joyous time as you can imagine. She met the rest of my family, and we enjoyed doing all the things with her I had loved as a child. We bundled her up and took her out to play in the snow and sledded down little hillsides; decorated the tree and baked cookies; had friends over and went to church. And there was even a quiet moment between Dad and me on that trip.

Over the years, when Dad and I talked together in person, it was our custom to drink tea. Mom would take the time to fix a pot and usually served Dad's favorite homemade chocolate chip cookies. He had an infinite appetite for chocolate. We'd visit over tea with Mom before adjourning to Dad's study to have our question-and-answer time. Mom was so patient, always supportive, and ready to bring us snacks or make us a little more comfortable.

During that Christmastime visit, I remember wanting to reassure Dad. "Dad, I got it that this process could potentially be really difficult. That it might stir up some pretty bad memories. So, I want us to make a deal. If I ever ask you something you can't answer or you don't want to answer, just let me know you want to pass on that question. Okay?"

At that, he put his hand on mine, looked at me with the clearest, bluest eyes I will ever see in this world, and said, "I will answer all of your questions."

In the beginning, I had much to learn about Dad's homeland of Indonesia. An archipelago my family had called home for generations. From my life as an American, I could hardly imagine calling such a far-away place home. Dad said to understand his story, I'd have to understand Dutch Colonial life. He believed this would be difficult because of my perspective as a modern woman, so he did the best he could to enlighten me over the years. However, parts of me cringed as I read the words he'd written on the page, and yet, it was his experience, however politically incorrect. And I needed to understand and honor the way he told his own story.

February 20, 2010

Dear Laura,

I have written five pages to answer your questions which I am enclosing.

It will be difficult for you to understand living in the tropics in the Dutch colonial environment. There is a 300-year-history of Dutch government that made the Dutch East Indies a source of wealth for them. The Dutch are practical people and hard workers transplanted into an environment where you don't have to work very hard to live. There are no winters. A thatched roof of palm leaves supported by bamboo poles and beams keeps the rain out. One banana tree will grow to produce enough bananas to feed a family and bananas are a perfect food.

There were also certain principles of Dutch Government such as "Apartheid" – which meant keeping apart from the native people who lived there. You can imagine the Dutch sailors surrounded by bare-breasted native women. Part of "keeping apart" meant that the men at that time could work in the Indies only seven years before returning to the Netherlands. They would have to leave the children in foster care or at boarding school if they wanted to return.

Historically in the 1600's, seven Dutchmen could build a sailboat. Then these seven men could sail to the Indies and return with a ship full of spices and retire for life. This took only six months to build, six months to sail, getting the spices took only another six months and they returned in six months, which added up to two years. This concept resulted in the seven-year rule—you work and then return.

There is more. Of course, you could not prevent the Dutch men from living with Indonesian women, but any children were called Indo-Europeans and were shunned to the effect that they were not allowed into the Dutch schools in Indonesia. You can see the problem that was caused by shunning this group that became numerous.

Love, Daddy

"At the time of the Japanese invasion of Java, there were six million Dutchmen controlling a vast geographic area spanning from Seattle to Miami. How were the Dutch able to keep control over the area? They had a philosophy of trade which was simple, you give us what we want, we give you what you want," Dad said.

"Back then, windmills in Indonesia generated more horsepower per capita than anywhere in the world. The power of the saw brought planks from around the world, from the Baltic countries, and Holland, to be cut in Indonesia. There they could cut 24/7. It was the cheapest place to cut wood in the world at this period in time," he continued.

As he spoke more about the business of the Dutch East India Company, he said something provocative that drove home the history of the islands in a way he never had before.

"Can you imagine a world without spices?" Dad asked.

Europeans didn't have pepper, but they did have salt. But even salt was rare during the 1600s and it became one of the world's most precious trading commodities.[12] Once the exotic spices from Indonesia came home to Europe, people loved the good tastes so much that they paid a fortune to have access to them. So those who could afford to pay were those who got to sample them. For years, Arabs dominated

---

12   https://time.com/3957460/a-brief-history-of-salt/

the spice trade on the Silk Road, a mostly overland route, until the Europeans arrived, first the Portuguese and then the Dutch. Indonesia was called The Spice Islands for a reason, and many of the adventurous made fortunes in the spice trade.

"One trip there and back could set you up for life. So, the Dutch maintained order with windmills and spices and trading with locals to give them what they wanted. The indigenous people there never had cooking utensils or clothes before the Europeans came," Dad said.

While all true, the impact of empire building on the world had played out during my lifetime. His references made me uncomfortable at times. But this was his history, and I needed to allow him to tell it in his own words. In his next sentence, we fast-forwarded about 500 years.

"Right after Pearl Harbor, everything in the country of Java still ran very well. Power, electricity, radio—all ran smoothly until The Battle of The Java Sea. The British and Dutch navy suffered a massive loss to the Japanese Imperial Army, and became part of the defeated forces," Dad said.

I began to get a greater sense of a term I'd heard called "the fog of war." In my mind, as a person who has never gone to war or been in a world at war, I would have thought that changes happened quickly. Especially changes that came with occupation. And in some instances, and in some places, they did. However, it took time for the noose to tighten around the little populous island of Java and the village of Bandung.

In that same conversation, Dad reflected on his wartime memories. "You know, those Zeros were so powerful. And the Japanese were so smart. They called the occupied area the Japanese Co-prosperity Sphere, which incorporated parts of China, Malaysia, and Indonesia.

When the Japanese occupied Bandung there were only hundreds of Japanese in a city of 100,000 people. You were allowed to keep working for them only if you wore an armband with the Japanese flag on it and only if you displayed a Japanese flag in the window. April 1942 is when they invaded. After that time, you didn't go outside," Dad said.

"Why wouldn't you go outside?" I asked.

"There was no need. No one went to school anymore. And there were roadblocks. The only person who ever left the house was my father. He was the only one who traveled to and from work and occasionally stopped at the store for food when it was available."

While I sat lost in thought, Dad looked at me and said, "Have you ever cut a salami?"

I nodded.

"The occupation was just the first slice that cut away at our freedom."

Over the decades, I noticed there were interesting patterns in Dad's answers. He did answer every question. When he didn't really know the answer, he'd let me know, then take his best guess. His recollections could come from all periods of time. Sometimes, when his memories became too difficult, he defaulted to talking about the general history of the time with stories he particularly enjoyed. Oftentimes, those stories spanned hundreds of years.

Dad had always been fascinated by history. This used to drive me crazy as a child when I would hear Dad tell long stories about the lives of MacArthur and Patton at our dinner table. But it wasn't until our correspondence that I began to fully understand the depth of his knowledge of WWII. I realized that a thirst to reconstruct the world he had been locked away from fueled his fascination.

Dad rarely spoke about the conditions of the camp (I would discover in the fullness of time that he was held in six different ones). The only answer Dad did offer was to watch the movie *The Bridge Over the River Kwai*, saying that the film portrayed conditions similar to those he'd experienced. As Dad was incapable of sharing the most gruesome details, I discovered plenty of published information about the camps where he was held to help me more fully understand.

It was no surprise that Dad used movies to express parts of his life that were otherwise too painful to talk about. He loved movies. I would come to learn that his passion for them had its roots in his experience as a refugee after the war when former POWs were allowed to watch all the movies they wanted. A few other movies Dad wanted us to watch together to help me understand his situation and his homeland were *Father Goose*, and *The Year of Living Dangerously*. Each movie gave a window into Dad's experience that I would never get otherwise.

A LOVE STORY

During the years that Dad and I wrote to each other, the Internet birthed email, texts, and instant messages. At the dawn of rapid communication, Dad favored snail mail. Even after he'd suffered a broken wrist on his right hand, his writing hand. Mom typed his emails as he never learned how to type or use a computer.

In addition to letters, Dad and I exchanged other things. I looked for any documentation that might have jogged his memory. Sometimes I'd send snippets from my research that had uncovered surprising details, like the record of the prison camp transfer to the temple in Japan where he had been held. He faithfully replied to my letters with his thoughts.

Dad began sending his replies from our family home in Oak Brook, then from their condo in Hinsdale, both suburbs of Chicago. Later, he sent letters from Florida where he and Mom had settled for the sunset of their lives. Dad's letters kept me riveted. He'd tell me that as the grandson and great-grandson of missionaries, letter writing came naturally. Missionaries were wonderful letter writers, he said, because of their longing for news of home and want of connection with far-away family and friends. In those days, most letters would take months to reach their destination.

Letters, newspapers, and newsreels in theaters were the only ways to get daily or weekly news back then until an invention called the radio changed the world forever. It's ironic that this story that began with a simple exchange of letters would have its roots in communication, specifically, the technology of radio.

Needless to say, when people asked where my dad was born (he had a heavy accent), their brows would wrinkle at my answer, "Indonesia." Frequently, the next question would be, "How did your family come to find themselves in that part of the world?"

* * *

My grandparents fell in love while attending the University of Freiburg in the southwestern tip of Germany, in the Black Forest, during the years right after World War I. Founded in 1457, the university is one of the oldest and most renowned in Germany. They met as part of an outdoor society called Wadervogel, a German word meaning "Wandering Bird", a group that promoted personal liberation through the exploration of nature, and leisure activities. In 1918, after the war, many young people were disenfranchised and looking for meaning in life. Wadervogel groups communed with nature in the woods and sprung up all around Germany in the 1890s as a protest against industrialization.

But when the Nazis rose to power, finding awe through nature was declared a crime against the state. Hiking was labeled elite, antisocial, and selfish—and so, the Wandervogel society had to disband. During the mid-1930s, the Nazis went so far as to make it illegal to hike from hostel to hostel in the German countryside. Even after WWI, over fifteen years earlier, the groups began to experience some push back from those in society who thought the act frivolous and too personal.

While Grandma and Grandpa enjoyed finding solace and spirituality hiking in the wonders of nature in the Black Forest, they were a world apart. He, an Iron Cross veteran of a brutal war, fresh from the signal corps, trying to find a professional footing in a war-ravaged, post-WWI Germany. She, born on Ulu Siau in The Celebes, a Dutch daughter of missionaries, who'd spent most of her life as a foster child of a German family, trying to survive long enough to attend university and make her own dreams come true. Women rarely attended university in the early twentieth century. Rarer still was the simple act of the pair's survival, since 8.5 million military deaths and around 13 million civilian deaths plagued Europe during WWI.

"In 1917, at the age of twenty-five, Grandpa was decorated with the Iron Cross 1st class and 2nd class and given the Legion of Honor Medal. My father only talked about what he did to earn those medals one time. Grandpa had to run over a field of dead bodies to carry telephone line."

Dear Laura,

I remember that Paps told me he was in the army for about 18 months and served on the Western Front[13]. Being a university student, he joined the Signal Corps, which at that time was charged to string wires from Headquarters to Field Commanders near the Front.

---

13   The Western Front was the line of fighting that occurred along the trenches that stretched throughout Belgium and northern France. It was the site of some of the largest battles of World War I, including the Second Battle of Ypres. The Second Battle of Ypres cost the lives of many people on both sides. German casualties totaled over 34,000, French casualties totaled about 18,000 and Canadian casualties totaled almost 6,000. In all, it is estimated that the British forces suffered nearly 60,000 casualties. https://www.history-crunch.com/second-battle-of-ypres-in-world-war-i.html#/

In a battle near the end of WWI, the telephone lines could not be strung and repaired, and the general was anxious to get his message to one commander. One of the general's aides told him that someone in his communication division regularly talked to his friend by radio who was at the Command Post where the general wanted to send the message. It was such a new concept, but Paps had a friend from the University who was a "Ham" operator, and they talked with each other on their radio sets.

As soon as the general found this out, he called Paps to headquarters and asked him to send the message to his friend to give to his Field Commander. Because of the message, the battle was won, and Paps earned his first Iron Cross. The general then asked to assemble radio equipment on a truck, which went with him, and the other radio trucks were sent to his Field Commanders. This was near the end of the war, and the radio could not influence the outcome, which was a disastrous defeat for Germany. Before WWI ended, Paps earned an Iron Cross First Class.

Paps was 26 years old at the end of the war and returned to the University of Freiburg to complete his degree. The university was barely functioning and the subjects that Alex needed to study were not very useful to someone who just provided the defeated German army with radio.

Love, Daddy

I had been told that my grandparents were Dutch, which was true, in a way. Grandpa had become a Dutch national in the late 1930s. But upon hearing this story, I realized that Grandpa had fought for the Germans. As an American, I knew he was on the wrong side of the war and needed to come to terms with that.

During the writing of this book, I've learned how many good people have been on the "wrong side" of things. And that "right" and "wrong" sides are not as black-and-white as we think. Instead, the two sides are populated by people caught up in the politics of countries and circumstances largely beyond their control, people whose fates were more often decided by chance. My heart ached for my family who were among these people. I couldn't imagine my young grandparents having to deal with so much violence and upheaval in their teens and early twenties. And yet, they persevered and even thrived. As you can imagine, after learning some of their story, I wanted and needed to understand more about their experience.

Having no idea of the violence of trench warfare that was a hallmark of WWI military operations at the time, I uncovered an account from another member of the Wadervogel group about a battle that Grandpa could have been in to understand what it must have been like for him on the battlefield.

"When day dawned, we were astonished to see, by degrees, what a sight surrounded us. The sunken road now appeared as nothing but a series of enormous shell-holes filled with pieces of uniform, weapons, and dead bodies. The ground all round, as far as the eye could see, was ploughed by shells. You could search in vain for one wretched blade of grass. This churned-up battlefield was ghastly. Among the living lay the dead. As we dug ourselves in, we found them in layers stacked one upon the top of another. One company after another had been shoved into the drum-fire and steadily annihilated."[14]

"After the war, things were so desperate in Germany that Paps had to shoot his dog; there was simply no food. He told me a story

---

14   Ernst Junger, (1895–1998) after a night march to the front line at Guillemont, September 3-6, 1916. A German author, highly decorated soldier, philosopher, and entomologist who became publicly known for his World War I memoir Storm of Steel, a graphic account of trench warfare.

about how he had to pay for a loaf of bread with a wheelbarrow full of money," Dad said.

At eleven o'clock on the eleventh day of the eleventh month of 1918, WWI ended. And so it was that on the eve of one world war and the dawn of another, Grandpa met Irene Kelling (known as "Reni"), my grandma. Grandpa had intense blue eyes and a large, handsome magnetic presence. He loved to sing and play the piano, as well as the guitar. Irene's large expressive blue eyes, wavy sunkissed brown hair and Mona Lisa smile made her a standout too. A love of hiking led to a love of each other.

"Grandpa fell in love with Grandma's legs. He enjoyed hiking behind her because he thought she had the most beautiful ankles," Dad said. I smiled.

I must have inherited my love of hiking from them, I thought.

Soon, they discovered they were expecting a baby and suddenly, their lives changed. In 1920 they wed and left university which put them in a precarious situation. Grandma had gotten her degree, but Grandpa had to leave one year short of completing his. Like most new moms, Grandma wanted to be close to family—only her family was a world away on the tiny island of Ulu (meaning "island") Siau in The Celebes, where my great-great-grandfather Fredrick Kelling had established a church. He translated the Heidelberg catechism and the New Testament in the Sangirese dialect of Siau.[15] The family served as missionaries there for three generations. The church is still going strong, and our family has helped with its upkeep over the years. Another story, best left for another day.

---

15   Aritonang, Jan Sihar, and Karel Steenbrink, eds. "How Christianity Obtained A Central Position In Minahasa Culture And Society." In *A History of Christianity in Indonesia*, 35:419–54. Brill, 2008. http://www.jstor.org/stable/10.1163/j.ctv4cbgb1.15.

It took a while to sort out when Grandma and Grandpa would leave Europe and how they might afford passage on an oceanliner. As time marched on, Grandma became farther along in her pregnancy, unbeknownst to her family in The Celebes. Eventually, my great-grandparents sent two tickets to the newlyweds to join them. When the happy day finally arrived, Grandma and Grandpa boarded a steam-powered oceanliner in Rotterdam and set sail, third class, to join Grandma's parents, the Kellings, on Ulu Siau, home to Karangetang (Api Siau), one of Indonesia's most active volcanoes.

However, on the passage to Java, the captain of their ship decided Grandma was too pregnant to sail any further and forced Grandma and Grandpa to disembark in the port of Batavia because there were no facilities or doctors on board to help with the birth. My grand-parents found themselves days away from delivering their first child, in a place where they knew no one and had no connections for work or living accommodations. Grandma wrote about the experience of being waylaid at Tanguman Priote harbor on Java in one of her letters (note: "Indian soil" is how she refers to Indonesia which was frequently referred to as "India" at the time), the following is an excerpt.

My beloved parents,

Both your children send you heart-felt greetings from Indian soil. It was a Sunday when we entered our old homeland, and we hope that this means a blessing for the future.

The journey from Rotterdam to Priote took us only 29 days, from the 14th of May to the 12th of June. Alex and I got only a little seasick. We were the last people who managed to get a place on the ship, there were only two places left, both 3rd class and in different parts of the ship. Nevertheless, when we boarded at

Rotterdam we were assigned the only 3rd class cabin with only two bunks, all other cabins having had four bunks. It again shows that we are children of God. This joy was shared by Hettrekind, it was she who brought us from Middleharris, where we had spent a very nice week, to Rotterdam to board the ship . . .

Unfortunately, all my German diplomas aren't recognized here. Slowly but surely things will start moving . . . I'm sure that the Father in heaven will help us, and slowly I will learn to do as my darling does, not to worry about tomorrow, as is told to us in the Sermon on the Mount.

How much would Alex and I have liked to continue our journey from Priote to see you, and to get information about transport and fares to Siau, but we shied away from it, because we were told that the first seat in 2nd class would be $216, and if we had left on the 22nd of June we would have arrived at your place on the 18th of July, I almost couldn't believe it.

Much love, Reni

My heart ached at how similar my experience was to my grandma's in some ways. I also started out marriage and motherhood unexpectedly. By the time Dad had shared this part of the story, I was a young, happily married woman with two girls who were born in LA, raising them nearly a continent away from my family. I'd also been without my family, feeling like a stranger in a strange land, moving from Illinois to California with no idea how I'd support myself in my early twenties. My pregnancy, marriage, and move also occurred within months. It would be a few years before I would finish my industrial design education.

I couldn't imagine having to do all that without a place to live. I so loved our little treehouse in Echo Park, even though no one stopped by except visiting family for the first year or so. Unlike Grandma, I easily made some friends while attending Art Center College of Design. After reading Grandma's letters, I realized that we both embraced our experience as a great adventure, and were similar in the ways we found joy in our journeys.

During one of my visits with Dad, he remembered that he had stored some of Grandma's letters. It didn't take him long to bring them out of his extensive cache of files. (He kept files on everything and even wrote memorandums to himself, documenting certain events and ideas he wanted to archive for use someday.) I'll never forget when he pulled out Grandma's original letters and set them on my lap. I melted at the sight of Grandma Irene's handwriting; her words frozen in time. She died at the age of 60, two years before I was born so her letters were my only way of actually knowing her.

Unfortunately, I couldn't read the carefully preserved correspondence because they were written in German, one of the handful of languages Dad spoke. But as he was getting on in years, he couldn't translate all of her letters into English. So, I returned home to Los Angeles with copies of Grandma's letters and no way to read them—happy to have a piece of her to hold onto, but frustrated, too. Many of the answers I sought were only a translation away. Why would my Dutch grandmother write letters in German to her Dutch parents? And why couldn't Grandma and Grandpa just catch the next boat to Ulu Siau and live with her parents when the time was right?

Years later, when I finally hired a translator, I discovered that the letters were full of Grandma's love of the Heavenly Father. One by one, they gave me a window into the young family's arrival and detailed their extraordinary journey. In an ideal world, my grandparents would have pressed pause, made some money, and gotten on the first boat to live with Grandma's family. However, lives had to be lived. And in the living, best laid plans and desires often didn't come to pass. They had to secure jobs in the Dutch East Indies as outsiders—worse yet, as "Germans"—to support themselves and their growing family. There was no waiting until later. They had to bloom where they were planted. And so did I.

It was a matter of settling in. Of finding their way in a world that didn't want them and fitting into a colonial way of life that another war would obliterate in a matter of decades. Because Grandpa was German, every job lead went up in smoke. On the fourth day after their arrival, he once again left Grandma at the Hotel del Indies—a hotel they couldn't afford—to search for work. But three days of door slamming had sent him to the local toko for a bit of refreshment where, by happenstance, he spoke about his job search and The Great War with a Dutchman who also spoke German. Grandpa's acquaintance sat silent, enraptured.

After Grandpa shared his war story, the Dutchmen asked if he still had his Iron Crosses. When Grandpa said he did (he was never without them) the gentlemen told him to pin them to his chest and apply for a job at the *Post Telegraph and Telephone Company* (PTT). The man said they were looking for brave men and emphasized, *Don't bring them. Wear them, and any other medals you have. Have them pinned to your chest when you walk in the door.*

So Grandpa did as he requested. Stunned at the sight of the impressive medals Grandpa wore on his suit coat, PTT did offer him a job. He was to string a wire for a long-range radio station. The longer the wire, the more powerful the radio. Malabar, located south of Bandung in the mountains near the Mount Malabar volcano in Southeastern Java, was going to be the most powerful radio station in the world at 2400 KW. The wire needed to stretch about 2 kilometers between two mountain ridges.

Dear Laura,

No one would do it, not the Dutch or the Indonesians. But my father had been decorated with the Iron Cross in World War I and so this [stringing of wire across the mountains] was nothing to him. After he completed the challenge of stringing the wire he became famous. The Indonesians loved him and were very loyal.

The Germans and the Dutch never recognized him though because he had no college degree. And yet, in Indonesia he was a hero. He got a big bonus for completing the project and spent it all on a grand piano.

Racism raises its ugly head in different ways at different times. In pre-WWII Java if you were German you were second class, far below the Dutch colonials but higher than the Indonesians. And yet, Father treated the Indonesians as his equals and taught them everything he knew. It was by this virtue that the Indonesians, under Grandpa's tutelage, would come to regard him as legend.

Love, Daddy

* * *

Salemba, 18th June, 1921
My beloved parents,

Yesterday was a very eventful day. On Friedolien's birthday, for which we send our best wishes, Alex went with his documents to *the head of the telegraph office and asked whether in the area of wireless transmission they wouldn't have any use for him. I wish from the bottom of my heart that he gets the job immediately. And my main reason for that is a wonderful secret I want to share with you because . . . besides us you are the closest to it, and therefore you can look forward to it.*

Our dear Father in Heaven will give us in a couple of weeks a little child, and you can imagine how grateful and happy I was when on the morning of the 17th of June, Alex came to me and told me with a face full of joy that he swore the oath as a civil servant and for the time being will work as a radio technician with a starting salary of 350 per month in Bandoeng[16]. But at the same time the gentlemen told him that he would be a radio engineer with a higher salary as soon as they were convinced of the skills indicated by his German medals. Mr. Stolz said that we were in a very favorable position now that so many people were unemployed. Uncle Hennemann was really happy for us. Alex had to leave immediately today for Bandoeng to start his job there. We left Welterreden together, he for Bandoeng and I to Depok to Aunt Agathe and her bunch of children, who wanted me to stay there as soon as I arrived; but I only arrived on Tuesday, and then to the end of the vacation (28th June). Because before that I'd like to have a medical check-up with a good doctor. I'm not complaining about anything . . . .Love, Reni

* * *

Because Grandpa took the job, he and Grandma eventually ended up living in Bandung, the garden spot of Indonesia, where people went to retire. For many reasons, Grandma couldn't live at Malabar

---

16   The Dutch spelling of Bandung.

where Grandpa needed to live and work. The least concerned the appropriateness of a white woman who would soon have a newborn baby living among mostly indigenous people in such a remote place. Distant relatives offered her shelter in a pavilion on their property in Bandung until Grandpa could find an affordable place for them to live as a family. The provision the Lord had set forth in Grandpa's job was such an answer to prayer and yet it came at such an incredible cost for both of them.

His was a dangerous, grueling job. Even though it was lonely at times, he was happy to get away from the structure of Dutch society and lead a crew of men on a nearly impossible mission. When I asked how he accomplished the task of stringing the cable, Dad drew me a picture. He described how Grandpa constructed a cable car on a pulley system that ran over the gorge between two mountain tops. Then he used the cable car to attach the wire from one mountaintop to the other, erecting what would be the world's largest antenna at that time. It was a massive undertaking and several workers lost their lives in the process.

* * *

Earthquakes, volcanic eruptions, floods, elephants, and insects in these early days of radio were the enemies. That's if you survived stringing the cable from tree to tree and mountain to mountain through the jungle. These were the trailblazers, engineers and unskilled laborers cutting their way through the jungle to lay track or a wire which in those early days they fastened to live trees, kapok trees best of all, and they built, as their shelters and as the end stations of the wire line, huts of wood, bamboo was best. The wire opened the old, so it seemed, previously closed landscape.—*Engineers of Happy Land: Technology and Nationalism in a Colony* by Rudolf Mrázek

MEETING RENI

I met Grandma through her letters. Long gone will be the experience of a father handing his daughter original letters written in the hand of a grandmother she never knew. As I laughed and cried while reading them, I was part of a generation opening some of the last treasure chests of the written word, since most people only write in the ether these days. What a miracle it was that those fragile pieces of paper survived the war, and the turmoil afterward.

Meester Cornelis, 07-VII-1921

My beloved parents, by now you will have received Alex's surprising telegram, and I want to quickly tell you myself now about the great fortune that we have received from our Lord, a telegram is always a little half-cooked.

The little, sweet girl that arrived in this world on the night of Sunday, 26th of June, at 1 o'clock in the morning, and who carries the name of her two youngest aunts – Aletta Paula – and her dear grandfather, managed to surprise her own parents, who were expecting her only three or four weeks later. The same with

Dr. van Maanen, who performed a medical check-up on me on the 20th of June, which I had promised Alex to have before he left on the 18th to start his new job, and which turned out normal.

Since this left me pretty relaxed, I took up aunt Agathes' invitation and went to visit her and her bunch of children in Depok. I was only there a couple of days when Uncle George had to take me by car to Tjileini. It was unexpected, and I spent long and lonely hours, full of pain, beginning on Saturday afternoon until early Sunday morning.

However, things couldn't have turned out better, three hard-working nurses were with me, the doctor did an excellent job, and even my little Lettie child started to make noises when only her little head was visible and the rest of her body was still invisible for some time.

And then the most wonderful thing, on Sunday afternoon arrived my beloved Alex to visit me and our wonder child, if only for two short hours; how well did the little creature manage, or better, how well managed the Creator, giving us this little child on a Sunday, because under the week her father had to stay at his post up on Malabar.

So far the little one is healthy, praise be to God, and that I deserve the title of 'model patient,' which was bestowed to me by the doctor and the nurses, you can see by the fact that the day before yesterday I walked again for the first time, and yesterday I was allowed to leave the hospital.

Aunt and Uncle Hennemann were so kind to offer me and my baby shelter at their pavilion until Alex has found appropriate, cheap housing here in Bandoeng for us, preferably a pavilion, too.

His ways are wonderful and plenty, His means abundant, His actions are full of blessings, where He walks there is light.

"Many, O LORD my God, are thy wonderful works which thou hast done, and thy thoughts which are to us-ward: they cannot be reckoned up in order unto thee: if I would declare and speak of them, they are more than can be numbered."(Psalm 40:5) . . . I still feel exhausted after I walk or stand up, but that doesn't surprise at all. Fortunately, I'm able to feed the baby myself. And she likes it a lot, for instead of losing weight in the first week as would be expected she has put on 130 grams.

But I guess I have to tell you a little now about the way the little wonder child looks. The baby has long hair, a high forehead, both of which she inherited from her father, if it is possible to tell at all at this stage. She has very small, blue eyes, a broad nose, and an impressive, little mouth, which easily turns into a smirk when she doesn't feel well in her little stomach. But when the baby is happy her mouth is the size of a big pea.

She knows as well how to frown, and then she looks like her father, she then has a disapproving look. The little thing has tender, little fingers with tiny, beautiful nails, and her toes look the same.

She is everybody's treasure here in the Hennemann house. Alex immediately took two photos of our little Lettiechild. If they turn out okay, he will send them to you right away. Last Sunday he was with us again. Unfortunately, he had a cold. It is cold in Bandoeng, that he had to buy two blankets in order to spend the night with us. Apart from that, he must leave us at 07.30 in the morning, has to sit in a car which drives at neck-breaking speed to the radio station, and it is easy to get a cold that way, particularly since his suitcase with the heavy coat hadn't arrived yet. But it appears that he got it by now.

But now I'd like to express my gratitude to my dear mother for her welcoming letter addressed to us here in India, which I received together with a marvelous, long letter addressed to Mr. Gratz. How kind of you to think immediately about 'baboes' [nannies] for me. I gladly accept that offer, but I'd like to leave the decision to you whether to send two or three. I'm afraid that three 'baboes' would be too expensive for us, since Alex's salary is still pretty low . . . But you are the one who has the most experience in matters like this. I will try to learn some Sanskrit with Mandty; for I'm pretty worried that I will manage things in a wrong manner, since I can't communicate with them. I'd like to close this letter for today. I'll have to bathe little Lettie child, may God be with you.

I send you a hug, kisses and lots of love, Reni

Grandma quoted many other verses of scripture in the above letter—*Psalm 107:8; Exodus 34:6; John 10:10; Deuteronomy 28:2; Ephesians 1:3; and 1 John 1:5-7.* Within her letters she painted a world that I could never have imagined. Reading her words took my breath away. Reni felt so much more alive, more real than she had ever seemed before.

Dad said that Grandma missed Grandpa terribly after Aletta was born. For months Grandpa worked far away and tried to see her and their "little Lettiechild" when he could. She was told that the mountains at Malabar were no place for a white woman and baby to live. But she felt otherwise.

Dear Laura,

When he started to assemble the cable way to cross the gorge, Paps told me that monkeys surrounded him. They wanted to know what he was doing in their forest. He actually had to shout them away to get his work done.

In the meantime, Irene had a baby girl, named Aletta, on June 26, 1921. She was waiting and waiting for Alex, and when he did not come, Irene decided to go to Malabar, where Alex worked. So, with Aletta in her arms and after explaining her plight, she asked a man how much it would cost to take her on the perilous 100-mile journey, all uphill, climbing 3000 feet. The Betchak driver said it was too far and that he wouldn't go. So, she brought 100 guilders out of her pocket, and he agreed to take her immediately in a horse-drawn carriage.

He also needed money to take an extra horse with him. Irene negotiated the price, and they undertook the journey, which came as quite an accomplishment, for the driver taking a white woman and small child that distance with overnight stops. In many areas, the natives had never seen a white woman or a white child.

Alex could not believe his eyes when Irene and his new baby girl finally arrived at the work site. This created a problem for the local village chief. It was one thing to have a white man living in a hut with the native workers, but a white woman and baby needed special attention. The village chief solved the problem by giving Alex, Irene, and Aletta a new house which was being built for him. Alex and Irene were grateful, but, of course, it was built of bamboo. Bamboo posts, woven bamboo mats for walls and mat floor. Native houses are always built above the ground so there are steps leading to the house floor, to keep the rainwater out of the house.

After successfully stringing the antenna, the Radio Station Bandung went on the air and the signal was received in Amsterdam. This was a milestone in communication with the Mother Country; communication by wire instead of by mail via steam boat.

For his part in the effort, Alex received a bonus. This German man of 29 years went from starvation, with his mother and sisters in Germany, ending up with a wife and baby on the tropical island of Java in the jungle, surrounded by monkeys in a matter of months. He was homesick.

With the bonus in hand, he went into the town of Bandung. The custom in the Dutch East Indies was to allow Dutch Citizens to work for a contract of seven years. Then they had 1 year off with pay to return to Holland with their wives and children. If they wanted to return to the Indies, they had to sign another seven-year contract, leave the children in Holland to be educated, and when they returned, they normally ended up in other parts of the Dutch East Indies. So, when these seven years were up, there were a lot of sales of home belongings.

I remember an Indonesian boy sitting in the front yard beating a gong by a sign saying the house belongings were for sale. Sometimes big items did not sell and were picked up by Chinese shop owners.

Alex went looking for furniture for his bamboo house and went to one of these Chinese warehouses, where he saw a Steinway grand piano. It was dusty, and in a corner, when he asked the Chinese owner how much it cost, he was surprised that he could *afford it. Apparently, the Chinese owner was happy to get rid of it. Now, to transport it was another thing, but the Chinese man found a horse and cart and a driver who took it to the house in Malabar. When it arrived, the problem was how to support the weight on the flimsy bamboo floor. They had to build columns under the piano legs. Alex finally got his grand piano, and the natives heard Bach's Preludes and Fugues in the jungle.*

Of course, the effect on Irene was ambivalence. Alex came back with no bed and no crib, but then she saw how he responded to being able to play his favorite music, she forgave him and enjoyed the music with him. But this taught Irene a lesson, and from that day she did not rest until she had a real house near Bandung. A real house with the required tile floors and regular windows. But this starts another story."

Love, Daddy

Even though Grandpa would eventually become naturalized as a Dutch citizen before WWII, being a German made him an outcast in the Dutch Colony. Dad once wrote, "Basically, the Dutch <u>hated</u> the Germans and called them *Rottmoffen* (Rotten people)." And this attitude was reflected in their daily lives when they moved to Bandung. In the colonies on a Sunday afternoon, every house prepared tea for people who would drop by. One never invited people; guests simply arrived. Dad said that nobody ever came to visit my grandparents. But, Grandma always had a lavish tea prepared anyway and waited on the veranda just in case someone did visit. They lived a lonely life and weren't made to feel welcome. In the end, the social strata didn't matter. They were all the blue-eyed enemy to the Japanese.[17]

---

17 Friend, Theodore. The Blue-Eyed Enemy: Japan against the West in Java and Luzon, 1942-1945. 1988. Princeton Legacy Library. https://press.princeton.edu/books/hardcover/9780691632223/the-blue-eyed-enemy .

"Mother was nineteen when women got the vote. This kind of a person was who my mother was—liberated, independent, and outspoken. That cross is my mother's cross." He pointed to a unique black mahogany cross with a brass crucified Jesus and a small brass skull and crossbones, that hung on the wall of his living room. I took a picture of the cross that afternoon since it is one of the most interesting crosses I think I've ever seen. Before Dad died, he gave me the cross as a gift. It hangs on my wall at my writing desk.

Grandma's cross.

During our conversations and within our letters, Dad told me that Grandma was decorated by the Dutch Queen Wilhelmina in exile[18] for starting an Indonesian school for Indo-European girls. She felt a deep need in her heart to help the abandoned and shunned girls, who, through no fault of their own, were of Indonesian and European

---

18   When Germany occupied Holland on May 10, 1940 the queen of The Netherlands went into exile in London.

descent. Perhaps she'd felt a kinship to the Indo-European girls as she had been shunned herself by the Colonial Dutch when she arrived on Java.

"Your grandmother was Christian enough to see that all these girls could sew and cook," Dad said. And so, she worked to give them better lives through skills that could help them find jobs that would help them support themselves. The name of the school was I.E.V.A.— Indo European Vrouw (The Dutch word for "woman") Association."

"You know that your grandmother's father and grandfather were missionaries," Dad continued, "but your grandma's faith was also influenced by Rudolf Steiner who was the founder of Anthroposophy.[19] Another follower of Steiner, a woman named Mrs. Kolisko, visited from England to do experiments which she wanted to perform at the equator. And so, she came to live with the family for a time. She showed me the difference between planting a seed four days before the full moon, during the full moon, four days after the full moon, and during the new moon. I saw that the seeds grew the tallest when planted four days before the full moon and the others were only a fraction of the size. I would use these planting techniques later. Farmers know all of this and plant accordingly."

Dad was a fantastic gardener and didn't seem very surprised by what he had learned. I, on the other hand, a girl raised in the suburbs of Chicago, had never before heard of the moon's influence on plants. It seemed fantastical to me that four days one way or the other could make such a difference, but the energies that are all around us impact people and things in different ways. I would learn, as Dad and Grandpa did, that timing is everything. I sat in my seat across from Dad in his

19   "Rudolf Steiner described it [Anthroposophy] simply as "consciousness of our human situation" which becomes "a path from the mind and spirit in the human being to the mind and spirit in the cosmos." He added that "it arises as a need of the heart." https://anthroposophy.org/learn-more/

study in Florida and watched him lean back in his office chair relaxed, recollecting.

"This woman became a very good friend of the family," Dad said. "And so, when my sister, Aletta, wanted to leave Indonesia, Mrs. Kolisco was the lady that she was sent to in 1939. Aletta had just turned eighteen. Mrs. Kolisco was meant to watch over her. Only, I believe from Aletta's story that it didn't work out so well. Mrs. Kolisco wasn't there to pick her up when Aletta arrived in London, but that is another story."

Aletta arrived in London in September of 1939, as Germany invaded Poland beginning WWII, and only a year before The Blitz. However, that wasn't the first time Aletta had been to Europe. Surprisingly, Dad's stories unfolded in both the European and Pacific theaters of WWII.

Boarding School

In 1931, two years into the Great Depression, Grandma and Grandpa sent Dad and Aletta (at the ages of seven and ten years respectively) to boarding school in Europe, as was the practice for colonial children, where they were expected to study for about seven years. Since Grandpa was German, he wanted his children to go to the best school in his homeland. Both of my grandparents had attended Birklehof, a boarding school located in Hinterzarten within the Black Forest, not far from the University town of Freiburg where they'd met. So Dad and Aletta also attended Birklehof.

As the years passed, Dad wrote home about having to join a new group called the Hitler Youth. The shock of the news sent my grandparents on an around the world trip to see what was happening in Germany. To do so, they used Grandma's modest inheritance from her mother to buy tickets to visit their children. Grandpa took a year-long sabbatical from work as was his right after seven years of work in Indonesia. He'd been working there for twelve years at that point, so the sabbatical was long overdue. In 1933, Grandma and Grandpa embarked on a lengthy globetrotting journey to visit Dad and Aletta.

Dear Laura,

During his work of testing various radio equipment at the Radio Laboratory, Alex found that the radio equipment made in the United States by RCA was superior to that made by the Dutch manufacturer, Phillips. Alex corresponded with the Radio Corporation of America (RCA) and with Dr. Sarnoff, who started the Columbia Broadcasting Network (CBS). Mr. Sarnoff had quite a similar life as Alex. He was born in Minsk, Russia, came to the U.S. in 1900, learned the Morse code, became a wireless operator for the Marconi Wireless Telegraph Company, and, in 1912, picked up that the Titanic was sinking, and he stayed at his station for 72 hours, helping to direct ships to the sinking liner and its survivors.

Alex went back to Europe after 12 years in the Dutch East Indies to find out what was going on in Germany with Hitler at the helm. He took a leave of absence, and he and Irene traveled to Europe via China and Japan. They visited the World's Fair of 1933 (A Century of Progress) in Chicago, stopped in New York and stayed at the Waldorf Astoria Hotel, and went to visit Mr. Sarnoff at RCA. His office was not hard to find at the Radio City Skyscraper. Alex asked to see Mr. Sarnoff, who now was President of RCA, and had his office on the top floor of the building. Fortunately, his secretary remembered Alex's last name [Hasenstab], and Mr. Sarnoff welcomed him into his office.

They had a good conversation, and Sarnoff offered Alex a job at RCA, but, at that moment, with Irene at the Waldorf and his *trip already arranged to meet me and Aletta, he declined the offer. Alex mentioned he had a message for Phillips in Eindhoven, and Mr. Sarnoff called Phillips by the first established radio telephone and got through. Alex delivered his message.*

This telephone conversation with Phillips became important later when Alex decided that Germany was not for him anymore, and that he was going to stay in Holland and wanted a job. Phillips knew that RCA had been interested in Alex, and, therefore, offered him a job with the Hilversum National Radio Station, the Dutch version of the BBC. Hilversum broadcast Dutch news to their colonies in East Asia and South America and the Caribbean.

The Dutch engineers at the Hilversum Radio Station did not know what to do with this German colonial radio engineer with no degree. So, they gave Alex a clerical job, which he did not like. Alex went to his work, but early in 1935, he got notice from the Bandung Radio Lab that they could not extend his leave of absence, and they could only keep his job open for another month.

Love, Daddy

* * *

After Grandma and Grandpa took Dad and Aletta out of Birklehof, Grandpa spent most of his time in Hilversum, Holland, negotiating a job with Phillips. During this time Grandma, Dad, and Aletta traveled to Kassel, Germany, to visit Grandma's foster parents who were overjoyed to see the children. While there, Grandma taught Dad and Aletta to speak Dutch again (since they'd spent years speaking German at the boarding school) so they could enroll at the Dutch school in Hilversum, where Grandpa secured a job.

"With the legacy of your great-grandmother's passing, Grandma and Grandpa got to take an around the world trip. They went to LA and saw Bing Crosby's rehearsal," Uncle Reinier said when I spoke with him in 2010. He remembered being a young boy in the house Dad built for Grandma and him after the war in Wahroonga, a suburb of Sydney, Australia. He remembered that Dad built the garage first and that's where they lived while Dad finished building the rest of the house. While living in the garage, Reinier said that he came across a pad of paper from a Los Angeles hotel. He wasn't sure which one.

"Mams said she had heard Hitler speak and saw that your dad was forced to be a part of the Hitler Youth. Your grandma saw what was happening," Reinier continued, "And so they pulled the kids out of the school. Since this was during the time when your Grandpa had to take a sabbatical, he sought work in Hilversum, Holland, but didn't like the work and wanted to return to Indonesia. After your Grandma and Grandpa spent time in Hilversum, where I was born, they wanted to leave what they called the horrors of Europe for the heaven of Indonesia."

* * *

Dear Laura,

Alex decided to return to his old job in Bandung, which he loved. As time was of the essence, the fastest way to return to Bandung was by using the Russian Trans-Siberian Railroad, connecting with regular boat service between Shanghai and Batavia. This decision by Alex was hard on Irene, who was pregnant with Reinier. They decided that Irene would stay in Hilversum until

Reinier was born, then return by regular scheduled Dutch steamer to Batavia and Bandung.

Reinier was born in November, 1935, and it was quite an adventure to pack up our house in Hilversum with a small baby, and arrive at a new house in Bandung at Multituli Boulevard. Alex rented the house and bought a Ford Touring Car with a V-8 engine, which was housed in our own garage. The new car was his pride and joy, and he constantly tuned the carburetor to make it run smoothly.

When Alex returned to his old job in Bandung, he decided to become a naturalized Dutch citizen. Now, being Dutch, he could finally become a regular employee of the Dutch Government Colonial Service, with vacations and paid holidays. However, he still could not qualify for an engineer position because he never got his university degree. This was the reason he always reminded me to finish my degree when I was at the University of Sydney. In any case, Alex had always trained his Indonesian co-workers since he arrived in Indonesia. His Indonesians became good at what they did, and also, did not fit into the established hierarchy. This paid off in later years, when the Indonesians took over the Radio Laboratory and remembered Alex as their teacher.

Love, Daddy

* * *

In the late spring of 1936, Grandma, Aletta, Dad, and baby Reinier set sail from Rotterdam—the port of her original point of departure from Europe about fourteen years earlier, when she was a wide-eyed newlywed on the adventure of her life. Grandma made an adventure out of their journey, taking the children to see the pyramids before sailing through the Suez Canal, and stopping at other exotic locations on their trip back home to Java. Only four years later, Germany occupied Holland. Few families had found themselves in peril in both theaters of the war. Escape from one was lucky, escape from both proved impossible.

Aletta, Grandma Irene (Reni) and Dad on their voyage back to Indonesia from Germany 1936, posing with baby leopards in Africa.

PEARL HARBOR

Phone in one hand, a frantic KGU radio reporter climbed the stairs to the rooftop of the Advertiser Building in Honolulu, Hawaii.[20] When the cord to the phone wouldn't reach any further, he dropped the phone and stumbled down a few steely steps.

"Shit!"

The reporter reached for the receiver and heard the operator, "Hello? I am connecting you now . . . "

He righted himself and tugged at the phone carriage to find a little more line. In the distance, he spotted Pearl Harbor on fire.

"Mother of God!"

He spoke into the receiver, "One, two, three, four . . . hello NBC . . . this is *KGU* Honolulu, Hawaii. I'm speaking to you from the roof of the Advertiser Publishing Company building in downtown Honolulu . . . We have, ah, witnessed the severe bombing of Pearl Harbor by enemy planes, undoubtedly Japanese . . . this battle has been going on for nearly three hours."

Another battleship explodes.

---

20   http://historymatters.gmu.edu/d/5167

"This is no joke—it's a real war! The . . . ah . . . the public of Honolulu have been advised to stay in their homes and await instructions from the army and navy . . . "

Sudden static on the other end of the line surprised him.

"This is the telephone company operator, Sir."

The reporter stared at the destruction, dumbfounded at the interruption.

"We're clearing the line for an emergency call . . . ," she said.

"Well . . . I'm talking to New York, Ma'am. My microphone isn't functioning, and this is the only way for me to file my story . . . "

The phone went dead.

In the distance, the aftermath of the Battle of Pearl Harbor loomed. Battleships listed to one side, partially sunk fireballs. Black smoke filled the sky. A lone Japanese zero churned thick black smoke as it rose to the heavens.

Yesterday The United States of America was suddenly and deliberately attacked by the naval and air forces of the Empire of Japan. Last night Japanese forces attacked Hong Kong. Last night Japanese forces attacked Guam . . .

—President Roosevelt's address to congress, December 8, 1941[21]

Days later, on December 10, 1941, the Japanese sunk the British ships *Repulse* and the *Prince of Wales*, in the South China Sea, ending the Allied forces significant naval presence there. As the Japanese threat worsened during 1941, the engineers at Malabar built a nearly 500-foot bomb shelter to house radio equipment and keep it safe. It was

---

21   https://www.nps.gov/wwii/learn/historyculture/1941-address-before-congress.htm

easy for inexperienced radio technicians to dig the limestone soil. To move the equipment, they also built a road.

"After the completion of the work, the traditional offering (called slamatan) was observed but this time instead of a buffalo, a black goat was sacrificed. Much valuable material was brought to safety such as transmitters and large water-cooled lamps. A month or two later, however, they discovered that the area was very humid and additional measures needed to be taken to protect the transmitters from mold. After the war, the operations could be restarted immediately with the material out of the shelter, because the tunnel system outlived the Japanese bombardments."[22]

Singapore fell in mid-February of 1942. Days later, the Battle of the Java Sea, the largest naval engagement since WWI, twenty-six years before, was the prelude to the Japanese occupying Java in desperate fighting and would be followed in the days after by two other battles.

On 26 February, ABDA [American, British, Dutch, Australian Command] commander Admiral Karel Doorman gathered his multinational task force and sailed from Surabaya at the east end of Java, his intention to intercept a Japanese convoy sailing towards Java from the Makassar Strait. Doorman's force consisted of every warship available to him, including two heavy cruisers HMS Exeter and USS Houston, three light cruisers Hr Ms De Ruyter (flagship), Hr Ms Java, and HMAS Perth, and nine destroyers; HMS Electra, HMS Encounter, HMS Jupiter, Hr Ms Kortenaer, Hr Ms Witte de With, USS Alden, USS John D. Edwards, USS John D. Ford and USS Paul Jones. The Japanese convoy was escorted by two heavy cruisers HIJMS's Nachi

---

22 Van Der Wal, Ineke, *The Temple with the Chrysanthemums: Dutch Prisoners of War in Tokyo*, Independently published, 2017. (note: In this book my dad is inaccurately called Reinier. My uncle Reinier is inaccurately called Hans. Quotes have been edited slightly for grammar and tense) pg. 148.

and Haguro, two light cruisers Naka and Jintsu, and fourteen destroyers Yudachi, Samidare, Murasame, Harusame, Minegumo, Asagumo, Yukikaze, Tokitsukaze, Amatsukaze, Hatsukaze, Yamakaze, Kawakaze, Sazanami, and Ushio, all under the command of Rear Admiral Shoji Nishimura of the Japanese 3rd Fleet . . .

The ABDA fleet was essentially wiped out after three sea battles [(Java Sea 1, Sunda Strait, Java Sea 2/Bawean Island], with 11 allied warships sunk and over 2,000 officers and sailors lost. Without a naval fleet to deter the Japanese invasion force, American and British forces began falling back to Australia, hence marking the practical fall of the Malay barrier. Unfortunately, the only strategic goal achieved by the decimation of the ADBA fleet was to delay the Japanese invasion of Java by just one single day; the remnants of Dutch and British troops eventually surrendering on 9 March. In just three tumultuous months, Japanese forces had effectively overrun all of Asia."[23]

Dad was a soldier in the Dutch army by the time the Japanese bore down on the island, tasked with identifying Japanese aircraft and communications. He got word out to local citizens about changing events.

---

23   https://ww2db.com/battle_spec.php?battle_id=23

Dad, 1942, Java.

Dear Laura,

Some of my classmates had already joined the army, one went to the Netherlands to join the air force and was shot down. In the beginning of 1942, some of our teachers went into the Dutch East Indies Army Reserves. This army had all Dutch officers, but Indonesian soldiers. They were from the island of Ambon and were fierce fighters. However, the Dutch East Indies Army was no match for the Japanese.

By February 1942, our school was shut down. In fact, we had already passed our final exams, and my mother visited the principal, Dr. Gisolf, and received a letter stating that I had completed the Gymnasium B curriculum and listed the subjects that I had taken. Gymnasium B included Maths as well as languages, but no drawing courses, which became important later to steer me to engineering.

With nothing to do, I stayed home. When the Japanese took over Bandung, the General in charge told all Dutch they could continue to work to keep the electricity and other services going, but only those Dutch were allowed outside their homes to go to work and had to wear armbands with a Japanese flag on it.

So, I had to stay home and I couldn't ride my bike to school anymore, you see. I was bored. All our Indonesian workers left. We had maids for cooking, cleaning, laundry, gardeners, the usual servants for a Dutch Colonial home. I became very busy helping Mams to keep our villa going. We started to close big portions of the house, but the buying of groceries to feed ourselves became a problem. Paps helped because he was allowed to go to work and picked up food when it was available.

Our villa was at a crossroads. The main road led to a bridge across the Tjitarum River, and the other one to Villa Isola, where the Dutch Commander surrendered to the Japanese General. The same road intersected with the road leading to our high school, the Christelyk Gymnasium. I traveled the road on my bike every day, so I was very familiar with our neighborhood. Our property bounded the crossroads on the right and toward the left was a kampong, or Indonesian village. Our gardener, Sukio, lived there and was a village official, and he asked for permission for his villagers to pray and bring offerings to our Holy Tree, which was near the crossroads.

After I could not leave our property, I started gardening and learned from our gardener. I was fluent in the local Malay dialect.

I'd sneak to the kampong and the people there were good to me.
Eventually, I considered myself part of the kampong and forgot
that my white skin gave me away.

    Love,

    Daddy

Just after the New Year in 1942, the PTT (Post Telephone &
Telegraph Company, the company Grandpa worked for) countered
Japanese propaganda by developing jamming transmitters and a special
post with the ability to listen in on those broadcasts in case of any specific threats against them. By that March, about three weeks after Dad
turned 18, The Battle of Java began and lasted for twelve days. 35,000
Japanese ground forces landed in the east and the west of the island.

"The Allied forces, commanded by Royal Netherlands East Indies
Army General Hein Ter Poorten, totalled about 25,000 poorly trained
Indonesian troops as well as 7,000 British, Australian, and American
men, under the command of British Major General H. D. W. Sitwell
(3,500 British were predominantly anti-aircraft units, though one
armored unit, the British 3rd Hussars, was present. The 2,500 Aus-
tralians were of Blackforce of Brigadier Arthur Blackburn. The 1,000
Americans were of the 2nd Battalion of the 131st Field Artillery, a
Texas National Guard unit, and was attached to Blackforce.)"[24]

By March 8, Ter Poorten surrendered all of Java to the Japanese.
Late that evening, Bert Garthoff ended his broadcast at the radio
station—

"Blacked-out communications have left events on Java in doubt
tonight. This, the last message from Radio Bandung: "*Wij sluiten nu.*

---

24   https://ww2db.com/battle_spec.php?battle_id=23

Vaarwel tot betere tijden. Leve de Koningin! (We are now shutting down. Good-bye till better times. Long live the Queen!)"[25]

It would be his last broadcast from The Dutch radio station NIROM from a temporary transmitter at Ciumbuleuit. They ended their program as they always had, with the Dutch National Anthem. The Japanese executed three NIROM employees in retaliation.[26]

On March 12, 1942, the Allies surrendered Java to Lieutenant General Masao Maruyama, having suffered around 5,000 casualties.[27]

* * *

"The Japanese were a brilliant occupying force, using only 100,000 soldiers to occupy the whole of Java," Dad said during one of our visits. "They did it with bicycles armed with guns that were equipped with large bayonets. The Japanese enrolled "essential workers." These were people who were integral to the daily functioning of public services like utilities. If you were 'lucky' enough, you were given the 'choice' of becoming an essential worker or being carted off to the camps with the rest of the Dutch. Grandpa and many of the other radio engineers became essential workers."

"*The Japanese derive part of their effectiveness from the fear they instill: after a successful attack, the military often behead several prisoners of war to keep the rest in check. All ranks of the KNIL* [Royal Netherlands East India Army] *know about this practice. In some cases, the Japanese even decide to take no prisoners of war at all; they just kill everybody. This happens (sic) to a group of soldiers in the mountains.*"[28]

---

25   https://www.nytimes.com/1942/03/08/archives/dutch-driven-back-last-bandung-mes-sage-is-ended-with-long-live-the.html "Wij sluiten nu. Vaarwel tot betere tijden. Leve de Koningin!"

26   https://en.wikipedia.org/wiki/NIROM *Garthoff later told that the station's employees were told by the Japanese authorities to "carry on as usual."*

27   https://ww2db.com/battle_spec.php?battle_id=23

28   Van Der Wal, Ineke, *The Temple with the Chrysanthemums: Dutch Prisoners of War in Tokyo,* Independently published, 2017. (pg. 154)

Occupation

Dear Laura,

The Japanese superior navy defeated the Allied navy, which mainly consisted of the British Battleships the Prince of Wales and the Repulse. Japanese suicide bombers (Kamikazi) flew their planes into the smokestacks of the two battleships and sank them both. The Allied destroyers were no match for the Japanese battleships, and were defeated in the Battle of the Java Sea on February 27, 1942.

It was not long thereafter when the Japanese Navy captured the Dutch Naval Base at Surabaya. In the meantime, I continued my final year at the Lyceum (high school) hoping to graduate. I'd just turned 18 a few weeks before, and I biked to our school every day. It was a long bike ride over a steep hill. On April 9, 1942, the Japanese Commander took over our school in order to use it for his soldiers.

Love, Daddy

"I know why my legs are so strong, because I rode my bike a half an hour uphill to get to school every day," Dad said. "I loved riding my bike. I hated being forced to stay home."

One day, Dad saw a regiment of Japanese soldiers ride by the house as he'd seen day after day since the occupation. Frustrated that they could ride their bikes on that road, and he couldn't, Dad hesitated and then made a break for it, pedaling hard out of the driveway and onto the road. A road he hadn't been allowed to ride for weeks.

The race was on. Dad caught the soldiers on a steep hill. His tire spun dangerously close to the soldiers' bikes. They had guns strapped to their backs.

"I'd never encountered people that looked like them before," Dad had said during one of our conversations.

A Japanese flag flew over his school. As Dad slowed down at the sight, a young Indonesian man called Sukio, the family gardener, appeared out of nowhere. He wore his pointed weaved bamboo hat and had a princely aura, despite being the poorest of men. Sukio immediately corralled Dad before he could bike through the gate of the school.

"This is not wise," Sukio said. They walked the main road together, leaving the bike behind.

Dad kicked a rock onto the road. "You know how hard I've worked to get into university! I can't even go to school now!?"

A little way down the road, soldiers with machine guns drawn, surrounded a car.

"What's happening?" Dad said.

"Roadblock."

Dad stopped in his tracks, surveying the road. "Where is everyone?"

"You're not safe walking the roads. Listen to your mother. She told you to stay home. Do as she says. You walk? There's problem. Big problem. Understand?" Sukio said.

Sukio walked faster. Dad followed, looking back over his shoulder from time to time, until the roadblock disappeared from view.

"It's all these soldiers' fault! My life's frozen!" Dad stopped in his tracks.

Sukio pulled Dad aside, off the main road. "That stunt, your little race? It could have killed you! Don't you understand? Everything's changed. Everything."

"I had to do something! I haven't done anything wrong. I want to go back to school. I want to graduate. I don't want to be a prisoner in my own home! It's not fair!"

Sukio stood, speechless. There was no way to help Dad understand what was coming. Instead, he motioned Dad to follow him. Sukio's steps were sure. Dad's were not. When he walked into the rice paddies, Dad followed.

Sukio said, "There's something you need to see . . . "

Their walk through the rice paddies was a wonder, a freedom never allowed before. The clear lines about what Dad could and couldn't do blurred as the colonial way of life crumbled after the occupation.

"The Dutch East Indies society is quite hierarchical with three populations that live separately from each other: Europeans, foreign Orientals (Chinese, Arab, British Indian, and indigenous people. The Europeans live mainly in the large, newly built residential areas north of the railway line, the Chinese mainly live in *Pasar Baru*, southwest of the railway line. Due to the rapid growth and expansion of Bandung, the *kampongs*, the residential areas of the indigenous population, shrink down to one third of their original size."[29]

29   Ibid. (pg. 81)

What a joy it was to walk freely in nature after being cooped up at home for so long. Exploring something new felt like a tonic. Dad breathed it all in—the tangy scent of wet, saturated earth and the heavy, muggy tropical air of Java. His eyes lingered at the sight of rice shoots poking out of the muddy water. While the sight enchanted Dad, Sukio didn't break his barefoot stride.

Dad quickened his pace to follow Sukio out of the rice paddies and onto a jungle path, which led to a huge Banyan tree.[30] The massive tree looked alive with arm-like tendrils that dropped to Earth. A large black-and-white checked sarong had been wrapped around its trunk. Dad ran his hand over the twisted bark and cloth. The bumpy texture of the ancient tree comforted him. It had survived for hundreds of years. Just beyond Sukio, smoke encircled a small temple that sat beside the tree. The temple was filled with brightly colored baskets and adornments. A musky, pleasing scent of incense filled the air.

"It's good to finally see such beauty, is it not?" Sukio said.

Dad nodded. "But why is the tree wrapped in cloth?"

"To honor it. This is a Holy Tree."

Dad took a step back and looked up through the Banyan tree's many hanging branches, falling all around him, looking as if they might be poised to give him a hug.

"The sarong honors good," Sukio said, pointing to a white check, "and evil," he continued, pointing to a black one.

Dad walked closer to the temple, examining its offerings—woven bamboo baskets filled with flowers, eggs, coconuts, and rice. Incense sticks burned and their trails of smoke rose, disappearing into the maze of branches.

"A great spirit lives inside this tree," Sukio said.

---

30   The Banyan tree is depicted on the Indonesian National Coat of Arms, called Garuda Pancasila.

"A good spirit?" Dad asked.

"Good lives equally with evil. The left hand with the right. The day with the night. We honor both worlds. They exist together."

"But don't you just want evil to go away?" Dad said.

"You see with clouded vision. What have I told you about evil?"

"Without evil, I would never know what is good," Dad said by rote.

Sukio picked some plants from the jungle floor, clipped their leaves, and trimmed the stems. He then raised up a handful.

"Remember this plant. It's called daun paku. See the shape of its leaves?"

Dad looked carefully at the fern leaves and nodded, with a question in his eyes.

Sukio crushed the herbs, handed them to Dad, then they ate them.

"This will keep your body healthy. It's everywhere. If you feel sick you must eat it, Understand?"

"You haven't answered my question," Dad said. He jumped at the sound of distant gunfire.

"Even at its worst, evil exists to point to good. There is great beauty in destruction. Learn to appreciate its beauty," Sukio said, a look of desperation in his eyes.

At the sound of more gunfire, Dad ran through the jungle. He slipped, fell, and punched the mud. Sukio followed close behind then stopped. With a smirk, he said, "Laugh when you fall. And when you are sad, sing—like the songbirds."

Sukio took Dad by the hand and helped him get free of the mud. Together, they walked out of the jungle. Still shaken from the gunfire, they crossed a dirt road by a warung, a tiny road-side restaurant. Small tokos, little outdoor stores, dotted the street.

Caged songbirds hung on the perimeter of a nearby toko. Sukio ordered two cups of tea and handed Dad one before squatting at the roadside. He squatted like Sukio, joining him with some difficulty. Close by, locals laughed and joked over their lunches. More machine-gun wielding Japanese soldiers cycled down the road. Suddenly, the laughing stopped, and all eyes were on Dad. Sukio continued to calmly sip his tea. Sweat beaded on his brow.

"Seeing the Holy Tree and the world as it really is, is good, is it not?"

"It's not boring," Dad said.

Sukio walked over to one of the caged songbirds. When he whistled, the bird instantly sang beautifully in return. "Remember, Hans, birds always sing after a storm."

"You're the only servant who hasn't left us," Dad said.

Black cars with Japanese flags flying roared down the street.

After a few seconds, Sukio took Dad back into the jungle.

The days were long, but the nights were even longer during the first months of the occupation. The colonists had tried to find a new normal, to make sense of the nonsensical. One night, Dad couldn't sleep because enchanting, haunting music played in the distance. He told me that the jungle came alive at night with an orchestra of sounds. But the sounds that piqued Dad's curiosity weren't natural, yet they were familiar. He'd heard them since he was a boy. The discordant music played sporadically, coming from the nearby kampong. He'd been told it was gamelan music, and it played during festivals of celebration and solemnity. A kind of chanting always accompanied the celebrations, too.

That night, Dad decided to follow the music. Gongs and cymbals drowned out the jungle's orchestra of monkey shrieks, bird caws, and insect chirps. Sukio followed on the overgrown path as the jungle's orchestra hit a crescendo. When they reached the kampong, they squatted together in front of a stage. Dad raised his eyes to where a giant white sheet had been stretched between bamboo poles. In front of the stage, seated in the dirt, sat elegantly dressed members of a gamelan group. Some played gongs, others played something that looked like xylophones, and in the center, a man sat chanting.

Wayang shadow puppets began to play out an ancient Sanskrit saga called the *Ramayana*, a love story about a prince called Rama, and his wife, Sita, a kind of Romeo and Juliet tale. Dad had never seen the likes of the exotic play before. Its sights and sounds completely captivated him.

"Sometimes, what we think is bad, isn't really bad at all," Sukio said.

"This is the most exciting thing that's happened since the air raids," Dad said.

"Boredom has its place," Sukio replied.

Smoke from flickering oil lamps drifted over the sheet. Behind it, intricate puppets moved, casting shadows on the stage. A man sat center-stage, cross-legged, swaying as he sang, channeling the gods.

"The Dalang chants stories of the *Ramayana*. He's a mystic. His voice is magic," Sukio said.

At that moment, some village boys squatted beside Dad, handing him an Angklung, a small wooden instrument made of different lengths of bamboo rods that sit in a bamboo cradle. One of the boys rocked the rods. The instruction turned into a mini-jam session. Dad tried to get comfortable squatting like the other boys, but he ended up sitting in the dirt.

Puppet shadows, gamelan music, and the Dalang's mystical chants hypnotized Dad. The shadow puppet play about Rama and Sita's star-crossed love cast a spell. The music and the Dalang's voice lulled Dad into a kind of dream. He watched wide-eyed as Rama drew a magic circle on the ground to protect Sita, saving her from an evil spirit.

*　*　*

Dear Laura,

A tropical night is always noisy. Shrieking and things going on, all the different sounds just blend. Animal sounds, human sounds. And the gamelan music itself. And yes, it would go on all night. I was a teenager when I first saw the shadow puppet show. Every night in the evening it was their entertainment. Like a young boy's jam session. Angklung-different pieces of bamboo of different lengths you shake them a little.

There was a sacred tree. A huge tree outside of our rented villa that we had to leave behind after the occupation. Emil [Dad's uncle by marriage, the husband of Irene's sister, Lettie, Aletta's namesake] was a real estate man and found this house for us. It had a beautiful atrium with a fountain and looked like an Italian villa. I had one corner and my parents had another corner. The rooms were beautiful, we brought our furniture there and the view was gorgeous. We looked out on beautiful rice fields. It over-looked Tangkuban Perahu, "Boat Mountain" so named because it looked like it was an upside-down boat.

Love, Daddy

Dad said the estate where he lived was called Leeuwensberg, meaning *Lion's Mountain* in Dutch. Uncle Reiner gave me a little more detail into how the family ended up living at the estate, saying, "We rented it from fleeing middle management. Dutch who all escaped before the Japanese occupied Java. Your grandpa could have left but he chose to stay."

Many people stayed. When Grandpa returned from Europe in the mid-1930s, after seeing the horrors of Hitler's Germany first-hand, he had asked Emil, a proud German, to naturalize Dutch. Because Emil didn't, he was thrown into a POW camp as soon as Hitler invaded Holland in May, 1940, about a year and a half before the Japanese Occupation of Java.

"Lettie, a Dutch woman and your grandma's sister, was considered German because she had married Emil. So, Lettie was left to fend for herself after Emil was thrown in prison," Reinier said. Then he went on to say that Grandma would have suffered the same fate if Grandpa hadn't naturalized Dutch after their trip to get Dad and Aletta out of Germany and back home to Java. I couldn't imagine Lettie's heartache and the terror that came with her precarious situation. Reinier further explained that Lettie's oldest son, Deter, was shanghaied at the age of sixteen and put on a German U-boat in Surabaya, a city in eastern Java.

Reinier said, "Lettie begged the captain to leave him with her, as he was the only man left in the family. She told the captain that her husband had been taken by the Dutch and sent to a British POW camp in India as a prisoner on a boat that had been sunk. Officially it had sunk, but Emil happened not to be on the boat that she had thought." What happened to Lettie, Emil, and their children, is another story, for another day.

Essential Worker

Grandpa set his elbow on the ledge of the open window of his Chevrolet. An armband with a Japanese flag had been sown on his sleeve. Middle-aged, he had an eerie countenance with unnaturally blue eyes. His wiry, long white hair stood on end in the breeze. As he drove by bamboo-and-barbed-wire fences of newly constructed prison camps, Japanese soldiers on bicycles swarmed his vehicle. Sunlight flickered off soldiers' bayonets into the rearview mirror, momentarily blinding Grandpa. He parked at the entrance to the PTT office, where he had worked for nearly two decades. But it was hardly another day at the office. When he got out of his car a Japanese soldier gestured to Grandpa's hair and said, "Welcome, Einstein."

Grandpa took steps toward the Japanese soldier but Indonesian scientists encircled their former boss and mentor before there was a confrontation.

The first scientist whispered, "No trouble . . . or you'll end up in the camps like everyone else." He searched Grandpa's eyes. "We'll be lost without you."

"Don't teach us everything . . . that way, you see, they can't take you away," another scientist whispered.

Grandpa's Indonesian protégés ushered him into the radio station then returned to work.

William Van Osten, a colleague a few years older than Grandpa, gripped him by the elbow. Van Osten led Grandpa away from soldiers who'd also entered the radio station. He escorted Grandpa into the transmission room for some privacy.

"You know what's at stake. Don't be a fool!" Van Osten said.

Grandpa pulled out of his friend's grip easily and said, "We've built the most powerful radio station on the planet! I won't help them steal it from the free world. The air has gone silent, don't you get it? All we'll broadcast is Japanese ravings. Propaganda!"

Van Osten turned down the volume on Grandpa's speech with his hands, then motioned his friend to come closer. They huddled together.

"You know what that attitude will cost?!" Van Osten said.

"There's a fine line between being an essential worker and collaboration," Grandpa replied.

"It's war, Alexander. Survival means blurring that line," Van Osten said. His gaze caught the sight of more soldiers through the window, presumably gathering to infiltrate the building. They'd lost control of their precious radio station.

Grandpa shook his head.

"What can one man do to fight this madness?" Van Osten asked.

"Whatever he can. Anything he can."

Grandpa worked with several scientists and Mr. Wim Einthoven was one of them. Einthoven, whose father won the Nobel Prize for inventing the electrocardiograph, had been a pioneer in radiotelegraphy and invested most of his life in the invention of the string galvanometer, essential to long-range radio which short wave ironically eclipsed in the 1930s. Late in 1927, after the sudden death of Dr. Ir. C.J. De Groot, Einthoven became the scientific successor at Malabar. He had been hand-picked by De Groot only a few years before to continue his work when the time came.

The engineers of the radio laboratory in Bandung put up resistance in the weeks that followed the occupation. Eventually the Kempeitai summoned all of the employees of the radio station to meet in one room of the laboratory. As the engineers stood in shock, the Japanese secret police surrounded them with their guns drawn. One of the Kempeitai officers yelled something in Japanese as he approached Mr. Schippers, who the officer simply picked out of the group.

"Schippers was with me at the radio conference in Cairo years ago. His room was also searched by the Japanese. How much do the Japanese know?" Wim Enithoven whispered to his colleague Klass Dijkstra.

The Kempeitai officer unleashed his fury at the outburst. He left his intended target and instead placed the barrel of his revolver on the forehead of Einthoven. Einthoven raised his chin in defiance. The Kempeitai officer lowered his gun then directed the barrel at Schippers' head.

"You choose . . . " The secret policeman stated matter-of-factly to Schippers, "A bullet through your head or your heart?"

Schippers froze. He shook, looking at his colleagues. As he closed his eyes he said, "Heart."

The Kempeitai officer pulled the trigger. Blood pooled on Shipper's white shirt before he slumped forward. His body soon hit the ground.

Death would be their only escape.

"Never speak of the work that you do," the officer said.

Soon an "economist" who wore a uniform, carried a Samurai sword, and knew little about radio technology, was assigned to the radio laboratory. In short order, the Japanese had total control over the largest radio station in the Pacific.

* * *

Dear Laura,

My father continued to go to the office as in the past, and as he did not have a car anymore, someone picked him up. The Japanese Commander asked all Dutch to remain in their essential jobs and they were issued arm bands picturing the Japanese flag. Also, a message in Japanese characters with a flag was posted on our front door indicating that our house was the residence of an essential worker and should not be disturbed. So, life went on pretty "normal" under Japanese rule.

Your grandpa was not encumbered by the notion that Indonesians were inferior and could not be taught. Alex treated his Indonesian workers at the laboratory as coworkers and taught them. After 15 years, Alex's superior Dutch graduate engineers envied him for his knowledge and cooperation with Indonesians. Now came the Japanese Sumitomo Engineers who were put in charge of the radio lab and could only speak German, but no Dutch. And the Indonesians became the bosses with the Japanese.

Love, Daddy

* * *

On September 24, 1942, Glenn Miller played his final show called *The Moonlight Serenade* on CBS radio. "Live from the Central Theater in Passaic, New Jersey, we bring you Glenn Miller and his Orchestra."

Thirty-eight-year-old Glenn Miller took center stage. "Naturally, we're very reluctant to give up our moonlight serenades, after such a pleasant association with Chesterfield for such a long time. But, since I gotta date with Uncle Sam coming up, I can sincerely say I'd rather have Harry James take over than anyone I know. He's got a swell sponsor, great product and with Helen Forest and that band of his, I know he's going to do a wonderful job. Sounds to me like a right combination. So, next Tuesday it'll be Harry James."

"Captain Miller, speaking for the folks that make Chesterfields, I'm sure everyone agrees that you're doing a mighty fine thing in joining the army. A lot of good luck to you, Glenn."

"Thank you very much, Larry, it makes me feel a little sad to leave Mary and Tex, Skip, the Modernaires, this wonderful gang of boys in the band, but there are a lot of swell guys in the outfit I'm going in and . . . maybe all of us can get together when this thing is all over. In the meantime, I'll see you all in the army, and we'll say goodbye the best way we know how."

Wild applause, shouts, and whistles greeted the soon-to-be Captain Glenn Miller, as they played *Moonlight Serenade* for the last time.

"This is Larry Brach, saying good night, goodbye, and good luck to all of you for Glenn Miller and the gang. And don't forget that starting next Tuesday and every Tuesday, Wednesday, and Thursday from then on the nation's number one trumpeter, Harry James, and his Chesterfield Music Makers will be on hand to entertain you—same station, same time. In the meantime, remember to make your next pack Chesterfields. This is the Columbia Broadcasting System."[31]

Glenn Miller would never return. On a foggy afternoon in December 1944, after entertaining the troops, Miller took off from England heading for France when his plane vanished over the English Channel. He was never found.

* * *

A world away, my family could no longer listen to the radio because the Japanese had issued orders that Europeans couldn't possess one. Where Grandpa worked in the radio laboratory these rules also applied and the Japanese confiscated those that weren't directly needed for their work. It would mean death to listen to a radio, but it was possible, although extremely dangerous, to listen in secret since opportunities presented themselves often.

> *"Mr. Einthoven, however (who finds it very hard to adjust to the new situation) was so imprudent to have a listening device installed in his office, apparently under the opinion that the order did not apply to him. It was typical that our 'economist,', who had noticed this of course, did not object. But the Kempeitai (the dreaded military police) are of a different opinion, because that very night he was taken from his home and brought to their headquarters. They beat him with belts on his legs before interrogating him, but he is nevertheless released after one and a half hours, and is allowed to walk back home. This*

---

31   https://www.youtube.com/watch?v=l8v5uRUqdoE "Glenn Miller's farewell before joining the U.S. Army, 24 September 1942."

time they show mercy, although the traces of the 'interrogation' remain visible for a long time. Later it turns out that one of the indigenous spies—it is apparent that there are lots of them—has betrayed him."

—Klaas Dijkstra, *Radio Malabar*

THE FIRST TIME
GRANDPA SAVED DAD'S LIFE

I needed to fill in important gaps of Dad's wartime memories. Gleaning those details was the most frustrating and yet magical part of our journey. At times I hit brick walls where I had to leave the story alone for years at a time. Other times, much-needed information came to me serendipitously, when I least expected it.

About a handful of years after Dad and I had been writing to each other, in 1991, I took a trip to Olympia, WA, to visit my Uncle Reinier with my young daughters. My family had attended a wedding in Portland and since we were only a few hours drive away, I thought it would be nice to visit my dad's brother for a few days. The girls and I made the trip alone. Reinier and I had rarely seen or spoken to each other over the years. But, I'd recently seen him at my sister's wedding. And a few years before that, he reached out for my help when his son needed a few things delivered to him while on a school trip to Los Angeles.

Twenty years earlier, when I was seven years old, I met Reinier, his wife, Beverly, and my two cousins for the first time. They came to see us in Chicago for a short visit. Before Dad died, he gave me our family's beautifully carved, wooden *Gestabok* (Icelandic for "Guest-book") where our relatives, guests, and visitors from all over the world signed sweet messages to our family. I treasure the book with its many signatures of folks who enjoyed Mom and Dad's hospitality at parties and special events. In 1971, Reinier signed and dated it, with a note that said "love to you all." As I grew, Reinier and I exchanged cards over the holidays. Some he beautifully painted with watercolors. He and Dad both enjoyed painting.

It was fun to see how different Dad and Reinier were and how similar. At the time of our visit, Reinier had a tall, slight, athletic stature and the gifts of curiosity and storytelling, like Dad. Also like Dad, Reinier was playful, happy, and kind with me and my girls. After playing with some toys, we all walked the rocky beach outside his home where we spotted his kayak. While my Dad took the train to work each day as a hydroelectric engineer, Reinier paddled across the inlet of the Olympic Peninsula to work as a professor at The Evergreen State College. He spent his career teaching Native American studies and also raised awareness about the lives and customs of the Native Americans of the Pacific Northwest.

I found my uncle to be a down-to-earth person who lived life simply. During our visit he told me that he and his wife, Beverly, decided to raise their children without any television so they had plenty of time to pursue their passions. Over the years, Reinier and his sons have been a constant source of inspiration. They have creative, brilliant minds, are a lot of fun, and have been a wonderful support.

That night over dinner, after the girls went to play in another room close by, Reinier asked, "Has Hans ever spoken about the war with you?"

The question took me aback a bit. "Rarely," I said. "We've only begun to talk about it."

Then Reinier immediately reflected on powerful incidents that he himself had witnessed as a boy during the war. Outwardly, Reinier had been much more affected by the trauma of WWII than my dad. And yet, unlike Dad, he was much more capable of talking about his emotional experiences. Reiner was the first one who gave me a window into the more chilling and frightening details about their wartime experience. He had just turned six at the time of Pearl Harbor and was eleven years younger than Dad.

"Hans was held in a men's military camp. They were rounding up all the men eighteen and over and your Dad was seventeen. The Japanese military's code of conduct was to never get caught. And so, prisoners were considered less than human, and the camp conditions were horrendous," Reinier said.

"Grandpa saved your dad's life by negotiating to get him out of the prison camp. The Japanese could have just shot your grandpa on the spot instead of negotiating with him," Reinier said with a penetrating gaze, adding, "Grandpa saved your dad's life two times. This was the second."

The second time Grandpa saved Dad's life. Those powerful words sank into my soul. It was the first time I really understood how close Dad and the family came to dying. How brushes with death happen in fleeting moments when split-second decisions can grant or end life just as easily.

Over the years, I would learn that Uncle Reinier had suffered much as a child during the war years and as a refugee. Dad had become like a father to him in Grandpa's absence because Grandpa had to return to Indonesia after the war to secure his pension. In addition to attending university in Sydney, Dad worked to help support Reinier and Grandma. He bought land in Wahroonga, a suburb of Sydney, and built a house for all of them to live in. When Dad immigrated to the United States in 1951, Reinier was only sixteen. A year later Grandpa returned to Australia; the first time Reinier had seen his father in seven years.

But my uncle found happiness at the age of 20 when Dad and Mom sponsored him to come to America and live with them only a year after they were married. Reinier often says that because of their kindness, he owes Mom and Dad a debt of gratitude that he can never repay. He arrived in the United States in June, 1955, after a 21-day voyage from Sydney, thrilled to immigrate. However, he had fallen in love with Beverly while living in Australia and wanted to marry her.

In the years after the Korean War, Reinier was able to join the U.S. military. Mom's brother, my Uncle Ron, was a U.S. Marine and Reinier became friends with him. When Reinier told Ron that he wanted to join the army, Ron suggested the Air Force instead. That way, Reinier might have the opportunity to fly to Australia and see the woman he loved. Reinier took Ron's advice and joined the Air Force (unfortunately, Ron died in a car accident only a few years later). Reinier was serendipitously assigned to Hawaii and flew to see Beverly often, leading to a beautiful courtship and eventually marriage. Sadly, when Reinier and I had our chat in 1991, he had become a widower years earlier.

Shortly after my visit with Reinier, Dad wrote to me with his recollections about the incident where Grandpa saved his life for the first time. (Decades passed before Dad would write to me about the second.)

In the heat of the day, Dad pulled weeds around some of his newly planted tomato seedlings in the once manicured garden outside the family villa in Bandung. The simple act of normalcy amid the chaos took on a moment of the spiritual. Steam rose from Tangkuban Perahu in the distance. An eerie silence engulfed Dad as he patted the soil with his bare hands. When he finished, he stared at the road, still absent of cars and people. He walked over to the garden shack and put a hand rake and shovel on their proper nails, joining the rest of the organized tools in the shed. Sukio's pointed bamboo hat lay upturned on the potting table.

Grandma walked to the shed and stared at her son. An exotic beauty of forty-four years, life in the tropics had painted her fair features.

"Where did you get the seedlings?" she asked.

"Sukio."

Grandma turned pale.

Dad lifted his chin and asked, "Where is he?"

"He's gone. You're in charge of the garden now," Grandma said. She searched her surroundings on her walk back to the villa.

Dad picked Sukio's hat up off the potting table and put it on, whispering to himself, "You'd never just leave me."

Just beyond the rim of the too-large hat, a black car raced up the driveway. On either side of the car, small Japanese flags flapped in the wind. It skidded to a stop in front of the villa beside Grandpa's blue Chevrolet. Soldiers got out of the shiny car and yelled at Dad in a language he didn't understand so he stayed silent. When one of the soldiers pointed a gun at Dad, he pointed to the villa, hoping the soldier would leave him alone.

Dear Laura,

One afternoon I was weeding in front of our house, when a number of cars with Japanese soldiers drove up and saw our car in the garage. As it turned out they took the wrong fork in the road near our house and went right instead of going left, ending up in our front yard.

They spoke no English, and I had no knowledge of Japanese. One of the soldiers wanted the keys to our car. I did not have them and motioned to the front door. The soldier saw my Mido Automatic watch I had received as an early graduation present from my dad on my birthday, and he stripped it from my arm.

My father came to the front door and saw what was happening and held the keys for the car in his hand and the soldier tried to grab them. But my father pointed to my watch on the soldier's arm and gestured to return it to me. Then the soldier took his gun and pointed it at my father's chest, but my father was still not ready to give him the car keys before my watch was returned to me.

Fortunately, another car pulled up and a Japanese officer stepped out and gave a command to the soldiers to step back. This officer spoke English, and my mother, who had come to the front door, spoke English too. The Japanese officer said that they were just requisitioning our car and would give a receipt for it. My father said if I give you the car, you can at least give my son his watch back from that soldier. The officer called the soldier and had him give my watch back. He apologized for the behavior of his soldiers and said they were Korean and not Japanese. I was happy to have my watch back.

This incident made me a lot more careful in how I behaved. I now never left our home, except to buy groceries at a local shop called a TOKO. Over the months, even these were harder and harder to get. My father and mother had hired some people from the neighboring village. Also, the headman of the kampong [village] had come to us to explain that we had a Holy Tree on our property and asked permission for the villagers to bring flowers and gifts to the tree.

When we could no longer get any rice at the local store, we got rice from the village. The village provided help for our garden. Our gardener helped me to plant a vegetable garden and showed me how to plant tomato plants.

Love, Daddy

CAPTURED

Dad reached for his violin and played in a sunny corner of the living room of the family villa. Grandma and Grandpa sat at a table not too far away. She clutched a framed photo. At her feet, uncle Reinier played with some palm fronds.

"I should've never let Aletta go to London. There's been no letter. If she were alive, there'd have been a letter."

Dad stopped playing.

"But there was a letter," Grandpa said.

"Years ago . . . "

"It was full of her joy . . . eurythmy, and the family she befriended. The family will keep her safe," Grandpa said. "Trust in that."

"No one's safe in London. No one's safe here. I don't know if Aletta is alive . . . or . . . "

Grandpa placed his hand on his wife's chest. "What does your heart say?"

"Our family . . . is . . . falling apart," Grandma said.

A car horn honked. Grandpa rose, kissed Grandma's forehead, and handed her his handkerchief.

Grandma patted her tears dry and smiled. A glimmer of hope in her eyes.

Dad slowly ran the bow across his violin strings again, the beauty of the music gave an air of normality to their chaotic lives until honks from a waiting car caused Grandpa to scowl. He glared through the window then took his wife's hand in his and gave it a kiss.

Grandpa walked slowly to the front door and breathed deep, as if inhaling Dad's music before he left. When the door shut, Dad stopped playing. He put his violin down and walked into the deserted kitchen where Grandma was. It had once been a bustling place, where the cook filled the villa with delicious scents of coconut, curry, and rice. Grandma stared into the empty pantry with a blank expression.

"We've run out of sugar."

* * *

Dear Laura,

The Japanese came eight months or so before I was captured. I considered myself part of the kampong and forgot that my white skin gave me away. I stayed away from the highways and walked on the local village pathways in the rice fields. One of those pathways led under the bridge to a kampong that had a toko, or grocery store.

On that Fateful Day, Mother had run out of sugar, and I decided to go and get some. I was just a kid and wanted to get past the roadblock and get the sugar as an adventure. They had checkpoints to pick up the Dutch. I used the local pathway along the river at the back of our property and went around the Japanese checkpoint on the highway. I had done that for months.

But, one of the guards saw me in the grocery store and knew I was not supposed to be there. So, he came up to me and asked me where I was from, and soon a car came, and they took me away to a Holding Area in an old Dutch Colonial House and put me in a room with other Dutch men. The home was typical for Dutch Homes with tiled floors. I stayed there some days and slept on the bare tile floor.

Then I was taken to the Central Police Station and put into a room with lots of other Dutch men. I just had my normal clothes on and no identification. The next day, they didn't know what to do with us. More and more people came and eventually you could no longer sit down in the room. We were taken to The Palace Hotel, which was converted to a prison. It was an Indonesian camp under Japanese command . . . and was transferred to a Prison Camp, where the concrete floor was warmer than the tiles, and we were given mats to sleep on. That became my way of living for the next years.

I ended up in the suburban camp established for Dutchmen. This area was a fenced area with a barbed wire fence about 6 ft. high in the suburb called Tjimahi. This was the Tjimahi POW camp where I was to spend the next few years. My dad did not know what happened to me . . . Things were pretty grim in the camp.

Every day started with Revile, when we had to count down in Japanese: Ichi (1), Ni (2), San (3), Shi (4), etc. and bow to the Emperor. Each prisoner bowed low to the ground as they said their number. Bowing low was a crucial part of Tenko. One of us did not bow low enough and got a beating with a bamboo stick. It was tough to watch, but it taught me a lesson. I followed the rules. If they wanted me to bow, I bowed the required amount. The camp taught me a lesson of survival, scrounging for food and obeying rules.

Love, Daddy

* * *

Dad wrote a graph on my paper indicating the years 1942, 1943, 1944 and 1945 and tried to figure out when and where he was during that time. These years of captivity were a puzzle for us to solve together. Dad had times of being very lucid, remembering certain things clearly and other times of great confusion, when he wouldn't have much to say or would say very little. But he never wanted to stop talking.

There were two things that stood out when Dad told me about his capture. First, there was no escape for Dad or any of the Dutch prisoners. Because of the color of their skin, the Japanese easily spotted the Dutch and killed those trying to escape. And second, Dad would begin to live in an otherworldly place where people died daily from starvation, disease, and brutality while he tried to survive.

"In the code of the Samurai, known as Bushido, is *The Way of the Warrior*," Dad said, "We were all traitors not to die for our country. As prisoners, we were less than human in their eyes. This was at the heart of a clash of civilizations."

DIFFERENT LIVES

During the writing of this book, Dad and I went through many changes. About the time Dad and Mom would go through one of their biggest—moving from Chicago to Florida at the ages of 84 and 80 respectively—I divorced my husband of nearly 28 years. The agony of losing my husband and best friend, the life we had built together, and the death of all the hopes and dreams I had for our family was one kind of pain.

In the aftermath, though, I experienced a new kind of pain that came with the business of divorce. I knew I had to be savvy in legal ways I never had before, so I asked Dad for advice. One day, while playing chess together, I told Dad I felt like I was in the chess game of my life with all the divorce proceedings. "Do you have any advice for getting through it all?"

He didn't miss a beat, stared at me with those beautiful crystal blue eyes and said, "The queen is the most powerful piece on the chessboard."

His words gave me all the encouragement I needed. I still keep them in my pocket. Dad had an art for saying exactly what I needed to hear when I needed to hear it. In this picture, only a few months before his death, he was more playful than he had ever been. Even wearing bling he never wore before. His golden chain made me smile almost as big as he did.

"The queen is the most powerful piece on the chessboard."
Dad during one of our chess games at his home in Largo, FL.

During this time, I remember asking Dad about his favorite song. It seemed odd that I didn't know. Suddenly I wanted to be sure to know so many things, especially the music he loved. I wanted to be sure to play it at his memorial service one day, though I never mentioned that to him.

He smiled and said, "*The Windmills of My Mind.*"

When I asked why, he said, "Because I've lived many, different lives."

He even counted them up for me—nine. I got goosebumps hearing the count. Unimaginable twists of fate and miracles led to him becoming my dad. I only had an inkling of what it might be like to live two lives—as a married lady, and as a newly single one. I don't think I would've gotten through my divorce with such joy and clarity without his wisdom and all the fun we shared during our journeys of self-discovery.

While divorce is common in this day and age, the personal process was anything but. Those were the years of big holiday parties and welcoming new members into our family. I looked forward to becoming a grandma one day and to enjoying a quiet life dedicated to my family.

Years before my divorce, during the crash of 2008, I'd left my multimedia job at the *Los Angeles Times* as my travel and lifestyle writing began to take off. I wanted to support my then-husband's new project management business venture of building and renovating hotels. That meant we needed to travel to where the work was because of the dire economic times. We were excited about traveling together to experience new places and enjoy being empty nesters at such a young age (we were both 45). About four years into what I thought was the romantic next chapter of our marriage, it ended abruptly.

Eight months later, a tortured attempt at reconciliation only revealed more lies and betrayals. But, I loved him deeply (with time, though, I would come to realize that I only deeply loved the idea of who I thought he was). In the midst of the chaos, it took me time to figure out what to do. He said things that didn't make sense all the time, like how I needed to immediately trust him. He asked the impossible of me, perhaps as a way of forcing an end to our relationship.

The only thing more impossible than staying was leaving. However, he gave me the gift of being awful. And I thank God for that because it gave me clarity. Two years after the marriage came crashing down at Christmastime, I received my divorce papers. Even then my heart ached terribly for the man I thought I married, the one I'd loved for thirty years; the life I thought we built together; and the many happy memories that seemed to torture me.

They say if you love someone, set them free. And the divorce was partly that, partly to give him the freedom to be his authentic self with whomever he wanted. But it was also about loving and honoring myself. I couldn't go where he led. I needed to be the strong one and end our marriage which was the hardest thing I'd ever done.

But, where would I go? I'd suffered too much trauma in our home to stay there. Everywhere I looked I remembered our confrontations. I remember the afternoon when my then-husband said the words that finally shook me from the ambivalence that had haunted me.

"You say I should just trust you," I said, bravely confronting him. "Immediately. The thing is that's unrealistic under these circumstances. Trust has to be earned. You blew it out of the water. Why are their numbers still on your phone? I mean, really?"

Anger rose up inside of him making his face red. "I don't know why they are still there!"

"Let's get away. I think this is the year," I said. I decided to do the riskiest thing I knew at the time—ask him a question that would help me understand whether there might be a glimmer of hope for us. It all rode on his answer.

"I'd like to go to Indonesia to research the story. I want you to come away with me?"

He stayed silent.

"It would only be a few weeks. We could look into hospitality projects over there too. It would be another one of our fun adventures," I said.

"I don't think I'll be able to go. You should just go alone," he said.

I nodded. When things got too cruel, I seemed to lose my voice.

"I'll be in the city all day. I'll text you when I'm on my way home," he said.

I couldn't look at him.

"Look Laura, we can't be together all the time. I need my autonomy. My job makes your writing possible. You can't survive without me."

You can't survive without me. I knew at that moment writing would be the key to how I would survive. I would create a new life for myself with my writing. As he left for the day, I realized that I would need to leave my home and everything I loved and worked for behind in order to survive my heartbreak. In a heartbeat, I lost one life and had to endure in order to find another. My home and my idea of home vanished. For a longtime, I became a stranger in my own life. But, as Reni had done, I tried to embrace the adventure.

CRYSTAL BEAR

On a hot, August day in 2013, my messy house was littered with thirty years of memories strewn across a carpeted part of a terra cotta tile floor—a wedding portrait of us as a young husband and wife; a framed photo composite of each of my daughters in every grade from Kindergarten to their senior year portraits; a photo of the whole family smiling, arm-in-arm at the base of a waterfall in Costa Rica. I'd hastily stacked our wedding china on top of the kitchen table. It had set every holiday and celebratory family meal we'd had over our lifetime together.

Where does love go to die? I asked myself. *Where should I go?*

Disheveled, I packed my entire life in an hour. My naturally feisty spark was clearly under strain. Empty boxes sat everywhere. I packed up some photos, froze, then cried. Confused, I stared over the mound of stuff, traumatized. Out of the middle of the pile I picked up a very ugly crystal bear with unusually large ears and arms that looked more like boobs. One of the boobs had partially broken off.

When we had become engaged we were in a long-distance relationship. My fiancé had just moved away to Los Angeles after we'd dated at the University of Illinois for about two years. So we decided that I would open all our wedding gifts in Chicago before the wedding. But I wanted to save one of them so we could open it together. I'll never forget how hard we laughed when we opened it. Of all the gifts to open together! It was really comical. The crystal bear became a standing joke between us and everyone in the family knew it. The bear was fine when we opened it. But one of its "boobs" shattered soon after our wedding when we moved into our home in Echo Park.

I stared much too long at that crystal bear on that hot August day in 2013. I slid my new cell phone out of my pocket as I cradled the heavy, broken bear and called my sister. A busy professional woman with three kids, she lived in Florida and had recently visited me as my world was imploding. I paced the floor, hugging the bear . . . *please pick up . . . please pick up . . . please pick up . . .*

When she did, I didn't wait for her to talk and immediately said, "It's the only wedding present we opened together. Of course it's broken. It should have been a sign!"

"What are you talking about?" Suzy said.

"The bear."

Silence.

"You know . . . the *crystal bear?*"

"Yeah. I'll fly out this afternoon," Suzy said.

"I can't breathe, Suz . . . "

"Sit down. Take some deep breaths . . . are you sitting?"

I sat, face-to-face with the bear, and said, "Breathing isn't going to help."

My sallow reflection in the bear caused me to look deeper into the undamaged crystal. Seemingly talking to my own reflection, I said, "I try to pack something or check on something and in the middle of packing or checking . . . I forget . . . what I'm doing. I remember him telling me that he took his wedding ring off every time. I remember him yelling at me . . . then I sat down. And I can't remember what I need to do."

I picked up a beautiful gold and glass clock off our mantel, another wedding present, and packed it into a box filled with pottery, a giant Easter bunny, bowls, and Christmas reindeer my children made as kids.

"Laura . . . "

An incoming text rattled the phone in my hand.

"What if he's on his way home?!" I nervously checked my texts.

A picture of a beautiful, scantily dressed young woman flashed a gorgeous smile. I grabbed my chest and doubled over.

"Is it . . . him?" Suzy asked.

"It's another young hottie sending a pic to MC Lars . . . "

"Who?"

"The rapper who used to have my new cell phone number. Since I picked the number when I bought my new cell phone, beautiful young gals send texts to me randomly. And people want to know where and when I'll be on stage at the next concert."

"I love you," Suzy said.

"My heart . . . Jesus!"

"Are you having palpitations again?"

I sobbed, still doubled over.

"You should wait . . . until you're stronger . . . until your heart can take it," Suzy said.

I straightened up and grabbed my chest, then I ran to the bathroom.

"What are you doing right now? I need to know!" Suzy said.

I squatted and threw up into the toilet, barely making it in time. "Dying," I said, flushing.

I sat on my butt and pressed my back against the wall, with my elbow on the toilet seat. I stared at the photo of the young girl in the text.

"When is he coming home?" Suzy said.

"I don't know. I mean . . . I'm not sure. He's usually . . . he's gone all day. Up in the city. In San Francisco. But things feel weird. Weirder than normal lately. I'm terrified he'll be here any minute . . . "

"How long is he usually gone?"

"All day, you know . . . "

"Okay. Take it easy. Why should today be different?"

"Because everything's different," I said, sobbing. I walked back to the living room, pacing. Looking over everything piled up in the room, still unpacked. "Everything I thought was real was a lie. Everything. I can't trust anything. Not even myself."

"You can trust me," Suzy said.

Me (6) and Suzy (4) ready for our ballet recital in 1969,
I was a seashell and she was a butterfly.

I looked out the floor-to-ceiling windows at the Ventana Wilderness, the coastal mountains of Carmel Valley.

Another text rattle.

"Damn!" I said.

"Laura? What? Is he home?"

"Another hot girl sending a pic to the rapper . . . ."

Suzy tried not to laugh. "You know this will be funny in ten years."

"God is messing with me." I grabbed my heart in pain. *What is God trying to tell me . . . Lighten up?*

"Get a drink of water. Do you need me to fly out there?"

"I need to make a list . . . " I said. (Why on earth I didn't just say yes to Suzy is beyond me. I was a complete wreck.)

"A list sounds like a good thing . . . ," Suzy said.

I stared at the view again. "This was supposed to be our forever home. Where we'd grow old together. I loved this place. We had the architect do the drawings for the addition for our future grandkids and everything . . . "

Silence on the other end.

"Talk to me about the list," Suzy said.

I couldn't speak.

"Laur? The list, tell me about the list."

"The list . . . like, three things. I'll write down three things," I said.

"Good. That's good and then?"

Still staring at the view, a tear rolled down my cheek. "I'll pack those things. I'll cross them off. I'll make another list. Of another three things. Then I'll get them. Then I'll pack them and then I'll cross them off the list . . . ," I said.

"Sounds great, Laura. Go get a piece of paper."

I grabbed a post-it note pad and a pen. I started to write but froze when the pen hit the paper and said, "I don't know what to write."

"You can't pack everything. Not now. Just pick the things you'll need," Suzy said.

"Kids school photos . . . ," I wrote every word carefully, intensely. Like each letter would be my last.

"You'll need professional clothes . . . " Suzy said.

"Pirate statue . . . " I continued.

"Financial documents," Suzy said.

" . . . my green glob of glass . . . " I said.

"Laura . . . "

I walked out the front door and rounded the corner of my home to my vegetable garden. I plucked a large, concrete pirate head out of the tomatoes and carried it to the winding driveway where I placed it behind the driver's seat of my Subaru.

"Laura . . . are you okay?"

I saw my tree swing hanging in one of the oak trees in the orchard. I froze.

"Laura . . . are you okay?"

I walked to the swing and climbed on it.

"I will be . . . " I swayed slightly on the swing.

"I can be there tonight," Suzy said.

As I stared at the coastal mountains of the Ventana Wilderness, I said, "I'll just keep making lists."

"I love you," I said. Then I hung up.

With great effort I packed everything three things at a time, including the tree swing. I crossed things off the lists I wrote and threw Post-It notes away. I teared up and doubled over after every trip I made to the car. My Australian Shepherd, Oso, followed me everywhere. I looked around the messy house for the last time and left a note for my husband. "I love you but I can't trust you. Will let you know when I'm settled. Love, Laura"

When I crossed the threshold for the last time, my cell phone rang. It was my husband. I let it go to voicemail. Shakily I made my way to the car. When I closed the hatchback Oso gave me his paw. I got down on the gravel and gave him a huge hug, sobbing. Oso looked at me as if to ask me what was wrong. As if to say "Let's play."

"Take good care of him. He'll need you now more than ever." I sobbed into his fur. He kept panting, and smiling.

"Thanks for taking care of me this year. I don't know what I would have done without you."

Oso licked my face. I got in the car and checked my voicemail, terrified my husband would be there any minute.

"I just called to say I love you," he said.

I folded over my steering wheel. Another text for the rapper rattled my phone again. I waved to Oso as I pulled out of the driveway. He plopped in the gravel, and put his head between his paws.

LOS ANGELES

I called my girls and let them know I'd left. (Finally, they would say.)
I told them that I love them very much. They asked if I was okay. I
told them I would be and just needed some time to be alone for a few
weeks. They told me they loved me. Then I called my brothers. My
sister. My parents. And my best friend Katherine who asked me to
stay with her for a while. It was the longest drive of my life, but I was
beginning to feel what it was like to breathe a little easier. I was amazed
at how putting distance between me and my husband felt good.

Red-eyed and exhausted, I wheeled my suitcase up to Katherine's
house.

"Wow. Come here. The guest room is all set."

I paused to hug my friend and took a deep breath. "Thanks so
much," I said.

"Come on . . . " she took a bag out of my hands and walked me
to the guest room. It was filled with a bunch of stuff including what
could be best described as her husband's briefcase collection which
made the room feel a little like a museum.

That night we sat in the backyard.

"So, what was the last straw?" Katherine said.

"I asked him to show me if he deleted all of their numbers off his phone. Three of them I knew were still there. He denied knowing they weren't deleted. He said his life made my life possible."

"He said that?

I stared at the moon, a huge disk in the sky.

"His exact words were . . . my job makes your writing possible."

Katherine sat back in her chair. "He stopped seeing you as a person," she said.

"I guess the signs must have been there the whole time. I didn't see them."

"Nobody saw them. Nobody."

"He scares me. It's like he was working to make me lose myself. Making me feel I couldn't live without him."

"As your old boss, let me tell you that's complete bullshit."

"I know, but, there's a part of me that believes him."

"Not the part that packed your shit and got your ass down here to Los Angeles."

"I don't think the moon has looked as beautiful as it does tonight," I said.

Katherine stared at the moon too.

"Can I get you anything?"

"I feel like my life is over."

"One life is over," Katherine said.

"I don't know how to live without him," I said.

"The past two years wasn't really living. It was a God damn rollercoaster that almost killed you," she said.

"I don't even remember packing the car . . . I don't have a plan. Everything was a lie."

"You have your girls."

"Yeah . . . ." I started sobbing. "I don't want to leave this world without knowing true love. It's what life's all about. It's what I thought I had."

Katherine hugged me.

"I'm glad you're here. You stay as long as you want."

"I don't know what I'd do without a place to land right now . . . thanks."

"Listen, do you want a glass of wine? Tea?"

"Tea. I guess . . . "

Katherine went back into the house.

"Lord, watch over me . . . .I know you can hear me. Thank you for getting me out of there," I said. I cried so hard I couldn't speak. A silent cry that shook my whole body. The kind that shook my soul. I spotted a shooting star and made a wish that I would be able to live by my pen and find true love one day.

The next day I finished a cup of coffee while Katherine's shy, blond, blue-eyed boy latched onto her leg as she did the dishes. Her husband, casually dressed for his job working on dark projects for a global aerospace defense and security company said, "Get ready for the War of the Roses." He chuckled then slapped Katherine's butt as he left for work. Katherine gave me a look.

"You should eat something," she said.

I stared into space.

"Eggs? Cereal? Toast?"

"I can't."

I stumbled into the cluttered guest room. There was no space for my suitcase, backpack, and the chest of silver I'd gotten on my sixteenth birthday. My things mixed with all of her husband's briefcases and the family's odds and ends. I opened the drawers of the bureau. Every one was full of old documents. I climbed over the bed to check out the closet, full of clothes. I headed out to my car anyway. I brought in some hanging clothes and stuffed them into the closet. Then I went back out and I dug things out of the car, setting them on the strip of grass along the curb of the very upscale, manicured neighborhood. Cars passed by. I set more and more stuff out on Katherine's lawn.

"Ry and I are going to the park later. Do you want to come?"

"Sure."

"Can I help?"

I kept digging. "I just have to find my computer." I pulled my old Mac out and set it on the lawn. Then I shuffled around in the car, face-deep in mounds of stuff, trying to find the mouse. I pulled out a hair brush and set a basket of DVDs on the grass. Another car drove by, slowing at the sight of the scene that started to look like a yard sale.

In Need of a Home

I sat opposite Jeff, a sixty-ish, skinny, efficient man with an air of calm about him amidst the chaos of his busy lawyer's office. He seemed to exude goodwill. As he finished the conversation he was having on the phone, I looked around at all his family photos.

Jeff hung up and said, "Alright where were we?"

"Serving him."

"Yeah. Well, here's the deal. If you serve first then the trial can be held here in LA."

"First?"

"Does he know where you are, who you're staying with?"

"No."

"Good. Make sure he doesn't have a clue where you are. Find a place to live right away. Make sure to keep it private, don't tell him where you're living. We need an address for you before we can serve him. Where do you want to live?"

I gave him a doe-in-the-headlights stare.

"For now," he added.

"I think I'll just live close to where I raised the kids. I'm not sure . . . "

"LA county, Ventura county . . . .doesn't really matter, I work in both jurisdictions. Just be sure wherever you live, it makes sense for you."

"Nothing makes sense . . . "

"Listen, Laura. I've been divorced. It's a rollercoaster ride. One day you're fine. The next minute you're not. You've got to be sure to protect yourself. Especially from his manipulation."

"That's why I'm here."

"Just live as cheaply as you can."

"Got it," I said, staring at Jeff's family photos again.

He forced a smile. "Hey, second time was a charm for me."

His cell phone goes off. The ring is an alarm that sounds like a submarine being attacked. Over the alarm it screams "It's the wife! It's the wife!" with more submarine alarms.

Jeff silenced it. We both smiled.

He shrugged, adding, "I'll get back to her."

Grateful not to have to hear the conversation of a loving husband and wife I sat back in my chair.

"Once you have an address then we can serve him."

"That might be tricky."

"Why?"

"I have no idea where he is from one day to the next. It's not like he has an office he goes to everyday. Every Sunday we'd sit around the table and figure out which city we'd need to travel to for work. We have projects in Northern California and Oregon."

"One step at a time. Right now you need a place to live. We don't want him serving you first and filing in Monterey County. That would cost you a fortune. But, I'm open to going up there if we have to."

Jeff hugged me, then I left his office. On my way to my car I whispered, "I'm not afraid. I'm not afraid . . . "

With the help of friends, I looked at apartments on the Westside of LA, all way out of my price range. The few that were in my price range were super sketchy. In between searches I'd usually go back to Katherine's and breakdown. After couch surfing for a few weeks at her place, I decided it was time to try and make one of my dreams come true. I wanted to live by the water in a beach community, so I set my sights on Malibu. It was a pie-in-the-sky idea, but I thought I'd shoot for the stars. I was so tired of feeling shitty all the time.

After checking out places that didn't work, I visited the Serra Retreat in Malibu, a gorgeous place of respite for busy people. Lucky for me, on that day I drove right up the cliff to the retreat center and parked on a ridge overlooking the Pacific. When I noticed a labyrinth with an incredible view of the ocean, I got out of my car.

Candice's name on my Caller ID took my breath away. I looked toward the heavens in silent prayer then answered. "Hey, sweetheart . . . "

"Mom, where are you?"

I sat on a bench beside the labyrinth, "I'm getting some air. How are you?"

"I'm worried about you."

I walked by the stations of the cross, taking a very long look at the statue of Jesus being glorified. "I'm in good hands, honey."

"Are you at Katherine's?"

"No, I'm sort of traveling around right now," I said, starting to tear up.

"Mom?"

I choked back a tear, "Yes, sweet pea . . . "

"I got to thinking about it . . . You know how Dad always said guys are idiots? Remember? I mean from the time we were little girls he always said guys are idiots."

Stunned at the recollection, I forced an answer, "Yeah."

"And you always told him to stop saying that. That guys aren't idiots. You always defended them?"

"Yes."

"Well . . . he was talking about himself," Candice said.

I cried. It was one of those lightning-bolt moments. Like she'd just solved a riddle I couldn't. As much as my daughter's insight spoke to the truth of my life, it sickened me and saddened me too.

"I love you, sweetheart."

"I'm worried about you," Candice said again.

"I'll be fine, honey. I just need . . . a little time to myself."

"Okay. I'm here for you, Mom."

"I know sweetheart. Thank you. I'll call you soon."

I hung up and looked out at the Pacific for a long time. Then I walked the labyrinth.

When you walk a labyrinth you're supposed to go slowly as if each step is sacred. It's best to walk intentionally and leave something in the center of the labyrinth that no longer serves you. Then on the walk out of the labyrinth you take a new insight with you. I knew nothing of this practice at the time. The labyrinth just called. After walking it, I felt a little better. This would be the beginning of me walking many labyrinths.

That night, my eyes red from lack of sleep and constant crying for weeks, I slumped over my phone as I sat in Katherine's patio chair, frantically hovering over the Craigslist App—apartment hunting, room hunting . . . *anything* and *everywhere* hunting. I'd widened my search to include Pasadena and all of Ventura County.

"How's it going?" Katherine said.

"You know, when we were on our 'romantic second chapter', as empty-nesters . . . " I said, using air quotes and rolling my eyes . . . "

Katherine nodded.

"We were so young when we got married. When Margaux headed to college, we decided we'd only work and live in places they put on postcards."

"Yeah. I remember when you told me about that. I thought you guys were the happiest married couple I knew."

"I've always wanted to live in Malibu . . . "

"Find anything?"

Katherine took a seat, intrigued.

"I'm checking a few places out this afternoon. Just seeing if anything else came up since I looked the other day."

"You are? What time? Let me come with you . . . "

"I meet with the realtor at 1."

"Crap. I have to pick my little guy up from school. Whatever happened to that house you found, that ridiculous deal?"

"Rented in a heartbeat. Anything reasonable in Malibu goes so freaking fast. Would've been perfect."

"Something'll come up."

"Yeah, but I'm frightened. I've only got like 5K. I'm hoping it'll last until things get worked out through the lawyers. I've never gone through this before. No idea how this works."

"I wish I could help."

"You already are," I said with a knowing glance.

"You can stay here as long as you like, you know that right? Take your time," she said.

"I wish I could. I need an address. Someplace I can use on legal documents. I guess we're in some kind of race and I have to serve him first or it'll cost me a fortune. I swear I can't even think about how hard this is going to be."

"One step at a time."

"I don't think I can live without him."

"I know."

"I don't know if I can live around here where I raised my kids. There might be too many ghosts . . . too many memories."

"Well, they don't put this town on postcards, anyway . . . so . . . "

I managed a small smile.

Malibu Barbie

That afternoon I drove from appointment to appointment in my still-packed car all around the overpriced-offerings in the Malibu area. Disheartened, I walked into a Realtor's office. Other people inside were inquiring about mansions. Soon a realtor named MaryAnn, a sixty-ish lady with a thick New York accent, greeted me. She was kind but not hopeful that she'd be able to find anything in Malibu in my price range. I was honestly surprised she gave me the time of day and didn't just laugh me out of the office.

After we checked out ones that wouldn't fly, MaryAnn said, "Okay, honey, I got one more. It's adorable and right on the water. Close to your price range, still on the high side. Wanna check it out?"

"Sure."

We got into our cars and headed to the beach in a caravan. I got my hopes up when we parked off Pacific Coast Highway (PCH) and stepped out onto a property with lots of little beach houses. I couldn't believe my luck. It felt like destiny. When MaryAnn opened a gate, I walked out over the water to the apartment. It's a closet. 200 sq. ft. You have to go outside to change your mind.

"Isn't this great?" MaryAnn said.

"Yeah. Great," I said, taking in the ocean view. Listening to the waves crashing just below the apartment. I walked around the small space, concentrating so hard you could almost hear the wheels turning. "I can't believe the location."

"Cable and internet are included and so is the furniture."

A white plastic murphy bed across from a white plastic built-in housed a TV leftover from the 70s.

"You like that TV, huh? I bet I could get the owner to throw that in for you too," MaryAnn said.

"Where would my kids stay? They'll be coming to visit," I said.

"That's what hotels are for!" she said.

Concentrating harder, I took a bunch of photos of the apartment with my cell. After I walked off the dimensions, I checked out the bathroom. The kitchen was basically a hot plate and small hotel refrigerator.

"You wanted a writer's retreat, right?" she said.

"I do." I walked out onto a little deck that jutted out over the ocean as I watched the waves crash below.

"What a view!"

"How much?" I asked.

"I got you a real deal doll! $2300. You can move in tomorrow!"

I wrung my hands and stared at the horizon. It was only a closet. But it was by the sea. It would be *my* closet-by-the-sea.

"I'll take it."

"I'll call the owner. We'll set something up for you to sign papers tomorrow. We'll need first and last month's rent and a security deposit, which should be around 6K."

The Realtor gave me a head-to-toe stare.

"That's not going to be a problem, is it, doll?"

"Nope," I said, choking back a panic attack.

We shook hands.

"See ya tomorrow doll."

I speed-dialed my lawyer's office as I drove back to tell Katherine the good news.

"I need to talk to Jeff, if he's available."

"One moment . . . "

I drove so fast that I screeched to a stop when a light on PCH turned red.

"Hello, Laura," Jeff said.

"So I found a place that's around $2300 a month. Do you think that's affordable for me right now?"

"Cheaper would be better. You got an address yet?"

"Nope. I will tomorrow. Thanks, Jeff."

I hung up the phone. I passed mansions and memory after happy memory on PCH—Moonshadows, Geofrey's, and the Old Colony liquor store.

The next night I drove over the Santa Monica Mountains from Katherine's place to Malibu again. I had high hopes when I parked at a shopping mall across the street from MaryAnn's office and the Pacific Ocean. I lowered all the windows and enjoyed the cool ocean breezes. Lucky to find a place to park, I took a big breath, turned off the ignition, and checked the time. Since I had a few minutes before the meeting, I wanted to listen to some music. But when I turned the key in the ignition, nothing. I tried again. Nothing. Worse yet, the car wouldn't lock. It was still filled with most of the things I'd packed into it the day I left my marriage.

Don't cry, I told myself. I got out of the car and stared at Mary-Ann's office. To make the lease signing on time, I had to leave the car and trust that no one would steal the car or anything inside of it. Shaking my head, I walked across the street to MaryAnn's office and took a seat, trying not to look like I was about to lose everything I had in the world. Again.

"And you're waiting for?" the snooty receptionist said, looking down on me from her desk as if I was a homeless person who'd just crept in. Which is exactly what I was.

"MaryAnn," I said.

The receptionist shot me a pitiful look on her way out of the room. My leg began to jack-hammer up and down.

"Hey, doll. Would you like some water?" Maryann said.

"Yeah, thanks. Where's your bathroom?"

"Right around the corner, doll. The owner isn't here yet. Something about a delay on the set."

I nodded and hurried to the bathroom where I doubled over and almost threw up. Inspirational and motivational posters with beach scenes hung on the walls—*Believe & Succeed: Success is a journey. Whatever sour pear, it is your determination to succeed that will get you there.*

You can't survive without me. I shook my head trying to erase my soon-to-be-ex's voice and stared at myself in the bathroom mirror. "You can do this. You can do this. Just sign on the dotted line. It will all work itself out," I whispered.

My keys rattled in my pocket. Tears welled-up in my eyes. I tucked my tank top into my jeans, ran my fingers through my hair to smooth out my wind-blown look and headed back into the office.

"We have to run your credit, doll. Are we going to find any surprises," MaryAnn said.

"No."

"Just need to know the name and phone number of your last employer," she said.

"I owned a corporation."

"Got it doll. Need somebody at the company that will verify," MaryAnn said.

I went pale. It was our corporation. He was the CEO and I was Secretary. As I told MaryAnn his phone number, my voice turned into a whisper.

"Doll, you ok?" MaryAnn said.

I nodded. Time went by. Lots and lots of time. I looked around the office at her awards. It began to get darker outside.

"This is Daryl. It's his listing," MaryAnn said.

"Yeah, well things are kind of held up because we can't find someone who speaks Spanish to talk to his mother," Daryl said. He was in his thirties with surfer good looks starting to age him a little too quickly.

"Mother?" I said.

"Yeah. The tenant went MIA . . . " he said.

MaryAnn tried to put on a brave face.

"I don't get it."

"You remember the notice on the sliding door, right? That's an eviction notice," MaryAnn said.

"So you're in the eviction process with this guy?"

The Realtors glanced at each other.

"Look, I gotta go. I need a place ASAP. This isn't going to work for me. Thanks," I said, getting choked up.

"Just give it another few weeks. I'm sure we can work something out."

"I don't have two weeks." I got so emotional I could barely speak. "It's just. Um. My car broke down." (I left out the fact that my car and everything in it was probably getting ripped off right about then.)

"What? Oh, no. Where is it, doll?" MaryAnn said.

"It's across the road. I need to call AAA."

"Doll, I feel bad. I'm sorry the owner was a no-show. And for the . . . ," MaryAnn said.

"Yeah. I'm sorry too. Where are you staying?" Daryl said.

"Over the hill. In Ventura County."

"Here's my cell, I'd be happy to give you a ride," he said.

I thanked him, took the card, and left quickly. When I felt the ocean breeze on my face, I took a deep breath and called AAA, grateful to see my car was still in the parking lot. While I checked to see if anything had been stolen, the mechanic arrived and opened the hood.

"Yep. Needs a new battery," he said.

I breathed a sigh of relief, still nervously peering inside the car windows doing an inventory. I was pretty sure nothing was taken. A miracle.

The mechanic got on his phone. Lots of yups, uh-huhs and got-its.

When he hung up, he said, "Well, I've got some bad news and some not-so-bad news."

My stomach sank. "Give me the bad news."

"Well, we don't have your battery in stock."

"Wow. I'm staying over the hill," I said.

"Okay. Here's what we'll do. I'll jump you here, but don't stop. You know . . . like don't turn your engine off . . . for anything. Just drive right to where you live. Call AAA from there in the morning, they'll fix it."

I got in the car right away and watched as the mechanic rigged jumper cables as night fell. As soon as I turned over the engine, I pressed on the gas.

"Just keep the gas on for a few more minutes then drive home," the mechanic said as he wound jumper cables around his arm.

I wish I had one.

"Remember, don't stop for anything," he cautioned.

"Thanks for your help," I said, keeping my foot on the gas. Then, my cell phone rang.

"Hey, Malibu Barbie. How'd it go?" Katherine said.

"Well, not great, I'll see you in a bit. Car problems. I might need your help if she craps out on me."

"K, drive safe."

I watched the mechanic pull out of the parking lot as my cell rang again and I answered.

"You okay, doll? Need a ride anywhere?" MaryAnn said.

"No, thanks. Very sweet of you. I'm going to be just fine. I got a mechanic to jump it."

"Great. Well, call if you need anything," she said.

"Anything at all," Daryl said.

"Will do. Thanks."

In the sunset's afterglow, I drove praying the car would have enough juice to reach my friend's house. As I drove through the winding Santa Monica Mountains, my tears flowed. When I reached the valley on the other side, I had coincidentally been driving on the street that would take me past the church our family had attended. The girls had grown up there.

Don't stop, the mechanic's advice played in my mind.

STILL, SMALL VOICE

As I drove closer to the church, my life felt so chaotic, like it was spinning out of control. I decided to hell with it, I'm going to church. Prayer would be the only way to center the whirlwinds of my grief and disappointment that night. It was as if the Lord himself brought me there to comfort me. I risked pulling into the parking lot and into a parking space right in front of the church garden where we'd blessed our pets over the years on the Feast Day of St. Francis and picked pomegranates to make pomegranate jelly at Christmastime. Then, I broke down and had a real snot cry.

"Lord, I don't know where to go or what to do. You came for me. You got me out of there. Now, Lord, give me a sign. Help me to know where to go next. Help me find a place to live. Help me find a home. Lord, I'm yours."

I just bent over my steering wheel and sobbed.

"Lord, I can't do this alone."

After a while, I walked up to the sanctuary doors. To my surprise they were open. I sat in the empty church and knelt in prayer, as I had done so often over the years from the time the girls were little to the time they graduated from high school and we became empty nesters. After I prayed, I flipped a Bible open to a random verse. And then I began to whisper to God.

"There's where the kids sang in the choir. And where my husband and I gave speeches about the Mexico outreach program. And there's where my legs always used to shake when I was a Lector. Remember how Hank, our vicar, used to always be so particular about the pronunciations of every Biblical name? And it always seemed like I got the verses to read that were filled with the ones that were the hardest to pronounce? Remember how we brought Snow and Christmas, the girls' cats, for the blessing of the animals?"

I sobbed, trying to gain my composure while I sat alone in the sanctuary. My solitude in the sanctuary felt sacred. A gift from God. I was able to speak with Him about my grief in a way I couldn't anywhere else.

"Lord, I feel myself walking so delicately upon the earth. It's as if each step might be my last."

Just then, a man with boyish good looks, in his mid-thirties, dressed in cargo shorts and a polo entered the sanctuary from the sacristy. Thankfully, he didn't know me. *I must look like a wreck*, I thought. He smiled, then gave me my privacy.

"Lord, I love him. I'll always love him. I don't think I'll be able to live without him. Give me the strength, Father, to know your will for my life since I'm no longer going to be a wife. Teach me how to be a good example for my daughters, oh Lord. In Jesus' holy name I pray. Amen."

I gathered all my strength to slowly get off my knees, I crossed myself, then walked out of the sanctuary. In the darkness I made my way to the car. Then the young man I saw earlier emerged from the garden.

"Hello," he said.

I wiped tears away from my eyes. "Oh . . . hi."

"I'm Father Brian. We have a laying on of the hands tonight. A healing service. I'd like to invite you to come."

"Thank you, Father. But I just came to pray."

"Feel free to join us," he said with a smile. "Service starts in fifteen minutes."

"Thanks."

I opened my car door and sat in the driver's seat, thinking. As I dried the last of my tears, a whisper said, *go inside*—that still, small voice we are told to pay attention to in our faith. I wouldn't be able to start the car again anyway. It was hot. *Go in the church and get some peace*, my little voice said. Driving right by the church couldn't have been a coincidence. After I caught a glimpse of my sorry-looking self in the rearview, I almost ignored that voice. But then, I opened my door and walked into church.

The service was simple, held just off the main sanctuary in a small chapel with only a handful of people. I took my seat and stared at the flaming sacred candles which cast a familiar golden glow that had inspired me as my family and I had worshiped there over the years. Yet, I'd never sat in that small section of the church before. It was just left of the main altar, called the "overflow spot" where people who came too late to find a seat in the main congregation would be ushered, often by my soon-to-be-ex husband, during big celebrations on the liturgical calendar like Easter, Christmas, and Epiphany, the church's namesake.

As I tried to stop the flood of memories and calm my racing heart with slow, deep breaths, my gaze fell on the beautiful old organ from the 1800s behind the main altar. Our family helped to finance its transport from a church in the east with a donation that inscribed our names on one of its pipes. I remembered the girls as acolytes, wearing their red and white vestments, lighting the candles before the altar, and singing in the choir.

When the laying on of hands service began, I was teased back from memory to the painful present. The familiar back and forth of the liturgy between pastor and congregants helped calm my beating heart. In the glow of the candles, peace began to envelop me but also unleashed a deep sadness of all that I'd lost. All that our family had lost. I don't remember the scriptures Father Brian read that evening but they seemed to speak directly to me and offered comfort.

We took communion then gathered in a circle, taking turns to pray and lay hands on each other after each of us spoke about our particular affliction. This was my first laying on of hands service and I didn't know what to expect. My heart raced. My malady wasn't anything physical. Mine was spiritual. When my turn came, I laid bare my broken heart in a way I never had before, emotionally and filled with anguish. And yet, the vulnerability didn't feel strange. More like a cleansing. A release.

That late summer evening, as people laid their hands on me and prayed for my comfort and guidance, I felt God's peace. Like a warm balm had been rubbed over my heart. The feeling seemed beautiful and strange. I'd been hypervigilant for so long. For years. The constant condition of alertness had left me in a regular state of panic, even when there was no need. I wouldn't know it at the time, but this was the beginning of my great adventure with God. My job was to pray and follow Him wherever He led.

After the service, I said some pleasant goodbyes to the gracious strangers I'd met. We all gave well wishes to each other as we walked back to our cars. I looked at the stars before I sat behind the wheel. When I turned the key over in the ignition, the car started and I smiled and said, "Thanks, Lord."

As I drove down the road to Katherine's house after the healing ceremony, I noticed apartment complexes I never really paid much attention to before. Applying for an apartment was tricky as I didn't have much money and didn't have a job but did have great credit. Somehow, and I still don't know how, I was able to lease an affordable apartment within walking distance from the church and across the street from a great coffee shop that would keep me alive with lattes and tuna salad sandwiches.

My love of cooking left me during those tumultuous times and would take years to return. So much of my joy came from celebrating over meals and hosting parties at my home. I inherited that joy of cooking from Mom. But cooking reminded me of what I'd lost.

That first night in my apartment it was just me, Dad's bench, and a brand new bed. This was what starting over at fifty looked like. The apartment I rented became my sanctuary and had a balcony where I could look out at the sunset. Even though I decided to ultimately attend another church, I would walk to our old church in the afternoons and sit in its garden as I healed my broken heart. I enjoyed walking around the fountain and talking with God. Especially on days when I needed His wisdom to help me overcome so many challenges and make more difficult decisions.

I missed my daughters terribly, but they were adults by that time with their own jobs and lives. I needed time and space to rebuild mine far away from where I'd experienced so much pain. Their visits on long weekends were a treasure. I couldn't imagine what they were going through. But, as heartsick and directionless as I felt at the time, I knew that they needed a mother who was happy and fulfilled and on a solid footing. If I was doing well, the odds were that they would also do well.

A few weeks later, when I did eventually sit down with the new vicar, who I knew well, she counseled me by reading Romans 8:28— "And we know that in all things God works for the good of those who love him, who have been called according to his purpose." In *all* things. Not just some things. But, this verse was hard for me to understand in my circumstances. I thought my purpose was to be a wife, mother, and a supportive spouse. When God didn't heal my marriage, it was clear He had more (and very different) plans for me than I did. Ones I couldn't fathom. If I loved God, I needed to trust His will. Not mine. I couldn't quite see how any good could come of my situation back then, but prayed that I would someday. Even though the verse seemed impossible to understand in my situation, the promise of a future where I'd be happy and whole again gave me comfort.

THE RIGHT TRACK

My alma mater, Art Center College of Design in Pasadena, had been a blessing when I was a young married woman, so I decided to take some night classes there and prayed they would give me the clarity I would need to find my future. Like cooking, in the months after the break up of my marriage I was also unable to write, except to journal. My published clips (articles I had published in magazines and newspapers) were old and they hadn't paid particularly well. I questioned how I would ever get back into the world of writing and how I would ever make a living doing what I loved. It had been years since I sold an article.

About a month later, I found a mentor in Tony Luna who taught a class called "Finding a Meaningful Career" at Art Center where we focused on our next career move. The class was for mid-career professionals in the arts who needed to make a career change due to burnout, technological advances, or some kind of required retraining. It was a class of seekers and we all learned and discovered together.

Tony had once studied to be a priest and his classes were full of wisdom and encouragement that helped illuminate my path. I remember when he said that enthusiasm is a word made up of the Greek words "en theos", which means "in God." I'll never forget when I realized that so much of my enthusiasm, inspired by the Holy Spirit, had been stolen by my circumstances.

Through more classes—like one that taught meditation, even over master artworks at The Norton Simon Museum; a storyboarding class that taught how to layout feature films in illustrations (that I sucked at, but helped me launch my screenwriting career); and Bible studies; along with long walks in nature, therapy, prayer, lunches with friends, and lots of those tuna salad sandwiches and lattes—I realized that I was not my circumstances and that joy is a choice. No one can steal my joy unless I let them. Practicing how to choose joy, like Dad had, eventually became part of my new adventure.

I was raw when I arrived at Tony's class at the Art Center at Night campus on a September evening, only a month after I had left my marriage. Even though it was far from the main campus where I attended in my twenties, I had flashbacks during Tony's class. My then-husband brought baby Candice to visit me as I worked late nights in the shop to finish constructing a model of my latest product design. In my mind, I could hear the saws buzzing and smell fiberglass catalyzing. They both stood in the hallway, all smiles, waving at me through the shop windows.

I remembered moments like the 4th of July right after Margaux was born, when I also gave birth to my freelance Industrial Design business. Together with my mom, we all watched the Rose Bowl fireworks from our perch at the old sculpture garden at Art Center's main campus. In the twilight, Margaux slept in her bassinet, Mom sat in a lawn chair and the rest of us sat on a blanket. The burly, usually surly, shop director melted at the sight of our new baby girl and sat with us for a while, giving us his giddy congratulations.

I'd worked hard to finish my education and help provide for our family. At the time, I was one of two women in the Industrial Design major. While I attended, I was the only student with a baby at the distinguished school. As memories of my first experiences at Art Center came flooding back nearly three decades later, I realized how happy I was back then, even though my then-husband and I were working so very hard. He called me "moonlight" and I called him "sunlight." I was a creature of the night, working on school projects, and he was a creature of the day working a job for a large construction company.

It took a long time for those kinds of happy memories to stop making me sad, especially as I found myself right back at Art Center trying to find my way in life again, this time as a middle-aged woman. But one day, a dear author friend would gently ease my suffering when she said, "Happy memories are good things." I would eventually learn how to stop suffering at their recollection and chose to honor the happiness that they brought by being joyful each time I remembered them. I had many, many happy memories. All gifts from God.

But in those early days, while taking classes at Art Center at Night, they still haunted me. I didn't understand how having a life filled with so many happy memories could lead to a divorce. It didn't make sense in my mind. Nothing about my situation made sense. I spent a lot of time trying to understand what had happened. But I soon would understand that it's impossible to make sense of the nonsensical. The process of trying to do so robs one of so much energy. It's enough to call it what it is and leave it be.

Even though being at the school was a kind of trigger for my pain, it was the perfect place for me to grow. I'll never forget what Tony said about how to choose the right professional relationships and how to know which ones are the ones you want to have.

"Think of a good relationship as a stool. And the stool has three legs—good communication; based on respect; set on a foundation of trust. If any one of those legs are missing, the relationship is not a good one. So notice these aspects and choose your relationships wisely," he said.

The analogy perfectly described why my marriage ended—we no longer had a leg to stand on. The epiphany calmed and yet also alarmed me. Yet, I began to open my heart to new ways of experiencing life after the constant barrage of painful, complicated intrigues that led to the heartache that ended my marriage. I had become weary from them all.

The class began to heal me in profound and simple ways, helping me find my strengths. I learned how to leverage my professional assets by exploring patterns that developed over time in my personal and professional life. Through that exercise and in doing some soul-searching and lots of reflection, it became obvious that my faith, writing, and helping people were my calling. I just needed to find a career that would marry them all.

As I searched, I did a deep dive back into the story about Dad. After working as a multimedia designer and graphic designer for over twenty years, then supporting my husband in his dream of having his own business, I decided it was time to get back in touch with my own dreams and make them come true. I wanted to be a writer and I wanted to live on the beach. I had no idea how, but I allowed my enthusiasm to lead the way. Years earlier, I had published my first travel article about Romania while working at the *Los Angeles Times*. I would build my career on that.

But, the world wanted me to be something else. Especially my ex's divorce lawyer who required me to take a test given by a vocational training counselor to determine my earning capacity. I'll never forget telling the man who administered my test about my professional ambitions.

"What work will you do to support yourself?" he asked.

"I want to be a writer," I said.

"But, *writer* isn't on any of my charts," he said.

"That's not my problem," I said.

"But I can't quantify your potential income," he said. "What kind of writing?"

"Books and screenplays," I said.

He got very concerned. "How much do they make?"

"Some make a lot, others don't," I said.

So many people wanted to keep me in a box. I needed tenacity to confront the forces that insisted I be anything but a writer. I was on the verge of beginning one of those different lives Dad talked about. And in his stories, I would find the courage I needed to move on, no matter how difficult and gut-wrenching it became. At that time, in the fall of 2013, the idea of taking a trip to Indonesia and Australia to research this story seemed impossible, a pipe dream.

PROPAGANDA

"Hakko Ichiu (Eight Corners of the World Under One Roof)."

—Japanese War Slogan

"We can do it"

—Rosie the Riveter

In a world where I can stream radio from Bandung as I write, I did not know the significance of radio or the balance of power it held in WWII for those who manipulated broadcasts to their best effect.[32] I needed to learn more since keeping the propaganda machine going was one of the reasons Dad gave for the capture and forced work of Grandpa.

Inspiring quotes like the ones above spurred on the war. The Japanese war slogan harkened back to Emperor Jimmu, the first emperor of Japan. In an 8th century literary collection, he referenced the idea

---

32   "In modern war there are four main fronts—military, diplomatic, economic and propagandist." —Time, Oct. 1939

that "eight corners of the world be united under one roof,"[33] creating a brotherhood of races. If a picture is worth a thousand words, then the images created during World War II would speak endless volumes.

The war was taken from the battlefield into the hearts and minds of those on the home front. Words are powerful, but some of the images in wartime posters drew attention more vividly, attracting an audience on a wider scale. Posters urged citizens to ration resources, "help our troops" by increasing the workforce and war production, and everywhere simple slogans aimed at increasing national pride—posted at subways, bus stops, train stations, and on every billboard and street corner. Ads to buy war bonds or join the armed forces were printed in nearly every magazine and newspaper. So, even if one covered one's ears to the messages broadcast over the airwaves, one couldn't escape the constant visual bombardment.

Radio and film, however, may have been the most effective means of reaching the audience. These new technologies sent information over a much greater scale. Moving pictures and audible words and music brought to life what was only still and static in a book or poster. In 1942, the Academy Award for best documentary went to Frank Capra's *Why We Fight*, which was the first of a series of war documentaries he made under the commission of the U.S. military.

Not to be outdone, the Japanese had their own cinematic propaganda. Two popular wartime films, *Chocolate and Soldiers* and *The Story of Tank Commander Nishizumi*, captured the attention of Japanese audiences. They showed weakness and hardship associated with war and a lot of sacrifice, more than American films, and included empathetic characters. The Japanese propaganda campaign was not

---

33   https://www.nytimes.com/1970/10/25/archives/the-japanese-challenge-the-japanese-challenge.html

only directed toward the United States, but also toward Asian countries whom they sought to conquer.

During the time that the Japanese began studying the culture and customs of the West, America was going through a period of territorial expansion that saw its borders extend to the Pacific. Japan became increasingly more interested in Western culture during America's expansion phase. In many ways, Japan took on a great number of the ideas and methods of American expansionism, and, consciously or subconsciously, incorporated them into their own methods of conquest throughout Asia.

Media and propaganda were powerful and often silent weapons that targeted human emotions and psyches, and often caused people to feel and think things that they otherwise wouldn't if not exposed to them. Politics and military actions can only do so much, but if they are driven by human emotions and impulses, they are driven further. And propaganda was the driving force of human emotion during World War II.[34]

* * *

Inside the largest radio station in Tokyo, a woman with painted red lips spoke into a microphone. "You listening, boneheads? Better surrender now. Hey black men, you cannot go in the front door of a store in your own country. We are your friends. Surrender to us now."

Just as she stops talking, The Glenn Miller Orchestra plays *When You Wish Upon a Star*.

After the song fades, she continues, "Hello you fighting orphans in the Pacific, this is your favorite playmate Orphan Ann of Radio

34   Navarro, Anthony V. "A Critical Comparison Between Japanese and American Propaganda during World War II" https://www.geocities.ws/films4/propagandaww2.htm . Accessed November, 2024.

Tokyo. How's tricks? Reception okay? Why, it better be, because this is all-request night."[35]

On an island somewhere in the South Pacific, dozens of American GIs gather around a single radio, the size of a bread box, jostling to get the best position. John, Stanley and Art gathered around the radio, listening. They couldn't get enough of her.

"And I've got a pretty nice program for my favorite little family, the wandering boneheads of the Pacific Islands. The first request is made by none other than the boss. And guess what? He wants Bonnie Baker in *My Resistance is Low*. My, what taste you have, sir."[36]

"Well, I'll be damned!" John said, wide-eyed.

"She's swell. Some geisha girl!" Art said with a smile.

"She's messing with you, son," Stanley said, rolling his eyes.

"She can have me," Art replied.

"Our Tokyo Rose, huh boys?" John said.

Catcalls rose up from the guys who huddled a little closer to the radio, while she played more big band music. The night sky behind their huddle lit up unnaturally.

Art laughed, "Oh, yeah, baby I like it like that . . . "

After more bombs and explosions, Stanley yelled, "Take cover!"

The air thick with gunpowder, they ran, disappearing into fox-holes. After a minute, John and Art peered out.

John spotted a "Kilroy" on the side of Art's helmet and smiled at the cartoonish legendary WWII American GI superhero who always "got there first" to win every battle.

---

35   "Hello, You Fighting Orphans": "Tokyo Rose" Woos U.S. Sailors and Marines http://his-torymatters.gmu.edu/d/5140/
36   https://www.dyarstraights.com/orphan_ann/NikkeiW7.pdf

"Brother, I hope Kilroy'll hurry up and win this thing so we can take that magic carpet we came in on and get the hell back home!" John said.

Back in the radio studio, Tokyo Rose stood poised at the microphone.

"Don't wait to die. While the bombs fall, let me take your hand, kiss your gentle cheeks and murmur. Before the terror comes, let me walk beside you in garden deep in petalled sleep. Let me, while there is still a time and place. Feel soft against me and rest . . . rest your warm hand on my breast."

Ron and John exchange horrified looks.

"What kind of shit is that!" John said.

"This could be it, brother."

A whirring noise sent the men down into their foxhole again. Bombs exploded just beyond. Smoke filled the air. Their radio fell silent.

* * *

Inside a torpedo factory in middle-America, an assembly line stopped, a never-ending parade of torpedoes flanked by a line of Rosie the Riveters. The women, glad for the break, paused as President Roosevelt's piped-in speech echoed through the factory.

"This war must be waged and is being waged with the greatest and most persistent intensity. Everything we are and have is at stake. Everything we are and have will be given. We have no question of the ultimate victory. We have no question but cost. Our losses will be heavy. But we and our allies will go on fighting together until ultimate and total victory. Further attempts will be made and are

being made to slow our progress. And I would make a very serious warning against the poisonous effects of enemy propaganda. Of the wedges they attempt to drive between us and our allies . . . "

One of the Rosies reached into her overalls and pulled out a jar of red nail polish. She opened it up and painted the torpedo in front of her—a cartoon character holding onto a fence with his big nose hanging over it, and the words "Kilroy was here."

"The President said we should give 'em everything we have, right?" she winked. "Kilroy always gets there first!"

They smiled as the assembly line started up again, watching the graffitied torpedo inch closer to the enemy.

HERBS

Uncle Reinier told me about the treacherous conditions Dad suffered after his capture by the Japanese. Grandpa's best friend, Mr. Van Osten, was in prison with Dad at one point. Reinier said, "The man had horrible dysentery and the vegetables your dad grew saved the man's life." Apparently, prisoners who were able, grew various herbs and vegetables. I wasn't sure if Dad's was a secret garden or if it was out in the open until he wrote about it in one of his letters.

Dear Laura,

I also received permission to make a vegetable garden, which I put behind the prison kitchen. We had plenty of land and I surveyed the property and found the back quite overgrown, which is normal for the Indies. The fence consisted of bamboo piles, 6 ft. high, with barbed wire nailed to the bamboo. There were two fences with a wall between them, where the guards patrolled. There also were watchtowers at intervals. I had never heard of anyone escaping from our camp. The reason was our white skin. If we could get out, there was nowhere to go. The surrounding Indonesians would soon see you and alert the guards.

Love, Daddy

Every year when I was growing up, Dad created a large garden at the back of our property and filled it with as many crops as possible. He taught us kids how to plant and grow all kinds of vegetables. And, of course, we would use our wooden benches to make it easy to care for the garden. He didn't like us sitting on the ground and wanted us to be comfortable.

Our soil in suburban Chicago was heavy with clay, nothing like the fertile soil of Indonesia. After the snow melted, a big part of our lives involved preparing the garden by enriching the soil. I remember how much Dad tilled the soil and made a point of properly amending it to grow the best fruits and vegetables. He took such great care in picking out the perfect fertilizer and selecting the best stock at the nursery.

What I remember most were his tomatoes. Grandpa Stanley, Mom's dad, enjoyed walking out to the garden with a salt shaker and picked Dad's delicious tomatoes, eating them right on the spot. Dad grew rows of them and loved carrots and chives too. One year he taught us how to grow delicious raspberries. Then there was the year he tried growing peanuts. But that didn't go very well, because when I weeded the garden one day, I ended up weeding the peanuts too. Dad never got angry with me, but that little episode left him speechless. I blamed Suzy. We still laugh about it to this day. Just the sight of a peanut can crack us up.

As I learned more about Dad's past, it made me appreciate his passion for gardening. Used to a tropical climate, rich with exotic fruits and lush with long growing seasons, he had to get used to the fierce climate of Chicago. One might think that he'd just forget about growing things, it would be such a bother. But working the earth had been his lifeblood so he had a special relationship with our garden and the land. It was his sanctuary where he made sense of the chaos around him, I suppose. The one constant. Homes came and went, places got bombed, volcanoes erupted . . . but the garden, the soil always remained. Dad spent long hours taking care of the plants and spent many more sitting with Mom on the back porch or the garden patio appreciating all the beauty they'd created.

Dad wore a large bamboo conical pointed hat and a brown or gray long sleeve work shirt and matching pants while he gardened. His complexion was usually very tan from his work travels to tropical countries and time spent in our garden. Occasionally, people in our neighborhood would stop their cars while Dad worked in the front yard and asked him if they could hire him. They assumed he was a gardener, not a homeowner. Perhaps it was because of his hat, or how hard he worked, or because of Dad's tan. It flattered him that the neighbors thought so much of his gardening and made him laugh too.

Dad handed down his love of the land to us kids. As a child, when Dad and I worked the soil and planted seeds together, I had no idea that his love of gardening had been born out of starvation. Many years later, Dad would remember and I would learn that he was transferred to many camps during his time as a POW, but he spent much of his time at a prison camp called Tjimahi.

* * *

1943 TJIMAHI POW CAMP, JAPANESE OCCUPIED JAVA

In darkness, Dad clutched some wet herbs he retrieved from his garden and ran. Out of breath, he opened the door to his cell block, a one-time warehouse. Monsoonal rain poured over the steel roof. A sea of pained prisoners laid on the ground. All of them old guys, each occupying a five-foot-by-seven-foot space. Prisoners rubbed their aching arms and legs as they writhed on flea-infested tatami mats, the only comfort some had to shield their bodies from the broken-up concrete floor.

Dad took his spot beside Van Osten and placed some daun paku into the old guy's curled up hands. He helped his father's best friend eat them.

"Where's Playboy?" Dad asked, wide-eyed.

"No idea," Van Osten whispered, lying in a fetal position.

Distraught, Dad crushed the wet herbs.

He pulled scraps of Van Osten's shirt off his bloody wounds, and dabbed them with the herbal paste.

"Here, place these under your tongue," Dad said, helping Van Osten put some herbs into his mouth. The old man licked them off of Dad's fingers.

Other prisoners gathered around Dad and Van Osten, all old men. One prisoner, called Storyteller, had rugged good looks despite years of captivity. Another, Bridge Player, was an emaciated bald man. Storyteller tapped Dad on the shoulder.

"A long time ago, boy, I once met a mystic . . . ," Storyteller said.

Bridge Player grabbed his stomach. "Mystic? Don't you have stories about food? For once tell us a story about food!"

"That reminds me . . . ," Storyteller said.

"No more damn stories, the boy needs to learn how to play," Bridge Player said, shuffling a deck of cards, turning toward Dad. "Would you like to play? Our fourth is . . . "

"On holiday," Storyteller quickly said with a nod to Bridge Player.

An eerie silence returned after the tin-tapping monsoonal rains ceased.

Bridge Player dealt cards in four piles with his good hand which took some time, something they had too much of.

Dad stayed at Van Osten's side.

Storyteller dabbed at blood dripping from a cut on his swollen hand and turned to Dad, saying, "The game's played in tricks, my boy."

"Look alive now, kid!" Bridge Player said.

"Where's Playboy?" Dad asked, unsettled this time, scanning the warehouse.

Bridge Player motioned Dad to lean in closer with one hand, his other too swollen to use.

"The oven,"[37] Bridge Player said.

Dad's gaze darted around the cell block in disbelief.

"Think it's your lucky day, boy?" Bridge Player said, shuffling.

"I'd rather be lucky than smart," Dad said, slinking back to his mat. He settled in as best as he could among the rubble, taking pains to not cut his skin on the broken concrete.

"Watch your knees, boy. Cuts turn septic. Fast," Bridge Player said, holding up his bad hand, a little too cheerfully.

"Back to that mystic. He knew about life!" Storyteller said.

"Girls! What about girls? You ever been with a girl, boy?" Bridge Player said.

A beat. Dad shook his head.

"A boy shouldn't die without knowing the pleasure of women!" Bridge Player slammed his cards down. Van Osten fanned his cards, visibly shaking.

"Kid, you be my partner," Bridge Player said. Then he turned to look at Storyteller boasting, "The boy's going to win on his first time out. You'll see. He's lucky. The boy's lucky."

---

37   A hole dug in the dirt under the sun with a metal lid. Prisoners were placed in "the oven" as punishment.

Van Osten tapped Dad on the knee and whispered, "What cards am I holding?"

Dad shrugged.

Van Osten smiled with a wince.

"Boy," Bridge Player said, turning to Dad, "I had a woman in Bangkok. Got after her from underneath, twirled her around and around in a swing. A real beauty!" He gestured wildly, tipping his hand, blood dripped down his arm. Dad put his cards down then reached over to dab Bridge Player's wounds with some herbs.

"That's all the mystic this boy needs! He'll become enlightened, alright . . . in the moans of a woman," Bridge Player said, not taking his eyes off of Dad.

As Dad's eyes went wide, the cell block door slammed open. Japanese officers infiltrated the building, swarming around some prisoners. They dragged them out of the warehouse kicking and screaming.

Storyteller shook his head.

Dad picked up his cards. Bridge Player and Storyteller squatted for a minute then fell on their butts.

"Damn!" Bridge Player rubbed his butt.

"I'll tell you what I dream of . . . ," Van Osten said.

"Women in Bangkok?" Bridge Player said, with a far-away look in his eye.

"Rice without rat droppings?" Storyteller smiled.

Van Osten rubbed his cut-up knees and winced in pain.

"Something to sit upon," Van Osten said.

Dad thought about home as he tried to sleep. What it used to feel like when he was served freshly squeezed orange juice after he awakened each morning. He dreamed about his bed and the family villa, and the idea of home began to represent something like heaven to him.

He missed his family. He missed his home. He wondered if he might die in the camp, and his family would never know where he had gone. He wondered if his family was still alive.

"Boy," Van Osten said to Dad, motioning for him to come closer. "I heard there's a job in the kitchen. Get that job, and you won't starve, my boy. Hurry, don't wait . . . "

*   *   *

Dad didn't talk too much about his fellow prisoners, but he did speak about how they had taught him how to play bridge. Mom and Dad played frequently with friends. And they taught us kids how to play too. I have fond memories of us all playing bridge together on Sunday evenings.

I didn't know how Dad learned to play bridge as a prisoner until decades into our letter writing. Dad said learning card games was a good way to pass the endless amounts of time spent as a prisoner and break up the monotony. But, card games weren't all the old men taught him.

Dad also talked about how the men told wild stories about their many manly adventures that often took place on the world stage. Their tales opened Dad's eyes to the ways of women and the world, exposing him to ideas about life he'd never heard before. There was a gleam in Dad's eyes when he told me a few of those stories.

SURVIVAL

While Dad was in prison, Grandma, Grandpa and Reinier had been forced to leave the family villa. They were relocated to Tjiboenit prison camp. All the PTT (Post Telephone and Telegraph) families, twenty-one people in all, were summoned to the camp. A fence was built around their accommodations with guards stationed at various points and contact with other prisoners was prohibited.

Grandma worked at the stove boiling some water when she heard a loud knock at the back door. Reinier ran to her side. Grandpa waited a minute before opening it. Sukio, the gardener, stood on the other side. Grandpa let him in then shut the door.

"Hans is alive . . . " Sukio tried to whisper, but the news was too good to muffle.

"Thank our Father in Heaven!" Grandma crossed herself. Shocked, she hurried to the kitchen.

"Alive?! How do you know? What have you discovered? Who have you contacted?" Grandpa said.

Grandma handed Sukio a glass of water and he gulped it down. Bright red marks ringed Sukio's wrists.

"The jungle has eyes. You risk too much!" Grandpa said, placing his hand on Sukio's shoulder.

"Hans was first taken to The Palace Hotel, a converted prison now. Before that, he was held at Camp Pasar Andir, then, most recently . . . "

"How many prisons are there?" Grandma said, horrified, melting into a chair at the kitchen table. Reinier scooted out of her arms. He ran to his father's side.

"Too many to count. But now, his trail's gone cold," Sukio said.

"Thank you for this news," Grandma said, hopefully.

But Grandpa was filled with anger. "Leave the rest to me," he said.

"What can you do?" Grandma said, "You're always watched. Constantly escorted . . . "

Trembling, Grandma offered Sukio another glass of water. After downing it in one go, he bowed to her in gratitude then stared out the open window into the night.

"Hope begins in the dark," Sukio said.

Somewhere out there, in the darkness, Dad remembered Sukio as he crouched over his garden beside the prison kitchen. But this time herbs weren't what Dad had come for. When he sensed the coast was clear, he made a run for it.

Dad crouched along the bamboo-and-barbed-wire fence, wanting to hide from the prison guards. Slowly, deliberately, he wiggled one rusty nail out of place, then another, being careful to only pilfer nails that didn't alter the fence's integrity.

"*Dare ga iru*, (Who's there)?" a guard barked somewhere in the darkness.

Dad hit the dirt and tossed the nails out of his hands. The guard pointed his flashlight in Dad's direction.

"*Jibun o misete* (Show yourself)!" Another guard said, searching outside the kitchen with his gun drawn.

The beam from the flashlight lit up the dirt in front of Dad. He held his breath. As the guards approached, still in search of Dad, some yelling on the other side of the prison camp caused the guards to stop searching and scurry away toward the noise. Finally, Dad let out a long breath and searched in every direction to make sure no one else was around. When Dad saw he was alone, he began to hunt for his pilfered nails. One by one, he scooped them out of the dirt. Then, he carefully retreated into the shadows and snuck back into his cell block.

The next day started out the same as every other. Boredom and heat combined to burn away more memories of what life was like before imprisonment. Just another day to count. Another day lost. After tenko, Van Osten writhed back and forth on his mat. Dad knelt beside him and Playboy.

"It's hopeless. I'm beyond your remedies, my boy," Van Osten said, so dehydrated, he could barely talk.

Dad nodded. Playboy laid motionless on his mat, staring at the ceiling.

"Why do they call you Playboy?" Dad asked.

Thunder crashed and rain poured.

Playboy stayed silent as Storyteller dealt four piles of cards, saying, "Because, Son, there was a time when those blue eyes of his could convince a woman of anything."

Leaks in the roof began to drench groups of prisoners.

"Lovely day for bridge, isn't it?" Bridge Player said.

Playboy began to moan, rolling from side to side.

"Indeed," Storyteller said in Bridge Player's direction. "Playboy and I always make a good team."

"Can't you see he's almost dead?" Dad said.

"Perception is reality, my boy," Storyteller said. "Never underestimate the power of revenge."

Bridge Player laughed, "Or lust," he said.

"Bump in the road, my boy. Bump in the road," Storyteller said, whacking Playboy with his fanned cards.

*　*　*

Grandpa examined transmission equipment with his Indonesian superior.

"Damn vacuum tubes keep failing. Typical of inferior equipment in the torrid weather of the tropics. I kept telling them the tubes manufactured by RCA are superior, but Phillips was all they wanted to use," he said.

The Indonesian engineer sighed. "Yes. Yes. However . . . repairing them is the task at hand. You must fix the tubes. You must do what you can with what you have."

"Or, nothing at all. Perhaps fate has stepped in and dealt our occupiers a blow we never could have on our own," Grandpa said.

"They'll kill you for not fixing the equipment."

"Hmm." Grandpa said, he and the Indonesian scientist put their heads together.

"Has there been any word about my son?" Grandpa whispered.

"A few of my friends have infiltrated some of the local prison camps as cooks. They've found nothing, so far. Teacher, you must prepare for the worst . . . "

"I'll search the prisons myself!"

A Japanese officer entered the laboratory during Grandpa's outburst.

"Talk of prison, Einstein?" The officer said.

The Indonesian scientist took his place at Grandpa's side. Alexander glared at the officer.

"How's your lovely wife?" The officer taunted.

Grandpa stood silent. His eyes betrayed his calm facade, trying like hell not to take the bait.

"Imagine your future. You are in a men's camp. Your beautiful wife and young son in a women's camp. You and all the other prisoners in camp left without your manhood. Eternally questioning whether your wives, sons, and daughters are dead. Or . . . worse."

Grandpa took a few steps closer to the officer, dwarfing him.

"The code of the Samurai dictates choosing death over dishonor," the officer continued.

Grandpa returned to working on the broken vacuum tubes that had lost their seal. The officer walked up behind him as he worked.

"You have been bestowed the honor of working for The Empire. By accepting this great honor, you will help to repent for the misery and suffering inflicted by your White race's exploitation of this paradise created by God."

Grandpa turned to face the officer and said, "And if I refuse?!"

"Evil is punished, and good is rewarded. Work for The Empire, in service of the entire Japanese Co-Prosperity Sphere—the New Order. Or refuse and your entire family meets your son's fate. I leave the choice to you."

Soldiers surrounded Grandpa and trained their guns on him.

His former student's forehead beaded with sweat.

"I need time," Grandpa said.

"I give you one day."

The Japanese officer spun on his heels in military fashion and exited the laboratory. Grandpa pulled out his worn, well-annotated pocket Bible with notes scrawled on every page.

DAD'S FIRST BENCH

Dear Laura,

We had [were housed in] an old warehouse with a broken up concrete floor—no beds. Each of us had an assigned space of 5 ft. by 7 ft., where we were supposed to stay day and night, except for regular visits to the mess hall. The food was atrocious.

The main food was the cheapest food, which was sago. Sago flour is produced from Sago Palm Trees and comes from the spongy center of the palm tree trunk, which is split open to remove the spongy pith. About 800 lbs. of flour is produced from each palm tree.

In our camp, we were given Sago with palm sugar for breakfast. The palm sugar was cooked with the Sago. For lunch we got Sago with cooked vegetables, and the same for dinner. You can imagine that we all lost weight and any food from outside was precious.

As I remember, after being in the Prison Camp almost 2 years, my mindset had accepted that I would not get out. Therefore, I accepted my life there and made it as comfortable as possible. My big break was volunteering for kitchen duty as suggested by Van Osten. As I remember, I just stayed in the eating area doing small cleanup jobs on my own.

The food was cooked in open oil drums over wood fires. There were always drums that stood outside the kitchen and I would sneak behind the kitchen and scrape some sago from the drums. It was pretty sticky stuff. Soon, I was discovered and told that if I wanted to clean the drum, to apply to be a kitchen helper, which I did. Apparently, not too many others wanted to clean these drums, which was hard work.

This made life better for me as the scrapings were extra food. Eventually I got to be able to add some palm sugar called Gula Djawa. I knew it from our kitchen at home. It came in round discs about 4" diameter, and was wrapped in palm leaves.

One rule was that you could eat in the kitchen, but you could not take food out of the kitchen. Being in the kitchen certainly made my days a lot easier. I even found out that they cooked meat for the guards and sometimes I got a piece of meat to eat, and other leftovers.

Love, Daddy

* * *

Dad didn't really describe the kitchen in his stories. And while we talked about his experiences, I hadn't thought to ask very much about those specifics. But, in my research I discovered that these kitchens were often makeshift buildings.

" . . . large and grimy, resisting all efforts to keep them clean, and that they contained nothing more than open fire pits built out of concrete blocks. The kitchen was roofed over, an open structure without a chimney, so that the smoke, and there was always plenty of that, especially when the wood was wet, escaped on the sides. A chronic shortage of matches compounded the problems . . . stepping through cinders and ashes as they worked. They tried repeatedly to sweep the ashes down the hill, but their efforts were ineffective. No walls protected them from the monsoon rains or wind. The cooking utensils were equally primitive, consisting of large oil drums set up over the concrete blocks confining the fires, which were usually stoked with green and often wet wood."[38]

* * *

Day after day, Dad worked in the kitchen. Much of the year, rain pounded the steel roof of the large lean-to in the center of the prison camp. Sheltering from the weather was impossible. Either monsoonal rains blew through the rickety kitchen or steamy sunlight encroached into the little shade it provided. Dad choked back a yelp when he stepped on hot ash hidden in the dirt and soot by large, steel drums. A whirl of smoke formed a kind of tornado at the foot of the drums where Dad tended the fires necessary to cook the prisoners' sago rations.

No matter what the weather, after all the prisoners had been fed, Dad would climb on top of the empty drums to clean them. Holding onto the top edge of the drum, he precariously leaned inside, using his fingernails to scrape the sticky sago residue. No one else wanted to clean them because it was such a painstaking, foul job. Dad loaded some scrapings into the palm of his hand then paused to make sure the guards were out of sight. Carefully, he eased the scrapings into a few

38 Stutterheim, John K. "Chapter 11. The Benteng". *The Diary of Prisoner 17326: A Boy's Life in a Japanese Labor Camp*, New York, USA: Fordham University Press, 2012, pp. 79-88. https://doi.org/10.1515/9780823250141-013

small pouches he'd stowed away in the waistband of his frayed pants and quickly tucked them away.

When rain poured in sheets so thick, it provided the perfect cover for Dad to fashion planks out of firewood. Reaching into his pocket, Dad pulled out the nails he'd pilfered and used the back of an ax to drive them into the planks. His wooden bench was complete. He took a second to admire it. Then he concealed the bench as best he could by stacking firewood on top of it. Satisfied, Dad quickly walked through the rain and mud back to his cell block. Once inside, he found his spot and collapsed on his mat. Tending the fires in the kitchen in the crushing heat and humidity took its toll. Dad only had strength enough to pull the sago pouches out of his pants and shoved them toward his cellmates. They quickly grabbed the contraband and gobbled up the sticky scrapings.

"Bless you, my boy!" Storyteller said.

"Caviar? Again?" Bridge player smiled, licking his lips.

"Damn, Son!" Playboy said.

"Man can't live on this crap. Pure starch," Storyteller said.

"A man can't live without it," Bridge Player quipped.

"A lot like women . . . " Playboy said.

"A woman can keep a man alive," Storyteller said. He was the only prisoner in the group who hadn't put on weight since Dad had shared bits of stolen food with them.

Van Osten motioned Dad to come close to him. Dad reluctantly rose up off his mat and dragged himself alongside the feverish man.

"Your father is out there . . . looking for you . . . " Van Osten whispered, barely able to speak.

"Who's deal is it?" Bridge Player said.

Storyteller coughed and after his fit was over, he turned to Dad and said, "Do you know the story of The Taj Mahal? What about the pyramids, my boy?"

"I've seen the pyramids," Dad said.

"Really? I'll be damned!" Playboy said.

"I rode on a camel. With my sister and my mother," Dad said.

"Good for you! Regale us . . . " Storyteller said, coughing.

Dad rolled over, trying to crack a smile. "I can't tell the kind of tales you do, but one day I'll have those tales to tell," he said.

"Sure you will, Son," Playboy said.

Dad curled up on his mat out of exhaustion.

Storyteller, Playboy, and Bridge Player exchanged sad glances.

"I will see the Taj Mahal. I will take my bride there," Dad said in a whisper as he began to fall asleep.

"Of course you will," Van Osten whispered.

"And where else will you take your bride?" Bridge Player said with a tear in his eye.

"Wherever she wants," Dad said before drifting to sleep.

"Smart boy," Playboy said.

* * *

Van Osten stumbled. His once-grand clothing had disintegrated in the monsoons and heat, hanging in rags around his boney body. He removed a grimy monogrammed handkerchief from a loop where a belt should have been and dabbed at his forehead. Taking a long breath, he put one foot in front of the other carefully, purposefully.

When he reached Dad, Van Osten held two cigarettes in his badly sunburned, peeling hand. Before long, he shakily held up the cigarettes, pausing when they reached Dad's line of sight.

"They're all I have, my boy," Van Osten said.

Dad set his wooden bench down and pulled a cigarette from the old man's boney hands. The old prisoner reached into his pocket and gingerly pulled out a match. He flicked it along the top of the bench. His old eyes went wide when he puffed the flame into smoke.

As if in slow-motion, the old prisoner agonizingly lowered himself onto the bench. The process labored, his body stiff as if his muscles had forgotten how to sit. When Van Osten shakily steadied himself on the seat, an ear-to-ear smile graced the old man's face. A single tear left the corner of his eye. As he searched the heavens, his shoulders fell, and his legs flopped apart.

He raised the cigarette to his mouth again, still smiling. Though he was among the oldest of the prisoners and the poorest of souls, at that moment no one looked more regal. Playboy, Bridge Player, and Storyteller gathered around the king.

"How did you?" Playboy said.

"Where did you . . . ?" Bridge Player wondered.

"Firewood," Dad said.

"Well, the boy is magic," Storyteller said.

Van Osten examined the bench's construction without leaving his seat.

"Nails?" Van Osten said. "How on earth?" Van Osten stood up and motioned for his cellmates to take a turn. First Storyteller sat, then Playboy.

"Lord, it's better than sex!" Playboy said.

"My turn, damn it!" Bridge Player said.

"Build me a bench," Storyteller said.

Dad stared at him.

"Your magic lies in your hands. Mine? In connections. What have you wanted more than anything else?" Storyteller said.

"Freedom," Dad said.

"Besides that . . . " Storyteller pulled a scrap of paper and pencil stub from his pocket. He offered them to Dad who grabbed them.

"It's forbidden to have anything to write with. How did you get these?" Dad asked.

"Write whatever you want. Build me a bench, and I'll get your note to your family," Storyteller said.

As they shook on it, Storyteller pulled a box of Silvercity Cigarettes out of his pocket. "Life isn't worth living without them."

Dad crouched down, set the paper on the bench and scribbled a message. He folded it into a tiny rectangle and handed it to Storyteller who slid it into the cigarette carton.

"If we're caught, we'll be killed," Dad said.

"We're dead men anyway," Storyteller said.

Knowing The Stranger

When people ask about my family and I tell them about my Indonesian roots, most people respond in the same way—giving me the once over with questioning eyes. Almost immediately, I mention that my relatives were Dutch Colonials—oversimplifying their status—which seems to ease their confusion.

Like the strangers over the years who have had questions about my heritage, I similarly needed my curiosity satisfied. At the time Dad and I began our correspondence, my family history was something like a cross between a world history lesson featuring many people I'd only known by name, and a great mysterious adventure. I had to go deeper than the facts and stories I'd been told over the years, many much too short, lacking the kind of detail my questioning mind needed to tell the full story.

Over time, it seemed that our letters had set Dad on a path of personal exploration, and he began to feel more and more comfortable with his recollections. Our conversations caused him to write about his journey at different times in his life. Those stories were filled with surprising events and details I never knew before. Back then I realized for the first time that, in a sense, Dad had been a stranger to me. I'd known only the part of him that he chose to share, perhaps that's true for us all. We only let people know us as much as we wish to become known. After going through the process of discovery with Dad and my ghostwriting clients I've discovered that the greater truth reveals that we are sometimes even strangers to ourselves.

The idea of the strange seemed to be as deeply seated in my Dad's psyche as his ever-joyous nature. He alluded to this in the advice he gave me when I married at the age of twenty-two. Before my wedding, Dad told me that the key to a happy marriage was to "always treat each other like strangers." By that, he meant to always give each other the same courtesy as a stranger and not take each other for granted. There was such wisdom in his words even as they seemed odd to me back then.

But, in the fullness of time, I might add that we need to treat everyone we love like strangers. As if every day we are meeting them for the first time. This practice has helped me to create unimaginable, grace-filled moments of forgiveness. Dad modeled unimaginable, grace-filled forgiveness for my brothers, sister and I as we grew up. He never said a bad word about the Japanese and didn't harbor any resentment toward them. I tried to model his grace in the way I dealt with the break up of my marriage.

One time Dad shared a stunning story about grace. After the war, in the early 1950s, he secured a job as a hydroelectric engineer at the Harza Engineering Company in Chicago. One day, the president of Harza walked up to Dad and said, "Hans, I understand you spent some time in Japan. We have some important Japanese engineers coming to town and I'd like you to show them around the city."

"Of course," Dad said. He proceeded to come up with his signature detailed itineraries for each of the visiting Japanese engineers highlighting the wonderful architecture of downtown Chicago. A place that Dad called home for most of his life. The tour went wonderfully, and the Japanese engineers were very grateful, particularly enjoying how Dad honored them by observing their many customs and knowing their language.

Afterward, the president of the engineering firm, Mr. Harza, thanked Dad then apologized profusely. Somewhere along the way, Mr. Harza discovered why Dad had spent time in Japan. "I had no idea you were a POW, Hans. You should have let me know. I would never have asked you to give the tour." Dad simply said that it was his pleasure to show them the city. Little surprises and beautiful grace-filled gems like this kept showing up in our letters and visits.

Dad's words flowed in the cinematic way you'd expect when someone you love speaks of places you'd never been, populated with blood relatives you'd never know except in his stories. They called to the mysterious and adventurous inside of me, which found me wanting to travel back in time to fill in the blanks Dad couldn't. Since that would be impossible, in 2013 I set my sights on traveling to Java in the hopes his history would find me through clues and shadows of the past.

The man who had helped me learn everything from how to stand up straight, swim, dive, mow the lawn; weed and plant flowers, sail, grow vegetables and harvest them, play tennis, sketch, and build things like wooden shadow boxes—two hang on my walls at home: a kitchen scene with a girl baking pies, a girl enjoying a bubble bath (some of my favorite things)—this man was someone I'd just begun to get to know.

My only living links with the past besides Dad included my Aunt Aletta who lived in London, Reinier, and Great Uncle Emil and Aunt

Lettie who lived in Germany. Emil and Lettie came for a visit once when I was a little girl. This is what Great Uncle Emil wrote (translated from the German) in our *Gestbook*—

July 13-16 1972

> *It has been more than 35 years when we last saw you, when you were still a school boy. Today, you are the head of a happy family. It is a lucky day that we could spend days with Junie and the three children and have Junie and you spoil us. WE have both gotten gray and friends have made us thankful.*
> *God bless you all, Uncle Emil and Aunt Lettie.*

Emil was a lot of fun. One of the things I loved about him was how we played together when we went swimming at the pool. He threw me high into the air, plunging me back down into the water. I couldn't speak a word of German. Emil didn't speak English. But I knew he loved us and Aunt Lettie with all his heart, and he loved life with a gusto I had never experienced before.

Perhaps Emil's love of life came because he nearly lost his. One way the Dutch used to arrest Germans on Java after Germany had occupied Holland was to ask them to pronounce the phrase "Schap Scheerder," *sheep herder* in Dutch. It was such a difficult phrase to pronounce for Dutch-speaking Germans, that the exercise easily gave them away. After Hitler's occupation of The Netherlands, German men were taken from Java to camps in the British Empire in India.

Great Uncle Emil eventually stayed in Dehradun, the same camp as Austrian mountaineer Heinrich Harrer and his companion Peter Aufschnaiter, located in the Himalayan foothills and featured in the movie *Seven Years in Tibet*. After the German defeat, Uncle Emil walked home to Germany over the Himalayas in a part of the world where the Japanese used Indian Army POWs as living targets and feasted on their flesh.[39] And that is, as my dad would say, another story for another day.

39   Japanese ate Indian POWs, used them as live targets in WWII https://timesofindia.
      indiatimes.com/india/Japanese-ate-Indian-PoWs-used-them-as-live-targets-in-WWII/arti-
      cleshow/40017577.cms

A Leap of Faith

As Dad and I spoke and wrote to each other, nagging questions kept surfacing. *What exactly was the project or projects that Grandpa was forced to work on by the Japanese? How could I write this story without visiting its settings?* The first question nagged at me for decades. I dismissed the second as a matter of fact. After all, since I had to rebuild my life while getting divorced, how could I journey a world away to all the exotic locales involved?

But, Dad once said, "When there is a problem, it's important to see it to find the right solution."

I had the problem of trying to tell this story well. Traveling to all the locales seemed the logical thing to do. The trip would finally help me answer all my questions and finish the story. I prayed about it. I dreamed about it. And then I did something about it.

By 2014, this story (and my life) needed focus, and that's what I worked very hard to find on my first research trip to Indonesia. I decided to immerse myself in the world of the story, and made a plan to tour its present-day settings so I could reimagine them in the 1920s through the 1940s.

I not only intended to ground myself in the setting but also in its history. I figured that to properly tour Indonesia and Australia, my trip would have to be about five weeks—two weeks in Australia and three weeks in Indonesia. Since I'd never taken more than two weeks of vacation in my life, five weeks seemed a gloriously mind-blowing amount of time. But, with money so tight, how would I ever pull it off?

The idea of traveling halfway around the world seemed inevitable, extravagant, reckless, and maybe even a bit dangerous. I sat with that for some months and got a little visualization and confidence booster while reading Jen Sincero's book *You are a Badass*. And, as I became more of a badass, I found myself in a familiar paradox—the only thing more unimaginable than going was staying. But one day, I decided to go. Nothing would stop me. I wanted to give the trip all I had, no matter the consequences.

Then, I had to figure out the right time to travel to Indonesia. As my dad rightly pointed out, Indonesia had two seasons—monsoon (November to March) and dry (April to October). Prices for the sweet spot of July and August were so high that it was out of my ballpark, even though travel to Indonesia was relatively inexpensive.

As I weighed my options, imagining what it would be like to visit Indonesia in the desperate heat or legendary rains, I remembered how Dad lived outside with little shelter and even fewer clothes. If he could survive, I could. No matter what would come my way. While deep in my decision making, I visited with my younger daughter, Margaux for Thanksgiving where she was living at the time in Boulder, Colorado. During the visit she came up with a brilliant plan.

"Mom," she said, "if you fly out of LA on February 13, you'll arrive in Melbourne on the 15th and never even have to live the 14th."

Great idea. My unfortunately timed, ex-anniversary fell on Valentine's Day. We both knew I would be better off skipping that holiday. My soul needed to be far, far away. It might be rainy, but what the heck. I had my departure date, February 13, 2014.

I just had to figure out everything else. In addition to taking an inventory of all the settings I would need to visit, I tried to learn some Bahasa Indonesian. Other research included how I would safely travel to Indonesia as a woman alone, the most economical ways to travel, and which of the destinations in the story would be realistic for me to visit on a small budget during a five week window.

Ideally, I wanted to visit all the countries involved in Dad's POW story—Australia, Indonesia, Singapore, and Japan—but when I did the math, I decided Japan and Singapore would have to wait. They would be expensive and difficult to visit given my time and language constraints. I'm not good with learning foreign languages, and Bahasa seemed intimidating enough. With a Trans-Pacific trip to plan, a life to reboot, and a lot of turmoil with the divorce, I didn't want to set myself up to be overwhelmed.

I decided to arrange a tour with Intrepid Travel to help me see as much of Java as possible in the time I had. Unfortunately, the tour's itinerary only included one day in Bandung. This would give me precious little time to explore the remote ruins of Malabar (if I could find them)—where my Grandpa had gotten his first job on Java which led to his career as a radio engineer. I didn't really know what to do about getting to such a remote location in the time I had. I just knew I had to find a way.

When I mentioned that my Dad had been born in Bandung, Indonesians greeted me with the warmth and affection one might give a long lost relative. This happened time after time. The first time occurred while chatting with my hairdresser in Los Angeles about my upcoming research trip. He immediately told me that his wife's relatives lived in Bandung and said they'd be happy to meet me at the airport in Jakarta and show me all the places I desired. Beyond excited to discover a way to actually see Malabar with people I trusted, I took this as a sign that my ambitious trip, one I could hardly afford, had been destined.

Naively, I thought three weeks would be enough to gain an understanding of Indonesia, the island of Java, and the culture. I would come to discover that one could live three (or four or five) lifetimes in the archipelago and still not understand the complexities of the country made up of sixteen thousand islands.

I decided to spend a week in Australia to see friends in Melbourne then on to Sydney where Dad went to university after the war. Then, I'd tour Indonesia for three weeks and return to Australia for a week. I wanted to tour what was once Camp Columbia in Brisbane where my family became refugees after the war and decompress there before returning to Los Angeles. I had arranged everything. All I had left to do was pay for my air fare.

On New Year's Eve of 2013, about five months after I left my marriage, I made another one of the most powerful decisions of my life. Katherine and I drove to Meditation Mountain in Ojai. On the drive up from Ventura County, we pulled over at the side of the road at a beach in Carpinteria where I called Quantas and purchased the airline tickets I had reserved.

Katherine and I celebrated at the top of Meditation Mountain with a picnic of sandwiches from our favorite Ojai deli. I'd packed dragonfly champagne flutes for the occasion, and we had a toast to the promise of 2014 as the sun went down on 2013 over the majestic Topatopas. We sat back as the mountains turned a glorious pinkish purple, a sight that captured the imaginations of all kinds of people from the ancient Chumash to filmmakers, tourists to hippies, celebrities, and many artists who call Ojai home. This became a New Year's Eve tradition for us for several years.

When I chose to take big leaps in my life, many well-meaning friends and family, even acquaintances all had advice and opinions about my plans. Most were supportive, others curious, and some, at times, were afraid for me. I'll never forget what my cousin, David, said in Florida while the extended family celebrated Dad's 90th birthday in February, 2014, days before I was scheduled to take off for Australia (I received so many farewells there).

David and I had a great discussion about unique jobs that sound intriguing and passionate, laughing as we ranked careers on a scale of 1 to 10. 10 being most intriguing. After giving an accountant a 1 (I have a B.S. in Accountancy—that's another story, another life), and circus contortionist a 10, David turned to me and said, "Cousin, you're strong. Your attitude toward your new life is going to make all the difference. You know, some are glass half-empty people, and some are glass half-full people. But some people aren't limited by the glass. That's how I see you." He gave me a hug, and in that instant, I realized that I wasn't just on the journey of a lifetime, I was also in search of a life.

At the time of Dad's 90th birthday, I had begun to write this story as a screenplay. Because of the trauma I suffered when I left my marriage, I had lost my ability to write. When I told my friends the situation, they suggested that I consider writing a new way. Since I'd always been a fan of films, the idea intrigued me and I decided to learn screenwriting. I hired Glenn Benest, an excellent teacher who mainly writes horror movies. He helped me develop what is known as a "treatment" (summary) of the screenplay before I left on my first research trip in 2014. I like to write books cinematically, so the transition to screenplays felt natural, even as I had a lot to learn. With my treatment in hand, I packed my bags.

In the International terminal at LAX, Margaux gave me a call. "You ready to go?"

"Yeah, I think so," I had a huge lump in my throat. The whole trip seemed too big for me when I heard her voice, knowing I'd be a world away from her.

"What are you doing?"

"I bought my first Indonesian money," I said, so proud. "I just exchanged dollars for rupiah." The sight of the foreign currency made everything so real.

"What does it look like?"

"Pretty epic. Twenty bucks is like hundreds of thousands of rupiah," I said.

Margaux laughed.

"Guess where I just was?" I asked.

"Where?"

"At Duty Free!"

"What scent did you pick?" Margaux asked.

"Balenciaga Florabotanica."

"Very nice," Margaux said.

Ever since Candice and Margaux were little girls, whenever we went on international trips, we would always pick out a perfume for the journey at Duty Free. It was a special way to remember the trip when we returned home. A simple whiff of the scent flooded our hearts and minds with sweet memories.

What would I remember this time? I stood in a small hallway leading to the international terminal at LAX with my finger in my ear so I could hear Margaux's voice better. I was jolted by the fact that I didn't really have a home to return to. Not the kind I'd had before. My apartment didn't really feel like home. It was more of a place to land. A beginning. My return there wouldn't give me that beautiful feeling I once knew of "coming home," but that wouldn't be for a while. I had a lot of living to do before my return.

"Mom, you there?"

I started to get choked up.

"Yeah, I'm here. So, it's like you'll be with me on the trip. I'll think of you when I wear it," I said.

"You got something to put you to sleep on the flight?"

"Yeah, I'll keep my eyes peeled. Thanks for the reminder."

Margaux was quite the world traveler by then, having studied in Europe and traveled there for work. "Well, enjoy your flight, Mom. And let me know when you land in Melbourne, okay?"

"Sure, sweetheart. I'll send a text."

"Love you, Mom."

"Love you too, honey."

After checking out my snack options, I spotted something called Dream Water, a melatonin drink that I hoped would do the trick on the 16-hour flight to Melbourne. Finally, when it was time to board the plane, I saw a quote painted on the wall just outside my gate—

"If you always put limits on everything you do, physical or anything else, it will spread into your work and into your life. There are no limits. There are only plateaus, and you must not stay there."

— Bruce Lee

On my flight from LA to Melbourne, somewhere over the Pacific, what would have been my twenty-eighth anniversary disappeared over the International Date Line. At the beginning of the trip, I figured I could disappear too. Somewhere in the world. It was an idea that gave me great comfort. This confession alarms me now. What disappearing would look like, what the actual act would be, I had no clue. I needed to end the pain. A pain I nicknamed the black hole. A pain that had consumed me for nearly two years before I boarded the Qantas flight.

Feb. 15, 2014
Somewhere over the Tasmanian Sea

I fill out my customs form and state writer as my occupation, traveling primarily for business. This feels good. I flip through the in-flight magazine. Features include Isabelle Rosselini's stage performance of her award-winning short film series, Green Porno, explaining the sex life of insects. Costumed as insects and sea creatures, she acts out their reproductive habits. In this moment I realize anything is possible. Including and especially my dream, my very big dream of writing about my dad's experience as a Japanese prisoner of war during WWII. It took me years to realize that big dreams are my birthright. Heck, compared to the bizarre and weird glory of insects' sex lives, my dream seemed tame.

I love dreams. Everybody's crazy, hell-bent-for-glory dreams. It is my life-long dream to fly to Australia and Indonesia. Splurging on a research trip in order to write the story I've been trying to write for decades seemed crazy all these years. Why? I make a mental note to never define myself as crazy ever, ever again.

When I arrived in Melbourne, Dee picked me up at the airport and we drove to her home in Wood End. Dee, her husband Michael and I spent lots of time talking on their backyard deck, catching up. The next day, we went to a music festival at an old caravan (RV) park where Dee's son Nick played *Smells Like Teen Spirit* by Nirvana. Being surrounded by teenagers reminded me of all the fun I'd had when my girls were their age.

Dee and I even had time for a wonderful writing retreat at her country home in Montegeta with Molly, her goat. I'll always remember our champagne stroll when we talked about writing and my career plans while spotting kangaroos jumping in the bush—the very first kangaroos I'd ever seen in the wild. It was ridiculously exciting for me to spot them as evidenced by the many videos I took.[40]

There were so many things to love about OZ—the beautiful trip we made to the library in Melbourne; how everyone was so nice and funny; how flashlights are called torches there; how they had a haunted bit of road where cars put in neutral always drove backwards; how turning right in traffic was a lot more life affirming than turning left in America; how Aussies say "heap" when they mean "lots" and how I laughed a heap every time I heard it; how the key to making the proper Vegemite sandwich is to layer the Vegemite ever so thinly on toast; how making "a cuppa" meant we'd soon be talking for hours over tea, an incredible way to begin the day; and, the calls of the cockatoos and magpies filling the air. Oz seemed lyrical in a way the U.S. isn't.

When it was time for me to leave, Dee sat with me at the departure gate. We waited together until my plane was ready to board. I'll never forget what she said just before I got on the plane.

"Laura, the world is your oyster."

---

40   https://youtu.be/0Wu4Uz6BByY?si=10x1RwGDmKWN2k4e

We hugged. Her encouragement was wonderful to hear, but I had yet to believe it. When I took my seat on the plane to Sydney, I felt hollowed out, suspended between two worlds—the one I'd left and the one I longed to create.

FEBRUARY 19, 2014
SYDNEY, AUSTRALIA

Glebe is a great part of Sydney. My room at the guest house is $80/night, unheard of affordability in the city, and just a short walk up Ferry Rd. to an amazing bakery and lots of restaurants. The bus stop to the harbor (the 431 & 433 bus lines) is right in front of the bakery. I purchased my $15, 10-ride bus ticket at the news store across from the Glebe library and boarded the bus. The Writer's Walk leads up to the Opera House. One of my favorite plaques on the walk reads:

"Australian history is almost always picturesque, indeed it is so curious and strange that it is itself the chiefest novelty the country has to offer. It does not read like history, but like the most beautiful lies. And all of a fresh sort, not moldy old stale ones. It's full of surprises, and adventures and incongruities, and incredibilities, but they are all true, they all happened."

– Mark Twain

While I saw a late-night show at the Opera House, The QE2 anchored in Sydney Harbor. Along with hundreds of people lining the harbor, I waved to those on board and wished them well as they sailed out to sea. When the ship sounded its horn, we all hollered. In the midst of the spontaneous celebration with my new-found friends, I realized I'd left my safe harbor and set sail in the world, too.

February 20th, 2014
A hotel in Sydney

It's so horrible to think about the past. Especially when I see couples together. I'm sitting in this hotel lobby and I think that's what's making the painful feelings surface again. I can't be in hotels anymore since so much of our livelihood was renovating them and so many painful memories occurred in them. He didn't protect what we had. Maybe he didn't know what we had. Most people in the lobby are couples, or are at least part of a group.

Curiously, at this moment, thinking of my soon-to-be ex with someone else doesn't bother me as much as it had before. Because with time I've realized that it doesn't matter how many cool places you stay, or how many interesting cities you visit, or how many fabulous dinners or expensive bottles of wine you enjoy—if it's all a façade, a fake, phony. I'd rather live in the truth. I'd much rather take myself to the beautiful places I want to see and have adventures that are authentic. I have to learn or come to understand—that I am my own magic. That I don't need anyone else to make it for me.

A comedy of errors leads me to missing my tour two times today. But without missing it so many times, I might not have met Gabriella and Vidal. They are each other's ex's and found they can't be married, but love each other very much, so they travel together. They'd just traveled to Uganda because Gabriella loves gorillas and wanted to see them up close. This involved trekking for five hours with armed guards.

Gabriella and Vidal found their brave new world. I begin to look forward to mine.

There was no one to see me off from Sydney. I waited for my flight to Jakarta alone, and was the only white woman to board the plane. I'd gotten lost in Australia—a country where they spoke English, only days after I'd arrived. I shuddered to think about how I would cope in Indonesia, a country so very different from any place I'd ever visited before.

FEBRUARY 21, 2014
FLIGHT TO JAKARTA, INDONESIA SOMEWHERE OVER AUSTRALIA'S NORTHERN TERRITORY

My devotional reads:

"Do not cast away your confidence, which has a great reward. For you have need of endurance . . . " (Hebrews 10:35)

My heart tells me that I'm on a pilgrimage. I never really thought of this trip in that way. My heart is telling me that I'll find healing here. My job is to be myself. It's something I can't screw up. There's only one me and there's precious little time left. Living life authentically is all I'm interested in. I am brave. I am strong. I am not my circumstances. My soul could not be fooled. The wisdom of my soul is learning to trust the mystery of the unknown.

JAVA

Because Dad could only speculate about why the Japanese captured our family and forced Grandpa to work for the Japanese military, I suspected there was more to the story than Dad knew. To satisfy my nagging suspicion that the real reason still needed to be uncovered, I endeavored to experience as much of Java as I could. All the while looking for clues that would solve the mystery.

When Dad was born on Java in 1924, it was the world's most populated island with 50 million inhabitants. When I visited 90 years later, its population had grown to about 150 million. Java was then and still is the world's most populated island.

"Possession of any kind of illegal drug is punishable by *death*. Have a good day," the pilot of the flight said on my descent into Jakarta.

The word death hung in the air. My heart raced at the sight of the tarmack. I'd soon step onto the soil where my family had been imprisoned and where my world-traveling father had never returned. So much death had been inflicted on Java, an exotic island I'd heard so much about and of which I knew so very little. *What would happen to me?*

In Jakarta's crowded airport terminal, I got my bag and connected with my hairdresser's wife's family—a group of five people including their grandfather, Baba. Short and slight, a little hunched over with sparkling eyes and a few missing teeth, Baba walked with a cane. As the family gathered to sort out some details of our trip, an impeccably dressed woman walked over and smiled at me.

She said hello.

"Can I have your phone number and email?" She asked in perfect English. I thought she was with the family, so I didn't make anything of it. But I was in a bit of a hurry. I wondered if I could give it to her later, since I didn't have anything to write on. As the family and I began to migrate to the parking lot, she slipped me a piece of paper with her name and number.

"Call me," she said.

"Sure." I smiled, then caught up with my hairdresser's relatives. On our way to the car though, I noticed she'd disappeared. She wasn't part of the family. *That was weird.* Puzzled, I regrouped on our walk to the parking lot. On the way, Baba asked about my time in Australia and how I enjoyed the flight from Sydney.

I told him about Melbourne and my good friends Dee and Michael, and how Sydney was important because that's where my family settled after being rescued by the U.S. Marines, then evacuated from Japan after the war. I also told him about seeing Luna Park, where Dad flipped pancakes in order to afford a round-trip ticket to the United States, something the government required of all immigrants. They wanted to ensure that immigrants like my Dad could return to Australia if his job as a hydroelectric engineer didn't work out.

Soon we piled into a large, black Escalade and began the five-hour drive to Bandung. As night fell, I took in Jakarta's jammed streets on our ride toward the mountains (I thought Los Angeles traffic was bad, not even close). On the way, Baba told stories about how he was one of nineteen children, and had become a Christian as a boy. Since Java is about 98% Muslim I told him that I was surprised that he had converted to Christianity. He laughed and said he was too. Baba spoke the best English of the group. The others seemed to understand, but only spoke a few English words. They all laughed and smiled a lot.

The family sang much of the way from Jakarta to Bandung—Indonesian songs, mostly. When they spontaneously broke out in "Tell Laura I Love Her" (the 1950s Ray Peterson hit) it nearly brought me to tears. They seemed to love my name, as well as the song, and sang beautifully. The gesture made me feel like one of the family. Their warmth and playfulness helped me enjoy being between worlds, instead of being embarrassed by it. I would learn to playfully embrace the adventure of it all, the good and the bad. As they sang, I understood in new ways how my trip to Java would have never happened without one world ending.

Having a group of strangers sing to me about love choked me up, a little too much. I tried to hold back my tears, but the lyrics just overwhelmed my broken heart.

"Are you married?" The old man asked.

How do I answer? I thought. Technically, I still was. This would be the beginning of learning how to speak about myself and my divorce. It was the beginning of finding my own voice, apart from my failed relationship and difficult circumstances. It would also be the beginning of people asking me why I traveled alone.

"Not anymore," I said.

I rubbed the ring on my ring finger. People told me that even though I wanted to shed my wedding ring, I shouldn't if I was going to travel to Indonesia. They warned that the ring only needed to be a plain band, nothing fancy. Something to stem inquiries as to my marital status.

"Most Javanese look down upon divorce as a stain on a woman's character," I remembered my hairdresser saying, "You need to protect yourself from men who might think you are easy or immoral," as he put the finishing touches on my hair a few days before my trip.

"Do you know that woman at the airport?" Baba asked.

"No," I said. "I thought she was part of your family."

"Did she give you anything?" he asked.

"Yes, she gave me a piece of paper with her name and phone number on it."

"Give it to me."

So, I did. Baba ripped it up immediately and threw it out the window of the SUV.

"She's a witch," he said.

"What?" *He's joking, right?*

"You call that number, the next thing you know, you will be pulling money out of the ATM. All your money out of the ATM. She will hypnotize you and you won't even remember you gave her all your money. You must be careful. Very careful."

Shocked, I stared at the old man, speechless. *A witch? Really?* Two seconds after I landed, an Indonesian witch targeted me.

"They dress very nice to disarm you."

Check.

"If you were to call her, she would whisper things on the phone, and you would lose consciousness. Your mind wouldn't be your own."

Hmmm. I considered all that he said and felt a kind of heaviness in the center of my being. A knowing. I'd had a brush with danger and hadn't even known it. Just like I had in my marriage. Charming, beautiful deception. *Maybe I had a knack for courting danger and not knowing it?* I shivered. Suddenly, the great adventure felt a little too spooky. According to Baba, being blonde and blue-eyed made me stand out everywhere. I would be a target.

"You need to pay attention. Be on your guard," the old man said. *Be careful. Pay attention. Be on my guard.*

Completely exhausted, all I wanted to do was sleep when we arrived in Bandung in the wee hours of the morning. But my hosts had other plans. The women of the home had prepared a huge feast of Indonesian foods—chicken satay, tempeh, gado-gado, rice, cooked vegetables, homemade chutney, and fried fish with sweet and spicy peanut sauce. They sat me down and invited me to eat. All of it. None of them ate at all.

It didn't take me long to realize they had cooked it all for me. This was their incredible form of hospitality. It also didn't take me long to realize they were poor, and the gesture was an incredible effort on their part, as well as an honor. Try as I might, I couldn't eat but a fraction of the delicious food. I hadn't been eating well since I set out on my own. Even with the lattes and tuna sandwiches that kept me alive, I lost forty pounds. My stomach shrank during that time.

Whenever I stopped, they would insist, *"Makan, makan.* (Eat, eat.)"

And I did. Afterward, I encountered my first Indonesian squat toilet. It was in a room with a deep wash basin. After scratching my head for a while, I ventured back outside to look for Baba. How I wished one of the ladies knew enough English to make it possible to have had a female chat.

"How do you flush it?" I asked, blushing.

He smiled, and we both went back into the room. He filled a bucket with water in the washbasin, then dunked a cup into the water and poured it down the hole.

Oh. Um. Okay.

My hairdresser's wife's relatives were incredibly gracious hosts, giving me my own private bedroom while the family slept on mattresses in the open areas of the house. As I walked up to my room with my host's wife, I noticed their walls filled with precious family photos. The beauty of family. Stories told in moments. *This is what home is.* To the sound of the TV (that stayed on all evening with talent-show entertainment the kids loved), I went through my small backpack and found what I needed to get to bed at around 3 a.m.

As I settled in for the night, I looked out the window of my room at a patchwork of rooftops. *Who was this Laura?* I'd never known she existed before. A bold traveler in search of the truth. But, maybe that's who I'd always been, and I didn't really know her yet. There were so many things I needed to learn about living on my own and also about living in Indonesia.

The next day, after a cup of instant coffee, the tour I'd been dreaming of for so long finally began. I found it surprising that in a country known for some of the best coffee in the world, so many Indonesians drank instant. The first of many surprises that day.

As we drove through the streets of Bandung, we passed by extravagant colonial villas. And like most colonial homes, they were modeled after typical Javanese structures[41] featuring grand roofs and large overhangs to give plenty of shade from the blistering sun. We tried visiting the address where my family had once lived, but found that

---

41 https://indonesiadesign.com/story/the-history-of-java-vernacular-residential-architecture-simplified#:~:text=Javanese%20traditional%20house%20forms%20had,with%20heat%20and%20heavy%20rain.

the villa was no longer there and had been replaced by a convenience store. Over the years the street had expanded from a dirt road to a busy boulevard.

At one time, Bandung was known as the Paris of Java. A mountain getaway far from the heat and bustle of city life in seaside Jakarta, a little over 90 miles away. Still a distance best journeyed by rail. Life was extravagant in Bandung at the turn of the 20th century. Dutch colonials made their mark by constructing stately boulevards and public buildings featuring a signature colonial architecture, along with fountains, villas, gardens, and pools.

Bandung had an active club life, five cinemas, music, theater, and *Groote Postweg*, a thousand-person dance hall. There was also *The Braga*, a fashionable shopping district which included a lavish tearoom in an outdoor tropical setting, tailors, a tobacco store, a bakery known for its Dutch delicacies, a chocolatier, and a place to buy cars. The spring water from the Tjitaroem river fed the community swimming pool. Eventually a few Art Deco hotels accommodated tourists interested in visiting the region's stunning natural beauty, including vistas of the rice paddies, the Maribaya waterfall, and the gorgeous flora and fauna.

Even today, locals refer to Bandung as "Paris Van Java." Some historical structures still standing include the Governor's house, called *Gedung Sate*, originally built by the Dutch in the 1920s; what was once known as The Concordia Society building, a club for wealthy colonials where the European elite would have weekend holidays, now known as *Gedung Merdeka*; the old Savoy Homann Hotel with its classic Art Deco style; *Gedung Pkuan*, a Dutch Mansion constructed in the 1860s; and Villa Isola, Bandung's most famous Art Deco building designed by Wolff Schoemaker in 1933, now known as *Bumi Siliwangi*, part of the Indonesian University of Education. Completed within six months,

Villa Isola had originally been built for the media tycoon, Willem Ber-retty, who only lived there for a year due to his tragic death in a plane crash while flying over Syria.

I wanted to absorb as much of the culture and the beauty of the city as I could. Villa Isola was as beautiful as I'd seen in photos during my research, if a little worse for wear. As we walked around the grounds and sat on its steps, overlooking a vast expanse of grass in the crowded city, students busily buzzed around the building and met their friends. At that moment, the estate felt more like a student union than any-thing else. I tried to picture what it had looked like to my family in the 1930s when they lived down the street.

We then traveled on to see the great volcano, Tangkuban Perahu. *Tangkuban* means mountain and *perahu* means boat. The volcano had appeared like an upside-down boat to the villagers once-upon-a-time and that's how it got the name. The rainy day felt a bit cold as the young couple, my hosts for the day, drove us to the smoldering vol-cano, bringing us right to its caldera. The scent of sulfur overwhelmed me as I took my first steps out of the car. Vendors sold trinkets, food, and children's toys at stands that rimmed the parking lot. To get out of the rain, we headed up one of the viewing platforms to stunning views of the smoky crater.

The smoking caldera of Tangkuban Perahu, Bandung, Java.

I could sense the energy of the caldera and see the damage done by the latest explosion—a force of nature, wild and unpredictable, one that I couldn't fathom. It reminded me of the devastation I'd suffered so recently in my own life. The betrayals that had blown up my world. I could only imagine how my family felt when their world had blown up during the Japanese Occupation. My troubles seemed so small by comparison, and yet so very painful.

After a while, the wife of the man who drove us to the volcano asked if I cared for a warm drink, something with ginger in it. I thanked her for her thoughtfulness. The sweet concoction took the edge off the cold and the rain. I would come to learn that Indonesians have an incredible penchant for sweets, only equaled by Dad's.

I shot videos of the amazing site from a platform just above the crater. Billowing smoke made the volcano appear alive even as it lay dormant. It seemed to breathe sulfur and smoke. As I focused my camera, trying to document all that I saw, I got curious about what would happen next for me and the volcano. When would it explode again? It could be anytime. I wondered if that's how it felt for my family as things got worse and worse for them during the war. I couldn't imagine surviving such a disaster, natural or otherwise. And yet, there was a beauty in the destruction too. With each explosion, the volcano made the surrounding Parahyangan (land of God) Highlands more and more fertile.

As the day wore on, my need to visit Malabar became all-consuming. That was, after all, one of the main reasons I'd arranged to visit Bandung that day. The old radio station site was a distance outside of the city and would be impossible for me to see once my tour began. But, my hosts didn't want to go and instead wanted to drink tea. I was so disappointed; I felt like I must have done a poor job of communicating the importance of that part of the journey. When I tried to explain again over tea, they didn't seem inclined to change their minds. They said it was too far away, much farther than I imagined, and not a place I should visit. They made it sound dangerous.

Be careful. Pay attention. Be on my guard.

My heart felt heavy. I had come so far. Too far to let go of my dream of visiting Malabar. I needed to walk in that jungle and see firsthand where my family had begun their lives on Java. That day I learned an important lesson about travel and research. I didn't quite understand that because I wanted something to happen and had gone to great lengths to make it happen, it didn't necessarily mean it would happen. And then there were other times, when my travel plans would effortlessly fall into place and take me to people and places I didn't know I needed to discover.

Had I traveled across the world for nothing? I wondered as we sipped our tea together. The family and I enjoyed each other's company so much that I opened up to them about starting my new life. Disappointment was a difficult emotion for me to manage during my divorce, a trigger allowing raw emotion to flow, at times unchecked. Sometimes it's easier to tell strangers things that have been bottled up inside. Over sips of ginger tea, I confided to them about some of the heartache I'd lived through. I cried at one point and had to excuse myself to dry my tears. They might not have understood everything, but they knew the pain. Heartbreak is an international language.

The next morning, I thanked the sweet family for the incredible tour of Bandung. Just before they drove me back to Jakarta, I had a special moment alone with Baba.

"What do you do to stop the pain of a broken heart?" I asked him with all the wonder of a child.

"Sing!" he said, not missing a beat.

"Sing and dance!" he added with a huge smile. He put his cane down and danced around in a circle in his living room and invited me to do the same with a wave of his hand.

So, I joined in. I couldn't help it. The joy in his eyes radiated into my broken heart. I gave over to the sensations of my body, listening to our voices in song—not solving, needing, wanting, fixing, or thinking about anything other than the fun of it all. As we danced, a lightness of being began to open my heart to joy again. Though visceral and wonderful, I felt awkward. Maybe my silly song and dance, arms waving in the air as I belly laughed, made me feel that way. But maybe, just maybe, that awkward feeling came from the joy and pleasure brought on by Baba's invitation to dance. I'd somehow been an exile from the world of joy for so long.

I took Baba's advice to heart and promised myself to sing and dance much more as I packed my little bag and put it in their black SUV. He and his kind family drove me all the way back to Jakarta to the Dreamtel hotel that evening, where my tour of Java was scheduled to begin with Intrepid Travel at a welcome dinner the next night. I had wanted to arrive early to sightsee in Jakarta before the tour started, since we would depart for Bandung early the following morning. On my only day to tour Jakarta, I intended to soak up everything I could about the city.

The plan made sense, but when I woke up and had a steamy Jakarta Sunday to myself, I became insecure about touring the city alone. I hadn't gotten used to traveling by myself yet, so that might have been part of my unease. Maybe it was the witch; maybe it was the warnings from Baba; maybe it was being blonde and blue-eyed and not knowing the language; maybe it was knowing that my family had been in the wrong place at the wrong time on Java during World War II; but suddenly, as I entered the lobby of the hotel, armed with an Indonesian language book and a map as a reference for my cab driver—I hesitated.

INTREPID

A headline about the Kelud eruption[42] in the *Jakarta Post* took my breath away as I walked through the sleek lobby of the Dreamtel Hotel. The volcano was about eight-hundred miles east of Jakarta, near Yogyakarta, one of the destinations on my tour of Java. Ironically, Kelud erupted on what would have been my twenty-eighth anniversary as I flew from California to Australia, just ten days before I arrived in Jakarta.

By that Sunday morning, four people had died and 100,000 people had evacuated their homes. My mind reeled as I prayed for the victims. I froze while processing the headlines, unable to step out of the hotel and begin my day of touring the city. Instead, I took a seat in the lobby beside its ceiling-to-floor windows and stared at the street in front of the hotel, thinking about how short life really is. And how small the world really is. And how if we could just wrap our arms around each other more, we would weep less.

So soon after my experience of seeing the smoking caldera of Tangkuban Perahu, the headlines spoke to me personally and to the

---

42   https://www.scmp.com/news/asia/article/1427623/thousands-indonesians-flee-deadly-vol-cano-mount-kelud-erupts

power of my journey. Not only had my world blown up, but the world around me had seemingly erupted in my wake. As I gathered my courage to greet the day, I told myself that it's okay to be afraid of the unknown. To have courage even in the face of a sudden, devastating eruption.

The iconic temples of Borobudur and Prambanan had closed because of the disaster, places I'd looked forward to visiting in the coming weeks. I hoped they might reopen by the time the tour arrived at Yogyakarta, the city closest to the temples. At this point in my journey, I composed my traveling prayer—"Lord, please bestow good health, good weather, and good connections."

I tried to reassure myself about touring Jakarta alone. *What else might happen on my tour? Could Kelud erupt again? Whatever may come, I am not really ever alone because God is with me.* And that still, small, confident voice inside helped me remember that I'd had lots of experience traveling alone. I'd just visited Sydney on my own. Sure I'd gotten lost, but in the end, everything turned out fine.

A decade before, in 2005, I had visited Bucharest, Romania, alone prior to joining a delegation of artists and ethnographers invited to learn about Romanian culture on the eve of the country entering the European Union. My experience there resulted in my first published travel article for the *Los Angeles Times*. I remembered the thrill and beauty of touring the painted monasteries of Suceava and traveling through the gorgeous countryside of the Transylvanian alps. Another story for another day.

The only danger I'd encountered while in Romania happened when some boys surrounded me and a friend and began whispering. When I bent down low to try to hear what they were saying, they unzipped my backpack. I instinctively spun around which launched my cell phone into mid-air (thankfully my passport and money stayed secure). The boys fought over my cell until the winner scurried away into the streets of the city, followed by the losers. They'd soon discover the password-protected phone wasn't much of a prize. But the boys weren't the real criminals. They were forced to steal to meet payment quotas set by those who exploited them.

The loss of my phone meant that I was cut off from real-time communication with my family. The comfort of being able to speak to my then-husband and my girls whenever I wanted gave me the confidence I needed to travel alone so far away from home. After the theft, I made many unsuccessful attempts to call my then-husband from Romanian pay phones. I wanted to let him know that I wouldn't be calling at our prearranged time because my phone had been taken. I didn't want him to worry. The memory weighed on me from my seat in the lobby of the Dreamtel hotel and I wondered, *had he worried about me at all?*

Just a few years before I'd met my first husband, during my senior year of high school, I had been the Vice President of the American Field Service (AFS), a high school student exchange program founded after WWII to foster world peace and understanding through cultural exchange. I loved getting to know the international students that came to my suburban Chicago high school and longed to have the same experience abroad. But Dad wouldn't allow me to stay with strangers. Instead, he arranged a trip for me to have the cultural experience with the family of one of his Italian business contacts.

My exciting trip to Italy taught me much about life. My host mother sunbathed nude on a balcony in Arenzano. *People do that? Check.* A surprise reunion in Venice on the Rialto Bridge took my breath away. I ran into an old high school friend, who I hadn't seen since he went to college, and another friend, the handsome Venetian exchange student he'd hosted the year before. That night my Venetian friend whisked us all away on a fun and delicious insider's tour of Venice that could only be given by someone whose family lived there for hundreds of years.

A few weeks later, I'd become part of the worldwide drama of he United States air traffic controller's strike. When air travel ground to a halt, my airline transported me and the other passengers by bus to a hotel on Lake Como. There, I shared a room with a young gypsy woman who secured all the jewelry she sold by wearing it and hiding it in her large coat which she wore even while sleeping. I barely flew to Chicago in time to drive to the University of Illinois at Urbana-Champaign and move into my university dorm room in time to start classes.

Mom would sometimes hear my stories and say, "Laura, that could only happen to you."

Women travel alone all the time all over the world. I had been one of those women. But on that bright, sunny Jakarta morning, the news of the day stymied me. It felt odd not wanting to explore. World travel was in my blood, after all. Fresh on the heels of an incredible day of discovery in Bandung with newfound friends, I should have wanted to skip into the sunshine.

However, the way disappointment and heartache bubbled up inside of me while touring Bandung scared me. And my feelings upon reading the headlines and the memories they triggered surprised me. I seemed to be living on the edge of my emotions. If I was so fragile, why had I put myself out in the world in such a big way? *Was I up to this?* In my heart, I knew I had to walk out of the hotel lobby and into the crowded city of Jakarta. I had to be brave. My family had once been so braver.

As I tried to muster the courage to walk out the door, I tried to have compassion for myself. *It's okay to be timid right now*, I thought. *Just try and do one thing at a time.* I took a deep breath, then ordered a cab at the front desk. While I waited for the cab I thought about how my grandparents had arrived in Jakarta. Had they felt the same unease? Would I get confused, like I had in Sydney, where I'd read the maps wrong? It took little to bring me to tears back then, including when I missed the bus in Sydney. I knew I had to become much stronger, especially when introducing myself to the people I would soon meet on the tour that evening.

Gradually, I got better at handling questions about who I was, what I did, and about my life in general. Initially my soon-to-be-ex appeared in my answers. But, in time, I kept the focus on me. *I am a writer.* It was true and felt natural. The only problem? I had never lived only by my pen before. My answer felt more like a declaration of the future than a statement about the present. But I owned it. Taking center stage in my life felt good.

I watched a cab pull up to the front of the hotel. And as I contemplated leaving the modern, air-conditioned, steel-and-glass confines of the hotel lobby for the unknown, I froze. But wasn't this trip all about overcoming fear? Mine and Dad's? That meant venturing into a city where I didn't know the language. That meant touring a country where I'd met people who'd never seen or met a western woman before. It meant learning as much about Java as I could in the time that I had. *Everything I do from now on would be about venturing to discover the unknown. Enjoy it—dance and sing.* I told myself.

I took a picture of the map of Old Batavia (the *Kota*) in my guidebook for easy access, figured Google Translate would help me communicate where I needed to go and stepped out into that Jakarta morning. The prickly heat and humidity gave me a *curl-up-in-a-ball* feeling. I had yet to try speaking Bahasa Indonesian on my own and wasn't sure how I would see all the sites I wanted to without speaking the language very well.

But when I took my seat in the well-maintained cab, a sort of supernatural peace came over me as the driver looked at me from the rearview mirror. In chicken-Indonesian, I told him the list of destinations I hoped to see that day. He told me his rates. In doing the math, it seemed better to just hire him as my driver for the day. A bit surprised, but happy, he pulled away from the curb.

My tour began with Monas—the Indonesian national monument commemorating the country's independence built by President Sukarno in 1961. As we pulled up to the monument and the taxi came to a stop, I was thrilled but terrified to take a tour without a native speaker beside me. However, my cab driver, Saipoel, wouldn't allow me to simply leave his cab unescorted. So, he became my guide too.

We walked to the striking obelisk in the center of Jakarta located in Merdeka Square. Over four-hundred-feet tall, Monas was constructed to symbolize the fight for Indonesian independence. Oddly, the walk up to the imposing monument settled my nerves. To my surprise, instead of going up, we descended some stairs into the National History Museum below the monument. There, we viewed elaborate low-relief sculptures and dioramas chronicling the long, complex history of Indonesia and the timeline of the country's struggle for independence and freedom from colonial rule. Depictions ranged from prehistoric times to the era of Majapahit and Sriwijaya, European colonization, the Japanese invasion in WWII, and the Indonesian Independence Proclamation on August 17, 1945.

After absorbing all I could of the history of the country, we climbed some stairs to a large outdoor mezzanine at the bottom of the obelisk. Stunning panoramic views of Jakarta spread out before us. I passed on going to the top of the tower because of long lines and the incredible heat. Throngs of school-aged kids were excited to get to the top. Their enthusiasm made me smile.

On our way back to the cab, I stopped in front of Monas. While reflecting on all that I had seen, a young female street performer dressed like a mummy with ghoulish white and black face paint smiled and motioned for me to come over. Smiling photos of others who'd taken their picture with her were on display. Her sign read, *Boleh poto poto sama Pocong? U* which is Javanese for "Can you take the same photo with Pocong?"

Me and the Pocong at Monas.

When Saipoel snapped this photo on my cell phone, the young girl surprised me (as pocongs will) by suddenly pretending to strangle me. I played along. At the time, I didn't know that a pocong is an Indonesian ghost that takes the form of a traditionally wrapped Muslim corpse. Indonesians believe that the soul of a dead person stays on Earth for forty days, and after that, if their shrouds are not released, the troubled soul will be doomed to haunt the world until someone releases them. It is believed that while some pocongs are playful, others are motivated to terrorize. Still others can appear like normal human beings, bringing messages to the living that they need to hear.

"*Kenapa kamu sendiri?* (Why are you alone?)" Saiopel asked, as he handed my phone back to me. He was slight with cheerful brown eyes. Much younger than I, he seemed very confident and had a knack for anticipating my every need during the day, wanting to make sure I stayed hydrated and out of the sun as much as possible. This proved very good advice as I would need a skin cancer operation about a year later.

Sometime during that day, Saiopel and I became friends. He had a very easy, caring way about him. During our time together, we asked each other big questions about life in the way people can when they know they'll never see each other again. We did our best speaking each other's language and discovered how similar we were in our differences. He was intrigued and sympathetic about my search to find the truth about what had happened to my family during WWII.

After we grabbed a bite to eat at a little food cart, Saipoel drove me to see Old Batavia, now called *Kota Tua Jakarta*, meaning Jakarta Old Town, a very small section of the city where Dutch colonial buildings are somewhat preserved. I walked around the old city with a special reverence, imagining my grandparents' unexpected arrival there—when

Jakarta was called Batavia, home to around 400,000 people, nothing like the modern metropolis of today. Later, we visited a few museums where Saipoel explained some Javanese customs and history.

During the afternoon we spent together, I happily stumbled upon a Wayang shadow puppet play performance. The flat puppets were made out of delicately carved water buffalo hide. When stretched over bone the hide looked like lace. The puppets were similar to the ones Dad had on display in his study. When I was young, Dad used to make plays with the puppets for my brothers, sister, and I. Later he did the same for my girls and all his grandchildren. Dad would hang up a bed sheet then have the audience sit in front of what would become the stage. Then, as puppeteer, he backlit the sheet, holding the puppets between the light and the cloth so we could see the puppets' intricate shadows. It would be a long time before Dad shared his story about the first shadow puppet play he ever saw—when he escaped from his home at night to the nearby kampong during the Japanese Occupation.

Saiopel and I had lost track of time and ended up touring the city until sunset. The last time I got into his cab, he held the front seat passenger door open (instead of the back) with a hopeful look. I took him up on the offer. After getting to know each other, it seemed silly to sit in the backseat. Instead of driving me back to my hotel, though, he drove us to a park where we parked and watched the sky turn different shades of pink and gold. As darkness descended, he leaned over and gave me a kiss. I wanted to explore my sensuality again and longed to feel safe enough to explore that part of myself.

He asked to spend the night with me. We had so much fun together all day that I could have easily said yes. But too many pocongs haunted me. When I turned him down, he was very sad. But, that was the way of it. I wasn't ready. We had one day together. And those unforgettable hours would have to be enough. He didn't take no for an answer very easily though, and that part sort of scared me. (By contrast, my ex took my final no very easily, not even a phone call.) Saiopel didn't want to drive me back to my hotel after spending all day taking me where I wanted to go. But, he finally relented.

"*Aku kamu cinta,*" he said as he drove up to my hotel.

I typed the words into Google Translate. It read, "I love you."

I smiled. Love is such a big word, and was so charged for me. Back then, I thought I may never be able to say "I love you" to anyone ever again. During my decades-long marriage, I thought I knew what it meant to love someone. But, in the wake of my impending divorce, I didn't trust myself in matters of love.

As Saiopel opened my door, my heart felt lighter and heavier at the same time. I didn't know what to say. I reached into my backpack and handed him the payment we'd agreed upon, but he refused to take the money. As I turned to walk up the steps and into the hotel lobby, my heart filled with so much gratitude and awe of all that Saiopel and I had seen and shared.

I went up to my room and freshened up before meeting my traveling companions for the next few weeks. A bit tired, I wanted to journal about all that I'd experienced that day but didn't have much time before I needed to join the tour. When I arrived at our meeting place in the lobby, our guide, Sukio, introduced himself then we all took turns making our introductions. He talked about our upcoming two-week journey east across the island of Java to Bali. That night we all went to dinner at a western restaurant, unlike the open-air roadside restaurants I'd gotten used to during my tours of Bandung and Jakarta. Eating in the western style felt strange that night, but it was part of the tour, and I went with it. In the two days since I'd arrived on Java, I had already started to assimilate to Indonesia. I remember saying *terima kasih* (thank you) to the server when she delivered my dinner to the table that night. It was the first word I learned in Bahasa. The people I'd just met on the tour were impressed with how I'd started to pick up the language. A few of them had seen me leave in the cab that morning and wanted to know where I'd gone during the day.

FEBRUARY 23, 2014
JAKARTA

I was touched that Saipoel wanted to be my guide. I mean, he didn't have to do anything but drive me where I wanted to go. Somehow we became friends and that doesn't happen every day. What a sweet way to tour the city and learn some Indonesian. We're texting back and forth. He seems to care so much about me, even as we will never see each other again and don't speak each other's language. He seems to care about me more than I've been cared about in a long time.

The next morning the tour group all gathered in front of the hotel for our transport to the train station. I stowed my bag, climbed some steps onto a small bus, took my seat, then looked out my window. Along with some other Indonesian men, Saipoel stood at the entrance of the hotel. Our eyes caught. We exchanged smiles. As our bus pulled away, he waved and smiled some more. Saipoel lived outside of the city and chose to sleep in his car that night in the parking garage of the hotel just to see me off, a total surprise. I'll be forever grateful for the kindness he extended me on that first day of my solo adventures on Java and the heartfelt, unexpected way he welcomed me to Indonesia.

His kindness gave me the confidence to continue seeking answers to the endless questions I had about this story.

When I took my seat on the train, I pondered so many things as the train car wound around the mountains into the jungle and up to Bandung. I imagined Grandma and baby Aletta traveling by horse-drawn carriage. The image gave me hope that somehow I'd still be able to make my pilgrimage to Malabar. On the train, I decided to ask Sukio how I might get there. He didn't hesitate to help, suggesting that I hire a private car. When I agreed, he arranged for a trusted driver to take me on the journey.

MY MALABAR

After arriving at the train station in Bandung and some serious luggage schlepping to our humble hotel for the night, I met my driver, Bokedi. He was professional and kind, so I got a good feeling about our trip together. My heart raced as I slid onto the black leather backseat of his freshly washed black Audi, thrilled to finally be on my way. Baba was right, Malabar was much farther from Bandung than I thought.

The adventure began on our drive into the remote jungle of *Gunung* (Mount) *Puntang*. So remote, Bokedi stopped often during our climb up the mountain to ask for directions from locals. It seemed curious that I'd hired Bokedi but he didn't know the way. Most people he asked only had a vague idea where we wanted to go. Others had never heard of Malabar. Occasionally, people gave him detailed directions. Bokedi would drive for a while and get lost again, needing more help. Always good-natured, he kept asking and driving, asking and driving.

Would we ever find it? What had I gotten myself into?

But my questions gave over to the adventure. As we drove closer and more off-road, my excitement grew. At our last stop, a local insisted on escorting us himself when he learned I was a descendent of one of the engineers who'd worked there. So Bokedi parked his car at the side of a rocky dirt road, and we followed our self-appointed guide into the jungle.

He was a slight, serious, chatty man who spoke with Bokedi almost constantly and carried a large pink umbrella. How I longed to know what they discussed. Soon, we came upon what looked like a park entrance sign. I took out my video camera and filmed everything. The sign illustrated many sites—Air Turgun, Buper, Gunung Api Purba (Malabar Vulcano), Kolam Cinta, Peninggalan Stasiun Radio Pemancar, (Legacy of the Transmitter Radio Station), Goa Belanda. The sign also displayed old pictures of Malabar which I recognized from some of the original photos in Dad's files.

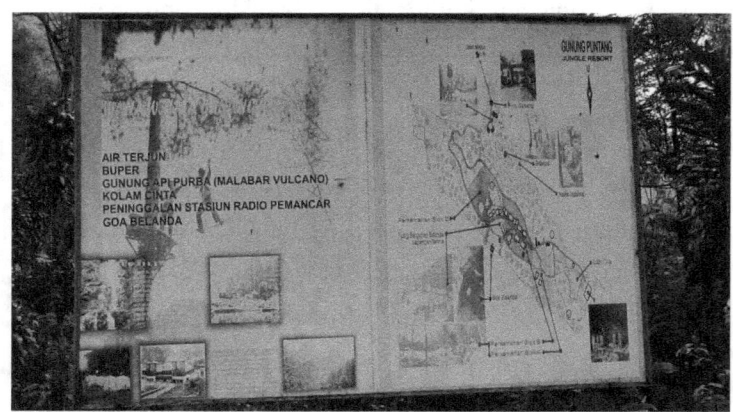

Malabar park entrance sign.

I didn't need Google Translate to know that we'd found Malabar and I thanked Bokedi and the local man with praying hands and a bow, saying "*Terima kasih*." They bowed in return and asked me to follow them. As we continued, climbing stone steps that nature had tried to reclaim, the three of us explored a vast jungle full of history, including my own. I remembered Dad's words from one of his letters.

> *. . . your grandfather had a good rapport with the Indonesians. They admired him because he did a job that no Indonesian would do which was to string the antennas from the two mountaintops. The longer the antenna, the more powerful the radio. Then, he constructed a cable car on a pulley and used this to attach the antenna from one mountain to the other . . .*

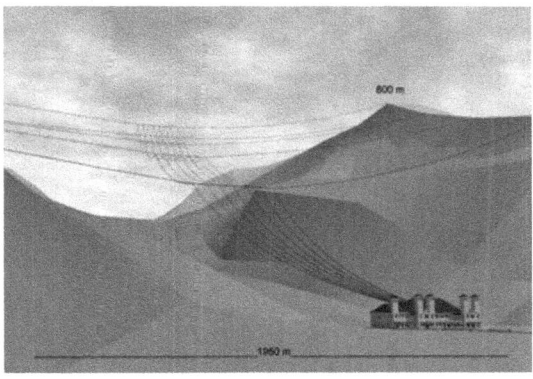

Schematic representation of Malabar's antenna system (Wikipedia).

When the mountain tops where Grandpa had done the impossible came into view, I stopped walking. My heart pounded. The sight of the gorge, free of any trace of the storied, once all-important long-range radio antenna helped me understand many things in new ways—how difficult it must have been for Grandpa to accomplish his mission and the fleeting nature of grand achievements.

The three of us spent hours at the site during a joyful, haunting discovery of Malabar. The beauty of the mountains enchanted as we walked among hundreds of highly poisonous yet intoxicatingly beautiful golden Angel's Trumpet flowers[43] blooming through a twist of wild jungle plants in infinite shades of green. As we got closer to the site, Malabar's ruins peeked out of the vast jungle.

Bokedi and our local guide at Kolam Cinta.

During the last months of 1945, in what's known as the Bersiap[44] period (sixteen months of violence that occurred in Indonesia shortly after the Japanese Surrender), the Japanese bombed the once pristine site of the powerful radio station and the small, exotic mountain paradise that had housed the community of engineers.

On our walk further into the jungle, the blown-up foundation of the radio station came into view. As my heart pounded, I paused in a moment of reverence. Like I would at a grave. Bokedi and the local gentlemen gave the same silent reverence. I traced the ruins of the great radio station with my eyes, spotting fragments of its foundation here and there that hadn't been overtaken by the jungle.

Knowing what Grandpa had gone through to secure his position at Malabar, how he risked his life to create the antenna, and how

---

43   Brugmansia Candida, Central Java, Indonesia
44   Bersiap is an Indonesian word, meaning "get ready" or "be prepared".

Grandma moved heaven and earth to join him there with baby Aletta, meant so much more as I stood in the middle of the vast jungle among the ruins. Dad's story was just that until I visited Malabar. The magnitude of what the family had gone through began to come alive in ways it never had before.

Malabar, circa 1923. Kolam Cinta in the foreground.

In my imagination, I superimposed Dad's old photos over the ruins. A stately building in the style of those I'd seen in Old Batavia rose out of them. I imagined bombs falling and how the building had blasted apart. What a shame something so grand had succumbed to the war. Reading about the site and researching its history didn't prepare me for the experience of encountering such a place.

My pilgrimage to Malabar gave me a kind of haunting closure. So far on my research trip, I'd been unable to walk into any of the places my family had inhabited. There seemed to be nothing physical I could hold onto. Every place they'd called home had either disappeared cr been destroyed. In the presence of the ruins, my heart had become an antenna tuned to the suffering of the past. It seemed more important than ever to illuminate the histories of the destroyed, abandoned, and decayed. Discovering all the settings of Dad's story became even more paramount.

As I stood in the shadow of the ruins of the bombed out radio station, I found myself wondering, *why*? Why had such an incredibly powerful radio station been necessary in the 1920s? Why did radio have to go to such extremes to create the signals? Why the desperate attempt to string wire over a 2000-meter gorge? I found my answers about a decade later on the event page[45] of a 100-year celebration of Malabar's first long-wave transmission to Holland's Queen Wilhelmina.

Malabar was vital for national security. The Netherlands had been beholden to Britain in one way or another for most of its cable telegraphic communication, which ran under the sea all over the world. Since the Second Boer War in Africa (1899-1902), the British government had exercised such extreme censorship on telegraphic communication that the Netherlands sought alternatives. Wireless was the best option being pursued when their plans got interrupted by WWI.

"The disadvantages of being dependent on foreign connections were again very noticeable, especially when the German submarine cable with which the coded telegraphic communication between The Netherlands and Indonesia was maintained, was destroyed. Indonesia was now only accessible via British cables and that meant a ban on the use of code words, and it meant censorship and huge delays.

The call for a wireless connection to Indonesia grew louder and louder. In response to this, shortly after the end of the First World War, the Dutch Government reported from Jakarta (former Batavia) they had

---

45   https://radioclublimburg.nl/mk/

started building a wireless telegraphy radio station that could communicate directly with the radio station in The Netherlands (PCG). Building the LongWave Radio Station Malabar, or 'the Gouvernements Zendstation Malabar', in Malabar near Bandoeng (Java, Indonesia) started in the year 1917. Dr. ir. C.J. de Groot designed a 2.4 MW long wave spark-gap transmitter, the original Poulsen arc transmitter design accordingly and about 60 - 80% of its power into the antenna. It took about 2 years to build the station. The long wave antenna was mounted in the Malabar gorge. The newly constructed antenna also had tremendous dimensions. The large long-wave antenna was supported by 5 inch steel cables stretched over the gorge of some 2.000 meters. The suspension points on the two foothills of the Gunung Malabar were located about 900 meters above the station. Five motor-driven winches on the south side, and corresponding counterweight conditions on the north side, served to keep the tensile stress of 10.000 kg constant.

The actual antenna wires consisted of copper wire wrapped non-ferrous carrier material of 7/8 inch strength. Due to the large surface area achieved in this way, Corona effects were encountered. The attachment to the carrier cable took place at a height of 700 meters by means of 2-meter-long insulators. The drawings show that roughly the eastern antenna cross-lines, which carried the antenna, were mounted at the slope of mount Gunung Poentang, and the western lines were anchored at the slope of mount Gunung Haroeman. The parallel antenna wires in the gorge started at 246 meters above the Malabar station level and sloping up to 715 meters. The station itself was at a level of 1.250 meters ASL."

The long wave antenna was mounted in the Malabar gorge. Grandpa's perilous job—without which the station would never have had such great power or prosperity—was reduced to a single sentence. How many sentences have incredible backstories? How many epics lie in the footnotes of history? How many stories have simply been eclipsed, just like long wave radio?

In 1920, some radio amateurs, who had been pushed to ever shorter waves by the growing number of official transmitters, discovered that with relatively little transmitting energy at wavelengths of 200 meters and higher (short-wave) one could bridge enormous distances. These radio waves had the nice property that they lost relatively little energy during their journey through the air. Moreover, these frequencies were much less affected by the noisy atmospheric disturbances that so often drowned out the long-wave radio signals. However, the professional radio world ignored this fact and stubbornly stuck to the generally accepted theory that only long-waves were suitable for reliable long-distance traffic. But more and more publications about record connections appeared in radio magazines. In 1925, a short-wave transmitter was built more or less unofficially in the PTT Laboratory on Parkstraat in The Hague. This transmitter operated on a 42-meter wavelength and had a power of only a few hundred watts (a fraction of the 2.4 MW in Malabar and the 400 kW station in Kootwijk). An aerial wire had been stretched from the laboratory attic to a nearby church tower. In the days after the first trial broadcast, a reception report arrived from Indonesia.[46]

Ironically, only two years after the Malabar Station (PKX) opened, long wave radio became history. Equipment that could fit on a dining room table broadcast more clearly, and reliably between Indonesia and The Netherlands on shortwave, eclipsing the giant of Malabar. Instead

---

46   Ibid.

of being relegated to a few precious hours at nighttime, a connection could be maintained twenty-four hours a day. And technology kept making bigger and bigger advancements.

By January 1929, people could telephone using the radio link between the two countries. This huge success came with an even bigger price tag. A few minutes could cost around a half a week's wages. Malabar adapted to become part of a larger network of radio transmitting and receiving sites in the Bandung region, first on long wave and later on short wave.[47]

Back at the site, I searched the sky above Malabar, imagining the Japanese Zeros on their mission of destruction. When my gaze returned to Earth, it settled on the intact, hauntingly beautiful *Kolam Cinta* (Love Pool), a heart-shaped pond once used to cool the generators of the radio station. A few teenagers sat on its cracked wall, dangling their feet over the side into the water. The engineers had constructed the pond in the shape of a heart that pointed toward home, to the Netherlands.

When we encountered the ghostly site of *Kolam Cinta*, Bokedi and the local guide had lots to say. But, Google Translate didn't work Ironically, we stood at the site of what was the most powerful wireless radio station in the world about one hundred years earlier and yet, in the present day, I couldn't get a wireless signal. I reached for my journal and asked Bokedi to make a drawing of what they were talking about so I could better understand.

He took my pen and drew the outline of the heart-shaped pond, and also a map of other places he wanted us to check out. Our local guide talked about the pond. Through Bokedi's translation, the local guide said that the gesture of love, pointing toward home, left a lasting

---

47   Ibid

impression on the locals who revere *Kolam Cinta*. Legend has it that if a couple visits and bathes in what is literally translated as the "Love Pool," their relationship will last. I smiled upon hearing the tradition. A bit of my broken heart melted away as I leaned on the Love Pool's wall within the shadow of the ruins of the bombed-out radio station, in the heart of the jungle.

The Japanese hadn't destroyed the heart of Malabar. Its survival took my breath away and soothed my spirit. *Kolam Cinta* was a metaphor for me, Dad, and maybe every war survivor. Try as they did, the occupiers couldn't destroy the hearts of their prisoners. How strong the human spirit is. And how beautiful the sight of the pond was in all its glory that day, nearly taken back by the jungle yet so full of life too. As I stood at the top of the heart and stared over *Kolam Cinta*, pointing in the direction of Holland, something crossed over inside of me. Since losing my home, I've wondered about what home means to me more than ever before. How I longed to be deeply anchored to a place my heart would always point to.

Staring out over the jungle, I imagined the thousands of miles between Indonesia and Holland, the distance a radio signal needed to travel to communicate. Awestruck by the engineers' invisible connections to their homeland through the radio waves, *Kolam Cinta*, and the beating of their own hearts, I realized home isn't a place, but resides in the heart. Perhaps our invisible connections are more sacred than the physical ones so easily destroyed over time. For the rest of the trip and many that would follow, I became intensely curious about the meaning of home.

Dad nearly gave his life protecting our childhood home when I was seventeen during a massive storm the night our sump pump failed. He bailed the rising water out of our sub-basement on his own and ended up suffering a massive heart attack that night. We almost lost Dad. But his doctors gave him a pacemaker. Dad later joked that he was the Energizer Bunny (after the drum-beating, pink furry creature featured in a commercial at the time).

"I'll get my batteries replaced every five years and live forever," Dad loved to say.

So many memories and echoes of conversations with Dad filled my mind as we continued our exploration of Malabar. Using Bokedi's hand-drawn map as a guide, we walked through the remains of the village of scientists where Grandpa and Grandma had lived. I imagined Grandpa playing Bach Fugues on his Steinway while we journeyed through the old compound. We frequently climbed stairs that led nowhere but to old plots of dirt where homes once stood. As we climbed one set of stairs, two yellow birds flew very close to me. They repeatedly encircled me and sang. I wasn't sure of their species, but as sunlight glistened through the jungle and danced on the birds' yellow feathers, the moment became spiritual. To me, they appeared to be love birds. I imagined them as the spirits of the grandparents I had never known, welcoming me to Java and encouraging me along my pilgrimage. Perhaps they wanted to let me know that I was at the site of their one-time home.

After my visit with the birds, we ventured to another part of the village. While I checked out the ruins of a nearly unrecognizable old swimming pool, Bokedi walked up to me and pointed to the drawing he'd made in my journal again. He mentioned we should investigate something else, something that suddenly eclipsed his easy-going, sunny demeanor. I followed him to a small opening in the mountain. He said there were several such caves that the Japanese used as hideouts during the war and where they committed atrocities. For that reason, many locals felt the spirits of the dead would forever haunt that jungle.

Our local guide standing outside one of many old Japanese bunkers in the jungles of Malabar.

My skin crawled as we stood at the entrance to one of the caves that were Japanese bunkers which littered the island of Java. A strong, visceral feeling came over me, warning me not to come any closer, which meant that I only had a very cursory view of the cave. I got weak in the knees and my heart raced. *No..no..no..no..get out of here!* . . . it seemed to say. Overcome, I told my guides I wanted to leave that place. The good that radiated from the heart-shaped pond lived together with the evil caves of the torturers. My discoveries at Malabar fueled my search for the reason the Dutch engineers and their families were captured. They also increased my desire to learn as much as I could about Java, her people, and soak up the natural and cultural beauty of the island.

After spending the day away from the tour group, I had to say goodbye to our local guide. We all drank hot ginger tea at a local toko before Bokedi and I hit the road back to Bandung. Visiting Malabar was another amazing dream that came true only because of the compassion and wisdom of complete strangers who wanted to help me.

* * *

Green Canyon, Cihideung, Java, Indonesia.

The next day, my tour group traveled to Pandagaran and we sailed through the Green Canyon, an otherworldly gorge filled with waterfalls, rapids, and rock formations bathed in the emerald green jungle. Afterward, a local Wayang puppet maker demonstrated his craft and told tales of the Hindu saga of *The Ramayana*, about Rama and Sita, their Romeo and Juliet. A day later, our guide, Sukio, invited us to his home for a delicious lunch prepared by his wife. When we arrived, people were playing a championship volleyball game right outside his front door.

Cave bats, Java.

Afterward, on a hike through a creepy jungle cave at twilight, spiders and scorpions crawled on its walls as bats hung over our heads. At the end of that day's adventure, we sat on a beach overlooking the ocean and watched tens of flying foxes take wing against the golden sky during their mysterious sunset ritual. Overjoyed to experience such natural beauty, my heart lightened at the sight of the flying foxes. Joy had been hard to come by before I took the trip. As night fell, fishing boat lights twinkled over the Java Sea.

After dinner, Tim, Derek, Hannah, and I rented a four-person pedal-powered open-air quadracycle and rode through the empty streets of Pandangaran. It was funny driving that thing because it took us a while to get the hang of pedaling in one direction. We had fun driving each other crazy as we tried to navigate the quiet streets and ended up laughing the whole time. We'd been touring for days, adhering to schedules so letting loose on a spontaneous ride through town was the perfect way to end the day.

Hannah, from London, was the youngest in the group and had been traveling for a few weeks before landing in Indonesia. She was a breath of fresh air, telling stories about all-night full moon parties in Thailand. I loved her energy and curiosity about the world. Tim, from New York, was a riot and always up for fun. This was his first trip to Asia too. Derek became a fast friend. He was well-traveled and enjoyed some much-needed downtime, a world away from his work life. We were all seekers of one kind or another.

As I walked back to my room after our ride that tranquil evening, I couldn't fathom the devastation that occurred when the tsunami hit in 2006, completely destroying Pandangaran. Sukio, told us the tale of how he had been leading a tour on the river in the Green Canyon when the Tsunami took over the island, and of his frantic search to discover that his wife and children were alive. It was equally hard to imagine The Battle of The Java Sea nearly seventy years earlier when *The Repulse* and *The Prince of Wales* would be sunk by the Japanese.

MARCH 1, 2014
PANDANGARAN, JAVA

It's evening prayer now. The call to worship is epic. As I drink a Bintang, prayerful echoes fill the night. I've been warned by Saipoel and my friends in Bandung to be careful in this part of Java. While I paid attention to the warnings, especially coming from the different Indonesians I know (who know nothing of each other), it somehow didn't impact me until now. I remember earlier today when Sukio showed us a guard tower and explained how the men take turns watching over the village each night.

MARCH 2, 2014

SELOLIMAN NATURE RESERVE, JAVA

The jungle hikes at Seloliman will stay in my imagination forever. So much to inspire. The great variety of life . . . the beauty of the wild. I thank God for waist-deep hikes in this jungle. Swallowed in nature, I'm blessed to experience the aliveness of an exotic world. A world Dad called home.

It's loud in the jungle, especially at night, just like Dad said. Full of hums and chirps, calls and caws, crescendos and croaks and howls. There are a million creatures out there and my mind's alive with the intoxication of sound! One of the most memorable experiences of my life—sitting here on the bed, under the mosquito netting, journaling to the jungle's symphony.

Go Big

'Cause the truth you might be running from is so small
But it's as big as the promise
The promise of a coming day

—"Southern Cross", Crosby, Stills & Nash

After navigating Jakarta on my own and traveling to Malabar on my own too, I began to understand that this story had its own timeline and wouldn't be told on mine. It hadn't occurred to me that the endeavor of writing this story would be so complex. I never gave myself that kind of grace. Instead, I drove myself, trying to beat the ever-ticking clock of Dad's lifetime. I would eventually learn that I had to forget (and not force) my personal agenda and instead trust where, when, and how the story led.

I needed to fully immerse myself in Java. And, I needed to know myself better. Throughout that first research trip to Java and then Bali, I wrote little letters to myself so I would remember everything I felt and experienced. One by one, each entry grew my confidence in my writing ability. And they led, like stepping stones, to mysteries about myself and my family's fate that would take another decade to unravel.

The day our tour reached Yogyakarta, Sukio told us that Borobudur and Prambanan had just opened to the public after Kelud's eruption. We couldn't believe our luck when we heard the news. To us, their opening was nothing short of a miracle. We only had that one day on our schedule to tour the famous temples. What a difference a day makes. One day earlier, we would have missed being able to experience the profound sense of history and spirituality held by those ancient, breathtaking jewels of Java.

Before entering the holy sites, I wrapped a sarong over my belly as requested by our guide. Indonesians believe the soul resides in the belly and they use the fabric as a form of protection. I liked wearing the sarong. It occurred to me as I tucked the batik fabric around my waist that I hadn't protected my soul enough. How could I protect something I thought so little about? But that day, I reflected on my soul and the importance of protecting something so beautiful.

The temples' overwhelming majesty quickly helped to raise my awareness to new levels of beauty. Their sheer size was hard to process. Every step I took seemed to transport me back in time to a place where Buddhist and Hindu kingdoms lived peacefully, side-by-side. The wanton ashen ruins of Prambanan, a World Heritage protected site, underscored how lucky we were to visit that day. A delicate layer of cinder blanketed every surface and gave me chills, an eerie reminder of the human toll and all that was lost during Kelud's recent eruption.

An ancient earthquake once destroyed Borobudur, burying it in ash before the jungle swallowed its massive stupa made of two million volcanic stone blocks. Thousands of years later, in the early 1900s, the Dutch unearthed the temple and began its restoration. The striking sight of seventy-two stupas in Borobudur's third level made me feel like I'd transcended the bonds of Earth and demanded a moment of silence and contemplation.

As my tour group and I walked among the stupas, dozens of well-dressed, uniformed school children got a kick out of practicing their English with us and charmed us with their smiles. Learning and sharing from each other surprised and delighted everyone that sunny morning. Then they insisted on an incredible spontaneous photoshoot which made our little band of travelers feel like celebrities.

Borobudur.

Scenes of meditation unfolded everywhere at Borobudur, with the faithful processing slowly, always in a clockwise direction. Seekers found peace in their rituals as they walked, singing and chanting, some with their eyes closed. The temple is a storybook of Buddhism told through thousands of sculptures carved in lava stone. Our guide said Buddhism is a way of life, rather than a religion, and stressed the importance of lessening the gap between the poor and the rich.

And yet, amidst Borobudur's beauty the devastation that had visited the region before we arrived haunted me. Lives had been lost and property destroyed. Our great good fortune at seeing the majestic temples was made even more wonderful in light of the eruption. A bittersweet metaphor for life, and perhaps the reason why Dad had been so joyful despite his tumultuous past. For what is sweeter? A moment of pleasure? Or pleasure after such loss?

When I left the temple, I entered the busy kingdom of Yogyakarta where motors (motorcycles) met horse buggies. Among the bustle, children riding in rickshaws put a smile on my face. Soon we explored a busy downtown market filled with fruits I'd never seen before, like rambutan and durian. All kinds of spices were on display, including rows of different varieties of ginger and turmeric. The blur of scents and sounds drew me into an exotic world of taste, causing me to reflect on the role of food in bringing good health. So the next afternoon, I took a class in the art of making ancient homemade wellness elixirs, called *Jamu*, meaning "a prayer for your good health" in Javanese. In the class I learned how to create mystical potions that can help cure various ailments and calm the body, mind, and spirit.

* * *

I'd already begun to open my heart to the joys of life on Java and gotten more comfortable with feeling good again as we traveled to the Kingdom of Yogyakarta, known as Jogja. The discoveries I made, personally and in my research, brought a new kind of magic into my life. I began to trust my instincts again and enjoy life more. Somehow, the darkness that seemed to have a grip on me began to loosen.

A bicycle tour guide named Ru helped me begin to see my way to the other side of my pain. He took me and a few others on a bike tour around Yogyakarta. We had so much fun pedaling through the rice paddies, watching the harvest, visiting a Lewak coffee house and joking around (pretty easy to do since Lewaks eat and then poop the coffee beans before they're dried and ground into the finest, most expensive coffee in the world. Ethical Lewak coffee is no joke, though).

I love bike riding. It's something I've loved ever since I was a little girl. But, I'd gotten away from it. A handful of years earlier, when I told my then-husband that I wanted to get back into riding a bike again, he got frustrated with me and said that bike riding was "his thing," not mine. At the time, his response seemed strange. Such a territorial view of something that could have brought us both joy should have been a signal that there was something more amiss. There were so many ways he could have responded, including being excited to ride together. His words hurt. Maybe that's why I just left it alone. But, why on earth did I?

Distancing myself from that memory made my bike ride through the rice paddies and visiting with various artisans that day so much sweeter. And, as I rode, I realized that no one could or should ever try to dissuade me from doing what I love. I could pedal all the way across Java, had I wished. During the ride, Ru made sure that my bike worked well, that I had water, shade, and anything else that I needed. He encouraged me to have fun and enjoy life. Ru's heartfelt concern for me caught me off guard. We rode for a few hours but it definitely felt like our time together ended too soon. Saying goodbye to Ru felt different. Not like saying goodbye to any other guide on the tour. But, it wasn't for long.

The next and final night in Jogja, Ru came to my rescue. When he found out my flashlight's batteries had died, he volunteered to help me buy some in town. Early the following morning, I'd be heading to a remote part of the island for a pre-dawn summit of Mt. Bromo. Since batteries wouldn't be available there, with Sukio's blessings, I hopped on the back of Ru's motor and he showed me around his kingdom. We had a spontaneous evening of fun that began with touring the palace grounds. As a rock concert ended, lit-up bicycle carts filled with happy Indonesian riders paraded around a circular street in front of the kingdom's walls. Later that night we couldn't find the right batteries for sale anywhere, which meant I had to buy a new torch (flashlight)—a metaphor for the new ways my light began to shine. My purchase of the torch with him was so symbolic. In a way, he had been my torch, opening my heart to the simple pleasure of riding a bike without shame.

When we left Jogja, Ru showed up to see me off at the train station. The gesture so very sweet and unexpected. Especially since I'd shut myself off to that kind of attention, let alone allow myself to feel the thrill of it. When he walked onto the train to say goodbye, I smiled. We exited the train car together and chatted briefly on the platform. I could feel my friends from the tour watching us. Ru looked wonderful. Too wonderful to leave. He asked me to come back to Jogja. To consider seeing him again. We held hands. It was hard to let go. We both knew that there was more to explore between us. It seemed too soon to say goodbye forever.

MARCH 4, 2014
MT. BROMO

My roommate Hannah and I sleepwalked into our clothes. Together with our traveling companions, we piled into five jeeps to take the dizzying, nighttime drive to summit Mt. Bromo. I sat in the far back seat of one of them. Every twist and turn sent mystery metal digging into my hip or thigh. My friends and I had braved many adventures on our tour together. This one was the earliest at 3 a.m. After a short hike to the summit, we waited, having no idea what beauty we'd witness. What wonders sat in the darkness below or the heavens above.

As I saw the Southern Cross for the first time, my friends and I sang the Crosby, Stills and Nash song of the same name. Under the curtain of stars I'd never seen before, I understood why I had come to Java—the truth I'd been running from was so strong, it was as big as the promise of the coming day.

In the pink and purple smoke of many shrouded volcano peaks, at the summit of Mt. Bromo, the sun rose. Revealing the beauty that comes out of the darkness. It was my sunrise. All mine. A new beginning. An invitation to do the very same thing within my own life. I am the sunrise illuminating the darkness—the web of my ex's lies that tried to convince me that black was white.

At that moment, I decided I'd always "Go Big." This big trip, this big sunrise called me to trust my big dreams. I'd no longer need to doubt or be frightened by them. Instead, I'd bravely keep on dreaming. Keep on living to discover myself and my passions in the face of catastrophe. I made an offering to the volcano to end my pain. I asked God to turn the flowers I tossed into the cauldron of the volcano at Mt. Bromo into happiness.

My offering to Mt. Bromo.

MARCH 4, 2014
KILABARU, JAVA

I just killed a spider for Hannah. She's adorable. A total sweetheart, she's extremely adventurous, but really upset by insects. At our last place in Seloliman Nature Preserve, our bathrooms were outside, and she had a wasp nest under her sink. She is staying alone in her room tonight (it was her night to have a room to herself, we all take turns). When she screamed and I was the one to kill the spider, I realized that I'd be killing my own spiders from now on. Once upon a time, my ex took care of that.

MARCH 5, 2014
KILABARU, JAVA

One of the most amazing memories of the trip so far was when I swam at the Hindu temple in Seloliman. It was completely spontaneous. I hiked to the temple with the other people on the tour, and before I knew it, I was swimming in the temple's holy water. I loved it. Every second of it. I just went in with my clothes on. The cool water felt amazing on my hot skin. There's such power in following my instincts, even though I have no idea where they might take me. All I know is that I'm more me when I pay attention to them. A few others joined in.

I was deeply sad at the temple (I think it had something to do with the fact that I would be killing all my own spiders from now on) and I wanted to wash the sadness away. After I went for a swim, another guy on the tour sat on the ledge of the pool, tapped me on the shoulder and asked how I was. The gesture was so very unexpected and so very nice. The kind of tenderness I wasn't used to.

Thunder's booming in the distance and is a comfort. I like the rhythm of the storms. We have no water in our room right now. Last night I blew a fuse when I plugged in my phone for a charge. In the last hotel the electricity didn't work at all. There's a peace to life in the darkness I never knew before. I've made friends with it.

MARCH 6, 2014
ON THE BUS TO TAKE THE FERRY TO BALI

I've heard about Bali my whole life and it seemed like an exotic place only other people would visit. But today, I'm going to set foot on the island. There were a million reasons to not go on this trip. To stay stuck in fear. To pull back, especially in the face of so much pain and uncertainty—but I didn't. I chose to Go Big, and this is my new philosophy. My new North Star. I've decided I don't want to live my life as I always have. I want to live differently. I'm not completely certain what this will look like. I've decided I'd like to travel and write and work incredibly hard to support myself with my pen (camera and computer too).

I would find that the real magic in my life lies in an elegant truth. An elegant truth it would take a trip around the world to discover.

Java, this ancient place of mystery and history, the island where my dad was born, the island where he fought for his survival during WWII, transformed me and my pain.

Calls of "hello"
Big smiles
Swimming in holy water
Offerings to volcano cauldrons
Beautiful simplicity
24/7 people in crowded squares
Life, life, life
Manic driving, bicycle rides,
Motors and torches
4:30 a.m. calls to prayer
Jungle shrieks and hums
I will miss it all
Everything
The bike ride with Hannah, Tim, and Derek
Through the nighttime streets of Pandangaran
Volleyball, 2 a.m. feasts
Clove cigarettes
Perfect strangers
Helping, caring
Kites catching flying foxes for dinner
Markets and the mystical
A witch's spell cast
A Holy Tree wrapped
The spirit world
A heartbeat away

Waiting to be felt

Waiting to speak

Listen

Living with duplicity

The black and the white

The left hand and the right

Good and evil

All have a place here,

Finding a balance

A great harvest ahead

Without fear

Without pain

Secure

In the joy

That comes from

GOING BIG

We've just passed a funeral. An amazing sight. The coffin is draped in green fabric and flowers loosely cover it. And, of course, I think about how short life is. And how little I was about to settle for just because I wasn't sure about the unknown.

It's my last few hours on Java and I'll take it home with me. Whenever I feel unclear or uncertain, I'll bring the harvest in the palm-tree fringed rice paddies to mind, trusting a rich harvest is ahead. I will take the ferry from Java to Bali today. My dear Indonesian friend warned me about the ferries.

"They sink a lot of the time. Go to Bali another way," she said. I pray extra-hard on the crossing, so breathtakingly beautiful.

MARCH 7, 2014
UBUD, BALI

The Hindu temples here have monuments at their entrances in the shape of hands in prayer. As you walk through, they bless you and as you leave, they wish you well. I went to the gardens of good and evil at the Goa Gajah temple in Ubud. I was kind of shocked how they acknowledge the evil spirits in this way, so different from the West where they are rarely talked about. I walked through the temple wearing a beautiful sarong wrapped Balinese-style.

As my guide, Ketut, and I walked through the temple, he told me that there was a small school in the Elephant Cave here. Once upon a time, in the Elephant Cave, the king taught boys about religion and philosophy. Ketut mentioned that the students were instructed in how to control their emotions because it is the only thing a person can control. He said that when there is a problem, that the problem always lies inside you, never inside another person.

The only two things a person should pray for from God, according to Ketut, are health and harmony in the family. When life is out of balance then there is a problem. The lesson reminded me that fear is something only I can control. I can't find happiness without harmony. It is up to me to find it within. It is up to me to turn my life around to be happy to get control over my emotions. To be solidly centered in who I am. It's up to me to find the balance.

The word "Bali" means "offering." I find myself here during a celebration for Ganesh, the God of wisdom, education, and good luck, a holiday for teachers and priests. I think it's no coincidence that I'm here on this day as I celebrate the incredible abundance of health, connection, good weather, experiences, and creativity in my life, and I pray for harmony within my family. I pray on this celebration day for the wisdom to see God's will for my life and to have faith to continually Go Big.

March 8, 2014

Ubud, Bali

I visited the holy springs at Tirta Empul on Hari Saraswati (a day in honor of Dewi Saraswati, Goddess of knowledge, music, arts, wisdom and learning). The springs were packed with people, and I wanted to go in, but didn't have anyone to leave my camera and purse with. But then, I noticed people with keys around their wrist. So, I searched for some lockers. I'm really glad I found them. After storing my things, I entered the holy water in my clothes. The guidebook said the Balinese people believe the waters have magical powers. I prayed for health and harmony and protection. It felt so great to surrender to the power of the fountains as I bathed my head in the holy water, so refreshing on this hot day. The beautiful flower offerings of plumeria and burning incense captivated me, especially seeing small streams of smoke wafting at the water's edge.

Jakarta Post Front Page March 11, 2014.

MARCH 9, 2014
UBUD, BALI

Word of the disappearing Malaysian Airlines flight MH370 plane shocked the world today, and Indonesia was in the spotlight for the search and rescue effort. As countries scoured the Java Sea for the missing plane, relatives contacted me and my friends to ask about our welfare.

They would ask if my next flight was a Malaysian Airlines flight. It's hard to put into words what it's like to go through such a global event at the heart of the event itself.

I think about how it's okay to be afraid of the unknown, even when planes disappear out of thin air. It's okay not to have any of the answers I want when I need them. It's part of the journey.

* * *

Back at home, people were concerned about me traveling far away to places so different from the U.S. The more I travel, the more I understand that the key to world peace is in the friendships we make. Because, in the end, barring anarchists, we all want the same things. We want to be happy. We want our children to be healthy. We want to be there for our friends. The more friends we have in the world, the more peace we bring to the world. I saw world travel as an essential way to foster world peace.

Hannah once told me during our time together, that there's a difference between going on vacation and traveling. She said we were travelers. And I believe it was at this point in the trip that I took inspiration from her and became a true traveler myself. Paying attention to my journey's cues and listening to where it wanted to take me. I had taken a break from everyone and everything I knew to concentrate on getting to the heart of Dad's story and to journey to the center of my heart, something that seemed to be equally shrouded in mystery. I had focused on answering the questions I had about Dad's life, but discovered that I also needed to find and answer the questions of my own heart.

But I didn't know how. At that time I was confused about so many things. Mark 8:35 had become important to me during this time. It basically says that if we try to hang onto our life, we will lose it. That we must lose our life to find our life. I felt like I had lost my life. At that time, I was like a planet drifting off into space, needing to find my sun. Something I could count on. Something to orbit around. A constant. What life would I find?

So when Tim, Derek, and Hannah said they were going to visit Ketut, the famous guru from the movie *Eat, Pray, Love*, I thought *why not?* We were about to say goodbye. They were due to leave Bali in a few days and I would be joining another tour. Seeing Ketut would be part of our last hurrah. I decided to have fun and just go with it.

KETUT

On the same day that we found out about the Malaysian Airlines airplane disappearing without a trace, my friends and I walked some winding roads out of Ubud to Ketut's place. It was a time of wanting to find answers to questions we all had about our futures. On the way, Tim and Hannah joked about how they were flying Malaysian Airlines the next day. When we finally arrived at Ketut's place, instead of getting the vibe that this would be a deeply personal experience, it was hilarious in so many ways. Visiting the guru from *Eat, Pray, Love* felt pretty over-the-top, including Ketut's moniker out front. Could we find a deeply spiritual experience there? We shrugged and were open to whatever came our way.

We actually had to take a number when we arrived. At that moment, I wished I hadn't bothered going. Taking a number to see a holy man didn't feel right. But, my friends insisted that I take one. A tsunami of people had inundated the poor holy guy after the popular book and movie adaptation. Beyond a central open-air temple at the typical Hindu family compound, Ketut held court on the tiled patio of his bungalow.

After my friends and I took our numbers we joined the crowd and sat together on a small wooden bench. Many tourists like us were seated, waiting their turn. I sighed, deciding to simply surrender to the experience. When a number was called, the person holding that number would sit cross-legged in front of Ketut and get a reading. Sometimes he'd hold people's hands. Other times, he'd stare at people in the eyes as he spoke with them. We quickly discovered that Ketut could barely speak English. Unlike us, many people had brought their own interpreters.

Something weird happened as I sat next to my friends. While watching the scene unfold at Ketut's, I suddenly longed for a holy man to speak an ancient truth that might bring me peace. Maybe he could help me find the answers I needed quickly so that I might write this story in Dad's lifetime. As I clenched my red number eight, I began to believe in the possibility that maybe, just maybe, Ketut had the power to help me find a healthy way to move past my heartache, and move on in my life.

After our numbers were called, we each sat cross-legged in front of Ketut on his tile patio. During my visit with Ketut, I found it really hard to understand him, but just the same, I enjoyed sitting in his joyful presence. How I wished I'd had an interpreter to help me discern all of his wisdom. Later that day, after my reading, I jotted down my interpretation of Ketut's insights about my life in my journal—

I am very lucky and will be very successful at what I do. I am an influencer. He is happy that I came and asked me to be his wife. (Ha!) I will marry again. I will live until I am 100. Whatever I do, I will be successful and very happy. All good things are coming to me. He asked me to smile. I have three lines in my brow which means good fortune for my life. Love and light is with me. I am very smart. I will have more than enough money. Come to Bali again and stay.

Afterward, I felt I had another riddle to solve. If everything that I understood him to say was true, why did I feel like the most unlucky woman in the world? If I was so "smart" how had I been deceived for so long by my ex? At that time in my life, I felt far from the success and happiness Ketut felt sure I would enjoy. His were wonderful words to hear, of course. But how could I believe him when my past made me feel like such a failure? And, the money he spoke of had yet to flow into my life. I didn't even have a job other than writing this story, reconnecting to my writing career, and getting a foothold in the world of screenwriting.

But, I loved meeting Ketut. His smile warmed my heart. Just to sit so close to him and share the energy of someone who wanted nothing but the best for me was worth the 250,000 rupiah ($20). Besides, my friends and I had a blast. While they were also confused by a lot of what Ketut said, they seemed to get something positive from his insights. The filmmaker in me enjoyed inhabiting one of the actual settings of the successful screen adaptation of the famous book.

As I walked back to Ubud with my friends, we had a good laugh when I let them know Ketut had asked me to be his wife. I wondered how many women he asked to be his wife every day and how many wives he actually had. What a joker. The memory always puts a smile on my face. He was so old, playful, and funny. Sadly, he would die only a few years later, in 2016, the same year as my dad.

During that visit, the only things I thought really fed my soul were the belly laughs and good times with my friends. But the idea that the visit might give me life-altering insights really made me begin to crave that kind of experience. I didn't think much more about that, until about a week later, on my next tour which focused on Bali. I became friends with Amy, Giovanna, and Sofia, who lived in Fiji, Brazil, and Belgium respectively. At some point I told them about my fun visit with Ketut.

Instead of laughing it off, they said, "Oh, my god! We have to go see that guy."

So, I arranged for the visit and an interpreter. Because of our schedule and Ketut's, the only day they could see him was the morning they were scheduled to fly home. I knew we had to get to Ketut's early to be first in line because of the tight timing of their visit. But, holy men don't live by the clock. That day he opened late.

Even though my friends got numbers two, three, and four, the readings went slowly that day. It seemed they wouldn't have enough time for even one of them to visit with Ketut. But, it all worked out. Even though the interpreter missed their readings, my friends didn't care. They enjoyed every minute with Ketut and loved the whole experience. As they rushed to get to the airport, we said our goodbyes and they thanked me for arranging everything. That's when the interpreter, Wayang, showed up.

I politely thanked him for coming, and said that my friends were already headed to the airport. "But, it is your turn," Wayang said. "Don't you want to see Ketut?"

No. I already had, I explained. But had I? I had only heard what I could discern. Maybe there was more. Part of me wanted to know word for word what Ketut said. Part of me didn't. I told Wayang that I was just there to help my friends and hadn't thought about seeing Ketut again. I would feel weird waiting there with an interpreter I didn't know, at the back of the line without my friends. But Wayang insisted. So I got a number and waited, again.

As I took my seat, Wayang said, "So, what is your problem?"

It was a straightforward question. Afterall, why else would someone journey to see Ketut unless they had one, right? Still, sharing my "problem" (which I couldn't even articulate at the time) with a perfect stranger was, well, a little jarring. But, my curiosity got the better of me, as it often does, and so I told him I'd think about it and let him know.

The wait was a lot longer than I expected, another thing I had to learn about Indonesia. There is no rushing around, which was a good thing since the rushing part of my nature needed to be tempered to help me find my center again. Wayang had taken two hours to arrive at Ketut's when I made arrangements for my friends to have an interpreter. But, I could hardly have a problem with any of those things. What choice did I have? When my patience wore thin, I tried to remind myself to trust and be patient. Like earlier that day, when I decided to spend more time in Indonesia. I had to surrender my passport in Ubud and trust that it would be sent to Jakarta and returned with my granted visa extension within a week. Yet another time I had to take things on faith, wait, and trust at a time when my ability to trust had been at an all time low.

Finally, my number was called. Wayang accompanied me on a walk up to the tile veranda of Ketut's bungalow. Once again, I sat cross-legged in front of Ketut as I had before. Wayang sat beside and a little bit behind me and told Ketut my problem in Indonesian. Honestly, I can't remember what I asked Wayang to say to Ketut that day.

But, I remember what Ketut said. I needed to forgive by keeping myself very full with good activity so that I could cleanse my imagination from my ex and from bad thoughts. Ketut knew I was a writer (which gave me the chills since I never mentioned it) and said I will be rich and very lucky. He kept saying how beautiful I am and how very smart I am. That I am an influencer. Ketut said lots of things, including the fact that my ex was still in love with me. He even added that if I wanted to, I could marry him again. If not, I could marry again but he cautioned me not to unless my ex would give his blessing.

Uh, what? I didn't know what to think about what Ketut said about my ex. To say his words shocked me would be an understatement. And yet, I did need to forgive. I did need to find a way forward.

Cleanse my imagination.

Good activity.

The idea that my imagination needed to be cleansed felt like a lightning bolt to my heart. I didn't know what to do with that insight at the time. Had I been unable to write as I always had because my imagination was clouded? The idea that my imagination could be cleansed fascinated me. I wanted to know how. The suggestion to do "good activity" also resonated.

But, I didn't need to hear that my ex still loved me. I think Wayang felt my overwhelm. So much so that after we saw Ketut, Wayang reiterated, "You need good activity. Your job is to forget through good activity."

Then, as if he knew the magnitude of the task before me, he added, "My brother-in-law can help you. He's a famous holy man. Many people come from all over the world to see him. I will ask to see if he will help you. If so, would you be interested in seeing him?"

Hmmmm. I had planned to stay in Bali until my passport was sent back to Ubud with the visa extension. After I'd learned so much about Indonesia, my dad, and myself during my tours I had a level of exhaustion I hadn't experienced before. There was a lot to process. I wanted to relax and pamper myself.

My plans at the time didn't include meeting with the in-demand holy man brother-in-law of an interpreter I'd just met who said his relative might be able to help me heal from my heartache. Yet, there was something so caring about the way Wayang wouldn't let me dismiss my own needs when he showed up at Ketut's.

And, Wayang went even further. He wanted to help me solve my "problem." I needed to give words to what was keeping me so heartbroken. This writer couldn't put her pain into words back then. Perhaps, some things are better left unspoken. And yet, identifying my pain would be the biggest step to breaking its hold over me. Wayang seemed to understand my urgent need to get beyond the massive rupture in my life and forced the need for me to articulate what I couldn't before.

As I considered Wayang's offer, the opportunity to see his brother-in-law seemed extraordinary, as if the universe had conspired to fulfill my desire to have ancient wisdom spoken into my life. Was this offer a Divine Appointment? I wasn't sure back then. But, I trusted meeting Wayang and the idea that if my broken heart was meant to be healed by his brother-in-law, then it would happen effortlessly, and fit in easily between all the other things I wanted to do during those precious weeks.

I felt the need to meditate, spend time alone, practice yoga, enjoy the food (my appetite actually began to return) and relax as much as possible. I wanted to travel to Lombok, or possibly the Gili islands, to snorkel and try freediving, because I loved snorkeling at Pulau Menjangan the week before.

Menjangan is a tiny island only five miles off Bali's western shores, part of West Bali's National Park Conservation Area. Snorkeling with Amy, Giovana, and Sofia, the silence of the sea, and the freedom I felt underwater helped me playfully enjoy life in a way I hadn't before. I wanted that feeling again—exploring an awesome, colorful underwater world full of surprises.

Snorkeling at Pulau Menjangan.

I was also enchanted with the idea of spending Nyepi Day (some-thing like a Balinese New Year's Day), a day of silence, in Bali. The idea came to me while riding on the back of Wayang's motorcycle through tiny villages outside of Ubud. I had hired him to be my driver for a few days after my reading with Ketut so I could see more of Bali. During these rides on his motor, I spotted boys constructing huge demons that rivaled any Hollywood creation. I began to film what captivated me about the ritual.

When I asked Wayang why the boys created the monsters, he said they represented Bhuta Kala, malicious spirits that inhabit Bali on Nyepi who turn people toward evil. Nyepi is a time for the dolls to capture the evil spirits. It is believed that the monsters symbolize all the negative traits of humans (greed, gluttony, lust, envy, pride, anger, laziness). The Balinese believe that it is only when they've burned the monsters on the night before Nyepi that they rid themselves and the island of the negative forces robbing positive energy from their lives.

Nyepi gives people the opportunity to begin to renew their commitment to living a life free from those negative forces with a day of silent self-reflection. During Nyepi, the Balinese restrict anything that might interfere with this commitment—no fires are lit and lights must be kept low (or turned off completely), there is no working, entertainment, or traveling, and for some, no talking or eating.

Each village funds the construction of the demons, called Ogoh-ogoh monsters because they want to keep their people safe and protect them from harm. *Ogoh-Ogoh* means "to shake" in Balinese because the monsters are shaken during a great procession of monsters before they are ceremoniously burned on the night before Nyepi. Is there anything better for most boys than making larger-than-life monsters? The Ogoh-ogoh demons looked like doodles from school papers brought to life.

On the island of Bali, night is considered the time for supernatural beings. Bhuta Kala and witches fill the darkness. Older Balinese see the night as a dangerous time for traveling outside the family compound. My Balinese friends told me that even to this day, I would not see a Balinese family out with their young children at twilight because it is the time when evil spirits can take control over people's lives.

Nyepi, 2014 Ubud.

The designs of the Ogoh-ogoh spoke to their creators' incredible imaginations and their craftsmanship spoke to how seriously villagers take their monsters. Most were big-breasted ghouls with fangs, some with blue skin, and others with very long hair and nails. Motoring the streets of Ubud felt surreal as we passed demon after demon in varying states of construction.

Witnessing the boys' creative process was as fascinating to me as seeing the finished creatures parade down the streets of Ubud the night before Nyepi. The actual day of Nyepi is determined when the *Tilem Kesanga* falls, the darkest moon. And it was only ten days away. It seemed the powers of good and evil were everywhere on display—in my own life, in Dad's story, in Kelud's eruption, in witches at airports, in the disappearance of an entire airplane, in the construction of Ogoh-ogoh dolls on seemingly every street corner in Bali, and in the words and wisdom of Ketut.

WAYANG & THE HOLY MAN

My first meeting with Wayang's brother-in-law, the holy man, had to be postponed because of a massive thunderstorm. People don't go out in that kind of storm in Indonesia. Instead, I watched nature's incredible fury with other guests in the open-air restaurant at my hotel. We lost power twice that evening. As lightning tore up the sky and thunder rattled the center of my still broken heart, I remembered what Wayang had said at lunch earlier that day as I filmed boys creating their Ogoh-ogoh dolls.

"It's a choice. If you choose to be with the bad spirits, your life will be bad. You must choose good. Do good activities." Wayang's profound words rattled around my heart along with the thunder.

Choose Good. Do good activities. I thought about myself, my ex, and our choices.

The battle of good and evil was alive and well, and on full display in Bali. Rather than fearing, pushing away, marginalizing, or denying evil the way the western world can, Balinese acknowledge and accept evil as a part of everyday life. They even make offerings to it. *It is what it is,* they seem to say.

As I experienced their matter-of-factness around evil, somehow its power over my life began to diminish. This refreshing, freeing development helped me enjoy life more. I began to believe that good really could come from evil.

In my own life, the battle between good and evil was hard to detect. But when I finally did become aware of the way evil had crept into my life, my inability to simply accept (rather than battle) it almost destroyed me.

* * *

The next night, on March 18th, 2014, at 5:30 p.m., I rode on the back of Wayang's motorcycle. First we drove through villages where teenage boys busily finished up their Ogoh-ogoh monsters. Then we continued our ride into the countryside, way off the beaten path. Reflections of the lazy afternoon sun in the delicate rivulets among green shoots of growing rice plants captivated me. I had longed to walk among the rice paddies during my trip to Bali, but hadn't yet. The stunning views on the drive eased the what-am-I-doing feeling that I had in the pit of my stomach.

When we arrived, his brother-in-law gave me a beautiful smile as he invited me to enter his traditional Balinese compound and meet his wife and family. Wayang and I entered together and toured the compound. The holy man and his relations were so very kind to me as I sorted out the mysteries of Dad's story and began to identify the ones in my own life. This would begin four days of healing a terrible ache not only inflicted by my own experiences, but also from the generational suffering my family had endured during the war.

I'll never forget how I sat cross-legged facing him as we meditated on the tiled patio just outside of his open-air bungalow. After a long while, we opened our eyes at the same time. My heart felt as muggy as the hot, tropical air typical of an Indonesian afternoon. The air felt heavy, like the feeling in my heart that wouldn't seem to go away.

Back then, I found myself haunted by wanting to know lots of . . . *Whys?* Why had the family been captured with other families and forced to move from Indonesia to Tokyo? What project had Grandpa been forced to work on? Why had my life fallen apart so spectacularly? I guessed my "problem" not only included finding the answers to the questions I had about Dad's story, but also to my questions about life. Some I didn't even know I had. I'll never forget his surprising response to the first question I asked.

"Why do bad things happen to good people?" I asked.

He smiled such a sweet, serene smile and said, "Laura, you see with clouded vision. What you have experienced isn't bad. It is, in fact, good."

Shortly after our discussion on the topic, he would observe that "Why?" isn't a spiritual question. His words disarmed me and took me by surprise (as much of his advice did). Eventually, he and others I met on my world travels helped me understand that harmony is what lies at the cave of great love. I remembered what Ketut, the guide at the Elephant Cave, said when we toured the gardens of good and evil at the Goa Gajah temple when I first arrived in Ubud.

"The only two things a person should pray for from God are health and harmony in the family. When life is out of balance then there is a problem."

My ex and I had arrived at a completely unharmonious place so there was no way back for us. I also needed to recognize that while I considered my ex's behavior bad, he and I are only human. He simply made choices that led me to make choices.

"Judging is for your god," the holy man said. He is Hindu. The fact that we observed different religions didn't matter at the time. However, a number of years later, I wondered if my experience was okay with "my god." When I spoke to a woman who ran a wonderful Bible study at my church in Los Angeles about my concern, she smiled and said, "The Lord can use anyone to speak truth into our lives."

To this day, I believe that Wayang's brother-in-law and I engaged in what felt like holy conversations. He said that to let go of judgment I needed to meditate with God, be happy, and take care of myself (what Mom would say to me every time I spoke to her in the last years of her life). I would need to listen to my heart, my intuition (that still, small voice), and pay attention (what Baba had said when I first arrived on Java). He said that he would help me develop a practice to invite these disciplines into my life and referred to the practice as having a love affair with God.

"Smile while you pray. And smile at your family, those that would do your harm, friends, life. God wants to see you smile. Spend one minute a day with God," he said.

I loved the notion of God loving my smile. Spending one minute with God didn't seem like very much time. And yet, how often had I gone days, weeks, months, without spending meaningful time with God?

His insights seemed simple, yet mind-blowing. Making my work and life an offering to God was something I hadn't really thought about before I met the holy man. We would soon begin a practice of finding the good in everything, where I did *This is good because . . .* exercises. At first it was pretty hard for me to reframe things. But after a while, it got easier.

The loneliness I feel is good, because it is just a stepping stone to my freedom.

The tears that come are good, because they are a release. The only way to let it all go is to feel deeply and release it.

"When my duties and my pleasure and my desires and my interests are in total alignment I know I'm on the right path," he said.

During that first night, the hours passed quickly between us. At some point during the evening, he said that the last time he spoke English was fifteen years prior. "I am not speaking English with my mind, but with my heart," he said. I had never heard anyone say anything like that before. He had been gifted with the ability to communicate with me (after what happened with Ketut, I was very grateful). He also mentioned that he only sees people he's called to see. He believed that the universe brought us together because we had known each other in another lifetime. But, my faith didn't allow for any such possibility. Still, there was an undeniable, deep connection between us. I believed that the Holy Spirit was at work in our conversations.

My heart felt lighter. I had begun to leave some of the heaviness of my past behind. Riding on the back of Wayang's motorcycle on the way back to my hotel the first night I worked with his brother-in-law, I reflected on how strongly I wanted the kind of guidance I'd received. How weirdly compelled I felt to hire a translator for Amy, Giovana, and Sofia's readings even though I had an idea that it might not work out for them timing-wise. How that led to meeting Wayang and his encouragement to see Ketut one more time, which led to my meeting the holy man. It became clear that there was a power at work that was fulfilling some of my deepest desires. While this thrilled and inspired me, it also felt humbling and at times even a little bit scary.

One afternoon, when Wayang had taken me to one of the villages near Ubud to film boys working on their Ogoh-ogoh dolls, an athletic, tan, silver-haired man bounded up the stairs of the covered patio where I stood and introduced himself with a smile.

"What do you do?" he asked.

"I'm a writer."

His smile widened as if he'd been expecting me. "I don't believe in hazard," he said in a Belgian-French accent. "This is destiny."

He is a filmmaker with a mischievous smile and adventurer good looks who had just returned from Kalamantan (the Indonesian portion of Borneo) where he filmed orangutans. You know, like you do. As we walked around the monsters, admiring their construction, he asked if I'd walked among the rice paddies yet. I said I wanted to, but hadn't had the time to figure out the best place to take that walk. He invited me to walk the rice paddies with him the following day. I smiled and accepted. Then he asked me to meet him for drinks that night. My heart smiled at the second invitation in as many minutes. Of course, I said yes.

The next morning, he picked me up on his motorcycle. He said he knew of the perfect spot and we walked the rice paddies together, only he didn't walk. His was a kind of purposeful stroll, much faster than I'd imagined in my dreams. When the going got really slippery, I laughed, trying to keep up with him. I felt so blessed to have the moment I'd dreamt about, in a beautiful rice paddy that seemed to go on forever.

We were able to communicate deeply in spite of our language barriers—he spoke French, Bahasa Indonesian, and a little English;

I spoke English, a little Bahasa, and very little French. Bahasa was relatively easy for me to learn because there is no past or future tense. Indonesians only speak in the present. The metaphor wasn't lost on me. God seemed to pull out all the stops to help me learn how to live in the present, inviting me to leave my rumination and worries about the future behind.

Our very relaxed day unfolded wonderfully. Walking barefoot together in the rice paddies was definitely on my bucket list of romantic experiences. But, it didn't include slipping and falling in the mud. A lot.

When I did, he laughed, "You like to be in full contact with nature, don't you?"

His endearing ways of saying things just added to the lightheartedness of it all. I loved the way he joked about our "mud bath" and "foot massage" (which was more about getting the mud from between our toes than anything really massage-like). What some people paid quite a bit of money for at exclusive resorts, we'd done for free. I loved the feel of squishy mud under my feet and the way it bubbled up between my toes. We were like a couple kids at play.

Full-contact rice paddy walk, Ubud, Bali, 2014.

After enjoying a light lunch at a roadside warung, we rode back to Ubud on his motorcycle. The powerful muscles in his forearms flexed as he steered us around every bend in the road, skirting the rice paddies. As my grip tightened around his waist to stay secure on the bike, I felt his strong abs underneath his shirt. I shouldn't have been surprised that a man who played with orangutans in the jungle had a rigorous workout ethic.

My arms lingered around his waist as we rolled to a stop at the side of the road by a local tourist office. I had to pick up my passport with my visa extension that afternoon, so he offered to drop me off. He mentioned something about needing to visit a friend that evening.

"I'll see you tomorrow. Come with me! I'm filming a tooth filing ceremony," he said.

The rite of passage in Bali involves a holy man filing the incisors and the points off the canine teeth, which the Balinese believe are a symbol of evil. The ritual is performed to rid the young person's (aged 6-18) spirit of six evil traits—lust, greed, anger, drunkenness, confusion and jealousy. Again, I was made aware of evil's presence. Again, Balinese thwarted evil through an ancient custom.

"Sure," I said. Even though I had no idea what a tooth filing ceremony was at the time, it sounded intriguing. "Thanks for today."

He smiled and gave me a twinkle-eyed look from under his silvery blonde bangs, and said, "The pleasure was all mine."

The whole day we spent together felt so damn good. We didn't make any specific plans to see each other again, but somehow I knew we would. I guess I didn't believe in "hazard" either. That night, when I returned to my hotel after a concert at the Arma Museum, the front desk said a man had left a note for me. Intrigued, I unfolded the paper with a smile. My rice-paddy buddy said that he was sorry he missed me because he wanted to take me out to dinner. He also thanked me for the wonderful day we spent together and told me to give him a call so we could make arrangements for the teeth-filing ceremony the next day. He wrote down his phone number. But, I couldn't read his handwriting.

Our attraction was kind of intense because we had so much in common. I liked that when we first met, he listened to how I wanted to walk through the rice paddies and made that dream come true. And I liked the way he left the note. And the way he held my hand when I needed to secure my footing in the mud. I found it oddly charming that he didn't dote on me at all. We both had cousins who climbed Everest, and both wanted to go to Kathmandu one day. We had kids around the same age. He lived close to my Belgian host daughter who lived with our family in California for a year when she was in high school.

Still, his larger than life presence was a bit overwhelming. He'd lived in Indonesia off and on for years. I was a newcomer. He rented a local house. I stayed in a hotel. He spent lots of time in Bali over the years, going back and forth between Bali and Belgium, his two happy places. I admired how he knew himself so well. I was in search of my happy places. He seemed to belong to his homes in ways I longed for in my own life. I loved that we were both filmmakers. I was interested in making documentaries and new to screenwriting. His films had won awards. We both shared a love of writing, traveling, and good times. It seemed he always wanted to get to the bottom of something, and I loved that. His dedication to finding his answers inspired me to keep finding mine. He was curious about the story I wanted to tell about my family.

A few days after our rice paddy walk, we reconnected and he showed me some of his films—the orangutans, volcanic eruption survivor stories. We kept in touch through emails and over Facebook. Destiny handed us a few more encounters in Belgium and Bali over the next few years. Our brief but spectacular times together over the years always made me laugh and inspired me to make more of my dreams come true (and learn more French).

* * *

The next day, I met with the holy man again.

"Know yourself. Make that belief your boyfriend," he said. That got my attention.

"When I climb to the top of a holy mountain, I never stop to drink and eat or take pictures. I do all those things on the way down," he said.

A metaphor for how I was to climb my mountain, I supposed. To prioritize the climb and not get distracted. He also said to keep life simple. To demonstrate this, he asked me to take a short walk while he watched. After doing so, he shook his head in disapproval.

"Am I walking wrong?" I asked.

"No, Laura, you need to walk sure," he said. "Walk with intention."

Walk sure. At a time when I questioned everything, were my feet doing the same? *How do I walk with intention? What does that mean?*

"We are all energy . . . " he went on, "your energy is happy and positive." He explained that I was to get in touch with my energy as I meditated. To breathe it in. To feel my smile in my solar plexus. To joyfully contemplate the important things in life . . . love, light, and liberation. We meditated off and on during the day and spoke with each other between our meditations.

At one point, he formulated a special kind of incense for me to burn so I could get back in touch with my happy, positive energy. After he lit it, he blew the musky scent my way. It wafted in the air all around us.

"You lost yourself in the first part of your life, Laura. You will need to find yourself again," he said. "When you were seven or eight years old, it was an age of happiness for you and when you were truly yourself. You went on an adventure and got lost. Many people were worried about you."

I instantly thought about my sister Suzy and the long bike ride we took while camping with my brothers' Boy Scout troop in Wisconsin. Suzy and I, along with other little sisters were adopted members of the troop. We went on lots of camping trips, attended courts of honor, and filled in whenever possible—like when we'd pretend to be accident victims so the boys could earn their first-aid merit badge.

During that trip in Wisconsin, Suzy and I got a little bored at the campsite and decided to go for a bike ride. It was wonderful to be on our own. We had such a great time riding through the woods that we didn't pay attention to the route we'd taken and didn't know how to get back to the campsite. Just as darkness descended, we found our way back. Our parents and all the adults were relieved so we didn't get in too much trouble. The memory of our long-forgotten adventure made me smile. A smile I felt in my heart. How much fun Suzy and I have had over the years. We've always been there for each other and continue to go on adventures together whenever we can.

As the incense continued to burn, we meditated to help lighten my heart. "You carry too much weight with you," he said, adding, "Laura, you don't need to take everyone with you. You must lighten your load. You are on a walk to the west. Do not listen to those who tell you to walk to the east. Stay close to those people who are walking in your same direction. You need space. Whenever you don't get space, you need to find it again."

We meditated again then he shared his simple philosophy of life, "I do what I like, and I like what I do." He flashed a beautiful smile.

Another time after meditating, I opened my eyes and he said, "Laura, every problem has a solution. Little problems are never big problems."

He pointed to a corner where four tiles met on his patio floor and said, "If this is the problem, you will never find the solution here."

"You must go over here . . . " he said, dragging his finger across the tiles to another spot, "away from the problem to find its solution."

I kept his advice in my pocket over the following years and used it when the going got rough. I remembered that to overcome my problems I would need to do things differently than what led me to the problems. I would have to go outside of my problems.

As I absorbed his wisdom, my burdens began to lighten. Burdens like: the idea that I wasn't capable enough to tell this story; the shame of betrayals; grieving a life I had loved and one that would never be; feeling alone; fears around where I'd live; if I'd ever have a home again; what that would look like; how I'd make the dream of supporting myself as a writer come true; how I'd have to kill my own spiders; that I was some kind of witch magnet; that I'd have to be the one to change all my clocks in the fall and spring; having to be alone in the middle of the night when earthquakes struck in California; having to be all alone in the middle of my life; figuring out the real reason why my family was taken to Japan; and why my grandpa was forced to work for the Sumitomo Corporation.

While still seated on his tile veranda, the holy man pointed to the floor and said, "It only takes one grain of sugar and . . . look, this ant will find it. Be like sugar. The people with problems will find you, they will seek you out and you will help people suffer less."

As I sat there on the tile meditating with him that day, I felt stronger than I had ever been because I was becoming more myself than ever before. He helped me remember who I am and helped me see through my clouded vision. Like he said, I had been on a walk to the east for far too long. I'd met myself in my heartache and there would be no going back. He was right, my heartache was good because the pain helped me remember and return me to my true nature.

"You lived half of your life lost to yourself and have finally awakened," he said.

It was a kind of birth and, of course, the process led to exhaustion. He said that if I was willing, he'd like to accompany me to the holy waters at the Tirta Empul Temple because he wanted to perform a purification ceremony for me. He sensed that my body needed this to keep it healthy. The idea would be for me to release all the negative energy in the holy waters so that I could be healed of anything that might be causing trouble in my body.

I instinctively said yes.

When we had parted that day, he said, "Laura, you will always be okay. It isn't important whether you win or lose. What is important is that you are yourself while you live this life and make your decisions based on love, light, and liberation."

His words were like a balm to my soul. I needed to hear someone tell me that I would be okay. And for the first time I really believed that I would find myself again. My period of confusion wouldn't last forever. I'd begun the journey to my true self. To peace.

* * *

That night in a restaurant in Ubud, *Lawrence of Arabia* played silently on the television at the bar. It was one of Dad's favorite movies and I found the moment oddly inspiring. It made me think of my next adventure in the world. Would it be one of the heart? One of the spirit? One of physical strength? Perhaps it would be all three. I laughed at life for the first time in a long time that night. Smiling at what might come my way, instead of being frightened by it.

I was due to meet up with a friend to say goodbye before she went back home to Singapore. As I waited for her, I watched men and women flirt with each other at the restaurant. It brought to mind all the ways men had touched my life as I began my walk to the west. They held a special place in my heart because they were the ones who helped me learn how to open up to love again.

A few of those encounters replayed in my mind—a man walking across a crowded bar in Los Angeles filled with costumed, (mostly intoxicated) Halloween party goers. I wore a flapper costume. He was dressed as a sheik (heck, he might have actually been a sheik) and said, "You are the most beautiful woman in the room. I want to make you my queen. Would you like to dance?" And we did, until the cops broke up the party early in the morning and we "escaped" together. Another said, "If you don't have any plans, I will take you to eat cobra." And another, "I don't believe in hazard." And yet another, "Step by step you will get to know me."

Would I have traded these experiences for a marriage that would have never been harmonious? The answer was definitely no. To move on, I needed to simply keep looking forward. *I came to Indonesia to write this story. And I will,* I promised myself. I only hoped that I could tell it in time for Dad to read it.

MARCH 24, 2014
UBUD, BALI

So, the advice about life that I get from time to time is to do one thing every day that scares me. Today I've done two, and after breakfast, I think I'll do a third. I've been resting and refueling here in Ubud, which gets its name from a Balinese word, ubad, which means medicine. I'm about to leave this place soon and head for the Gilis [Gili Islands] for a few days of fun in the sun where there aren't any cars or motorcycles. I'm going to enjoy the sunsets and look at the stars. I just booked my passage to Gili Air and will return to Ubud for Nyepi Day. That was the second thing that scared me.

The first was calling Wayang to confirm that I would allow him to perform the healing ceremony at Tirta Empul Temple . . . Going to that ceremony scares me a little bit, but if it will get rid of all the negative stuff and open my heart up then I'll try anything. I think it's best that I head to the Gilis afterward and get some distance from the power of Bali. It's a good power, I just need to go remote for a while. I have no idea where I'm staying, but I think that will be okay. I'm packing up again, and it feels good.

Now, about that ticket to Jogja [Yogyakarta] . . . I think to live big, I might go and write the screenplay there. Two weeks is a long time to extend my trip, but it will be fun, and I know I'll learn a lot about myself and get a solid start on writing Dad's story as a screenplay while I'm there. I can't force the writing, I'll bless it when it comes.

Every wonderful word will be an offering to God. Something good is happening here. The flow is good. The flow is all that matters. The flow is what life is all about. Go big. Live big. I have to remind myself to live expansively.

Wayang snapped this photo before my purification ceremony at the Tirta Empul Temple, Tampaksiring, Bali.

The day of my purification ceremony, I had one of the most transformative spiritual days of my life. Wayang and his brother-in-law had prepared gorgeous, exotic offerings on my behalf and brought them with us to the Tirta Empul Temple. They included a large, weaved bamboo basket filled with homemade, colorful delectable treats like cakes and coconut, fruits, plumeria, and incense. This time, the springs weren't packed with people as they had been when I visited them earlier on my trip.

Together, the holy man and I entered the holy water. He swam before me in the waters and showed me how to rest my head under the fountains, first bowing to them as he faced the waterfalls and then turning to let his head lean back and allow the water to flow over his forehead and body. At each fountain, I closed my eyes as he had, and bathed under the waterfalls in the same way.

As water flowed over my body, he said, "Imagine yourself healthy and vibrant. Pay attention to what God has to say to you."

I prayed again for health and harmony in my family and for protection. The whole bathing ritual seemed to go in slow motion as I surrendered to the water and was fully present as it flowed over my body. At the time, I wished I could have shot a video to remember the experience, but the ceremony plays in my mind so vividly even today that no video was necessary.

During the purification in the holy water, I remembered how Dad immediately told me that I was worthy after I confided in him regarding some of my ex's betrayals. But I don't think I really believed my worth until that warm afternoon of the purification ceremony with the holy man and Wayang—strangers only a handful of days prior— who wanted nothing but the best for me. They wanted me to be happy and free of the darkness that had visited me. They wanted me to be well and showed me more love and care than I could absorb. And they did it all out of the goodness of their hearts. Their incredible act of kindness overwhelmed me.

Afterward, they brought the elaborate offering to a priest in honor of my purification. The priest took us aside to a special, private part of the temple and asked me to kneel. He said well-wishing words over me in Balinese, praying as incense blew smoke rings around us.

The day will be one of those deathbed moments for me. At least what I imagine will happen when every beautiful memory from my life will play like a movie in my mind. I allowed myself to believe what he had said. *I will always be okay. What is important is that I am myself as I live this life and that I make my decisions based on love, light, and liberation.*

"Only put good thoughts in your head. Only speak good thoughts out of your heart," he said.

MARCH 25, 2014
UBUD, BALI

My purification ceremony was one of the deepest spiritual experiences of my life. Be strong. Be Happy. Don't look back. I feel free. Unburdened. Liberated from my problems and bad memories. The solution is love and simplicity. Make every decision based on what God is—love, light and liberation. Consume less. Suffer less. Be true to myself. My practice will include daily meditation, yoga, and doing good things. Yoga is God within. If I do these things, I will know myself and I will never be afraid, scared, or powerless. I will harness my power through prayer. God will answer. All I need to do is ask and it will be given. This is certain. I need to know my direction—if I am on a walk to the west, don't listen to those who whisper to walk to the east. Do not negotiate. With love, keep to my own path. Know thy path. My heart is my home. God lives in my heart. He will guide me and be with me. Do not take everyone with me wherever I go. This is my problem. Take care of myself. I will only be able to help others to suffer less when I am strong.

After the ceremony, I couldn't believe that I almost didn't go out of my fear of the unknown—about what the ceremony would be, maybe even angering God. I didn't want to worship idols or anything. But the way I looked at it, God led me there. He didn't lead me to Bali to be afraid of the world. He led me there to embrace it. To *Go Big*, what He whispered at Mt. Bromo.

When we parted, the holy man gave me some silver rings to wear, one with an amethyst and one with a moonstone. They had the Balinese symbol for God imprinted on them and he said that I should wear them for protection. He told me to keep my life simple and remember what is truly important. He told me that all I need is enough and that I will always have enough. The idea of "enough" fascinated me. I got curious about what is enough.

"Never go back," the holy man said. His last words to me were an invitation to return to Bali and visit him when I found my path. I promised that I would.

I also promised myself that I would never go back to the fear or the world of lies that caused so much of my confusion and pain. I was finally free to go forward. It took two and a half years, a leap of faith on three continents, and lots of new friends to help me begin to let the past go and open up to happiness. I finally understood that I didn't lose myself and promised to always honor my inner wisdom. I would always Go Big.

Going Big meant learning how to listen to the whispers of my heart. Even if it meant doing things that made me afraid or didn't make sense. Going Big meant learning how to recognize its whispers and how to find and trust my own voice. It meant getting quiet and tuning into the still small voice inside, one that I'd tuned out for far too long. It meant following where the voice led, not relying on my own understanding or timeframes. It meant continuing to pray the powerful prayer the older lady shared with me at the beginning of my trip to Indonesia—*Lord, please bring me the people I need and bring me to the people who need me*—and meaning it. When God answered, Going Big meant having the faith to go where He led.

GILI AIR

I took a short ferry ride to Gili Air (one of three tiny islands close to Bali that include Gili Trawangan and Gili Meno), happy to enjoy the simplicity of life there. In addition to its stunning, endless panoramic views of unnaturally blue seas, cars and motorcycles are not allowed on the island. Some of the Gili islands are known for partying, but I'd heard that Gili Air was the most laid back (mostly true). When I walked off the ferry, I took a horse-drawn carriage to my hotel and then collapsed in the sand.

MARCH 26, 2014
SOMEWHERE ON THE BEACH, GILI AIR
The boat ride on the way over to the island was incredible, not just for the epic beauty of the indigo ocean and the fast friends I made aboard, but also for the incredible messages I received on the passage, some from the present and some out of the past. An Indonesian song played, one I hadn't heard before, and the lyrics went—*If you lose your way*

tonight, that's how you know your path is right, and that was followed by the Hawaiian version of *Somewhere Over The Rainbow*.

The first lyric reminded me of how important it is to lose our way in life. That when things blow up or change in ways we can't even imagine, there's a kind of beauty in the loss. In my case, in the fullness of time, I would realize that the twists and turns in Dad's life and mine deepened our relationship with the Lord, ourselves, and each other. The Bible says we will have trouble in this life, it's not if . . . it's when. My belief is that God uses troubles to bring us into a deeper relationship with Him and ourselves.

The second lyric reminded me of an afternoon Suzy and I spent on Zuma beach. She'd come out to California to visit me so she could help me unpack the U-Haul truck my soon-to-be-ex drove down to Los Angeles. Seeing my things all crammed into that truck overwhelmed me. Unpacking those memories was harder still. When I opened the door to the driver's side of the truck, I saw that he had placed my special Halloween mug on the dash. It was so thoughtful, especially since my coffee mug collection irritated him. I had too many, he would say, and he didn't like drinking from them. I loved that mug. I guess he wanted to be sure it didn't break.

I cried when I saw it perched on the dash, wishing he'd been as careful with my heart. *Maybe it would have been better to not have anything at all*, I thought. The act of my soon-to-be-ex bringing me my things was a little unexpected, especially since he drove the truck down from Northern California. He parked the truck at a storage facility where I picked it up. I'd end up storing most of my things at that facility for years.

In the middle of the heartache of unpacking, Suzy and I took a hike to my "dream beach" at Point Dume in Malibu, tucked away from the larger beaches. I'd go there from time to time to lay in the sand and try to dream again. Suzy and I walked arm-in-arm and sang *Somewhere Over The Rainbow* together. She sang and danced in musical theater in Chicago before she had her kids. On the deserted beach, with our feet wet in the sand, I listened to her beautiful voice and began to cry away tears I had for the ending of the life I had loved and the man I had loved.

After a while we collapsed in the warm sand, stretched out, and talked and talked. Eventually we propped ourselves up on our elbows to check out the panorama of sandy cliffs and turquoise blue Pacific waters. Right in front of us, we couldn't miss a very ripped guy in a very tight speedo playing in the waves. His back was covered in tattoos, like an essay had been written on his back. It didn't take long for him to smile and wave at us. As he walked up to where we sat on the beach, we spotted a very large tattoo on his lower abdomen that disappeared into his speedo. We looked at each other as he approached, our eyes wide. He asked where we were from. We asked him about the tattoos on his back.

"It's my Tiger Tirade," he said. "I have a sister and I hate what the M*ther F*cker did to his wife. So I created a tirade, check it out, every word describes him and his despicable behavior. Every word starts with a *T*." He turned his body and let us read his back.

"You want to walk with me to the nude beach and get stoned?" he asked, nodding his head to the south.

Suzy and I smiled and politely said we had to get back home, but thanked him for the invitation. He smiled and handed us his card in case we wanted to take pole dancing classes with him. With the speedo, we thought he might have been a tourist from Europe, but he ended up being from Encino. He also didn't want to leave without showing us the elephant tattoo that peeked out above his speedo, especially its trunk. We passed on that too.

It was an odd meeting and one I hadn't thought about in a long time. Suzy and I cracked up at the absurdity of life and how we can laugh at it together so easily as we walked down the beach to some stairs. Next to them, a young woman dressed in black with a cat on a leash stood in the sand. She wore a unique black leather necklace with a large white bone as a charm. On our way up the stairs, we asked about her necklace. She told us the bone was from a racoon and she wore it for protection. As Suzy and I climbed the stairs we hugged each other.

These memories came up for me on my bike ride around Gili Air. Of all the people Suzy and I could have met on the beach that day, we met the tiger tattoo guy. *I don't believe in hazard.* As I pedaled the tiny island, sort of hard to do with all the sand, I needed something to eat and stopped at the Matahari II Bungalows for a painkiller, a beautiful mixed drink.

While sipping my cold painkiller, I thought about a question I asked the holy man, "Do you think if I was a more spiritual person I would have stayed with him?"

Instead of an answer, he told me a story—There is an old woman in her house who lost her glasses.

"Where are my glasses?" she says. She feels around in the dark for her glasses and then she looks out at the garden and she searches for them in the garden.

Her son stops by and asks her what is wrong. She says she lost her glasses. He says, "Where were you when you last had them?"

"In the house," she says.

"Then why are you searching for them here?"

"Because it's dark in the house," she says.

The holy man said that my ex was the old woman.

I took another sip of my painkiller and reflected on the story again. I liked the story. It made me feel more at ease. His message seemed to be that I did everything I could to try and understand him and what we were to each other. There is so much open for interpretation, it seemed to suggest that no matter what I did he'd still be searching for something he'll never find because he is afraid of the dark, his own demons. And that awareness gave me so much compassion for him.

"You chose wisely, Laura. The most spiritual person in the world would have done exactly as you did. Leave and live," he said.

* * *

On Gili Air I made it my mission to become a better freediver. I noticed when I snorkeled off of Bali that I could have gotten even more stunning photos if I had the ability to dive much deeper. So, I arranged for some instruction when I first arrived. The next day, I took to the water with my freediving instructor Sean, a handsome, tan, Irishman.

The morning of my dives, while we were on land and before we took a boat ride and jumped into the water together, Sean helped me learn how to breathe (filling up my lungs to their capacity and letting the air out slowly), how to conserve energy on the dive, and how to trust my instincts. He told me before our first dive together that he would never leave my side. He would always be there. Sean seemed to know exactly what was going on in my mind—a battle with my own fear, and my own perceived limitations.

On my first dive I tried using flippers, but I could only descend four meters (thirteen feet). I wasn't out of breath though. Instead, I'd looked up and saw just how far I'd descended and got scared. Sean told me that he didn't care about my fear. He said that I would get over it and that to be a good freediver I just needed practice. Freediving was a perfect metaphor for everything I needed to learn then—how to breathe, how to focus, how to relax, and how to trust my instincts.

The dives taught me a lot about having faith—choosing to believe that I would overcome my fear of deep diving on one breath, trusting that one breath would also get me back to the surface, believing Sean was right about me and my abilities, surrendering to the breath and where it would take me, allowing peace to infuse my dive so I could go deeper. I would need to have that same kind of faith in myself, my perceptions, choices, dreams, and people to Go Big in my life on my walk to the west.

I had trouble with one of my ears on an early attempt. Just before I dove the deepest, Sean said that if my ears didn't equalize, then diving deep wouldn't be possible. Some days are just like that, he explained. When ears hurt due to a lack of pressure equalization, it's important to return to the surface. I decided to keep trying.

To help me conserve my energy, we used a line for my descent. I hoped on this attempt I'd go all the way through the crystal blue water to the white sand below. After breathing deeply on the surface, I surrendered to doing everything I'd been taught—staying calm and conserving my energy—all as Sean accompanied me.

Hand over hand, I descended into the water and looked into Sean's proud, encouraging green eyes. It seemed I could see miles in every direction underwater. The silence was what I loved the most about freediving. It allowed me to be more in tune with the adventures of my heart. A heart that once had such seriously high blood pressure it sent me to the cardiologist a year earlier, only a few months before I left my marriage. Mercifully, the malady disappeared once I settled in Los Angeles.

But in the middle of the descent, Sean returned to the surface. I had no idea why, especially when he told me he would be with me every step of the way. That he'd never leave me. But I kept calm and continued to descend. When I finally reached the bottom of the Bali Sea, thirty-six feet down, I stretched out over the white sand and stared up at the ocean's surface. Sunlight bounced above me on beautiful waves and shone through the water in streaks, rippling in pools of light over the white sandy seafloor.

I celebrated my moment alone at the bottom of the sea by lingering, fully capturing the memory as I nestled in the sand. It was meaningful that after so many attempts, I peacefully accomplished my deepest dive on my own. Somewhere down there I fully realized that alone, I am enough and worthy of having big dreams and making them come true. That they aren't "silly," "crazy," "irresponsible" or any of the things others had tried to paint them. This knowing infused my spirit and filled my heart. It set me on a path to believing that I could accomplish so many more "impossible" things.

When I returned to the surface, Sean yelled, "Recovery!" A command to help me remember to take special shallow breaths, so I wouldn't black out. It was hard to stay in control and not instinctively gasp for air. Once I recovered, Sean said how proud he was of me. He apologized for leaving me, but his ears wouldn't clear. The pain forced him to ascend in the middle of my descent. I told him that I was fine when he left. I smiled to myself at that moment. Having a man promise one thing and do another no longer held any power over me.

I liked the idea of having a recovery period after every freedive. Hearing Sean shout *recovery* in his Irish accent each time I resurfaced made it that much clearer to me that I'd actually been recovering from the deep dive that my life had taken for years without knowing it.

Once I'd recovered from my deepest dive, as we floated in the water, Sean said, "I knew you hadn't come close to running out of air."

When he saw the look of surprise in my eyes, he added, "You were very slow on your ascent. You could have gone much deeper had you wished or believed you could."

* * *

MARCH 28, 2014
GILI AIR

Always Take The Weather With You played at an open air bar/dance club down the beach from where I am staying. I sat on the beach in front of a bonfire with a group of new friends. We'd met earlier that night at a seaside BBQ at my hotel and ended up going to the dance club afterward. At the bonfire, we were all talking about our lives. How they'd all met, where we might all be going. Laughing a lot. I traveled alone, but found I was never really alone. That is this research trip's great gift, the company and wisdom of new friends.

They were from Sweden, a guy and four girls. The guy and his girlfriend were very sweet and invited me to have dinner with them at the BBQ. What struck me about him was how gentlemanly he was, making sure I had a glass of wine and that I knew everyone. Later that night I would discover the heartache he'd suffered. The gal I spoke with most of the night is an artist-yogi. Much later that night, a few Spanish gals and I would dance barefoot on the beach until morning.

The holy man said that in life three things are certain: Everyone will die, everyone will grow older, everyone will lose all that they have.

I hope to dance barefoot on the beach. Often.

On Gili Air I made the decision to give myself the time and space to write the screenplay on Java. What better place to write than in

Jogja. It seemed important that this story be written on Java and I decided to spend two weeks writing there.

On my way to Jogja, I would return to Bali to experience Nyepi, when the entire island would go dark and quiet. Never had I spent a twenty-four hour period in silence. Most of my friends would laugh at that idea. Me? Not talk for 24 hours? Yeah, right. But, Nyepi was healing in a way that I didn't expect and provided the perfect environment to rejuvenate and reflect on where I'd been and where I was headed. My experience of Nyepi was life-changing.

* * *

MARCH 31, 2014
PONDOK PUNDI VILLAGE INN, UBUD
NYEPI

I'm not supposed to be outside, but I have to look at the stars. Bathed in silence, I stare at the kind of darkened sky most people will never see in this light-filled world. It's more than a moment of "unplugging," it's freeing. Nothing needs to be done or thought about or planned for in the next twenty-four hours. In the streets meat and alcohol offerings are left for evil spirits to feed on in the hopes that they will pass by "deserted" Bali.

I love my rings. I love that the holy man made both of them He picked out the stones, prayed over them, meditated on them and picked them for me. I love that he gave me a ring with an amethyst and the Balinese symbol of God. He said that the amethyst would open up my crown chakra so I'll always be in communication with God. He also said that my stones are diamonds and white sapphires and that I should never wear any jewelry unless it is precious. He told me that I need to wear a ring with a stone the color of the stars. He said that white sapphires are extremely rare. The stone in the second ring he gave me is a moonstone. White is the color of purity and kindness. He said that white is Monday's color. White daisies symbolize loyal love.

When I got off the boat from the Gilis and reached The Pondok Pundi Village Inn earlier this afternoon—only a few inns were open as most of the tourists left Bali for Nyepi—I was asked for my meal preferences for the entire next day. The hotel concierge explained that I was to return to the inn before midnight and afterwards I was not to go outside. I was not to use electricity. The staff would bring my meals to me. I was to observe the four abstinences:

"amati geni" no lighting fires or using lights

"amati karya" refraining from working

"amati lelanguan" refraining from indulging in leisure activities

"amati lelungan" refraining from traveling outside the house

Bali hopes that in the silence all the evil spirits will fly over their island. As they sit inside, they reflect on how to purify their minds and their bodies with yoga and meditation.

Nyepi comes from the Balinese word "sepi" which means silent. Village crossroads are where evil spirits are believed to linger. The evening before Nyepi, a ceremony much like a parade occurs in the villages where the Ogoh-ogoh monsters representing demons and symbolizing evil are paraded then burned. Cock fighting is permitted that night too because the spilling of blood is necessary for purification. Banging pots and pans, tin cans, and honking horns also forces the evil spirits to get disoriented and leave the villages.

That night, I went to the parade of the Ogoh-ogoh monsters and witnessed the Balinese purifying their villages of evil and realized I have been doing the same for the past eighteen months. I've been trying to cleanse myself of the evils of betrayal, manipulation, false-love, deception, fear, doubt, guilt, depression, pain, agony and suffering. Pain has purified my heart and taught it how to suffer less. My heart has learned to listen to its soul. My heart has recognized I almost gave myself away. Evil did not win because my heart and soul would not be deceived. In the end, I chose to live in the truth.

In addition to pain, I've also been purified by love. The love of people who held onto my dreams when I could no longer see them. People who've helped me believe that life will be more glorious on the other side of the pain. All my friends and family and new friends and family, strangers who I now love and who love and believe in me.

JOGJA

When I returned to the kingdom of Yogyakarta (Jogja), I booked a room at the d'Omah. "Omah" means *home* in Indonesian. In many ways, I came home to myself on Java. The peaceful and healing experience reminded me about who I am—playful, passionate, fun, joy-filled, enthusiastic, spontaneous, deep, loving, kind, and hopeful. I rediscovered those parts of myself again as I wrote during the day and toured the kingdom with Ru each evening. With the treatment I'd written in LA before the trip, the screenplay began to take shape over long writing sessions infused with the world's best ginger tea.

As I began to put the story together and learn more about myself, I typed about a world that didn't exist anymore. All the while, I tried to discern what home meant to me. Would anywhere feel like home? Would I ever belong somewhere? Would I ever feel safe again? Home meant so much more to the Javanese than it did to me at the time, filled with rich symbolism about connection all on display at the d'Omah.

Javanese homes are replicas of the human form. So, it's not surprising that people in Java treat the house just like a human being, both have a cosmic harmony with each other. The Javanese call it *manjing warangka*, meaning "God enters into humans, humans enter into God."[48]

For example, the top [of the house] is a world untouched by humans. It is the overarching sky which covers the middle and bottom of the house. The form of elevated roof points upward. The roof is often identified with Meru, the mountain peak in the Himalayas which is considered the abode of the gods at the center of the universe. Because the place [roof] is not for everyday activities, its existence is more sacred and transcendental in nature. The top is high and is believed to bring magic into the living space. The human personification of this section is the head, or in the arrangement of the Borobudur temple, called arupadhatu [meaning "formless world" where desires and sensations have disappeared and the pure spirits live.].[49]

* * *

APRIL 4, 2014
D'OMAH, JOGJA

Ru keeps saying . . . "Step by step you will know who I am." I like that idea. I often see Ru as regal even though he has no material wealth. He lives simply, deeply. I sometimes think of Yul Bryner when I look at him. His kind of kingly way of walking and how he cares for me, the way he speaks of love and life.

APRIL 5, 2014
D'OMAH, JOGJA

My playlist is growing. My message this morning is about place and satisfaction. Ru has been my torch in so many ways, lighting up what

---

48   Slamet Subiyantoro. *The Interpretation of Joglo Building House Art in the Javanese Cultural Tradition*. Department Fine Arts, Faculty Education of Language and Art, FKIP University Sebelas Maret (UNS) Surakarta, Indonesia. (edited)

49   The Interpretation of Joglo Building House Art in the Javanese Cultural Tradition

was dead inside of me. Cherishing me in ways I've never been cherished before. An ocean away from the island of barely being tolerated, manipulated, and deceived. Where I lived for far too long. God is so good. I cherish our many magic memories of street bands, the Wayang Shadow Puppet play and Prambanan lit up by lightning, reggae bands, political demonstrations, chocolate, and more chocolate and even more chocolate, french fries, SMS, cycling in the rice fields, motoring with a particle mask on, little warungs, carriage rides to the Sultan's Palace, rose candy, the batik purse he gave me. And his "slow and steady" reminders when I would test my physical limits in order to see everything I could. Dancing and the freedom to be who I am. I finally found some peace. I am who I've always been, playful, passionate, fun, joy-filled, enthusiastic, spontaneous, deep, loving, kind and hopeful.

In my meditation this morning I received a message about pleasure. Ru certainly has done some incredible things to make me happy. That's all he wants, he says. And just that simplicity about our relationship is beautiful. So many things about us don't make sense to my old self. But it is what lives in the heart that's important, more than anything. He's been a good friend to me. A ray of light even though part of me isn't ready for this kind of closeness yet. And another part of me is judging it and him and me and us. Judgment is a form of fear. I have learned a lot from Ru. How to open my heart, how to let go and live my life, how to have fun, how to be me.

I guess when you get over the fear and shock of losing everything you have, true riches find you. For me that looks like trusting in myself, the capacity to dream, priceless experiences, and having faith in the unseen. As long as I am true to myself, I'll always be rich. I'll always have enough. The old ways are being left behind and the new ways are finding me.

A few days after I arrived at the d'Omah, I received an email from my friend Derek.

"Would you be free in a few weeks to help at the dental clinic in Kathmandu?" Derek asked. "Our non-medical worker got injured in a ski accident."

I had to read the word *Kathmandu* over a few times to make sure that was what he wrote. My heart beat faster. I would be taking care of kids as they waited to see a dentist and help out with administrative work. Little did I know, but the role would also happily involve playing lots of string games, coloring pictures with the kids, keeping records of the visits, and even giving fluoride treatments.

When would I get another opportunity to do such important humanitarian work and visit Nepal? Never. What an experience it would be. And what a joy to be called to help such a worthy cause. I had to say yes. So I researched flights and figured out a way I could make it work. But when the opportunity for me to go to Nepal came up, Ru became different. Possessive in a way I wasn't ready for. Even though he knew I would leave Java soon, anyway. My trip to Nepal just meant that my departure moved up a few days. I wasn't ready to compromise what I needed to accomplish in my life. I had just begun to learn how to live life again. What we had seemed so perfect in some ways. And yet there were so many differences.

"Your time would be better spent on a young woman who could give you plenty of children," I said.

He balked at the suggestion, of course.

A few days later, we watched young people try to walk blindfolded between two trees at night. Legend has it that if they walked from one tree to another while blindfolded, they'd have good fortune. The simple act of trying brought so much joy, whether they made it or not. As they stumbled in the dark, I hoped beyond hope that they'd make it. The fun of watching them was so addictive, but we finally pulled ourselves away from the spectacle. Soon, we motored to a club and danced to Bob Marley and German reggae. We danced to *Aku Cinta Indonesia*, sung in German and Bahasa, a love song to Indonesia—

> *I love Indonesia*
> *and may God always give you*
> *blessings and your heart's desire to achieve success*
> *may you always be given ease*
> *hey my friend oh my brother*
> *the story doesn't end when you leave*
> *you bring back sweet memories*
> *that will last forever*
> *as warm as the smile of the archipelago*

April 11, 2014
Breakfast terrace of the D'Omah, Jogja

Last night amazed me. I was so happy to see Ru after a rather boring dinner with some Europeans. And it was then I realized what Ru and I share. Life is such a crap shoot. And he's really made me happy—gone out of his way to do so time and again in the short time we'd known each other. In the month since we'd met and the week we've been getting to know each other, everything we've done seemed incredible. Every afternoon we've gone on one adventure or another. Late tonight, I went for a swim in my pool and afterward I got cold. He arranged for ginger tea for both of us even though the kitchen had closed. So thoughtful. And the way he looks at me. I just melt, seriously melt. Our carriage ride today was incredible because we got to hold hands. PDAs are forbidden here (especially between a white woman and an

Indonesian man). My life feels so much lighter now. I can't wait to get the tattoo. I really hope I can find a place that will do a good job. I don't want to forget all that I've learned on my journey to Indonesia. The feeling. The peace. Who I am. I want something to take home, something real, so this incredible journey won't ever seem like a dream. Or that it's over.

* * *

"I am enjoy with you," Ru said.

I am in joy with you. Our travels together took us to so many joyful places. Before we would leave to tour around the kingdom, Ru would ask, "Check. Make sure. Do you have everything you need?" I tend to move a mile a minute and get easily distracted sometimes. The reminder was so much like a tour guide, and yet so very loving. I try to remember to ask myself that very important (Ru made it sound urgent) question of myself to this day. I don't ask it enough.

Check. Make sure. Do I have everything I need? Then we'd be off on a hundred adventures in Jogja that would help me remember myself. Trust my perceptions. Get in tune to my wants and needs and listen to them.

Ru had tears in his eyes when I talked to him about what I wanted written on my body. He didn't like the idea. But when he understood how important it was to me, he arranged for me to meet his friend, a talented tattoo artist named Heru. I wanted a permanent reminder of all that I had learned. I wanted to see the Javanese words and remember to always Go Big, to never go back, to walk to the west, and not carry everyone with me.

When I met Heru, we discussed so many things like the color, size, style, and location of my tattoo. He didn't speak very good English so the process took some time. When we first met, I didn't really think I could make him understand what I wanted clearly enough for him to create the tattoo. So, I tried meeting with him a second time. I had a hard time explaining the font (the style I wanted the letters to have) and the color. He had more of a heavy hand and I wanted my tattoo to be lighter, thinner. It took some time, but after our second meeting I felt sure he knew what I wanted.

After that meeting, Ru pulled me aside and said, "Laura, you have to be sure. It has to be perfect."

And, of course, he was right. He wanted to be sure I got exactly what I wanted. And the exercise of being in touch with my wants and needs and going through the process of art directing was exactly what I needed. I had gotten so far away from myself. So much so that at one point I didn't even know how I'd purchase a computer printer by myself, or what car to buy. Forget about the creation of a permanent mark on my body. When we settled on the details, I couldn't wait for Heru to create the tattoo the following day. But it was bittersweet. It would be my last day on Java.

I got to thinking about what Ru said about perfection, and how there's beauty in the imperfections too. The happy accidents, the things beyond our control like who you love and why. And like circumstances that found me holding onto Ru for dear life that mimicked the way I might have held onto a husband in childbirth. While the needle drove into my skin, Ru winced as if my pain was his. As we stared into each others' eyes, I thought no man would look at me like that again. No man would brush my hair off my face, kiss my forehead, or hold my hand like he did. Afterward, I chain smoked clove cigarettes and drank Bintang to take the edge off. He didn't smoke or drink. He didn't say a word. He just let me be me.

We had different words to describe our feelings for each other. His, *aku sayang kamu*; and mine, cherish. New words for both of us and that felt perfect. Love wasn't a word I could use back then.

* * *

APRIL 14, 2014
AIRPORT JOGJA, JAVA

Now when I write with a pen, I see words in a whole new way. Sometimes I feel my skin burn in the spots where Heru tattooed me yesterday. Saying goodbye to Ru at the airport seemed impossible and inevitable all at the same time. We never actually got to say a "real" goodbye. Which is merciful, I guess, as I couldn't imagine saying goodbye. He took me to the airport the day of my flight. When I realized I needed to check in for my flight earlier than I expected, I was just going to take care of that and then have our last coffee together at a place across the street from the airport. But I got caught up in protocols and the airport officials wouldn't let me leave the terminal. Ru stood outside the building and walked up to the window when it started taking too long. I walked up to him and we stared at each other through the glass. We didn't need any words. We held our hands up to each other. The look in his eyes said it all—*Selamat tinggal* (the kind of goodbye when one person is staying where they are . . . a long separation.) And then he flashed a gorgeous smile. From the day I first arrived in Jogja, it had been a place of miracles. I thought about nothing else when I boarded the plane.

NEPAL

APRIL 14, 2014
OVER THE ARABIAN DESERT AT SUNRISE

The sun's rays catch the slopes of drifts in the Arabian desert, painting the sand pink and gold. From my window on my Etihad flight plots of land are carved into the desert pointing east, at angles with roads. Roads with no traffic. And I realize that I have nothing, yet I have everything. This is my dream come true. Writing and traveling, meeting amazing people.

APRIL 14, 2023
BOUDHA, KATHMANDU

The times they are a changin' is playing. A Bob Dylan song that seemed to become the anthem of my life. It caught my ear as Derek and I enjoyed drinking tea while the locals lit what looked like thousands of candles around the Boudhanath stupa on their New Year's Day in the year that they marked as 2072. In Bali, I just celebrated Nyepi (their New Year) which the Balinese numbered 1936. The moon was full and the stupa was beautiful. I bought three bottles of water as the people I met wished me a Happy New Year. And with all these new year celebrations I was beginning to feel there was a message from the universe that a new year is beginning for me. And it will be beautiful. Tomorrow we will tour the sights around Kathmandu. My tattoo is getting a lot of compliments and feels better every day. Tonight when I put cream on it I missed Ru's kisses. And I realize, by contrast, I don't miss my ex's. And that seems good. Ru is so very young and so very old at the same time. So self-assured and so very much like a boy too.

Derek handed me a book called *Arresting God in Kathmandu*. It's a great gift. A sweet gesture, so thoughtful. Somehow and in some way, after spending decades together, my ex hardly knew me. And yet we had begun to know each other in such fun-filled joy so long ago. It seemed impossible that I hardly knew him. And yet the man I left was a stranger to me. We are only known as much as we allow ourselves to be known.

APRIL 15, 2014
SHECHEN GUEST HOUSE & RABSEL GARDEN CAFÉ
BOUDHA, KATHMANDU

I was so happy to get Ru's call today. He said he took my friend Micha and her boyfriend for a cycling trip that morning and they loved it. The people at the d'Omah wanted to know where I was, and Ru told them that I was in Kathmandu. Later today I saw a picture of Bob Marley and it said "One Love." The sight of it reminded me of dancing to the song with Ru. And I could feel his finger on my heart telling me that we shared one love. And I really miss him. I'm here and part of me wishes I was there, riding on his motor with him squeezing my hand

and holding onto my thigh. And it's so great to have someone care about me so deeply. Who tells me to save my energy. I just feel like I'm being powered by the Holy Spirit. I am trusting wherever it leads. I am learning to choose faith over fear. And I think this will be the best Easter ever. Easter in Kathmandu.

Every worker at the dental clinic had the opportunity to trek the Everest Base Camp trail after we completed our humanitarian work to provide dental care to "yakland" kids (children who live above 10,000 feet) some who were orphaned due to the ten-year civil war there and others who had been victims of human trafficking. In the end, the clinic served over 300 people in all, mostly children.

One day during the clinic, mid-morning, my new friend Jody and I headed out of the classroom-turned clinic, cups of tea in hand, to a small concrete platform at the top of a small staircase to get a bit of sun and take a break. While we were chatting and watching some of the kids playing on the asphalt below us, a charming older woman walked up the stairs and greeted us with a beautiful warm smile. She looked so familiar as she shook my hand. She said she was happy to meet us and how wonderful it was that we were there working at the clinic. She said she lived in the village and wanted to stop by to see the clinic and say hello. I found out later that day that the nice lady I met was Jane Goodall. This was only one of the many miracles that happened while in Nepal.

Me, Kathy, and Linda walking to the clinic from our guesthouse in
Boudhanath.

The volunteers and kids that worked at the clinic in
Boudhanath, April 2014.

As we wound down the clinic, I was conflicted about trekking
the Everest Base Camp Trail. I had read about it before I arrived and
wanted to go badly, but I'd previously made arrangements to meet my

daughter, Margaux, in Thailand. Since my itinerary wouldn't allow me to complete the whole trek, I thought that I wouldn't be able to go. However, my new friend, Kathy, a retired midwife, and Derek both insisted that I trek with the group.

"It's the experience of a lifetime and you can't miss it," Derek said.

When he put it like that, I couldn't refuse. Even though I wasn't entirely sure I was capable of such a trek. I hadn't trained at all. But, I decided to Go Big. Those running the trek helped to make arrangements for me to return to Lukla in time to catch my flight to Thailand. I had to trust that everything would work out.

They even helped me get outfitted since I'd only packed clothes for the heat of Southeast Asia, not for the cold of the high Himalayas. I wasn't alone. Many of us in the group went on a great shopping adventure to Thamel, a buzzing bizarre outside of Kathmandu, filled with anything and everything anyone would possibly need for a trek— waterproof duffel bags, heavy coats, sleeping bags, backpacks, fleeces, pants, and survival gear. Touristy Thamel is full of nightlife, bars, and great restaurants that offer all kinds of cuisine from around the world. So the outfitting was a whirlwind—part party, part provisioning.

Boudhanath Stupa.

April 22, 2014
Kathmandu, Nepal

I just packed to trek on Everest! I am so excited I can't sleep. Today, Jim, one of the dentists volunteering here, said something that really resonated with me while we were having tea. "The eyes of the stupa are a symbol of awakening. Their field of blue is a symbol for emptiness— like the blue of a cloudless sky." I love the symbolism. It's incredible. I told him about the eyes that seem to stare back at me while meditating lately. Jim said that the things that come up when meditating all have to do with what's on the inside of me. And I best not be in a rush to figure it all out. I told him how the eyes I see when I meditate look like the eyes of the stupa. I didn't know anything about stupas when I arrived in Nepal a little over a week ago. I couldn't help but be taken aback at my first sight of them. That's when Jim said that it is purely internal what the eyes mean. And so when I go on this trek, I guess I can slowly ponder what the significance of the eyes are in my life. When Jim said they represent awakening, it struck a chord with me because that's exactly what I've done. I've woken up. But I didn't feel like I was asleep before. But now I know I was. I know that the old ways are falling away and that something new is breaking through.

The magical experience of trekking over vast suspended bridges across cavernous mountain passes, among prayer flags whipping in the wind left me breathless. As we trekked, I overheard our guides peacefully chanting in a low voice, at times only in whispers, "*Om mani, padme hum* (The jewel in the heart of the Lotus)."

By reciting OM MANI PADME HUM, you can achieve all your wishes for happiness, not only for the happiness of this life but for the happiness of all your coming future lives, and also for the ultimate happiness that comes with cessation of the oceans of Samsaric sufferings and their causes, karma and delusion, and even their negative imprints. Cessation of all negative imprints makes it impossible for delusions to arise again, which makes it impossible for negative karma to be accumulated, which makes it impossible for suffering to happen. There is then great liberation, or full enlightenment.[50]

I knew nothing of the chant or what it meant. I just listened at first and didn't question its meaning. Linda, my roommate and a physician from the Denver area who had volunteered for many dental

---

50   **Lama Yeshe Wisdom Archive,** https://www.lamayeshe.com/article/chapter/6-benefits-reciting-om-mani-padme-hum#:~:text=By%20reciting%20OM%20MANI%20PAD-ME,karma%20and%20delusion%2C%20and%20even

clinics, told me that the practice was about contemplating the brilliance of a diamond in the Lotus, and how that opened up awareness into greater ways of being. I knew nothing of Buddhist teachings or the spirituality of the people in Nepal. But the Lord had brought me there to learn and even helped me to celebrate Easter in Kathmandu in a way I will never forget. Another story for another day.

The beauty of the whispered mantras as we trekked up each stage of the Everest Base Camp trail, higher and higher, (for a total change in elevation of 6,339 feet to the heights of 15,000 feet), filled my spirit with peace and a kind of centering that wouldn't have come any other way. Everyone I met at the clinic and the ones I got to know better on the trek were incredibly kind.

They shared their knowledge of the culture, answered my many questions about the Buddhist traditions, dental practices, and encouraged my endeavors even as it seemed I set my sights on things that I perceived to be beyond my reach (like writing and publishing this book and supporting myself as a writer). The friends I made along the way held my dreams in their hearts and mirrored back to me, as so many others would in the years to come, that anything is possible, especially the beautiful dreams I envisioned for my as yet unknown future.

During one of the last stages of the trek, I bunked with Kathy. We are still friends to this day and have enjoyed seeing each other over the years. The night that we bunked together, we told each other stories about our lives long into the night as it was cold and the tea house beds were hard, the only cushion was our sleeping bags. That chilly night brought to mind the beauty and heat of Gili Air and I told her about freediving off the shores of the island, about a month before.

After hearing my free diving story, as we shivered together in our bunks in the Himalayan mountains on the Everest Base Camp trail,

Kathy said, "You descended thirty-six feet in the ocean in Indonesia and now you've nearly ascended twelve-thousand feet."

Her observation stunned me. I'd been so busy living the experience that I hadn't made that connection. It would take many years to try and comprehend all that I had been through on my travels. There was beautiful wisdom in Jim's words back at the Shechen Guest House before our trek—I best not be in a rush to figure it all out. And yet, the fact remained, the Lord had taken me from the bottom of the sea to the heights of the highest mountain on earth. He wanted me to hear those words and understand the power of my wishes and beliefs too.

I couldn't have gone bigger than Everest, Earth's highest mountain above sea level. The sight of Everest's summit on the trek took my breath away. The mountain was so large, I felt like I could reach out and touch it. Its gorgeous snow-capped peaks dared me to believe big things about myself and challenged me to follow my dreams, no matter how distant I believed them to be or how impossible. I knew then that anything is possible.

Everest and Me, April 2014.

And yet, during our trek, the beginning of the climbing season on Everest, one of the worst disasters in the history of the storied mountain unfolded. An avalanche took the lives of 16 sherpas and Everest went dark as a result, meaning no climbers could summit that season. The victims were family members and friends of our guides on the trail. So the loss was personal and we attended a few memorial services along our trek to help support the widows and children of the lost.

Many climbers had already trekked to Base Camp for their attempted summits before the tragedy. As we trekked, we saw the shocking sight of fully packed yaks descending with all the supplies of those mountaineers. Many helicopter flights evacuated hopeful summiters off of Everest. It was yet another life-and-death story I'd been caught up in during my travels. Again affirming the preciousness of life. And how we need to protect the ones we love. To be reckless with our loved ones isn't love at all. Only a year later, a devastating 7.8 earthquake would hit Nepal, killing 9,000 and maiming many others. It destroyed much of what I had seen in Kathmandu, Boudhanath, Thamel, and Bhaktapur. Thankfully, all the children I'd gotten to know were safe.

THAILAND

After trekking back to Lukla on time to make my flight to Thailand, I had one of the most important and joyful parts of my journey with my daughter Margaux in Phuket. Made that much more precious due to the epiphanies and tragedies I experienced on my trip. I wanted to hug her closer than ever. It had been months since we'd seen each other and I'd been in the world much longer than I'd planned.

We arranged a surprise serendipitous trip to Phuket since she was coincidentally in Vietnam on business while I was in Nepal. When we met up at our hotel overlooking the Andaman Sea, Margaux told me that she'd arranged a Mother's Day present, a day of cooking at The Phuket Thai Cookery School. It started at the local market with our charming guide who showed us how they made the freshest coconut milk and how to pick ingredients for our lunch.

Back at the school, after a few demos by the charming staff, we were let loose in their open-air kitchens to recreate the traditional Thai recipes they'd demonstrated. All of our ingredients had been measured out for us in our seaside kitchen—a cook's dream. The best cooking tip I received there has become a tradition in my own cooking ever since.

When squeezing the juice out of a lime (or lemon) squeeze it around the blade of a knife and the juice flows down the blade, beautifully. Cooking in new ways helped me open my heart to cooking again.

The beach at the cooking school.

The food seemed to flavor our passions too. This dream lunch had all the best ingredients: Thailand, a reunion with my daughter and the kind of exotic surprises that can only be found among kaffir limes, lemongrass, curries, the freshest of seafood, and grapefruit eggplants. Cooking and eating the five-course meal cast a spell over our food, conversations, and most importantly, our spirits.

Dreams and dining intertwine in my life. My daughter and I set a few of our own dreams in motion while enjoying our meal. Tom Kha Kai was our favorite course. As I raised my last chopsticks full of Phad Thai and looked to the sea, I gave thanks for the time Margaux and I had to spend together, another dream come true. During our weekend in Thailand, we had long conversations over beautiful sunsets, strolls on the beach, calming massages, and a boat ride to an exotic island as we swam and shared our struggles, hopes, and dreams with each other.

Me and Margaux cooking.

While challenging, 2014 was a year of miracles. I met myself in the world and it changed me in ways I could have never imagined. For me, the real magic in life happens when I trust myself and the unknown more than the plan. Back then, I thought my travels in 2014 were a wonderful experience I would always cherish. I thought I would look back fondly on the three months or so that I traveled in the world for the rest of my life. I had no idea that my first research trip was only a warmup of what was to come.

THE SECOND TIME
GRANDPA SAVED DAD'S LIFE

Inside the house in the detention area where Grandpa, Grandma, and Reinier lived, a concerned middle-aged, rail-thin man sat next to Grandma on the sofa where Reinier slept, his small head in her lap. He rifled through his bag, searching, then pulled out some vials.

"Give him these as soon as he wakes." The man handed some brown glass bottles to Grandma.

"What are they?" Grandma said.

"Medications to beat the complications from jaundice."

"What complications?"

"No need to worry. We'll pull him through."

A knock at the front door sent Grandpa walking into the room. Grandma went pale and set Reinier's head down on the sofa. He continued to sleep soundly.

With a nod from Grandpa, she walked to the door and answered.

A Dutch teenager stood at the doorway; someone they didn't recognize. He breathed heavily and handed Grandma a pack of cigarettes then left as quickly as he came. She watched him hide amongst some buildings before sneaking out of the camp in the shadow of a slow-moving truck as it left the compound. She quickly closed the door.

Grandma opened the carton and saw only cigarettes. But then, she removed each one. At the bottom of the carton she discovered a small scrap of paper. It had been folded so tightly she had difficulty prying it apart with her trembling hands.

Grandpa quickly came to her side, and they put their heads together to read the note.

"He's trying to tell us . . . .where he is . . . ," Grandpa said.

"He's alive!" Grandma said. Then, she read Dad's note aloud.

"Dear Paps and Mams, The boy who delivers this is the son of a man who sleeps next to me. He can also take something for me in return which he can put into a package for his father and then hand over to someone who is brought in here. In any package, please include a pair of shorts for me, some food (such as dengdeng [thinly cut dried meat with spices], kroepoek [like a potato chip made from tapioca flour and shrimp], etc.) and for my sleep mate some Silvercity cigarettes? I am in good health. Still work in the kitchen. I am hopeful to be free again soon. Many kisses for Rein-iertje, Paps, and Mams"

At the end of his note, Dad tried to indicate where he was held by the Japanese in relation to the family home. He listed major roads and the family villa at Leeuwensberg.

* * *

Dad drove home the horror of the war when he told me about smuggling his note out of the prison camp. Fascinating and heartbreakingly hopeful, his desperate attempt to communicate with the family came with such risk. And yet, how could Dad not want to do everything he could to let them know he was alive?

Many years would pass before Dad and I revisited the story and shared one of the most precious moments between us and a haunting moment in the writing of this book. In Florida, we had been talking together in his study when he pulled out a white, no-nonsense envelope from one of his files and handed it to me. I opened it and slid a tiny piece of paper into my hands. As I gingerly unfolded it, tiny German handwritten words filled the paper. This was Dad's note.

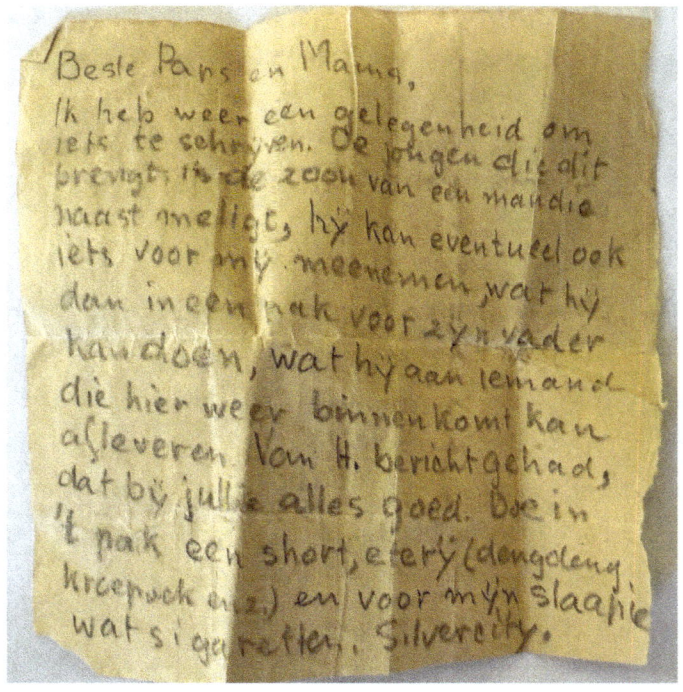

Dad's note, over 80 years old.

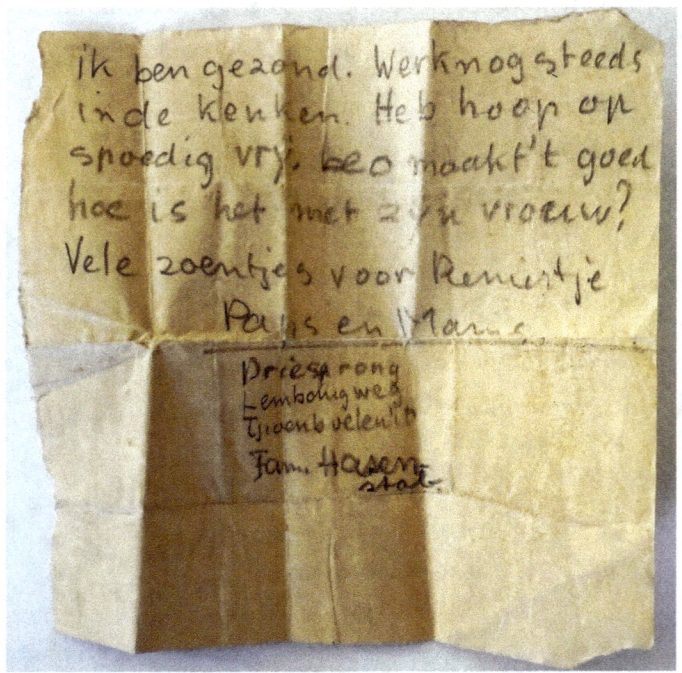

Dad's note, over 80 years old.

My heart broke when I touched Dad's note for the first time and examined its details, even as holding it inspired my writing and fueled my quest. I saw how many times Dad had folded the paper in a desperate attempt to hide his message in the pack of smuggled cigarettes. A fragment of paper that Dad, Grandma, and Grandpa touched was in the palm of my hands. The tie that binds. Immediately my thoughts went to how many people had tried the same thing and ended up dead. With all the family had gone through and would go through, that they survived is a miracle.

I sat with the weight and joy of holding Dad's precious note and becoming its keeper. My heart raced. That it survived long enough for Dad to pass it down to me seemed extraordinary. Somehow the tiny scrap of history survived the war and all the upheaval afterward. By the time Dad gave his note to me, he'd saved it for nearly seventy years. I wonder how it felt for him to let it go. As I held the tiny paper in my hand, I was comforted by the tangible reminder of how horror and hope can live together—a testimony to never giving up, no matter what our struggle. Dad had precious little hope to hold on to as a POW, and yet he had hope.

I hugged Dad.

As we sat and chatted some more, I marveled at all the things that had to go right for Grandma and Grandpa to read the note when so many other things had gone so terribly wrong: Dad had been smart and lucky enough to get a job in the prison camp kitchen to survive; he'd been resourceful enough to build a bench out of firewood, something of value that he could trade for the opportunity to get a message to the family; he'd been clear-headed enough to give Grandma and Grandpa his location; and, despite his circumstances, conditions, and situations he had hope that somehow his note would reach his parents after they'd been separated for years (and not be somehow intercepted which would get them all killed).

Dad didn't realize that Grandma and Grandpa had been forced to leave the family home and relocate to Tjiboenit camp. That the note courier found and gained access to my grandparents who were imprisoned in a camp-within-a-camp was another miracle.

Miracle upon miracle.

So many things have overwhelmed me in the telling of this story. It seems that epic stories have an element of the fantastical to them. They simply don't seem real. The few pieces of Dad's story that I can hold on to are the most precious. They are time machines that help me imagine it all. They are Ebenezers so I might remember God's favor and grace on our family. How human it is to overlook or even forget the many blessings bestowed upon us. Even the most incredible can fade over time. To have something to cling to, something to remind me of God's love for me and my family is its own kind of miracle.

The Israelites were about to cross the Jordan River into The Promised Land after wandering for 40 years. But they were afraid of being swept away in the high turbulent waters of the Jordan, and needed a reminder of God's miracles. So God dried up the Jordan (as he had the Red Sea years earlier) so the Israelites could cross into The Promised Land. He commanded that they create a 12-stone Ebenezer so they might never again forget how much God loves them.[51]

Our family's Ebenezer is Dad's note, now over eighty years old. Your family certainly has theirs. No matter what or who has let you down, the Lord is faithful. He is always with us. We are never alone. He is the same yesterday, today, and tomorrow. He is good. And all good things come from Him. I only studied this Bible story after my life had imploded about a handful of years after I became the keeper of Dad's note. Little did I know that I would be crossing my own Jordan so soon afterward, into my own Promised Land adventurously delivered from heartache and oppression to discover true freedom in my walk with Him.

---

51 "And Joshua set up twelve stones in the midst of the Jordan, in the place where the feet of the priests bearing the ark of the covenant had stood; and they are there to this day." (Joshua 4:9–10) "And those twelve stones, which they took out of the Jordan, Joshua set up at Gilgal. And he said to the people of Israel, "When your children ask their fathers in times to come, 'What do these stones mean?' then you shall let your children know, 'Israel passed over this Jordan on dry ground.' For the Lord your God dried up the waters of the Jordan for you until you passed over, as the Lord your God did to the Red Sea, which he dried up for us until we passed over, so that all the peoples of the earth may know that the hand of the Lord is mighty . . . " (Joshua 4:20–24)

Kempeitai

NOVEMBER, 1943

Grandpa sat at a large table, testing vacuum tubes. Two Indonesian scientists flanked him, observing.

A Japanese officer walked up to the table and smiled.

"It is time to choose, Einstein. Death in the camps? Or dishonor in Tokyo?" he said.

Grandpa put his instruments down and stood up, going chest-to-chest with the officer. The Indonesian scientists stepped back in horror.

"Death comes to all," Grandpa said.

The officer pulled a pistol out of his holster and pointed it between Grandpa's eyes.

"I'm not leaving Indonesia without my son," Grandpa said.

* * *

Prisoners streamed out of their warehouses for tenko at noon. When Dad and his cellmates had to walk past two Banyan trees, they saw a back-up of prisoners. Men in front of them stared. As Dad and the others got closer, the dead body of a man tied to one of the "punishment poles" came into view.

Pale, Dad grabbed his stomach. Storyteller fell to his knees. Dad and Bridge Player tried to bring Storyteller to his feet, but he punched them away.

"I don't know what the hell is going on, but I don't want you to die too," Bridge Player whispered. "Get up . . . . Walk!"

Dad and Bridge Player held Storyteller up, draping his arms over their shoulders. Hunched over, they walked him to his spot for tenko.

An umbrella-carrying assistant shaded the commandant from the blistering sun.

The count began as the sun beat down on Dad. He wobbled, and nearly passed out.

"Kyū-jū hachi (98)," one prisoner said.

"Kyū-jū kyū. (99)," the prisoner next to Dad said.

Dad's eyes opened and closed. Between worlds, his thoughts bordered on the real and the fantastic. The pause in the count horrified his cellmates. They didn't know what to do. Then Dad remembered where he was. What was at stake. What was real. With eyes wide, Dad made a mistake, saying, "Kyū-jū kyū (99)."

The commandant swiftly had Dad caned and scolded him in Japanese. Because Dad messed up the count, tenko began again and all the prisoners were forced to stand in the broiling sun that much longer. When the hellish tenko was finally over, the prisoners limped back into their cell blocks. Dad laid on his mat, sore all over. The old guys gathered around him, except for Storyteller.

"Hey son, one day this'll all be over. This shit can't last forever. One day soon these monsters will be dead and we will be free . . . " Playboy said.

Dad's eyes fluttered, but he turned away from the group. He laid in a lump on his mat and was drifting off to sleep when the door to the cell block slammed open. A group of prison guards entered. As they marched toward Dad, his cellmates gathered around him. But the soldiers beat them away with the butts of their guns.

"What's he done?" Storyteller said, wincing in pain, holding his side. A soldier slapped him.

Storyteller and the other cellmates sat in stunned silence as the soldiers dragged Dad out of the cell block. When they let go of him outside, Dad fell into the mud. Sunshine blinded him temporarily.

"On your feet!" one of them said.

Dad complied, shivering with fear in the steamy heat. He looked to the sky, as if in prayer, then felt the barrel of a gun in his back. The soldiers marched him through the camp. Delirious, Dad imagined songbirds flying around them as they walked through the mud and into the commandant's office. The commandant stood at his desk. His assistant took a step back at the sight of Dad.

The commandant put a glass of water down on the front edge of his desk and said, "Drink."

Dad had never seen the commandant up close before and took a long, hard look at him. As he did, Sukio's apparition appeared and walked behind the commandant.

"Birds always sing after a storm," Suko whispered.

Songbirds filled the Kapok tree outside the commandant's window.

Dad licked his lips constantly, willing hydration to pour into his body instead of evaporating out of him at lightning speed. Imaginary songbirds fluttered around the commandant. Sukio's apparition walked closer to Dad. As a few of the songbirds landed next to the glass on the desk, Dad's gaze settled on the water.

"Look at me when I'm talking to you!" the commandant said.

The roar of an engine got Dad's attention. He turned his head and caught sight of a black car with Japanese flags flying. It screeched to a stop just outside the open doors of the office. Two Kempeitai officers exited the vehicle.

"Drink!" the commandant demanded.

Dad hesitated at first, wondering if it might be poisoned. But refreshment was too compelling. A small gulp of water washed over his baked lips and cooled him to the core as it traveled through his hot body. He could feel every inch of the drink on its path to his stomach.

"Today is your lucky day," the commandant said, wiping his brow. "Mine too—you're not dead. Unlike every other prisoner here, you have some value to The Empire," the commandant said.

When the Kempeitai entered the office, the commandant bowed low to them. They exchanged words but Dad was too groggy to understand them.

After a brief discussion, the Kempeitai immediately walked Dad out of the office to the back door of the waiting car. An officer opened the door. Dad hesitated before shakily taking a seat inside.

The Kempeitai sat in the front seat. When the driver hit the gas, Dad looked out the back window. The prison camp and the commandant got smaller and smaller in the distance. Dad couldn't believe he was leaving the horror behind. He said a silent goodbye to his cellmates. Would he ever see them alive again? What would become of them? Dad wondered if the ride out of camp was all a dream, like Sukio and the songbirds. Where were they taking him? What would become of him? Was he going to another camp? A worse camp? Had he done something horribly wrong? Had something gone right?

Soon, they sped down a country road. Dad's eyes settled on the rice paddies. Watching their gentle curves helped him calm the fear that rose inside of him. A deep abiding feeling of dread had latched onto his heart, and seemed like it would never let go. Dad lowered his window, allowing fresh air to hit his face. The air smelled different. Months spent stoking the fires had colored his sensibilities: harsh acrid smoke was seemingly the only air he breathed. And when it didn't stink of smoke it stunk of men wilting in the sun, and in their bodies. Sick men, always with dysentery.

He hadn't smelled fresh air for so long. So very long. He closed his eyes as the hot breeze rushed over his body, and took deep breaths, bathing his lungs and psyche in the sensation of freedom. Dad dared to hope that the nightmare might be over, allowing himself to enjoy the cushioned backseat and resting out of the broiling sun. When he opened his eyes, he didn't recognize the route. In a dream-like state, his mind went back to the time he and Sukio had visited the holy tree.

"Good lives equally with evil. The left hand with the right. The day with the night. We honor both worlds. They exist together," Sukio said.

"But don't you just want evil to go away?"

"Even at its worst, evil exists only to make you aware of what is good."

Sukio's apparition told Dad something he had never heard before. "In English, evil spelled backwards is live—the key to overcoming a great evil. Live. And live well. Do good deeds."

When the car reached the end of a dirt road, the driver hit the brakes and came to a stop just outside the bamboo-and-barbed-wire fence of the Tjiboenit camp, where a camp within a camp held the engineers and their families. Each family lived in their own small homes isolated from the other prisoners. Soldiers opened the gate and bowed low to the Kempeitai's car as it drove to one of the small houses.

Soon, Grandma came into view.

Seeing his mother just inside the door of one of the houses, Dad jumped out of the car right before it came to a complete stop and ran to her, but he collapsed. Grandma ran to Dad and held him in her arms. Tears came to her eyes.

"Praise to our Heavenly Father!" Grandma said. "You're alive!"

"It's over, it's finally over . . . " Dad said.

"I never gave up hope. Not for one second," Grandma said, trying to restrain the horror she felt at seeing her bruised and emaciated son. She helped him to the front steps of their forced relocation living accommodation.

Dad stiffened and backed out of her hug. "You're skin and bones," he said. She walked him to the front stoop of the house and he sat with her.

"Where are we? Why aren't you home?" Dad said.

Too choked up to speak, Grandma just hugged him again. Dad looked at a line of homes behind the barbed wire. Other families walked out of them briefly, spotting him, then walked back inside.

"Who are they?" Dad asked.

Soon Reinier ran outside. Dad smiled at the sight of his younger brother and gave him a hug. At eight years old, Reinier had gotten older but hadn't grown very much in the years Dad had been imprisoned. When Grandpa walked out onto the porch, Dad raised his head. Beyond Grandpa, inside the place they lived, everything was disheveled. Some pictures and clothes had been thrown haphazardly in a few suitcases that sat open on the floor.

Grandpa said, "We leave for Japan tomorrow."

"Japan?" Dad could barely stand. Grandma helped him up the steps and into the house. As he entered the strange home, his Aunt Frieda, Grandma's sister, stopped her work of packing. "Welcome back," she said. She was a bit taller than Grandma, but with similar features. The sisters had been very close at one time. But somewhere along the way Dad remembered they had a falling out.

Seeing the look of surprise in Dad's eyes, Grandma said, "Tante Freida decided to stop working in the hospital. She is going to come with us to Japan."

* * *

Dear Laura,

The commandant told me that I'd have to go with the secret policemen. But as we drove, I didn't recognize the roads they took. I didn't know where I was headed. Then the Kempeitai brought me to a compound of homes behind barbed wire and bamboo gates where I'd never been before. I didn't recognize the house that they drove me up to, but I saw my family. I was so happy that it was over. It was only then that I learned that my family was forced to leave our home and had been living there for some time. My father told me we were leaving for Japan the next day. I didn't know why. Instead of coming home, I was a prisoner again. It was like a nightmare.

Love, Daddy

When Dad spoke to me about the trauma of being taken away from prison camp only to have the nightmare continue in ways he never thought imaginable, I shuddered. I didn't know about this part of the story. When I heard he was a Japanese POW captured in Java, I figured that he was a prisoner at one camp on the island. Instead, I discovered he had been held in a handful of different camps in Indonesia and then our family, along with four other families (twenty-two people in all) were transported to Japan.

Dad couldn't have known it then, but he would be spending the rest of the war with these families in close quarters, under house arrest, and cut off from the rest of the world. These were also some of the same people who wouldn't come over to their home for tea. People who had marginalized Grandpa for being German and Grandma by association. People who had discriminated against Grandpa because he lacked a diploma. The five families that lived behind the barbed wire at Tjiboenit camp, in a the camp-within-a-camp and would need to survive forced labor for the Sumitomo Corporation were—the Levenbachs, Lels, Leunissens, Hasenstabs, and Einthovens.

Hasenstab: Alexander, Irene, Hans, Reinier, Frieda Kelling

Levenbach: Riek, Geo, Fritz, Marijke, Hans

Lels: Annie, Henk, Paulien, Murk

Leunissen: Jan, Corry

Einthoven: Wim, Beb, Loukie, Wink, Tineke, Kate

Before leaving for Japan, the engineers were notified that they would be working for the Japanese army.

"Starting from the Japanese announcement, the five men were summoned regularly to the Japanese office near the camp to receive instructions. These instructions were given by one officer, who always brought an interpreter. At the last meeting, and after he had sent the interpreter away, he closed the door carefully and said in perfect English to the stunned men, 'Gentlemen, I'm sorry, I cannot do anything for you and I cannot prevent you from being sent to Japan, but I'll give you one piece of advice: when you are forced to go to work, work as slowly as possible and keep asking for more literature about your topics. The resources will be exhausted soon. I wish you all the best."[52]

Grandpa angrily refused to cooperate with the Japanese, as did the other engineers. They used all kinds of tactics to stop their transfer and get out of the work they would have to do for the Japanese army, especially as it seemed the tide had turned in the war, beginning with the battle of Midway, about a year and a half earlier. The engineers petitioned the Japanese to keep the women and children on Java, and even hoped the queen-in-exile might be able to exercise her power to stop the transfer. The response was to flat out let them know that their families were being taken as hostages to force them to do the work the Japanese needed them to perform.

* * *

April 5, 2010
Dear Laura,

As I mentioned before, Sumitomo arranged for the transport of our family to Japan. I remember that we went on a troopship in a convoy leaving Djakarta seaport. There were at least eight transport vessels and two were torpedoed in the Formosa Straits. We heard the explosions and saw the ships sink. And you know the rest of the story.

Love, Daddy

---

52   Van Der Wal, Ineke, *The Temple with the Chrysanthemums: Dutch Prisoners of War in Tokyo*, Independently published, 2017.

Dad said I knew the rest of the story . . . but, I didn't and neither did he. His idea that radio held the balance of power in the Pacific and that the engineers were needed to accomplish the ambitions of the Japanese to win a propaganda war, thereby securing Japan's ultimate victory, was plausible. However, something felt off. Call it intuition or just an unsettled feeling. I knew there was something more to the story.

Early on, I wondered about the specific projects the Japanese forced the engineers to work on day after day in captivity. The Dutch engineers had the capability of maintaining the radio equipment better than the Japanese. Inventing and applying some kind of new technology was another possibility. For context, I believe the Japanese POW Research Network puts it best:

"During World War 2, the Japanese Armed Forces captured about 140,000 Allied military personnel (Australia, Canada, Great Britain, India, Netherlands, New Zealand, and the United States) in the Southeast Asia and Pacific areas. They were forced to engage in the hard labor of constructing the railways, roads, airfields, etc. to be used by the Japanese Armed Forces in the Japanese occupied areas. Of the 140,000 Prisoners of War (POWs), about 36,000 were transported to the Japanese Mainland to supplement the shortage of the workforce, and compelled to work at the coal mines, mines, shipyards, munitions factories, etc.

They lived miserable lives, and by the time the war was over, a total of more than 30,000 POWs had died from starvation, diseases, and mistreatment within and outside of the Japanese Mainland. The POWs' mortality rate was as high as 27%.

Those POWs who survived the war and returned home have suffered from incurable mental and physical wounds and lived the postwar days harboring a deep hatred against Japan and the Japanese people, which turned out to be harsh emotions hard to restrain, and erupted as flashes of sudden and disturbing rage should anything happen between their countries and Japan, even 60 years since the war was over.

On the other hand, after the war, many Japanese who had been associated with the POW Camp administrations were prosecuted in the war crime tribunals for their mistreatment of the POWs, which left deep scars in the hearts and minds of the Japanese people as well. At any event, very little has been known about the Allied POWs. This is because at the time of the termination of war, the Japanese Armed Forces destroyed all documents related to the POW Camps. Furthermore, the Japanese Government had been negligent in keeping records of such historical facts during the war.

For the purpose of digging out those buried historical facts, the POW Research Network Japan was inaugurated in March 2002, and with about 70 members all over the country, we have carried out research and studies on the Allied POWs, civilian internees, war criminal trials, etc. by helping one another. In addition, we have worked on the interchanging activities with the ex-POWs and their families, and many other activities."[53]

---

53 http://www.powresearch.jp/en/about/index.html

Dear Dad

In 2015, I visited Dad a few times. He was frail. I had never seen him quite this way. He smiled more, even though he had to have every last one of his teeth pulled when he was ninety. His dentures didn't spoil his smile, still as big and beautiful as it had always been, but more childlike.

When I'd visit, Dad would hold my hand and sing to me, "When you're smiling, when you're smiling the whole world smiles with you. When you're laughing, when you're laughing . . . " He wobbled a bit as we walked the long hallways of his residence building, most often hand-in-hand. I remember being relieved that there were benches strategically placed on either side of the hall, just in case he'd need a rest on our way to Mom and Dad's apartment.

Once inside, Dad walked over to the phonograph, turned it on and carefully placed the needle on a 78 RPM recording of him playing the violin when he was a student at the University of Sydney. We sat and listened to it together. Music was his refuge. He had to have been living with more pain than one man should have to bear, both mentally and physically and yet, he smiled. Joy continued to be one of his greatest gifts, as was his deep compassion for others, the ability to find happiness in the midst of despair, and comfort in his pain.

In the months leading up to Dad's 92nd birthday he hadn't been well. His heart failure had worsened, sending him to the hospital more frequently. In February, 2016, about a week before I traveled to Florida to celebrate Dad's 92nd birthday, I workshopped the script I'd written about his life with Bill Boyer, an award-winning screenwriter, during a writers' retreat in Malibu.

When I met with Bill one-on-one, I was scratching my head over the ending of the screenplay. I told him that only months before, I'd discovered the most important missing piece of Dad's story while doing research in Indonesia—the truth about why the Dutch engineers and their families were taken prisoner and transferred from Indonesia to Japan. But, I struggled with how to incorporate the information into the script quickly. I couldn't come to terms with the enormity of the rewriting task.

Bill suggested that the script would write itself when I visited Dad for his birthday.

"The story isn't just your dad's," he said, "it's yours too."

This jolted me for a couple of reasons. Not only would editing the script to incorporate what I'd recently learned be impossible before Dad's birthday, but I hadn't shown up on the pages of the script at all. The idea of being part of the story hadn't occurred to me. But, Bill encouraged me, saying that a new version should be written to include my story, not just dad's.

After meeting with Bill, I took a stroll on the grounds of the beautiful venue of the screenwriting retreat and stared out at the Pacific Ocean. As I breathed in the salty air, I lifted my face to the sun and drank in the sunshine, realizing, yet again, that I'd have to go back to the drawing board and rewrite. My heart sank at that prospect, even though I knew Bill was right. I'd have an even bigger job of trying to put myself on the page. That wouldn't come easily. I'd hoped Dad would read this story in his lifetime. But, as the sun danced across the waves and the surf crashed on the cliffs below, I knew my dream would be impossible.

I'd run out of time to get the story "right." But I did have the ability to write Dad a letter about what I had serendipitously uncovered. I decided to give the surprising revelation to Dad in a letter that would be his birthday present. At an AirBnB in the hills of Malibu overlooking the Pacific Ocean, I sat in an adirondack chair in the sunshine, and typed Dad's letter. The act of placing all my research into one document gave me pause. Before that moment, the narrative had been in bits and pieces—within journals, emails, photos, and videos.

Dear Dad, I wrote then I spelled out how I discovered the answers to our most perplexing questions in black and white in the Malibu sun. I breathed a sigh of relief, believing for the first time that one day I would be able to fulfill my promise to tell Dad's story. Then, I signed Dad's birthday present, *Love Laura*, and took a deep breath.

Dad's 92nd birthday celebration in Florida.

FEBRUARY, 2016
MALIBU, CALIFORNIA
Dear Dad,

Happy birthday! I want to write to you to reveal The Lord's hand in our screenplay. This is my gift to you on your 92nd birthday. What a joy it will be to spend it with you.

Something had always nagged at me while we discussed the story about your experience and our family's fate in WWII. I understood the Japanese government forced the radio engineers to work for them, but I didn't understand exactly what they were working on. And, as you said, you never went to work with them. Because Grandpa never talked about what he did, you had no idea what he had worked on for the Sumitomo Corporation.

The idea that radio held the balance of power in the Pacific and that the engineers were needed to accomplish the ambitions of the Japanese to win a propaganda war thereby securing Japan's ultimate victory was a plausible one. I wrote an ending that reflected this premise. However, it always seemed like something was lacking in this ending. I wondered what specific projects the engineers worked on. The idea that they had the capability of maintaining radio equipment better than the Japanese was one plausible project. Applying some kind of new technology was another.

Yet, it didn't explain that when the firebombing of Tokyo occurred, Grandpa and the engineers and their families were carefully moved to Nagoya to the Buddhist temple. Something about this didn't add up in my mind. The radio station was in Tokyo. What could they possibly do for the Japanese government in Nagoya? Why were they being so protected and taken care of by the Japanese?

Radio projects, while plausible, fell flat for me. It felt like there was something more to the story. But the original draft of the screenplay was crafted around this idea which came from the plausible facts and inferences made by my primary research. However, The Lord would reveal to me an ending I was unable to uncover on my own.

He called me to many parts of the world in 2015. During my travels, Margaux let me know that she had work in Vietnam and was due to travel to Bali to meet some friends. So I thought it would be fun to rent an awesome place in Bali and have them join me there. Margaux and I had so enjoyed meeting up in Thailand the year before and we thought it would be fun to meet up again.

As I hiked El Camino de Santiago (Frances) that summer, I wasn't sure if Margaux and I were still on for our meet-up. Somewhere along the way I received a message from Margaux that said she wanted to know if I was "for sure" going to Bali. I said yes and made the final arrangements from my walk in Spain's Rioja region in Navarra. But, at the last minute, Margaux's company postponed her business trip, so she wasn't going to be in Asia as planned. Instead, she stayed with me in Paris and we had a wonderful time. We went to another cooking school and learned how to make croissants. After Margaux left, I questioned returning to Bali. There really was no reason to travel there since we'd met up in Paris.

But, I felt a strong instinct to go anyway. I wanted to write about my life-changing experience on the Camino and begin figuring out my freelance writing career (I had paused the writing of the screenplay since I had so many questions about the type of work Grandpa had been forced to do). What better place to write and center myself than in Bali, I thought. Indonesia had been a creative sanctuary for me the year before. So, I persevered. After I arrived in Ubud, I became friends with the landlord of the room I rented in one of his beautiful Balinese homes. A Dutchman, living full time in Bali, he asked if I was going to attend the Ubud Writers and Readers Festival. As it turned out, the festival was going to occur that week.

I don't believe in hazard. It felt like the Lord had arranged for me to visit Bali at that precise time and rent that exact place to take me to the festival. While signing up on the festival website, I discovered there were many "extra" programs I could participate in. One of them was a luncheon with Mpho Tutu, who would speak about her recent release, co-authored with her father, Desmond Tutu, *The Book of Forgiving.* When I read that Mpho was earning her doctorate in forgiveness, I was captivated. I'd been trying to learn to forgive, and longed to know more about how. Another breathtaking coincidence. I felt the Lord at work and signed up.

Here's how the luncheon was advertised:

"At this once-in-a-lifetime sit-down, the Reverend Canon Mpho Tutu will explore forgiveness; a concept she learnt first-hand from the closest the world has to an expert on it, her father Archbishop Desmond Tutu. Over a delicious lunch, hear tales told of her growing up with a Nobel Peace Prize laureate, and the ancient southern African beliefs that guide her life."

On Oct. 29, 2015, I went to the beautiful Maya Resort in Ubud to hear Mopho speak.

Maya Resort in Ubud.

Maya Resort in Ubud, where the luncheon was attended by 150 people.

I had just taken my seat when a Dutch woman and her husband sat next to me. We made casual conversation and I asked if she was a writer. When she said yes, I asked what she wrote. Her name is Seline

Hofker. She is the niece of Willem Gerard Hofker 1902-1981, who was a Dutch painter in Bali and was also imprisoned. His subjects were Balinese people and his artwork is on display at the Neka Art Museum in Ubud. She'd written a book about his life entitled *Wilem Gerard Hofker 1902-1981*.

Seline Hofker and me at the luncheon (credit: Seline's husband).

Drawing by W.G.Hofker (1902-1981), 'Djanger Dessa Renon Budung',
Bali. ©Pictoright Amsterdam 2025.

Drawing by W.G.Hofker (1902-1981), 'Ni Kenyung', Bali 1943.
©Pictoright Amsterdam 2025.

Seline Hofker with the painting by her uncle W.G.Hofker (1902-1981)
Title of the painting: 'Balinese sisters at the temple feast'.
©Pictoright Amsterdam 2025
Thank you Seline of The Hofker Archive
https://www.willemgerardhofker.com/

She told me her uncle had been imprisoned in different camps and that she did a great deal of research to discover where. After I explained that my dad was taken prisoner on Java, that his father was a radio scientist and forced to work for the Japanese government, her face went white. She said that in her research she kept running into a group of engineers who had been moved together. Even though those engineers had nothing to do with her research, that detail intrigued her.

Seline explained that she lives in the Hague and did her research at NIOD Netherlands Institute of War Documents in Amsterdam. She said that she discovered the project the engineers were working on when talking to the relatives of Willem Frederik Einthoven, who was the head scientist and worked with my grandfather.

"The project your grandfather and Willem Frederik Einthoven were working on was a remote detonation device for a nuclear weapon," she said.

This floored me. If true, then there's a much bigger story here. History that has to be told. I couldn't quite wrap my head around incorporating this new information into the story. I'd have to do more research and feared trying to make sense of the technology. I don't have a scientific background. I came up with all sorts of excuses why I couldn't dive in and rewrite the script. So it sat. I left Bali, went to Spain, Morocco, back to Spain then home to LA. Then I had a month-long visit with Candice and Margaux in December. My trip back to Malibu in January and a medical diagnosis kept me very busy.

The screenplay was all but forgotten until . . . on your birthday this year, I received an email from Seline, where she said among other things, this very powerful statement:

Dear Laura,

Long time you had to wait for a mail from me. But now I'm here. I never forgot about our meeting that I felt was very special.

How are you? And your father?

I can confirm that our meeting from last October in Bali was no coincidence. I checked my notes from a few years back and can tell you the 5 families incl. your grandfather Alexander Von Hasenstab were taken by the Japanese during the war to Tokyo. The name of the one family you were looking for is: Einthoven Willem Fredrik Einthoven (his father was a Nobel prize winner for physiology of medicine).

fam: Lels

fam: Levenbach

fam: Hasenstab

This information I was given from the daughter and grand-daughter of Willem F. Einthoven, whom I visited in 2010. The Einthovens were very good friends with the Hofkers in Indië [Indonesia] and Holland after the war. The children from Eintho-ven were Willem, Katy en Tineke. Maybe your father remembers playing with them?

I contacted the granddaughter today asking her for more infor-mation about the family and Tokyo. Let's see what she comes up with. I remember that she was planning to find out more about her grandparents. Also, her grandmother, wife of Willem Eintho-ven, was an interesting person. As first woman in Holland who was an architectural engineer.

Hope to stay in touch, and give you more info. you need for your movie!

Best wishes,

Seline Hofker

After I told Seline it was your birthday she sent this document over as a token of her affection and she wished you a happy birthday.

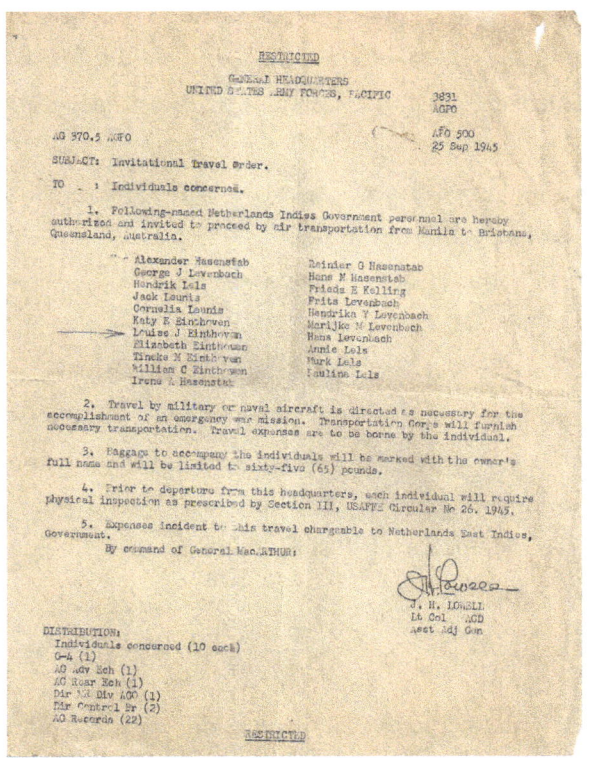

Travel document authorizing and inviting the families from Manila to Brisbane, Queensland, Australia. (As it turned out Dad had a copy of this same document in his files.)

I need to do more research to write the ending correctly. I have done a little research into this new information and have discovered that the Japanese military had a secret program to build a nuclear weapon.

Here is an excerpt from a recent article of note:

"Robert K. Wilcox, the L.A.-based author of "Japan's Secret War: Japan's Race Against Time to Build Its Own Atomic Bomb." Wilcox, who has been researching the program for decades, said Japan's problem was not a lack of know-how. "They knew the physics needed for creating the bomb and the engineering needed to build it," he said. "It was lack of element resources like uranium that was the real problem for them."[54]

Such supplies were not readily available in Japan, so its leaders looked toward occupied territories.

"In 1945, the Japanese navy alone spent a fortune to gather uranium," Wilcox said. "They needed a win-the-war weapon and an atomic bomb was seen as one of those." The Japanese government burned thousands of documents as the war was ending. Researchers believe many documents related to Japan's atomic bomb program were destroyed. U.S. occupation forces confiscated almost anything that remained. So the documents discovered in Japan have drawn intense interest."

"I happened to read a story in the New York Times about Japan possibly making an atomic bomb during the war. I'd never heard that. Was there a story or was it just a footnote? I made inquiries. I was led to a prominent scholar, Derek deSolla Price, a Yale historian of science, who told me there was much to be uncovered. I sold the concept for Japan's Secret War to a publisher who will go unnamed because it went from them to Morrow, who published it in 1985. I went to Japan. Fascinating. The Sword and The Chrysanthemum. Ferocity and delicacy. That's the Japanese dichotomy. For a month, I sipped tea and tried to extract information. The story was a sore spot for the Japanese who had only been portrayed as victims of the bomb. Like pulling teeth, the story unfolded. Yes they did have a program. It

---

54   http://www.latimes.com/world/asia/la-fg-japan-bomb-20150805-story.html

was more developed than most know. They would have used the bomb on us in a Hiroshima minute had it been ready. It almost was. The story was as much as I had hoped and more. I told it through the scientists and soldiers who lived it. If the Japanese and Germans had not been so suspicious of each other and had cooperated, they might have made the bomb before we did – a very controversial story. I worked so hard in Japan that I fell ill when I returned. Writing can be physically demanding. I exercise every day."

— Robert K. Wilcox, author *Japan's Secret War: Japan's Race Against Time to Build Its Own Atomic Bomb.*

I am currently researching this idea and finding more and more information to corroborate that they had a fully functioning bomb and successfully tested an atomic bomb—- "In a cave in a mountain near Konan, men worked against time, in final assembly of *genzai bakuden*, Japan's name for the atomic bomb. It was August 10, 1945 (Japanese time), only four days after an atomic bomb flashed in the sky over Hiroshima, and five days before Japan surrendered."[55]

I continue my research to find out exactly how the Dutch scientists' skills were exploited.

Here are some inspirational quotes from Mopho Tutu's luncheon:

"You can't give lip-service to transformation for transformation to occur."

"I can't honor the love for my husband and children by promoting hate. The only thing I can do to honor them is to love."

---

55   Wilcox, Robert K. *Japan's Secret War: Japan's Race Against Time to Build Its Own Atomic Bomb*

"Abusers can occupy a lot of psychic territory. Territory better given to building your new life."

"Forgiveness is somewhere that you get to when you get there."

"I am not going to allow you to define me, I refuse to collude. I refuse to allow you to hold me emotionally hostage."

And so, we see where the story has taken us, Dad. I love you and promise you that we will write this to the finish.

Love, Laura

Dad believed this answer to our ultimate question about why the families were taken as prisoners and transported from Indonesia to Japan. But many others did not, saying that if what I discovered were true, we would have heard of it by now. The granddaughter of Wim Einthoven who Seline mentioned in her email is named Ineke Van Der Wal. She would be a few years from publishing her book about her family's experience that would illuminate much more about the story. About a month after Dad's last birthday, we were in touch. I will never forget the email she sent.

March 29, 2016
Dear Laura,

Here I am at last. I will do my best to answer your queries.

The only document I was able to find about the work performed in the laboratories of Sumitomo during WWII by our grandfathers is in Leiden, at the KITLV - Koninklijk Instituut Taal- Land- en Volkenkunde, call number H1800 #22. This is a statement of Geo Levenbach concerning the work he performed. As the 5 engineers were always divided, I cannot say whether all engineers worked on these subjects. I am no physicist or engineer, so it is a total mystery what he is talking about. After the war he told me in a personal interview, that it is his conviction that the Japanese were working on an atomic bomb and that their work was supposed to be part of that project. In the book you mention Sumitomo is an important player in this quest. Geo Levenbach also said that there was hardly any electricity in Tokyo and that they needed lots of this for the vacuum installation that was requested. We know now that centrifuge is the best way to upgrade uranium, but in those days everybody was still looking desperately for the right procedure and it was thought that vacuum could play an important role.

The Japanese were also desperately looking for Radar and this was discussed already right after the transfer of the Bandoeng Laboratory to Sumitomo. It is unclear to me how that played out. It has always been a mystery why Sumitomo spared no expense to transfer 22 people to Japan and then let them perform work which an undergraduate student could have performed easily. Direct requests to Sumitomo never resulted in a straight answer. Radar was once suggested, but in the same interview it was said that my grandmother had written a letter, stating that Sumitomo was not to blame for the death of my grandfather. I can assure you that such a letter was never written. In short, Sumitomo never came clean.

The book you mention also states that the Riken laboratory - the one to develop the atomic bomb - was moved out of Tokyo to Korea once the heavy bombing of Tokyo started. This would mean that the work of our grandfathers was basically terminated . . .

I would love to meet you. Please let me know when you come to The Netherlands or whether we can meet somewhere in between. Paris maybe? Good luck in Spain. Best regards, from Ineke

A race was on between the United States, Japan, Germany, and later, the Soviet Union. And the prize was priceless—whoever built and used the atomic bomb first wouldn't face nuclear annihilation and would be the winner in a zero-sum game. If the Dutch PTT engineers did work on a remote detonation device for the Japanese army under the orders of the Sumitomo Corporation, did that prove the Japanese nuclear program was much more advanced than reported at the end of the war? Was there enough overlap in the science of radio technology to warrant having radio engineers develop a remote detonation device for an atomic bomb? Using the families as hostages to guarantee their cooperation with the Japanese army meant the work they were doing had a high level of importance to The Empire. The way Sumitomo guaranteed their safety was uncharacteristic of the treatment given to other POWs.

This story makes a case that Hiroshima and Nagasaki could have been San Francisco and Seattle. Were we only a breath away from annihilation? If so, America could have been close to losing the fight of her life.

"In August 1945, the U.S. dropped atom bombs on Hiroshima and Nagasaki. Now, as Japan and the rest of the world prepare to mark seven decades since the end of World War II in the Pacific, new evidence has emerged about the Japanese military's own secret program to build a nuclear weapon."[56]

— *The Los Angeles Times*, 2015

---

56 https://www.latimes.com/world/asia/la-fg-japan-bomb-20150805-story.html

HELL SHIP

As the engineers continued to try to delay, postpone, or change their fate, the waters of southeast Asia became more perilous. On January 24, 1944, under cover of night, the Kempeitai transported my family and the other four Dutch engineers' families by bus from Bandung to Jakarta where they were smuggled out of Tanjung Priok, the port of Jakarta, on a small Japanese cargo ship. When the hellacious night finally came, Dad had to say goodbye to the only homeland he had ever known and would never see again. Many of the engineers left extended family members behind in gruesome camps, not knowing if they would live or die.

Japanese soldiers led the families to the docks at the port in Jakarta. Dazed from dehydration and trembling with fear, throngs of male POWs, some only clothed in loincloths, crowded the docks. As the families joined the herd, wide-eyed prisoners parted, making way for the women and children. The condemned gave an uneasy deference with the haunted eyes of men who'd only survived by clinging to the desperate hope that they would see their wives and children again.

As the Kempeitai guards corralled the five families up the crowded gang plank to the cargo ship, they passed a few engineer POWs they knew. Horrified at their comrades' fate, they tried to communicate with them, but the guards forbade the engineers and their families to make contact with any of the other POWs. When it came time to board the unmarked vessel, the other Dutch POWs were lowered into the already overcrowded hold of the vessel. But the Kemapetai diverted the Dutch engineers and their families to two cabins above the deck of the ship. None of them were allowed to walk on deck. Blankets, life jackets, and rough seagrass pillows awaited them inside their cabins.

The port remained amazingly unharmed as they sailed by a few obvious shipwrecks. Their Japanese "guides"—Tsutsia, Takahashi and Kishida—let them know that their journey to Japan would involve a couple of passages. The first, and shorter passage, would take them to Singapore where they would disembark and wait several weeks for another vessel to take them the rest of the way. But the passage wasn't straightforward. The boat had to find safe harbors a few times. Once they fled Allied ships by sailing into the port of Palembang where the oil refinery of the Batavian Petroleum Company had fallen to the Japanese. After they anchored, Japanese on the distant dock waved to the Dutch families and made circles with their hands, a symbol of the rising sun.

Once safely moored in Singapore, Dad watched the horrific sight of the unloading of exhausted, hungry, male POWs from the hull of the ship—walking skeletons who had been forced by the Japanese to clean their toilets during the passage. The process of disembarking took hours. During their extended layover, the Dutch families were placed under house arrest in two rooms at the once grand Adelphi Hotel[57], at

---

57   https://www.nlb.gov.sg/main/article-detail?cmsuuid=2db6b69a-b42e-4886-a4af-
      13265197f392

Coleman Street and North Bridge Road across from a park and near St. Andrew's Cathedral.

The popularity of the Adelphi Hotel as a first-class establishment did not wane throughout its existence. Notably, while it was renamed as the Nanto Hotel during the Japanese Occupation of Singapore (1942-1945), its reputation continued to be recognized by the Japanese military.[58]

They were only allowed occasional supervised outings at a local park. While there, they were constantly reminded not to make contact with anyone outside their group, especially Singaporeans who found the Dutch people a curiosity. Their three "guides" always accompanied them and posted additional guards as sentries at the park's entry gates to make sure the families didn't make any contact with people outside their group. Doing so meant losing their outdoor privileges.

Dad rarely spoke of his time in Singapore, and when he did, it was only to say that he had spent some time there on the journey to Japan. Actually, he seemed quite confused about the passages he took from Indonesia to Japan.

Dear Laura,

When I got back with my parents, we had only a few days before we were transported to Tanjong Priok to board a Japanese freighter bound for Japan. After 10 days waiting in Singapore,[59] a troop ship took us on board and we crossed the Formosa Strait. "We" consisted of Alex, Irene, Hans, Reinier and Frieda along with the other engineers and their families. We got bunk beds, one on top of the other, the same as the Japanese soldiers, with poor ventilation.

---

58   "Success will crown efforts of our armies". Syonan Shimbun. November 13, 1942. Accessed 29 November 2022. Retrieved from NewspaperSG.

59   This recollection is inaccurate. They were in Singapore for six weeks.

We were confined to this area, but after a storm and an attack by U.S. submarines, we were allowed on deck. One of the ships in our convoy was sunk.

We had an inside cabin, but not enough beds, so I slept on deck when possible. I met Japanese soldiers on deck and started to learn to speak Japanese. I was always interested in different languages and realized that a new language is just a collection of words. So, I started to learn Japanese, one word at a time.

This boat journey was a great opportunity, because I learned the correct pronunciation, although I could not write it in the Japanese alphabet. As I continued talking to the Japanese on board, they became interested in teaching me, and they brought Japanese newspapers and pointed out the words that I had learned. This was the beginning of my becoming the future camp interpreter. In my old prison camp, I had started to learn to speak Japanese, and on shipboard, I had plenty of opportunities to practice. Some of the soldiers were friendly and helped me with words and sentences.

Our journey became part of a convoy of vessels after we left Singapore, and one night we saw one of our ships being torpedoed and sunk. All the ships were being bombed by the Americans. I saw a ship explode behind ours. The prisoners were all on the deck because we were about to evacuate the boat as the Japanese anticipated being bombed at any second. The crossing occurred in total darkness and so the nighttime crossing with the explosions was very dramatic.

As we got closer to Japan, it became more dangerous, and we were happy to land in Okinawa[60], and then near Nagasaki to take the train to Tokyo. Changing to Japanese food and chopsticks

---

60   This recollection is inaccurate. They docked in the Port of Moji, Kyushu.

*taught us a lesson but at least there was food. When we arrived
in Tokyo, we lived in a kind of Sumitomo Corporation employee
housing.[61]*

    Love, Daddy

I had gone for years wondering about the specific details of Dad's experience until Ineke Van Der Wal wrote her important book, *The Temple with the Chrysanthemums: Dutch Prisoners of War in Tokyo.* In the book she chronicled in detail the experience of the Dutch engineers and their families in Tokyo from the perspective of her grandmother, Beb Eninthoven, in a memoir of her life. Unfortunately, it was written in Dutch.

But in 2022, Seline, the woman who I'd met during our fateful luncheon in Bali in 2015 at the Ubud Writers and Readers Festival, let me know that Ineke's book had been translated into English. I was grateful to finally read Beb's account. However, precious little was written in her book about my family's experience as they were shunned by the group for perceived transgressions. The most serious included being German in their eyes, and as such, the family was treated as separate and apart from the others—a kind of prison within a prison for our family.

This attitude toward our family alarmed me when I first read Ineke's account, but then I remembered how Dad described the discrimination our family experienced in Java from the day they first arrived. I couldn't imagine having to adapt to a society that would always treat them unfairly, no matter what they did. A society that judged people not by who they were, but by their "inferior" accent and background. This coming during an era when people seen as the

---

61   This recollection is inaccurate. My research would uncover it was the Chilean Embassy.

"other" was justification for genocide. There is nothing written that explains what it must have been like to be held prisoner in such close quarters with people who disliked our family. I especially wonder about the toll it took on my grandmother and her sister, Frieda.

I don't know the psychology behind this kind of treatment. But, I believe that people sometimes need a way to take out their frustrations in traumatic circumstances. Finding a common "enemy" in our family would be one way for them to react during their chaotic, life-threatening situation. In the end, though, everyone was doing the best they could with the cards they had been dealt.

I'm incredibly grateful to Ineke and Beb for filling in so many blanks for me about the group's experience. I'm especially grateful that Ineke decided to translate her book into English so that I could have the opportunity to read her grandmother's account. Dad simply wasn't willing or able to speak very much about the details of the time he spent in Japan, let alone give the kind of rich detail in the way that Beb did.

Beb recollected the busy city of Singapore and talked of what she saw through the windows of the hotel and on their military-escorted outings to the park. She painted a picture of a bustling city with charcoal-fueled cars, crowded electric trams, and many Asian pedestrians. This last detail seems obvious to us. And yet, it wasn't one to be glossed over.

"From the park one can see the end of the bay and a row of graves with English names on them. The Dutch people are an attraction; local people come and watch, and wonder who the Europeans are. The Dutch, in turn, look at the Singapore people."[62]

---

62   Van Der Wal, Ineke, *The Temple with the Chrysanthemums: Dutch Prisoners of War in Tokyo*, Independently published, 2017. p. 177.

Beb also spoke of other encounters they had on their visits to the park in Singapore—police officers directing traffic and spotting an impressive Sikh[63] (also called a gurdwara) on a corner, Chinese shops, and how everyone in the hotel, the soldiers, and sailors were all Japanese. She mentioned spotting women she called "pariahs," dressed in blue, digging bomb shelters and others pulling rickshaws. She noted how the anniversary of the capture of Singapore by the Japanese was celebrated with a large procession on February 15 (only days after my dad's and grandpa's birthdays).

When Beb described the time in Singapore, the emphasis was on trying to educate the children. Her husband and leader of the engineers, Wim, taught his fourteen-year-old son, Wink, an entire book of trigonometry in the six weeks they were held at the hotel. With literally nothing to do for days upon days and then weeks upon weeks, eventually an intense boredom set in. Sometimes, the traffic below provided the only entertainment.

Beb wrote that their time in Singapore felt "interminable" as the families began to quarrel and created rivalries amongst themselves. Their food included sashimi, something they had never eaten before. Fresh fruit like papaya and pineapple were also brought to them everyday, only because Reinier and another in the group were severely jaundiced.

I remember how Dad had loved to carve pineapples when I was a girl. He went to great lengths to create a special spiral pattern eliminating each and every "eye" so there was little wasted in the carving and maximum pineapple to enjoy. I suspect that he took such unusual care and pride in serving pineapple this way because he'd learned the beautiful art during his captivity, undoubtedly to help his little brother Reinier.

---

63 https://www.worldgurudwaras.com/gurudwaras/central-sikh-temple-wadda-gurdwara-sin-gapore/

Beb mentioned a real win when they received the newspaper they'd been asking for, however it was a mixed blessing. While it contained news from the outside world, many were alarmed when they read about so many Japanese victories, including Burma, and many British deaths. Frustration grew when they wanted to know more about certain unfamiliar cities and locales mentioned, however no one had access to an atlas. I couldn't imagine Dad's frustration at not knowing his bearings and not being able to find out more about his surroundings.

Dad had a particular passion for atlases. We always had a globe and a large atlas book available at home as we grew up. I remember buying new globes and atlases to reflect the changes that had gone on in the world as new borders and countries were created over time. Dad even gave my first-husband and I an atlas as a wedding present.

Beb also wrote about random times Japanese soldiers or others walked into their rooms unannounced. One notable encounter included the time when men from the Sumitomo Corporation excitedly wanted to meet their new "colleagues" when they first arrived in Singapore. But the Dutch engineers gave them a rude welcome. Another time, their three "guards" wanted to talk politics.

Eventually the guards became close enough with the families that they confided their chilling task. Ineke wrote about Beb's recollections, saying, "The guards have orders to transport the entire group to Japan, and when in danger, they must sacrifice themselves for the group and tie everyone on rafts. The chance to be torpedoed appears to be the worst near Formosa (now Taiwan). Tsutsia sees this as a difficult assignment and is not looking forward to the next part of the journey."

The engineers and their families had hoped against hope for some sort of delay, some way to get out of their predicament. But it was clear that others were in control of their lives and there was little they could do. I can only imagine that reality setting in. Finally ending the interminable waiting at the Adelphi hotel meant that they'd be doomed to a perilous voyage of torpedo attacks and airstrikes. On March 8, 1944, the families were notified that they would be leaving Singapore the next day.

They took this seriously because the Japanese ordered them to give stool samples to check for diseases even though they had all been immunized for cholera, smallpox, and typhoid before they left Indonesia. They were so rushed that they secretly had to share their stool samples, because some of them couldn't eliminate in time. This provided a welcome moment of levity. Once they got the all-clear, they packed their luggage which soldiers promptly took away.

The next morning, they boarded a bus and headed to the busy port of Singapore. They were given some food for their first meal aboard the hell ship Teia Maru (帝亜丸), formerly the S.S. Aramis, once a French ocean liner which had been converted into an armed merchant cruiser after Japan seized the vessel in 1942. The families spotted their bags and picked up their heavy luggage for the required search by Japanese soldiers before boarding. But when their time came, red arm-banded Kempeitai officers closed in on the families and ushered them through the slog to their vessel. Almost immediately, a blackout signal sounded, and all the painted-black port holes needed to be closed and covered with blackout curtains.[64]

Dear Laura,

Because there were no markings on the Japanese ships to show they were carrying prisoners, we became targets for Allied

---

64   Van Der Wal, Ineke, *The Temple with the Chrysanthemums: Dutch Prisoners of War in Tokyo.* Independently published, 2017.

torpedoes. Prisoners killed on these Hell Ships lessened the burden of The Empire to care for us. Each cargo hold was jammed with prisoners in the hopes of killing as many of us as possible.

Love, Daddy

"Allied prisoners of war called them "hell ships," the requisitioned merchant vessels that the Japanese navy overloaded with POWs being relocated to internment on the Japanese Home Islands or elsewhere in the empire. The holds were floating dungeons, where inmates were denied air, space, light, bathroom facilities, and adequate food and water—especially water. Thirst and heat claimed many lives in the end, as did summary executions and beatings, yet the vast majority of deaths came as a result of so-called "friendly fire" from U.S. and Allied naval ships, submarines, and aircraft."[65]

For the first three days they sat at anchor in the port of Singapore, and no one was allowed on deck. Stifling conditions challenged the families and when a guard allowed them on deck for an hour, he was brutally reprimanded. Even on board, their movements were severely restricted. They were sequestered in one corner of the galley during mealtimes and weren't allowed on their part of the deck unless the ship was underway. Three days into the voyage, they were not allowed to bathe because it was too dangerous to be caught with no clothes on during an attack. Soon after, the Japanese turned the water off completely.

Dad rarely spoke about the voyage. He did mention that Grandma had been punched by one of the Kempeitai on the ship, but either chose not to reveal the details or just couldn't remember. Reinier

---

65   The Japanese "Hell Ships" of World War II https://www.history.navy.mil/browse-by-topic/wars-conflicts-and-operations/world-war-ii/1944/oryoku-maru.html

reckoned that as such a young boy during wartime his memories were easier to share because Dad faced a much more difficult experience. And yet, as the years wore on, it seemed Reinier suffered much more outward signs of trauma than Dad had. Even though my uncle's memories caused him anguish, he was curious about Dad's recollections, particularly in the years following Dad's death. Reinier called more often to check in with me and we enjoyed long conversations about our lives, his recollections, Dad's stories, and the progress of the book. While Reinier always seemed to enjoy our talks, he would also share how much trouble he had sleeping and how his anxiety had gotten worse over the years. Over time, it felt like our conversations were akin to pouring salt in a wound.

My heart went out to him. I walked a delicate line, wanting to answer his questions, know his stories, and yet not wanting to cause him undue pain. We've spoken less about the story as he has advanced in years. Whenever we speak on the phone or see each other in person his greetings are always so joyful and grateful. He has shown a sweet interest in my life, my writing, and my blended, growing family over the years.

During the visit I had with him in the 90s, Reinier talked about walking the decks of the hell ship as an eight-year-old boy. One of the Japanese soldiers placed him on his lap and showed him pictures of his own kids. Seeing the soldier's children made him seem less scary but made the experience of being held on the ship more confusing.

The passage was very cold. Onboard, Sumitomo provided warm clothes for the families since all they had were clothes for the tropics. But the men were too large to fit in most of them. Women weren't allowed to wear skirts and dresses. Unable to shower and with little access to food, they survived the ordeal by trying to sleep when they could in their clothes and lifejackets. They even wore their shoes in case they needed to muster on deck to evacuate in lifeboats since the ship could sink quickly. The adults would practice abandoning ship by placing the children in baskets and lowering them into the lifeboats. They became so familiar with the task that they could do the unthinkable job at a moment's notice in the dead of night, when they expected most of the attacks to occur.

Their ship was part of a convoy of sixteen ships made up of destroyers and oil tankers. While they knew they were sailing to Japan, information about the details of their passage were kept from them. The passage ended up taking sixteen days instead of the eight they expected because of the four submarine attacks they endured. Their ship was hit during one of the attacks, however the torpedo did not explode. Five of the ships in the convoy were destroyed during the passage, according to Beb.

"Any modern cargo vessel can survive a torpedo if it smashes fore or aft. Damaged ships being repaired in British yards today have limped home after being hit by more than one torpedo. But it takes only four or five minutes for any merchant ship to sink if the torpedo catches it amidships. Most cargo ships just break in two when hit in the middle, sink in three or four minutes—nine months' work shot to hell in four minutes."[66,67]

* * *

The Japanese didn't divulge the route to the families, but they observed the movements of the boat which sailed close to land,

---

66   *"MATTER OF MINUTES"*, Malaya Tribune, 12 July 1941, Page 6. Accessed 29 November 2022. Retrieved from NewspaperSG.

67   *The Pacific Strategy 1941-1945*. The National World War II Museum, New Orleans. Accessed December 1, 2022. https://www.nationalww2museum.org/war/articles/pacific-strategy-1941-1944

through the Malacca Straits then north across Indochina and beyond Cambodia. Most of the shoreline was natural, however at one point they spotted a large, deserted white monastery built into a rocky cliff along with a lighthouse and radio station. At various points, the convoy sought shelter in different bays in Indochina. On one occasion, a sea plane landed next to their ship delivering something, but the families had no idea what. They surmised that they had to seek safe harbor due to Allied aircraft being spotted in the region.

When the convoy crossed to Luzon—the largest and most populous island in the Philippines—they were attacked for the first time.

"At half past one at night the siren went off and they all made sure they quickly went upstairs. As soon as they arrived on deck the whole ship started to tremble, it was hit and it trembled for several minutes. They all stood at the railing and waited in silence, they were not allowed to talk, lights flashed around them and there was thundering noise everywhere. The ship fired a shot—it had a small auxiliary gun on the back—followed shortly by a second shot . . . It became clear to them that this was serious, because the men looking at the stars realized that their ship was now sailing due south at full speed heading back to where they came from. It all came unexpectedly, it was quick and then it was over and pitch-dark."[68]

During one of our chats, Dad talked about how one night during an attack, he stood on deck and saw an ocean full of ships on the Pacific. He talked of the stars, the beauty of the night and shared how he heard the sizzle of torpedoes as they headed for their boat, then missed. The situation heightened his senses and the way he told the story was more like a poet than a possible torpedo attack victim at the unknowing hands of the Allies.

---

68   Van Der Wal, Ineke, *The Temple with the Chrysanthemums: Dutch Prisoners of War in Tokyo*, Independently published, 2017. (pg. 186)

"The explosions looked like fireworks," Dad said.

An unreal, evil, yet captivating beauty bewitched Dad in that moment. Then, a torpedo hit a boat to their starboard. Dad said he grabbed the railing of his ship and struggled to walk on the deck. The engineers and families huddled together. Explosions turned the pitch-black darkness into daytime. Another torpedo sizzled through the water, a miss. With each attack a siren sounded, and they would awaken at night feeling their way out of the boat and onto the deck, counting the doors of the cabins as they walked to keep track of their whereabouts on the ship. The children had to be carried.

Surprisingly, the alarming, detailed account of my family's journey to Japan gave me closure. Finally understanding the pieces of the puzzle that had been missing for so long was like a tonic, satisfying my need to know the truth of their experience—especially around the torpedoing of their boat, the specific details of their voyage to Japan, and actual routes taken. I'd had nothing but my imagination to fill in the blanks for decades.

Finally learning these details helped me to move forward with the story, and yet these facts were also difficult to absorb and process, particularly the rare passages that mentioned my family in Ineke's book. Because our family had been ostracized, their point of view wasn't represented in the pages of the book. As I found myself filled with excitement at discovering some of the details of Dad's experience that he wouldn't or couldn't talk about, it began to sink in that much of what had happened to my family had been lost.

Ineke wrote about how the convoy continued on to what is now known as Kaohsiung, Taiwan. "After anchoring until the surviving ships were reunited, they set sail west to China when another attack changed their course. After they heard a thud that reverberated throughout the ship, more loud bangs sent them up the stairs to the deck where so many were assembled. The families had to shout *Kedomo! Kedomo!* (Children! Children!) to get the military to let them have more room. Just then they saw a gigantic wall of fire—one of the ships in their convoy had been hit. The Japanese screamed directions which the Dutch didn't understand. But their guides, Tsutsia and Takahashi, corralled the five families under their designated lifeboats and told them to *Doedoek* (Squat)! They did for hours until the dawn of the next day when they passed Okinawa toward China's East Coast."

As they sailed by Okinawa, they jammed on deck because of the constant threat of torpedo bombardment, however they had to suffer enduring gale-force Siberian winds. Because they cruised in pitch darkness, several of the destroyers in their convoy had near-miss collisions at sea. During their final passage in the inland Sea of Japan, they saw a crowded coast full of houses, factories, and a landscape peppered with red torii gates, entrances to Japanese temples. It was during this time that the Japanese confiscated a diary that one of the family members had been keeping.

It took some time to disembark from the *Teia Maru* once they found themselves at the end of their passage, at anchor at the port of Moji, on the southern Japanese island of Kyushu. They gathered their luggage to cries of *lekas, lekas* (quick, quick) in the lit-up harbor. They were startled yet grateful at the prospect of disembarking, and yet, as they needed to get their things together, it was difficult because they weren't used to living in light as they had been in total darkness for so long.

The back-and-forth process of leaving the ship by small boat to get clearance at a customs warehouse took days and proved endlessly aggravating and confusing. They were shuttled onto land and then back to the boat numerous times. It seemed as though they might be stuck in that kind of limbo for months.

Finally, the Japanese military cleared the families and allowed them to carry their luggage on a long walk to board a crowded, two-decker ferry which let them off across the harbor at Shimonoseki, on the main island of Honshu. After disembarking, they made another long walk to a station and boarded a train headed for Tokyo.

Would this be their final ride on their long, perilous journey?

Because the group stood out among the many Japanese on the ferry and at the train station, the families received a lot of attention. Rare colored Kimonos dotted the throngs of Japanese people who were dressed in mostly gray European dress. The women in Kimonos shuffled along in getas, outdoor wooden clog-like thongs, with two strips of wood attached to the bottom of their soles—something the Japanese would soon force the families to wear.

* * *

Only five months after my family disembarked, the *Teia Maru* sank:

"On 18 August 1944, TEIA MARU was on voyage in convoy HI-71 from Mako for Manila in Typhoon weather transporting troops and supplies for the defense of the Philippines. At 2312, U.S. submarine USS RASHER hits TEIA MARU with two torpedoes to her starboard side No.2 hold and engine room aft section. TEIA MARU catches fire and explodes at 23:40. 2,665 troops, civilians and crew are lost."[69]

---

69 https://www.wrecksite.eu/wreck.aspx?138479

CHILEAN EMBASSY, TOKYO

MARCH 25, 1944

Once on the train, they all had their own seats, however, the curtains needed to remain closed. Soon Tsutsia and Takahashi brought them some food in bamboo boxes, and they wrapped themselves up in their coats to try to stay warm and get some rest during the twenty-two-hour journey. They took an ancient route, what is now the high-speed Tokaido-Shinkansen rail line. It had its origins as feudal Japan's most important trading route to Tokyo.

They headed northeast past cities like Hiroshima, Akashi, Kobe, Osaka, Kyoto, Nagoya, and Hamamatsu. Finally, minutes after sunrise, they were allowed to open their curtains and get a first glimpse of Japan's bleak, overcrowded cities that soon opened up to landscapes of rolling green countryside. Just beyond plum trees in bloom, a distant view of snow-capped Mt. Fuji rose. After passing Yokohama, they arrived at the central train station in Tokyo—a small group of Dutch people among millions of the enemy.

At one point my family got lost because they had become separated from the group. Due to their disappearance, tensions escalated among the Japanese guards and the other families because they believed my family had tried to escape. They figured that since Grandpa had traveled through Tokyo about a decade before (when he returned to Indonesia to keep his job via the Trans-Siberian railroad and caught a boat out of Tokyo), he must have had contacts in Tokyo. But, our family had simply gotten lost.

Chaos ensued at the station when nothing seemed to be going to plan. Only after a long delay, did the Sumitomo representative arrive and instruct the group to take a commuter train to another part of the city. They traveled in two small groups and were reunited at the final stop, where they walked with their luggage, yet again, through the pitch-black city where blackout rules were strictly enforced, making tram tracks in the road difficult to spot. The young children of the Einthoven, Levenbach, and Lel's families were exhausted and had to be carried as it started to rain. Eventually the families were forced to stay at what was once the Chilean embassy, long vacated, located in a neighborhood with European architecture.

"The site was fenced in and there were several houses where beautifully landscaped gardens overlapped. There was a road with a driveway for cars, several garages and housing for the staff. The house where the Einthoven and Levenbach families lived is the largest on the terrain. Downstairs was a large dining room, a big sunroom, and a large reception hall. On the first floor there were four bedrooms, two for each family and a bathroom. The house was large and did not feel pleasant; the house where the other families lived was smaller.

The Hasenstab and Leunis families lived upstairs and the Lels family lived downstairs in two bedrooms and a sitting room. The houses were beautiful, but quite bare, as if Sumitomo had made the arrangements quickly. The large house was connected to a big kitchen, which Sumitomo used to provide food for receptions and dinners. Sometimes they would see a delivery van that picked up food for Sumitomo. It smelled good, but completely Japanese, a cuisine they were unfamiliar with. At first, there were Japanese people in two other houses on the property, but they left quickly. Some spoke briefly with the families, but all were afraid of being discovered because contact was strictly prohibited. They were decent people who were not hostile, but the intention clearly was to isolate the Dutch group and not to allow any contact with other people."[70]

Dear Laura,

Sumitomo arranged for us to stay at the empty Chilean Consulate Complex. It was surrounded by a wall and had a circular entrance drive with the main building in the center with two floors. Two other buildings were adjacent along the circular drive. We were given one building to stay in, and the other Dutch took rooms on the second floor of the main building. So, we were separated, I believe, because of my father's original background [being German]. We were fed in the dining room and any Sumitomo personnel stayed in the third house.

In the beginning, our conditions were a great improvement over Java and the ships. We had beds and were served regular meals in the dining room in the consulate building. The engineers were picked up in the morning and returned at night for several months. Then we started to hear the noise of airplanes bombing

---

70   Van Der Wal, Ineke, The Temple with the Chrysanthemums: Dutch Prisoners of War in Tokyo, Independently published, 2017. This English translation has been edited slightly and to reflect the past tense. pg. 196

part of Tokyo. We were in a distant suburb, and in the beginning
the bombing didn't affect us.
Love, Daddy

They were severely malnourished, and Sumitomo was appalled by their condition upon their arrival in Tokyo. Most were sickly and exhausted and lost a great deal of weight on the journey. The Japanese fed them well over the next days with much of the food coming from the Imperial Hotel. The fuel shortage in Japan meant that the central heating wasn't used except for the coldest months, and not run in March.

When they arrived, they met Mr. Hirata, their liaison with Sumitomo . . . The next day the men were given instructions by a high-ranking officer of Sumitomo. The men worked hard (13 consecutive days, the 14th day is free), or otherwise were severely punished. The men must swear an oath, which among other things stated that they would not try to escape. According to the Geneva Convention, such an oath was not allowed. The men made some money, but that money was not paid to them. Hirata controlled the money and if something needed to be paid, he provided for it."[71]

* * *

The oath to which the five men "employed" by Sumitomo must adhere. Non-adherence would be punished severely.

OATH

1. Regarding your personal conduct, you will be under the surveillance of the SUMITOMO COMMUNICATIONS INDUSTRY COMPANY, Ltd.—the said surveillance to be carried out at the

---

71 Ibid.

request of the Japanese authorities—and more particularly, you will be under the charge of the General Affairs Department of that Company.

Whatever you are directed to do by the said General Affairs Department, you shall attend to immediately, always considering it as an order coming from the Japanese Government, and shall not disobey or evade it through any misconduct.

2. As for your work and behaviour at the laboratory, you will be governed according to the rules and regulations issued by the laboratory.

3. Regarding your clothing, food, and dwelling, you are to take whatever is provided by the said Company and shall bear a portion of the cost and expenses thereof charged and arrived at by the said Company.

4. On your way back and forth between your home and laboratory, you are strictly prohibited from getting off the automobile in conveyance, and from riding together with any person other than those permitted by the Company.

5. You are strictly forbidden to go outside the designated area.

6. You are strictly prohibited from communicating with any person other than those in charge either over telephone or by telegram; and shall not communicate by letter with any people on the outside, nor listen to radio, nor take any photograph.

As to any reading matter, such as newspapers, magazines, and books, you may read only those that are permitted. [72]

---

[72] Ibid. pg. 195

* * *

Dear Laura,

In Tokyo, it was like a dream to be living in a civilized way, and a little bit unreal. The food was good, since we had a Japanese cook who had worked for the embassy. As it turned out, Sumitomo picked up the Dutch radio engineers, and, presumably, worked with them, and they returned every afternoon. I did my thing about the kitchen and offered to help the cook. He let me bring in supplies from the storeroom, which gave me an opportunity to spirit some supplies to our room, but there was really nothing that we wanted.

There was really nothing for me to do. I looked at the newspapers and tried to decipher the Katakana text. There was a small kitchen garden on a sloping piece of ground behind the kitchen of the main building. They grew green onions and cucumbers, and I started to put some rotten tomatoes in the ground to see if the seeds would germinate, and they did. The cook was impressed with my efforts and showed me what he used for fertilizers.

He had buried an old toilet in the ground, which could hold water which he filled with discarded fish bones after he fileted the fish for our meals. He used the fish soup to fertilize the kitchen plants. It smelled awful but the plants liked it. The toilet cover kept the stink out of the immediate area. Whenever you wanted some fertilizer, you opened the lid, scooped out some of the fluid with an old can and closed the lid. For my work, he gave me kitchen leftovers, which I took up to our rooms for Paps, Mams, Reinier, and Freida.

*As the months rolled around, conditions changed. The maids
left and the cook was the only one who remained as he lived in a
house on the grounds. Food became scarcer."*
	Love, Daddy

Dad would recall things and clarify his recollections over time.
At first, he recalled that they stayed in the French Embassy. However,
I did some online research in 2009 and discovered that the Dutch
families' movements within Japan had been recorded and according to
that document, the families were forced to live in the Chilean Embassy.
I consider it a miracle that I was somehow able to stumble upon that
information and have it confirmed in Ineke's book.

It pleased Dad to know the specific details that he couldn't recall.
He was surprised there was any accounting of them at all and that I
could discover such a thing on the Internet. I was too. I'd never gone
on such a scavenger hunt before, fueled by my desire to help Dad
remember, and also by my curiosity about more specific details of his
experience; details he had long buried.

* * *

Dad remembered soldiers standing guard outside their new
fenced-in accommodation at the former Chilean embassy. He and the
rest of the family set their bags down in the hallway. Those bags contained everything they owned in the world. Everything they had left.

Soon Reinier set off exploring the rooms, a child full of curiosity.
Far from the camps, he incredulously examined every corner of their
new accommodations. Grandpa helped Grandma and Frieda into one
of the bedrooms while Dad stared at the gardens outside. Glassy-eyed,

he followed his brother and watched him play. Reinier pulled Dad down onto a bed.

"We have real beds with sheets!"

Dad touched the fabric as if it was gold. Filthy and bruised, they stood in shock and began to rub the grime off of their hands and face. As Reinier settled into one of the beds and dozed off, Dad got a whiff of something delicious. Doubting his senses, he left his sleeping brother and followed his nose to the kitchen.

The chef, an elderly man named Hyokisan, glanced at Dad, then went back to chopping sweet potatoes. There were three cooks and two maids on staff at the compound.

Dad spoke in Japanese saying, "What are you cooking?"

That got Hyokisan's attention. He smiled and answered, "You speak well, I wonder, can you read?"

Dad shrugged his shoulders as if to say a little.

"Do you have a garden?" Dad said.

Hyokisan's eyes softened. He grabbed a newspaper and slid it across the kitchen counter. "Practice," he said.

Dad wrinkled his brow as he glanced at the paper filled with beautiful markings.

"When I was little, I learned Chinese. On Java, the Chinese shopkeepers set their list of prices on scrolls and sat them outside of their shops."

Hyokisan stopped chopping. He took in Dad's bruised, filthy body.

"I admired the beauty of the Chinese characters. So, Mams gave me lessons. I learned to paint them."

"You will read Japanese very well then. Chinese and Japanese use the same alphabet," Hyokisan said. He tossed chopped sweet potatoes in a pot of boiling water. Dad stared into the water and reached for them. Hyokisan grabbed Dad's wrist before he scalded his hand.

Dear Laura,

I was interested in Chinese characters as a young boy. I would see them at the shops growing up in Indonesia. All the shops in Indonesia were owned by the Chinese. And so, outside, they would list what was for sale and the prices. I loved the characters and asked my mom if I could learn how to write Chinese. She got me a teacher, and I learned. As soon as the Japanese saw I could actually write the Katakana characters, I was unique in their experience. I was interested in them. I was original in their experience. Katakana is the name of the Japanese alphabet.

In Samurai culture, we were all traitors to not die for our country. Foreigners like us were less than human in their eyes. We were scum. The Japanese soldiers admired Samurai. Samurai would commit suicide for an honorable death and never become prisoners of the enemy. There was a clash of civilizations.

Love, Daddy

* * *

" . . . at the end of May, a new resident appeared at the court, a special Kempeitai guard, Hamaichi Tanaka, who would live in the gate house with his family. From there he could look out over the group and the gate, which was erected soon after their arrival to prevent them from leaving the site. Tanaka accompanied the men to work . . . "[73]

Each day, the men took an hour and a half ride on crowded trains to Sumitomo's laboratories at Ikuta Noborito, where each of the

---

73   Ibid. pg. 200.

engineers received a design from the Japanese engineers and were asked to write long reports for the Japanese army. The only news they were able to get on these more and more crowded trips (due to a shortage of rail cars) were headlines that they could only memorize. During this time, they were able to understand that Paris had been liberated and that one of the important Japanese war ministers had been fired.[74]

All was not going well for Japan or for the engineers and their families. The winter of 1944-1945 would be the coldest in 40 years. To save calories, they bundled up and tried not to move. In February, Wim Einthoven contracted the flu and it spread to the rest of the families. They all seemed to get over it, however the flu returned after Wim decided to take a bath. He became very ill, and they summoned a doctor, but he didn't arrive right away and Wim died.

"The whole group is so crushed. Beb and Annie both feel that Wim died not only from pneumonia, but more because of his inability to adapt to their circumstances. This especially made a deep impression on them. The idea that he had to relinquish the Radio Laboratory to the Japanese and had to work for them. This was a huge inner struggle: he wanted to sabotage, but he knew he couldn't because he was also responsible for his wife and children. It is the tragedy of men who are unable to maintain control of their lives and ensure the safety of their children . . . Wink observed: 'What I believed has been the worst of all, is that he could do nothing about the situation. We had to wait. Maybe it was the intent of the Japanese to kill us in order to keep things secret and that we wouldn't learn anything until the very end.'"[75]

---

74 Ibid. Small edits made to reflect the past tense.
75 Ibid. page 228.

FIREBOMBING OF TOKYO

"Seventy years ago, on the night of 9-10 March, in the Japanese capital [Tokyo], 334 American B-29 bombers dropped thousands of tonnes of incendiary bombs on the city's crowded wooden neighbourhoods. They started a fire storm that burned at over 1,000 degrees and killed more than 100,000 people. It was an event that dwarfed even the atomic bombing of Hiroshima, yet it's been all but forgotten around the world—even in Japan."[76]

Tuesday, March 9, 2010, seemed a day like any other with Dad. However, once he began speaking about surviving the Firebombing of Tokyo, the day became anything but. When we would talk about his war experiences, his recollections often ran the gamut of history. But on that day, of all the stories he could have shared, he particularly spoke about the firebombing.

I had no idea that it was the 65th anniversary of the firebombing of Tokyo, and he never mentioned the fact when we spoke. Only when

---

76 Wingfield-Hayes, Rupert. WWII fire-bombing of Tokyo by U.S. Remembered 70 years on. BBC. https://www.bbc.com/news/av/world-asia-31809257 March, 2015. Accessed 2022.

I got back to the guest room at my sister's house (she kindly hosted me on almost every trip I made to Florida and we had so many good times, enough to fill another book) and Googled the firebombing did I put our conversation in its historical context. My random trip to see Mom and Dad coincidentally fell on the 65th anniversary. Had it not, who knows whether he would have shared his memories with me.

When I first arrived at Mom and Dad's home that day, we had breakfast in the dining room of their building. At the end of our meal, Mom asked me if I had received the itinerary for my visit with them. When I confessed I hadn't, she handed it to me when we got back to their apartment. It had been neatly typed as their itineraries always were. This was the very first time I remember absolutely loving the experience of receiving their itinerary. I had no idea how much I would miss them, or how little time was left.

After a few hours of conversing in the morning, we went to tea at a local place Mom and Dad enjoyed. Although Dad didn't care for the tea very much that day, saying it wasn't flavorful enough, he loved the scones and drenched his in clotted cream and strawberry sauce. After tea, we returned to their apartment again so Dad and I could continue our discussion.

"When the B-29 firebombs started, fires came so close to the houses," Dad said. "We were protected, but were transferred from the houses to a camp during the firebombing. We were taken to Kotakuji and were there from the firebombing until the liberation, less than six months."

His electric blue eyes stared out the window as if to find his next thoughts.

"The Japanese had no food. The war effort and constant bombing interrupted everything. I had not seen an egg for years—the only thing

I ate was sweet potatoes. When the bombing started, my father stopped working. The Japanese dug holes in the ground and buried everything they didn't want burned."

His revelations sent chills down my spine. Back then, I felt like these stories were gold. Understanding Dad in new ways brought to light a past that I could hardly guess at. One he didn't remember until we sat down to speak to each other day by day over the decades.

After our afternoon session back in 2010, Dad had a nap and Mom and I walked around a pond in their complex. They both enjoyed the view of it from their apartment. Mom and I sat together on a picnic bench, admiring the fountain in the middle of the pond, enjoying a sweet moment of stillness. *Far Niente*, as Dad would say. It meant the joy of doing nothing and was also the name of a fine wine he came to enjoy on his travels to see me and my family in Southern California.

I loved being with Mom during special, quiet moments like the one we had while sitting on the picnic bench that afternoon. I lived a continent away. And yet, when we saw each other again and again, it felt like no time had passed at all. Dad liked to tell stories and she often admiringly looked on. How many lovely stories of her own she had to tell. And what a strength and support she was in our endeavor to work to tell the family's story. How easy it was to sit together with Mom and talk about any and everything.

As we stared out over the pond and watched the patterns the fountain made in the water, every airborne drop and splash, I recalled how much Mom and Dad loved fountains. We had one in our yard growing up and it was a real event to set it up in the spring after the icy snow of winter had "gone to its reward" as Mom would say.

The fountain in our backyard garden, circa 1971
(Mike, Me, Mom, Dad, Suzy, and Mark).

We wheeled each part of the fountain out of the garage, three heavy concrete graduated bowls set one on top of the other, separated by bulbous pillars, the smallest of the bowls on top. The fountainhead, shaped as if winds had wound the petals of a flower around it, gently performed all summer, splashing water up through the center of the fountain then cascading droplets down the rims of the bowls until they pooled into the largest bowl at the bottom. Dad had poured a concrete foundation for the fountain to sit upon and Suzy and I placed our hands in the concrete side by side.

Dad and Mom loved fountains so much, at the turn of the millennium they purchased a beautiful one for the courtyard of my newly minted dream home in Dos Vientos, a lovely Spanish villa. I suppose I shouldn't have been surprised that they loved watching the water so much, as Dad spent his life designing hydroelectric projects.

"We love to walk around the pond two times together every day," Mom said as we enjoyed the view from the bench.

I remembered their walks on the winding path Dad and my brothers had constructed at our childhood home. Mom and Dad placed their arms around each others' waists and strolled together on summer nights enjoying the garden they had built together. How lovely the memory is today. Later, in the years before Mom passed away in 2020, she would often remind me how important it is to enjoy my surroundings.

> *Dear Laura,*
>
> *The B-29's flew very high, out of reach of the Japanese Zero fighters. Because of the great height, the bombing was not very accurate, but Tokyo is a large city, and the bombs were effective in starting large fires among the wood and paper houses of the city. The campaign continued, and, after some months, the fires became close . . . Sumitomo decided that the Tokyo location was too dangerous for their Dutch Radio Engineers, and they found an area in the hills above the city of Nagoya in the central Honshu Islands. Things were pretty disorganized after our train ride to Nagoya.*
>
> *Love, Daddy*

* * *

The deafening sound of buzzing propellers sent people scrambling. Fires erupted, with explosions that made the ground rumble. Air-raid sirens blared, and fire whipped throughout the wooden city of Tokyo.

"Welcome to a special edition of BBC News. The latest out of Tokyo . . . They set to work at once, sowing the sky with fire. Hell could be no hotter. Barely a quarter of an hour after the raid started, the fire, whipped by the wind, began to scythe its way through the density of that wooden city. A huge borealis grew over the quarters closer to the center, the bright light dispelled the night."

An evening sky of fire and smoke illuminated a swarm of B-29s flying over the city.

"B-29s long wings, sharp as blades, could be seen through the oblique columns of smoke rising from the city, suddenly reflecting the fire from the furnace below, black silhouettes gliding through the fiery sky to reappear farther on, shining golden against the dark roof of heaven."

Below, Japanese reacted to the spectacle with a combination of fascination and fright. As had been observed before, some buried their valuables in the dirt.

"The Japanese near me were out of doors or peering up from their holes, uttering cries of admiration—typically Japanese—at this grandiose, almost theatrical spectacle. Soon it was raining fire," Dad said, as he recounted the event.

Dad and the families watched as fire rained down on the embassy and its gardens. Soon, they realized that the fire wasn't local, but that they'd somehow been caught in a firestorm that burned the wooden home directly behind them. Then a bomb, covered in some kind of thatch (which they later discover was napalm[77]) landed in the garden. The thatch was on fire, but the bomb didn't explode.

---

[77]   *The atomic bomb wasn't the only weapon of mass destruction at Hiroshima and Nagasaki.* Boot, Max. The Washington Post. August 8, 2020. Accessed December 2022. https://www.washingtonpost.com/opinions/2020/08/08/b-29-not-atomic-bomb-was-first-weapon-mass-destruction/

Terrified, they feared the worst and wanted to prevent the fire from burning the embassy, where they were held. They put out fires as best they could with a bucket brigade from the second story, targeting a palm tree near the embassy. One of the Japanese cooks who beat the tree to try to put out the fire became deluged by the prisoners' bucket brigade. But, he said nothing about it. It was all hands on deck—captives and captors—all extinguishing the large fire together. Then they put out small ones that had flared up all over the embassy grounds.

The Japanese went on to chop down all the palm trees in the front yard of the embassy as they caused an extreme fire hazard. This left only three precious trees in the back garden, the families' one-time sanctuary which had been loved by all. By Ineke's account, my Dad chopped down the last of these palm trees in the backyard. While he did so to protect the families from the fire danger, she mentioned that his act caused the others in the group to alienate him, claiming that the trees were too beautiful to cut down, even in a firestorm. The madness also found Tenaka ranting about how valuable the trees were, at 1000 yen each.

* * *

The aircrews were afraid they were going to be slaughtered when they were sent to bomb Tokyo on March 9, 1945, but they were the ones who did the slaughtering. Their napalm bombs whipped up a firestorm that destroyed much of central Tokyo and killed some 100,000 people— fewer than at Hiroshima (roughly 130,000 dead) but more than at Nagasaki (more than 60,000 dead). Descriptions of the firebombing of Tokyo are as revolting as those of the atomic bombing of Hiroshima; even the aircrews were sickened by the smell of roasting human flesh.

The B-29s went on to target more than 60 of Japan's largest cities in similar fashion. They laid waste to 178 square miles—nearly three times the size of Washington, D.C.—and only 3.5 percent of the total area damage was inflicted by the atom bombs. If President Harry S. Truman was not overly troubled by the decision to use the atomic bomb, it was in part because he realized that the U.S. Army Air Forces had already been killing German and Japanese civilians en masse. It would not have mattered much to the average Japanese whether death came from atomic or napalm bombs. The major difference is that while it took 334 B-29s to demolish central Tokyo, only one B-29 was needed over Hiroshima and Nagasaki.[78]

People who took shelter in concrete buildings were roasted. People who tried to escape the fire by jumping into rivers were trampled to death by people who jumped on top of them. The water in shallow channels became so hot that people were cooked. The firestorms that ran through the streets caused tremendous heat and a lack of oxygen that caused people to be cremated alive. All these scenarios took place in less than six hours.[79]

* * *

A few weeks later, all eight of the Dutchmen who defended the embassy against the fire, including my dad, were rewarded with 50 yen each by Sumitomo representatives for their valiant service in protecting the property. They weren't able to do anything with the money though, and the gesture seemed odd.

---

78 Ibid.
79 Caidin, Martin. *A torch to the enemy — The Fire Raid on Tokyo*. Ballantine Books, New York, 1960.

By the beginning of April, the men returned to work as the conditions in Japan worsened. With the trams overrun, their commute to work was much harder because the rails had been incinerated. When firebombings returned in the middle of April, food and fuel supplies became extremely limited. Ineke mentions in her book about how the families added sawdust to give their bread some substance. She observed, "They are hungry but so is the Japanese population. But the Japanese have a stoic creed that believes not in material things and only in the strength of the spirit. It is believed that if the will is strong enough, the Japanese citizens will thrive. Illness is simply the result of a weakness of spirit."

"The personal tolls mounted as twenty-one people lived together, packed into two homes resulting in fist fights, disagreements between spouses, fighting the constant cold by keeping small hibachis lit, kids who have no freedom to explore and get away from their parents, and the seemingly hopeless situation, and total seclusion takes its toll. The men discover on their outings to and from work that the war isn't going well for the Japanese."[80]

In mid-April the Allies firebombed Tokyo again.

"Everyone is happy with the bombings: it is finally a sign that something is happening. Beb writes: 'We sit for hours in the shelter, but I see it as a gift for my birthday.' It is unfortunate that Wim cannot experience these bombings. They know that the chance of being hit by such a bomb is real, but their life chances are already slim, so when a bomb hits, at least it will all be over."[81]

---

80 Van Der Wal, Ineke, The Temple with the Chrysanthemums: Dutch Prisoners of War in Tokyo, Independently published, 2017. pg. 239
81 Ibid. pg. 238.

APRIL, 1945

On the deck of the destroyer, USS *Lardner,* the American flag flies at half-staff behind Marines listening to the radio. Ron and the rest of the soldiers stare out at the calm Pacific, bewildered.

"We interrupt this program to bring you a bulletin from CBS News . . . President Roosevelt is dead. The president died of a . . . .cerebral hemorrhage. All we know so far is that the president died at Warm Springs in Georgia . . . "

"It happens to everybody. The big ones too," one of the guys said.

"He was an awful smart guy . . . "

"Sure. But he's not the only smart guy. We've got others. Lots of them . . . " Ron said.

"I just feel like I got punched in the gut. For my money that guy was one of the greatest guys that ever lived. You can put him next to Lincoln or Washington . . . "

"The Germans and Japs identified Roosevelt with America so long they might think Roosevelt is America!"

"Yeah, well, we ain't dead in the water . . . not by a long shot!"

A palpable, eerie silence filled the moment of dread as their beloved leader was no more. As they swayed in the gentle ocean waves, a familiar voice with a tortured charm filled the air.

"This is the Zero Hour calling in The Pacific," Tokyo Rose's voice said over the radio. "Greetings everybody. This is your number one enemy, your favorite playmate Orphan Ann of Radio Tokyo. We are ready again for a vicious assault to your morale here in the South Pacific. I know you hate us. But don't let hate ruin a good time. It's poisoning the whole system. What you need is some good jive. It helps you relax. All set? Here's a song called, "Hey Pop, I don't want to go to work."

Kotakuji

"A demand has been made from the United States to transfer prisoners of war to safer areas in Japan. Sumitomo will be handing you over to the Ministry of the Interior."

The families didn't know what to think about their change in status. Was it good news?

"I'd like you to know that Holland has been liberated," Hirata said. "Don't worry. It won't last long."

What won't last long? Could they assume that their one-time jailer was admitting their imminent defeat? It gave them hope, and yet, would they survive until that day? So much was unknown. They had no power to affect an outcome in their lives except to do what they were told. Their blurry reality became even more drastic as the food dried up. The Japanese sent seven trunks for the families to pack their belongings. Since they ordered the families to take their quilts and blankets, they suspected they might have to sleep on the floor again. But where?

On May 15, 1945, the families traveled through the night by train and then by trucks to a destination unknown. Using their bedding to make the truck ride more comfortable, they had no idea where they were or where they were heading as they took the two-hour drive through a gorgeous countryside—a poor, populous place—filled with wild azaleas in full bloom, and bountiful and fragrant pink lilacs. Behind their truck they heard Japanese children call out, "*Oranda, Oranda* (Holland, Holland)!"[82]

Suddenly the truck came to a stop and Kempeitai officers instructed them to unload their suitcases at a fork in the road where a Torii gate marked a small walkway that wound through the country-side. The families walked through the gate and up a path. After they reached the temple, the children were put to sleep on a 20' x 40' front porch, the only space allotted to the 21 people who slept on 3' x 6' flea-infested tatami mats. Somehow, my family was later able to secure a small room for themselves within the temple.

The strange ceremony that welcomed them when they arrived included the Kempeitai giving the adults a long lecture in Japanese about forbidden things they must not do, with a warning not to venture more than 100 meters beyond the temple (a distance a little less than the size of a football field). Making trips to the nearby life-giving river out of the question.

Down the road, fifteen other Italian prisoners were held in a prison close to Kotakuji. Once Hitler invaded Italy, Italians in Japan had to make a terrible choice—sign allegiance to Mussolini or deal with the consequences. In 1943, Italian anthropologist Fosco Maraini

---

82   Van Der Wal, Ineke, The Temple with the Chrysanthemums: Dutch Prisoners of War in Tokyo, Independently published, 2017. pg. 241. Tenses adjusted.

and painter Topazia Aliata refused to sign their allegiance to Mussolini, so they were imprisoned with their three young daughters, Dacia (7), Yuki (4) and Toni (2).

The Dutch group was in utter shock to find themselves at the Kotakuji temple outside of Nagoya. Of course, they didn't know exactly where they were, yet. But a visit from Mr. Grenwell, an official at the Swedish Red Cross, would soon enlighten them. Because Sumitomo wasn't responsible for the prisoners anymore, the Japanese allowed Mr. Genwell to visit the families a few weeks after they arrived.

Grenwell knew about their detention because the Red Cross was located in the embassy district in Tokyo. However, the Japanese government never allowed the Red Cross to visit. He also brought the news that the Allies had destroyed the entire embassy district during a bombing attack on May 25th, only ten days after the families arrived at the temple. Through him, the families tried to send telegrams to let their relatives know that they were alive, but those went unanswered.

* * *

Sleeping on the ground again was very painful as they had lost so much weight. There was no padding on their body and so they were unable to find any comfort. Dad talked about how bad the fleas were, saying they were nearly impossible to eliminate, so there was no choice but to live with getting bitten. Outside, a single hammock provided a bit of a refuge from the fleas when the weather was good.

The primitive living conditions included no running water or sanitation. When the water well ran dry, the prisoners had to dig another well. When they did, the water wasn't potable, so they had to boil it before drinking. There was little left for bathing, so once a week they filled a bathtub with water and everyone had to wash in the same water without soap, which also had been a scarce commodity for some time. To boil the water, the men made stoves out of clay, but other than boiling water, there was precious little to cook.

They were starving for food and news. Dad once told me, "When you are starving, food is all you think about. It's constantly on your mind." And that went double for news. They were ready to risk their lives to find out whatever they could to keep their hopes up and stay alive.

They tried to live on what they could forage, like berries. They also began to appreciate the exceptional surroundings, and the welcomed camaraderie of the Italian prisoners from time to time. But even those moments of respite couldn't hide the fact that they might not survive. Without food, their days were numbered. Their rations had gotten down to 800 calories a day, at best. Foraging for food and news—activities they most engaged in—might kill them. But, they were dead men walking anyway.

Dear Laura,

We were assigned a wing with an open hall and one room. We ended up sleeping on futons and on the tatami straw floors. Here the food supply was a problem, because the monks did not have enough to eat themselves. We were lucky to get sweet potatoes and some stew they cooked up. My main problem was the flea infestation. The fleas lived in the tatami straw floors and I had a lot of trouble sleeping with the fleas crawling over me and biting me.

The temple was located on a hill and a village was down below. It was not very high, maybe 100 ft. and the slope and it was easy to walk from the temple to the village below. Adjacent to the temple were the temple gardens and vegetable areas, where Japanese women were harvesting sweet potatoes which provided the only source of sugar available. We could walk around but not leave the temple grounds I started my normal activities helping the women harvesting the sweet potatoes and harvesting some for myself, which I added to our meager rations, mainly noodles. I was pretty fluent in Japanese and could talk to the people . . .

All Europeans were segregated and put in special detention areas. One of them was close to the temple and mainly housed Italians, who had better accommodations as members of the Axis Powers. We were allowed to use their bath once a week. That Camp Commander also controlled the people housed at the temple. I was pretty good at speaking Japanese, and I had learned some Japanese Katakana script, and with my knowledge of Chinese characters, I could make out some information from the Japanese newspapers.

Love, Daddy

* * *

Shouts of Kempeitai officers came through the paper-thin walls.

Grandpa turned to Dad, "What are they saying?"

A Kempeitai officers shouted louder.

"They're complaining . . . ," Dad said.

"About . . . us?"

"It's about the monks, something about the monks," Dad said.

Grandpa sat on the floor and Dad joined him. Fleas jumped all over their legs and they swiped at hundreds of them. Grandma took a bedsheet out of her bag, unfolded it and placed it on the ground. Her dull eyes unnerved Grandpa as he and Dad scooted onto the sheet.

They heard a knock at the door. A few monks entered and bowed to Grandpa. One of them pulled a radio out from under his robes. He spoke softly in Japanese.

Dad translated, "He says they'd rather have a radio that works, if they're going to die anyway," Dad said.

Grandpa took the radio. He felt the weight of it, then stashed it under some flea-infested blankets. "Have him return in a few days," he said.

The monk raised prayerful hands, bowed, then left as two Kempeitai pointed their guns into the room. When one spoke to Dad in Japanese, Dad rose to his feet.

"What's going on?" Grandpa asked.

"They're taking me to see the Camp Commander," Dad said.

As Grandpa rushed to Dad's side, one of the officers pointed his gun at Grandpa, who froze immediately.

Dad walked out the door at gunpoint. The Kempeitai barked a command. Dad did what they said and flicked as many fleas off his feet and legs as he could. After examining Dad, the soldiers marched him a few short steps into the temple as the commander walked around him in a tight circle. Eyebrows raised, he gave Dad the once over.

The sixty-year-old man with a shaved head wore polished black boots.

"You speak Japanese. How did you learn?" he said.

"Prison."

"Many Dutch don't know Japanese."

Dad's gaze settled on some ancient scrolls mounted on the temple walls.

"Look at me when I'm talking to you!"

Weakened from hunger, Dad started to feel faint. Sukio's apparition appeared, and he walked behind the commander. Sukio looked over at Dad and whispered something only Dad could hear, "Lighten your life, sing like the songbirds."

Dad suddenly took a deep breath, trying to remember what it was like to be free, walking among the rice paddies. What it was like to eat food.

"Can you read Japanese?"

Dad hesitated, enraptured by the presence of the ghost of Sukio.

The commander rapt his cane on the temple floor.

Dad came to attention.

"I said, can you read Japanese?"

"Yes," Dad said.

A phantom songbird flew into the room and met with Sukio's gaze. The songbird landed on a monk's writing table. A blank parchment lay beside a brush and well of black ink. Dad picked up the brush as if to honor it. Sukio's apparition stood beside Dad, and gave him a peaceful, reassuring look. The songbird flew to the bamboo ceiling.

Dad dipped the brush into the ink as the commander walked behind him and stuck his neck out to peer over Dad's shoulder. Sukio made room for the commander.

Dad artfully drew the Japanese character for *beauty*. The commander's expression softened for a second. Dad, Sukio, and the commander silently regarded the character.

The commander slipped the brush out of Dad's grasp, painting effortlessly, beautifully.

"You are unusual in my experience. No blue-eyed boy knows the way of Bushidō."

Dad tilted his head. They regarded the character the commandant had painted.

"The Way of the Warrior. The ancient way. Death before defeat. Before dishonor. Of Bushidō's seven virtues only one, Meiyo, rules them all."

"Honor? What are the others?" Dad asked.

"Duty. Courage. Benevolence. Morality. Truthfulness. Loyalty."

The commander walked around the desk to face Dad. "You are now camp interpreter. You will translate whenever I wish and whatever I wish to communicate to your fellow prisoners. Begin with this . . . "

When the commandant handed Dad a piece of paper, Dad bowed very low.

The commander stared at some monks processing into the temple. As if in a trance, he continued, "As a Samurai, I must strengthen my character. As a human being, I must perfect my spirit."

* * *

Dear Laura,

Sumitomo decided that the Tokyo location was too dangerous for their Dutch Radio Engineers, and they found an area in the hills above the city of Nagoya in the central Honshu Islands. Things were pretty disorganized after our train ride to Nagoya. The Sumitomo Engineer found that there was not enough room for the Dutch families in the fenced-in area provided for the foreign detainees. There was a nearby Buddhist temple called Kotakuji that had some unused rooms, and we were taken there. There were only low Japanese style tables in the room as the Japanese sat on the Tatami woven floor. We slept right on the woven straw floor as was Japanese custom. What we did not bargain for was that the Tatami mats were infested with fleas. This made sleeping very uncomfortable. Fortunately, my mother had taken sheets from our Tokyo house with us, so we had at least a sheet between us and the fleas.

The temple was a working place of reverence with monks praying and ringing bells at intervals. We ate with the monks. The food was simple, mainly sweet potatoes and vegetables. The monks grew the sweet potatoes behind the temple. Rice was never served because it was exported to the Japanese troops spread out over the Greater Prosperity Sphere. Every day, one of our group went to the Main Camp and reported for the Dutch Families. After the fall of Mussolini, when the Italians no longer belonged to the Axis Powers, Italians came into our prison camp. Most could speak fluent Japanese, having been either in business or the Diplomatic Service in Japan. They were a source of news of the outside world, and we started to know that the war was coming to an end in Europe.

The big recollection was about the B-29 bombers. There were two days and nights when there were so many B-29s in the sky that I could not see any sky. In fact, the bombers flew wing to wing and maybe a plane's length behind each other. The amazing fact was that the U.S. had so many B-29s coming from different airfields to create this armada. In those two days they destroyed the City of Nagoya, which was about fifty miles south of the temple, with incendiary bombs

My father was intrigued by the Buddhist temple, the monks, and admired the scrolls that they had hanging. One was Buddha contemplating an apple. He also noticed a radio that was not *playing and found out from the monk that it was broken. My dad told the monk that he was a radio engineer and might be able to fix it. Apparently, it was a loose connection, and he was able to repair it. Word of repairing the temple radio spread around and people began bringing their broken radios to the temple for Paps to repair. Soon, he received many radios to repair, and from the ones he could not fix, he assembled a radio that received the BBC broadcast. My mother could understand the English broadcast. Of course, we had to keep it very quiet. With the radio and the newspaper, we heard about the two atom bombs at Hiroshima and Nagasaki.*

Love, Daddy

THE VOICE OF THE CRANE

KOTAKUJI TEMPLE, NAGOYA, JAPAN
AUGUST 15, 1945

"The enemy has begun to employ a new and most cruel bomb. Should we continue to fight, it would not only result in an ultimate collapse and obliteration of the Japanese nation, but would also lead to the total extinction of human civilization," Emperor Hirohito said over the makeshift POW camp loudspeakers.

As camp interpreter, Dad understood what the Emperor had said, but the other POWs didn't. Bewildered, they looked to Dad as the soldiers guarding them lowered their guns in disbelief.

"We've met a superior force and we must now bow to that superior force," The Emperor continued.

The commandant of the POW camp turned and bowed to my dad, a twenty-one-year-old prisoner, then handed Dad the keys to the camp. They felt heavy in Dad's boney hands. Stunned, Dad stood speechless. *Was this real?* How many times had fantasy felt like reality in his starved, punishing existence?

B-29s faintly buzzed in the distance, and grew louder. The terror in the commander's eyes gave Dad the clarity to understand the reality of the situation. He stared at the keys. He held freedom in the palm of his hand.

The commander looked Dad in the eyes and said, "What is your command?"

"I want to go to Kyoto," Dad said.

The commander's head tilted slightly to the side and his expression softened. As he kept his eyes trained on Dad, the thunder of B-29s became deafening. With 141-foot wingspans, 99-foot fuselages, each weighing 105,000 pounds, hundreds of the bombers soon blocked out the sun. The sight reminded Dad of the sky over Tokyo during the firebombing, when the same planes roared in formation, one after another, blotting out the blue sky.

As Dad's gaze followed one of the planes, white leaflets sprayed into the sky, forming a paper cloud. They fluttered down slowly, coming to rest on the temple grounds, landing in plum trees, on rooftops, and among sunflowers. Dad reached up and caught one mid-air then pulled it in close enough to read. He clung tightly to the paper and smiled.

* * * * *

I sat across from Dad in his study in Florida, when he carefully slipped a torn, dirty, once-crumpled leaflet out of one of his manila folders and handed it to me. I read the message The Allies had written in many languages, "Allied Prisoners : The Japanese Government has surrendered. You will be evacuated by ALLIED NATIONS forces as soon as possible . . . "

Then a thud shook the ground and knocked him off his feet. Belts, pants, and tin cans had exploded out of a giant wooden crate. A pool of ketchup oozed out of some of the cans and formed a large red puddle. Everyone nearby had been sprayed with ketchup. It looked like the scene of a mass shooting, without the guns. Without the blood.

The prisoners staggered toward each other in disbelief, trying to comprehend the unfolding scene. Dad bent down, scooped ketchup up out of the dirt with his bare hands and lapped it up. Soon, the other prisoners joined in. Dad couldn't stop slurping the ketchup mixed with mud and swallowed the tangy, gritty mess by the handful.

"The whole Japanese nation was notified of the Emperor's address on August 15th. It was broadcast over loudspeakers at 4 p.m., Tokyo time. Emperor Hirohito ordered an end to all hostilities, telling his people that they must "endure the unendurable and suffer the insufferable."[83]

* * *

Dear Laura,

Bowing is a Japanese custom, with a lot of tradition and meaning behind it. For instance, the deeper you bow, the more respect you show. For the Emperor to bow is extraordinary, as the Son of Heaven, he does not bow, every other Japanese person bowed to him. This was a common custom, even the highest general or admiral bowed to the Emperor. So the meaning of the words he spoke, saying that he, the Emperor, bowed to a Superior

---

[83] *Japan surrenders, bringing an end to WWII.* History.com Editors. History.com. A&E Television Networks. February 9, 2010. Last updated August 31, 2021. Accessed December 30, 2022. https://www.history.com/this-day-in-history/japan-surrenders

Power, meant that he surrendered to the United States. The prison commander and General MacArthur understood that.

Love Daddy

"None of us had ever heard the Emperor's voice before yesterday," the commander said as he walked to the window, staring at the temple garden.

Dad stood at attention on the other side of the commander's desk, a habit he found hard to break. His job as camp interpreter had given him a higher status than any other prisoner. And with the keys in his hand, Dad had even more power than the commander. The power to run the camp. The power to command the commander however he chose. The freedom to go anywhere he pleased.

"The Emperor is a God to us. His is the Voice of the Crane . . . the voice of authority. The final word," the commander said. Dazed, he stared out of the window as if he was in search of something that could help him comprehend the Emperor's shameful behavior.

Dad silently picked up one of many white leaflets sitting on the commander's desk and began to fold it.

"You can't surrender God! God doesn't bow to anyone!" the commander yelled, turning away from the window to face Dad. "It is not the Way of the Warrior," he whispered.

When Dad finished his last fold of the leaflet, he walked gingerly to the other side of the commander's desk. Dad bowed low, then handed him a white paper crane, a symbol of peace. The commander stared at the paper crane for a while, overcome. After regaining his composure, he twirled the crane slowly between his finger and thumb and raised it to the level of his eyes.

"As a boy, I was told that simply hearing the Emperor's voice would unleash The Gates of Hell," he said. The commander looked past the twirling crane at Dad, then whispered, "But Hell . . . was unleashed . . . by you." He bowed low to Dad. As low as Dad had been forced to bow to him and other camp commanders during his captivity.

President Truman announced the unconditional and unqualified surrender of the Japanese at 7:00 p.m. on August 14, 1945. August 15th would forever be known as V-J day (Victory over Japan Day). General MacArthur accepted the formal surrender for the United Nations. The war that began with the infamous attack on Pearl Harbor December 7, 1941, the largest and deadliest war in history, killing somewhere between 35 to 60 million people, involving thirty countries, had finally come to an end.

* * *

Dad told me the story about the commander giving him the keys to the camp during one of our visits.

"When Emperor Hirohito saw the devastation of the two atom bombs (one dropped on Hiroshima on August 6, 1945, and one dropped on Nagasaki three days later), it is reported that he asked his generals what they are going to do about it, and they replied: "Fight to the last man." Hirohito did not want an atom bomb dropped on Tokyo, and arranged for the broadcast. After the broadcast, the surrender was very clear to the Japanese commander of the camp who came to me and told me that I was now in charge and handed me the keys to the prison camp. I was the interpreter, and, therefore, he could talk to me. Amazingly, I took this in my stride and asked him to get me tickets to Kyoto. Of course I never went, because orders came for all of us to assemble at the beach at Hamamatsu for evacuation."

Dad took out some parchment paper, India Ink, and a brush. He carefully used the brush to paint a few symbols. One meant "man" and the other meant "country."

"The characters of the Chinese were similar to that of the Japanese," Dad said. "Their newspapers had these symbols in them, and the newspapers were brought into the camp. I learned the Japanese script language easily because I knew the Chinese characters."

"What was the name of the newspaper you translated?" I asked.

Dad shook his head and searched his memory, then the name came to him, "The Shimbun newspaper."

It is now called *The Asahi Shimbun*.[84]

"Dad," I asked. "In that moment when you were told you could ask for anything you wanted . . . .why didn't you just ask to get the hell out of Japan? Why did you want to arrange a trip to Kyoto?"

"The inquiring mind," he said, flashing his gorgeous smile. "Kyoto was known not to have been bombed because of the many temples there. I wanted to see a place that hadn't been bombed. I had seen too much devastation. I needed to see something beautiful."

"So, how did you get down to the beach to be rescued?"

"The Foreigners Camp near our Kotakuji temple prison was called Hirose. We received word about a week after the Emperor's Speech that we had to be prepared to go to the beach village Hamamatsu near Nagoya. Some cars came to pick us up. On this trip we drove through some of the streets of Nagoya and saw the results of the firebombing. I was surprised to see the streets clean and bricks of the destroyed buildings neatly stacked and I saw some walls still standing with glass from the windows molted down the brick walls."

---

84   http://www.asahi.com/english/

LIBERATION

After World War II ended in Europe, the Allies met at the Potsdam
Conference July 17, 1945, only three months after Truman became
president and less than a month before the Japanese Unconditional
Surrender. Potsdam was a suburb of Berlin, and all the Allied Powers
were represented: Truman, Churchill, and Stalin were the main nego-
tiators. They issued something called the Potsdam Declaration, "which
threatened a massive aerial and naval attack and land invasion" that
would "strike the final blows upon Japan," unless the Japanese agreed
to surrender.

The declaration laid out the Allies' non-negotiable terms for
peace, which included unconditional surrender, disarming of the Japanese military, and the occupation of Japan "until there is convincing
proof that Japan's war-making power is destroyed," trials for Japanese
war criminals, and the creation of a democratic system of government
with freedom of speech and other rights for citizens.

In exchange, Japan would be allowed to maintain industries that were unrelated to war and have access to raw materials, and eventually would be permitted to resume international trade."[85]

* * *

Dear Laura,

Truman started the [Potsdam] conference, and the Germans and Italians agreed to the unconditional surrender, but the Japanese representative could not commit to the unconditional surrender of the Emperor. Stalin agreed to leaving the Emperor in place, but Truman did not agree. He also said that the Russians should declare war on Japan. At this point, Truman was told that the U.S., at the Nevada testing grounds, had successfully exploded the atom bomb. Truman asked Churchill if he would like to share the atom bomb. Churchill said that after the European War was won, he did not need the atom bomb. The Potsdam Conference closed with the requirement of unconditional surrender by Japan.

Truman got word that we were ready to drop the atom bomb on Japan, and he authorized its use, which resulted in the dropping of the atom bomb on Hiroshima on August 6, 1945, by the crew aboard the "Enola Gay." A second atom bomb was dropped on Nagasaki three days later.

Now things changed very rapidly in our prison camp. I remember that day because the next day we were served rice for the first time in Japan. Then, on August 15, 1945, we were told to assemble at the main compound of the prison camp, where a loudspeaker was installed. We did not know the reason for the

85   Potsdam Conference. History.com Editors. History.com. A&E Networks. Updated November 15, 2022. Original: May 18, 2022. Accessed January 3, 2023. https://www.history.com/topics/world-war-ii/potsdam-conference

order, but a lot had happened in Tokyo after the second atom bomb had been dropped on Nagasaki.

Under the Imperial Palace in Tokyo was a conference room built in a bomb shelter deep below the palace for the Emperor and his family. After Hiroshima, Emperor Hirohito assembled all the chief Ministers, including Tojo and the Admiral of the Japanese Fleet, asking their advice about what to do. The Chiefs of the Army, Navy and Air Force all wanted to continue the war and try to defeat the enemy. Hirohito asked specific questions about what would happen if the next atom bomb was dropped on Tokyo. There were no good answers. Hirohito thanked the chiefs and asked for another meeting. He did not want his homeland destroyed.

Then, the second bomb was dropped on Nagasaki. Hirohito called his chiefs together and said that he wanted to talk to all the people by radio. Immediately, they said that the Emperor had not spoken over the radio, and the radio station was not convenient. Hirohito was adamant and told them to make everything ready for the Emperor's address to the people on August 15, 1945, and the notice had gone out that the Emperor wanted all people in Japan to assemble at a radio or loudspeaker at 4:00 p.m. on that day.

This was a very special occasion since the Emperor had never spoken to the people. He was a God to the Japanese, and not expected to talk. The broadcast was heard all over Japan, and it was picked up in all Japanese controlled areas. Hirohito said, "We have met a superior force, and I bow to the superior force." In Japan, this meant that the Emperor had surrendered to the Superior Force and the war was over.

The people were stunned, but the effect was immediate. The Commander of our prison camp came over to me and told me that he surrendered and turned the camp over to me. As I was the one who had been an interpreter with my broken Japanese, I took over and had a lot of help from everybody. I remember talking to the Camp Commander who asked me what I wanted to do. I remember telling him that I wanted to see Kyoto, which was known not to have been bombed because of the many temples. But, I never made it, because the Americans had told the Camp Commander to assemble all prisoners on the beach at Hamamatsu, which was close to Nagoya.

General MacArthur also heard the Emperor's speech, and, knowing the Oriental mind, knew that Japan had surrendered. He ordered an unarmed transport plane to take him to the Atsuki Airport, the main Air Force airport of Tokyo. All his fellow officers thought he was suicidal, but followed his orders. Soon his unarmed plane was intercepted by Zero Fighter Planes, but they escorted MacArthur's plane when they found out that he was flying to Atsuki Airport. In Japan, the Imperial Guard supplied an old Lincoln car, and the Army had posted shoulder to shoulder soldiers with guns facing the crowds, to make sure General MacArthur reached his destination.

The Japanese thought the General wanted to see the Emperor, but he stopped at the adjacent Imperial Hotel. Soon, Japanese Envoys came to him for the Peace Treaty. MacArthur replied that the Peace Treaty would be signed on American soil. The Battleship Missouri came into Tokyo Harbor, but then before signing, MacArthur ordered all POWs to be present when the surrender was signed by the Japanese on the battleship Missouri.

Even my family and I floated by that giant ship on the USS Lardner[86] after they rescued us off the beach at Hamamatsu. MacArthur ordered all POWs to be present because he knew this request would ensure that his second in command, Wainwright who'd been taken prisoner at Corregidor, would be returned alive.[87] Along with MacArthur and Wainwright the Dutch commander and British commanders who lost at The Battle of the Java Sea and the Japanese commander who won the battle were also aboard.

That particular order changed our lives, and it was the reason we were assembled at the beach at Hamamatsu and we could see ships in the distance. We waited at the beach after driving through Nagoya, which had been completely destroyed by fire. I saw some brick walls where the glass had melted and covered bricks below the window.

Before too long, there was a full-scale assault of U.S. Marines storming the beach. Apparently, they expected military resistance, but there were no Japanese soldiers around. Landing craft took us to a Hospital Ship, where we were stripped of our clothes, washed, deloused, given new clothes and belts. We all got new soldier uniforms. They did not fit very well because I was tall, but only weighed 85 pounds. Soon we were picked up by the U.S. Naval Destroyer USS Lardner, and then taken to Tokyo Bay to the Battleship Missouri.

I could not believe how tall the battleship was. We pulled into a temporary mooring, and I could not see the top of the overhanging steel hull. As it turned out, we came too late for the signing of the Peace Treaty, which had occurred the day before.

86   http://destroyerhistory.org/benson-gleavesclass/usslardner/
87   https://www.salon.com/2018/11/11/gen-douglas-macarthurs-escape-from-the-philippines/

*I still have the tag that the Hospital Ship doctor gave me. I
was listed as a Dutch Civilian from Camp Hirose. My diagnosis
was Malnutrition; Nationality: Dutch. The Tag was signed by
Examining medical Doctor: D.W. Johnson, MC USN, and read
"R TO Rescue Transferred to Destroyer September 5, 1945." This
tag I carried on the Destroyer going to the Battleship Missouri
in Tokyo Harbor, which eventually dropped us off, and we were
taken to the Atsuki Airport to go to the Manila Prisoner of War
Relocation Center. Many transports arrived and returned to
Manila. By September 12, we were on our way to Manila on
an empty transport plane and arrived at the Recovered Personnel
Replacement and Disposition Center in Manila.*

*In Manila we were taken to the POW Rehabilitation Center.
Life at the Rehabilitation Center was like a dream. We got a taste
of the superb organization of the U.S. Army. There were Quon-
set Barracks for us, and the tags that identified us as returning
POW's, and the PX was open to us free of charge. We could "buy"
anything we wanted. The food in the mess hall was unbelievable.
We had not seen eggs for years, and there were eggs, bacon, pancakes and syrup, as much as you could eat. So after some weeks, I
gained 13 pounds on my 6'2" frame increasing from 85 pounds
to 98 pounds.*

Love, Daddy

* * *

Beep-beep-beep-beep . . . Announcement of the Japanese Surrender. This dramatic event comes to us now by short wave from the
Pacific . . .

. . . Attention the peoples of the world, World War II is about to come to its official closing . . . we're on the Pacific Fleet Flagship USS Missouri in Tokyo Bay for the signing of the surrender of Japan.

Three years, eight months and twenty-five days since the attack on Pearl Harbor, we're 3700 miles from there . . . The Japanese delegation has just arrived—military men in formal military uniform.

The veranda deck of the USS *Missouri* stretches out before us. The ship's great guns are pointed skyward in honor of the victorious nations represented here. An interesting note: all former POWs are in attendance. A flotilla of humanity, once suffering . . . now liberated.

* * *

The battleship *Missouri*, 53,000-ton flagship of Admiral Halsey's Third Fleet, becomes the scene of an unforgettable ceremony, marking the complete and formal surrender of Japan. In the Bay of Tokyo itself, the United States destroyer *Buchanan* comes alongside, bringing representatives of the Allied powers to witness the final capitulation. General of the Army Douglas MacArthur, Supreme Allied Commander for the occupation of Japan, boards the Missouri. Fleet Admiral Nimitz Pacific Fleet Commander, and Admiral Halsey welcome MacArthur and his Chief of Staff General Sutherland aboard. Admiral Nimitz escorts General MacArthur to the *Missouri's* veranda deck where the 20-minute ceremony is to take place. It is Sunday, September 2nd, 1945.

Cameramen and reporters of many countries record this historic moment, as United Nations military leaders crowd aboard the *Missouri* and examine souvenir cards bearing the Japanese flag, special mementos of the occasion. And now, in a Navy launch, the Japanese surrender party arrives. They are headed by Agent Mamoru Shigemitsu, Foreign Minister of the Japanese surrender Cabinet, who was wounded by a Korean patriot in Shanghai years ago and walks on an artificial leg. The Japanese delegation lines up on the opposite side of the surrender table from the Allies. A war, which had entered its eighth terrible year in China, which had raged for three years and nine months for America and Britain, which was the brutal, costly eastern half of the most horrible worldwide war in human history, is now within minutes of ending for good. General MacArthur speaks.[88] [89]

* * *

"We are gathered here, representatives of the major warring powers, to conclude a solemn agreement whereby peace may be restored. The issues, involving divergent ideals and ideologies, have been determined on the battlefields of the world and hence are not for our discussion or debate. Nor is it for us here to meet, representing as we do a majority of the people of the Earth, in a spirit of distrust, malice, or hatred . . . .

It is my earnest hope and indeed the hope of all mankind that from this solemn occasion a better world shall emerge out of the blood and carnage of the past—a world founded upon faith and understanding—a world dedicated to the dignity of man and the fulfillment of his most cherished wish—for freedom, tolerance, and justice . . .

As supreme commander for the Allied powers, I announce my firm purpose, in the tradition of the countries I represent, to proceed in the discharge of my responsibilities with justice and tolerance . . .

---

88   https://www.archives.gov/files/social-media/transcripts/transcript-japanese-sign-final-sur-render-39079.pdf

89   https://www.youtube.com/watch?v=3b4A60dacq0

Then each national representative signed two copies of the instrument of surrender, one in English and the other in Japanese. When the last name was affixed, MacArthur said:

"Let us pray that peace now be restored to the world and that God will preserve it always. These proceedings are now closed."

With that, MacArthur draped an arm around the shoulder of Adm. William "Bull" Halsey and whispered, much less eloquently:

"Start 'em now."

His words triggered an order to orbiting warplanes—Navy fighters and Army Air Forces B-29s, hundreds of them. In wave after wave, they overflew the Missouri just as the sun broke through the overcast sky. World War II was over.[90]

* * *

Dear Laura,

"Now, I was in the same situation as I was when I had to learn Japanese. I did not know how to speak English, but surrounded by English speaking servicemen in the Rehabilitation Center in Manila, I learned more every day. It helped to read the newspapers, and the paperback novel of the detective, Mr. Moto. After 4 weeks, I could make myself understood.

The conditions in the center were unbelievable. We were identified by our Identification Tags as Returning Prisoners of War, and the Commandant had told all the support people to try to accommodate our every wish to make up for the Prison experience. With all that I had been exposed to, I decided I wanted to immigrate to the United States and requested a talk with the

90 https://www.stltoday.com/news/archives/sept-2-1945-surrender-on-the-battleship-missouri-the-end-to-world-war-ii-and/article_e5aedae4-ecd7-11ea-a679-537b806b5f1b.html

Rehabilitation Center Commandant. He saw me and I told him my request. He told me he could not help me but that I should go to the U.S. Consulate in Manila, and he provided me with a staff car. When I got there, I was requested to fill out forms, and they told me that I would be informed. Not until many years later in Australia did I find out how important that application was.

After going to Camp Columbia, attending and getting my degree in civil engineering from the University of Sydney, working for the Snowy Mountains Hydroelectric Authority, living in the house that I built at 127 Edgeworth David Avenue, in Wahroonga, Australia, I received a postcard from the American Consulate in Sydney that just asked me briefly to mark in the two squares below: one square for those who still wanted to immigrate to the U.S., and one for those who did not want to immigrate to the U.S. This postcard arrived 4 years after my application in Manila. Incredible!

Love, Daddy

I remember talking to Dad about the magnitude of this choice. He said that he talked to Grandma about it. At the time Grandpa was in Indonesia finishing a few more years of work in order to receive his pension. So at the time, Dad had been the provider for the family and like a father to my uncle.

"Which box should I check? I feel like an Australian now," Dad said.

"America is the future, son. Go to the United States," Grandma said.

Dad had spoken about his liberation when I interviewed him about the Firebombing of Tokyo. In the middle of his recollections, he fast forwarded to his rescue saying, "Can you imagine, 1.4 million GIs were ready for the invasion of Japan? There were 40,000 prisoners of war, not all there at the same time, but they all came through the camp in Manila. I befriended the American POWs and told them I wanted to learn English. One of the guys told me the best way to learn was to buy a book. So I went into the PX and got a book, *Mr. Moto's Dangerous Hours*, about a Japanese Detective. It really helped me, because there was a lot of dialogue."

And that summed Dad up perfectly. He needed to learn and so he found a way. Whenever he needed to learn he found a way. Nothing stopped him. Not war, not chaos. Not physical pain. Not rain or snow or volcanic eruptions. Nothing stopped him from experiencing joy on the next part of his journey. He found happiness and helped others to do the same, especially his children.

Going Home

In June, 2016, on my way from Europe to California to see my daughters, I visited Dad. On Father's Day, my brother, sister, and I all bought Dad a huge stuffed giraffe to keep in his hospital room. We called the giraffe Dr. Spotty. Dad had been in and out of the hospital sporadically with kidney failure as his heart failure progressed. We thought Dr. Spotty would brighten his spirits. Dad loved the gift and the idea that the giraffe would watch over him.

Dad with Dr. Spotty (From left Mark, Suzy, Mom and I).

It was also important to return to California to see my daughters, since I had been in Spain for months. I looked forward to reconnecting with my girls and having fun with them that summer. Candice's 30th birthday was a few weeks away and would be a great celebration. She'd invited me to the mountains where her dad's family has a cabin and where we spent many summer holidays together. It was a place full of loving memories, celebrations, and good times. I looked forward to reconnecting with the mountains again. I hadn't been there in years. In the meantime, I settled into an AirBnB near Seascape beach, close to where my girls lived. I had been traveling for a long time and looked forward to settling in and enjoying some relaxation and rest.

On my hike down to the beach on the night of July 16, 2016, I had an intriguing encounter with a fawn. I'd never seen one on a cliffside beach trail before. As soon as our eyes locked, it sprinted up the sandy cliff so fast it seemed unnatural. Even then, a curious feeling came over me. I wondered if Dad's spirit was saying goodbye. About a half an hour later, around 8 p.m., I sat on the beach and stared out at the ocean and the horizon beyond. The summer sun melted into the Pacific, painting the sky different shades of pink, purple, and tangerine. It was a typical summer night, and yet, I had an overwhelming urge to call my sister on the other side of the country, two time zones away.

"Hey Suzy . . . "

"Laura, Dad's gone home . . . ," Suzy said, crying. "I'm here with Mom . . . I just told her. I can't believe you just called."

We all sobbed.

"Laur . . . he died about a half an hour ago."

"Oh, Suz . . . "

"There was a terrible thunderstorm. And . . . there was no way to get Mom to see Dad before he went home. We tried. We thought about getting the car and getting her there anyway. But, it was too dangerous . . . "

Suzy told me the whole story. An afternoon of knowing what was coming. Calling her daughter, Rachel, so she could come to Dad's side and see him before he died. Coordinating it so Mom could say goodbye. Then, the massive thunderstorm. The Tampa area is known as the lightning capital of North America.

"It was such a force. I've never seen it storm so bad. Maybe Mom was meant to remember Dad the last time she saw him . . . and not . . . in . . . in the hospital." Her voice cracked.

Suzy spoke about how Dad reached out to Suzy and said his last word, "Maaa . . . "

Through her tears, Suzy said, "It was as if Dad thought I was Mom and he was telling her goodbye."

Through our sobs we said how much we love each other. After I hung up with Suzy, I called my daughters, crying, letting them know the news. As darkness descended, my daughter Margaux joined me on the beach.

She sat with me as we watched the darkness swallow the sun. Little bonfires dotted the beach and tourists lit fireworks. I looked out upon the waves, knowing Seascape would be a sacred place for me and that I would be tied to that beach, the Pacific, and the Monterey Bay for the rest of my life.

Margaux gave me a final hug on Seascape beach and we said our goodbyes. Not long after, I left the beach and took a long walk by the cliff where I saw the deer on my way back to my AirBnB. So many memories flooded my thoughts on that walk. I reflected on the time I took a walk at Zuma Beach with a friend of mine in LA right after I left my marriage. As we talked, a huge owl swooped down, just inches away from me. Then it landed on a streetlight in front of us. She said that it's important to pay attention to the animals that appear in our lives. She said every animal we encounter, especially the ones that come upon us in unusual ways, have messages for us.

When I returned to my AirBnB, I took some time to look into what an encounter with a deer could mean. Deer are symbols of gentleness, innocence, intuition, unconditional love, safety, strength, and protection. The description also mentioned that deer are highly sensitive and intuitively aware of subtle energies happening all around them. I felt so lost at that moment, yet comforted, too. Dad had one last message for me. *Dear Laura,* he seemed to say from another realm, *You are worthy, safe, loved and protected. I love you.* I still think about that haunting encounter with the deer every time I walk to the beach at Seascape.

Sadly, I missed Candice's birthday celebration in the mountains because I'd become very ill. I had a bad problem with my digestion since I'd returned from Spain and it just got worse. The condition became so debilitating, I had to see a doctor and he prescribed rest. I used the time while I rested to put together a slideshow of Dad's life, which turned out to be a tribute to Mom & Dad. Our family photos chronicled our happy lives as a loving family.

The celebration of life service for Dad was standing room only. Firefighters and policemen showed up to pay their respects. Suzy worked for the city government and many got to know Mom and Dad too. Dad had done a lot of volunteer work with the city. It was the first time so many members of our extended family had come together. My cousins came from Chicago along with Reinier, his sons and one of his grandsons. Dad had repeatedly said he wanted to live to 99 years old. He thought that was the largest number. 100 didn't have the same punch, he would say. He even drew pictures of the numbers as he got older. From the time he turned 90, he drew his age in black numbers on orange circles. He cut them out and taped them to his wall. A birthday countdown of sorts. 92 was his final number.

Dad's countdown.

We had his celebration of life service a day after Mom's birthday in early August. I rented a place in Seminole, close to Mom and Dad's apartment so I could help Mom navigate through life for about a month after the service. She was a very pragmatic woman and tried to soldier through everything she knew needed doing. At one point, we even looked and arranged for a new, smaller apartment for her to move into. I helped her downsize, which meant going through everything that had been precious to Dad. And, very sadly, dismantling his study. The place where so many of our visits took place. Where I would sleep for the first few weeks as I stayed with Mom to help her through.

Dad's study, Largo FL, July 2016.

I took a photo of Dad's study before I touched anything. The place of wonders I knew as a child had morphed a bit over the years, growing ever smaller and now even included his bed. Yet, most of the beautiful, cherished items Dad had curated still covered his walls. We had spent many hours over the years talking about his story there. On the wall next to a painting of rice paddies with a volcano in the distance, hung a Japanese scroll and a framed portrait of Mom as a bride.

"Darlin', take whatever you like," Mom casually said one afternoon.

Take what I like. It seemed wrong to break up his treasures. And yet, it was a way of keeping his memory alive and keeping him with me. I finally began the unthinkable job of deciding what to take, what to leave, what to throw away.

I packed a travel suitcase with a few of Dad's slides and as many of his files as I could—some contained books he'd compiled and written like "Method For Problem Solving Using Creativity," and files entitled "Happiness," and "Abraham Lincoln." I shipped what I couldn't carry, including more files and a silver-plated champagne bucket. Taking anything off Dad's wall was unthinkable. For it meant the end. Our discussions were over. Dad's study as I knew it would be no more. I would never be able to walk in and ask Dad another question.

Eventually, I placed my hands on Dad's beautiful image of Iguaçu, the world's largest broken waterfalls on the border between Brazil and Argentina. I remembered Dad describing how he took the photo. He wanted to get the foliage of the trees in the foreground to give the waterfall more impact and waited for a rainbow to appear before snapping the shot. The dramatic, beautiful image of the waterfall with a gorgeous, faint rainbow in its spray had captured my imagination since I was a young girl. It now hangs on my study wall. A constant reminder of the power of small things. How water droplets can come together to create unfathomable beauty and a stunning amount of power. Impossible beauty. Impossible joy. It's all possible.

Dad's photo of Iguaçu.

As I got ready at my AirBnB in Seminole to go to my sister's house to prepare for Mom's birthday celebration with the family, the day before Dad's memorial service, I received an intriguing message on my computer. A travel magazine on an online job board that I had registered with a few years prior wanted to hire me to write a few articles. This was the first request I had from that job board. It was also the first writing job I landed since my first travel article, *A visit to Dracula's castle in Romania*[91], was published by the *Los Angeles Times* about a decade earlier, two years after my trip to Romania. The assignment I received that day would be the beginning of that "other life" I'd been in search of for so long. I smiled knowing that somehow Dad had something to do with setting my career in motion. He was still with me. Our adventure hadn't ended. As a travel writer, I would still be his eyes in the world.

---

91   https://www.latimes.com/travel/la-trw-romania30nov04-story.html

"Mom, how did you survive the pain of your divorce?" Candice asked sobbing on the phone, while Mom slept in the other room. She'd just broken up with her boyfriend.

"I felt it. The only way to cross a mud puddle is to go through it. Then . . . ," I took a breath, "I realized I didn't want to give anyone that kind of power over my life. So I let it go."

Candice sniffled a little. "I don't get it," she said. "What do you mean about the mud puddle?"

"A little while ago, I met a missionary who had grown up in Tasmania. She told me that when she was a little girl and her family drove in the bush (remote areas), they sometimes encountered huge mud puddles in the road. People are tempted to go around them because they are a bit frightened of trying to drive through. They don't want to flood their jeep, and maybe stall out the car. But, trying to drive around a huge mud puddle never works because the squishiest part of the mud lay on the puddle's edge. If they drive that way, their jeep sinks and its wheels get stuck in the mud. The safest way is to actually drive in the center of the puddle, where the rainwater compacts and hardens the mud. The only way to cross the mud puddle is to drive through it."

"It's so hard, though," Candice said.

"I know. I'll be here for you every step of the muddy way," I said.

Then a loud chirp interrupted our call. It startled me and I let out a yelp.

"What's going on?" Candice said.

"It sounded like some bird just flew into the room," I said.

"What?"

After I did a little searching I found the culprit. "Oh, it's one of Dad's bird toys. Mystery solved," I said.

We laughed. *Lighten up*, Dad and the Lord seemed to say at that moment.

Dad always had a collection of toys. He was particularly fascinated with wind up toys. His toy bird never chirped randomly before, though. During the time I spent with Mom after Dad died, the bird continued to make random chirps. Always at the funniest times. Always lightening our spirits. That was Dad. Making things joyful.

And we needed that levity. I'd just helped Mom through one of the worst moments of her life where she confessed that she just wanted to die too. I had to convince her that being alive was a miracle. I needed to help guide her during those tender weeks. My job was to show her how to embrace this new chapter, however difficult. As I had to do not too long before.

But her pain seemed unfathomable. How would she turn the page after 62 years of marriage? Could she? Somehow we had entered into a sisterhood of heartache. Although we lost our spouses in very different ways, heartache is heartache. At the same time Mom ached for Dad, my daughter ached for her ex-boyfriend. We were three generations of heartache, loss, and pain.

Mom and I bonded like never before during that time. We laughed, ate ice cream with sprinkles on top, and held on to each other as she bravely drove through her mud puddle. But on the way through the mud, I also held her hand when she ended up in the hospital. Like Dad, she was diagnosed with heart failure a few weeks after he died. His was on the left side. Her's was on the right. She could live years with the condition, or not. It frightened me to think that I would lose her so soon.

IGUAÇU

"Come visit me," my dear friend, Tatiana, said. We'd met on the Camino in 2015, a year earlier, and became fast friends. Shortly after Dad died, she invited me to her home in Brazil, a posada (small boutique hotel) in the mountain town of San Francisco Xavier, a tiny city in the middle of Manticueira Mountains, not far from São Paulo. The pousada provides peace and tranquility for city-dwellers, as do the many waterfalls and hiking trails close by.

Even though I wasn't familiar with the region and didn't know much about Tatiana's home, I immediately said, "Sí, Claro." (Yes, of course.) I had a little "Sí" pin on my backpack that I'd bought in Spain, a great reminder to say yes whenever I might hesitate to Go Big. When I accepted Tatiana's kind invitation, I needed a break from everything, especially writing this story. By the time I boarded my red-eye flight from Tampa to São Paulo (with a stop in NYC), exhaustion had set in. Not only because I'd lost Dad and would never realize my dream of having him read this story, but also because the flurry of world travel over the previous three years had caught up with me.

Somewhere in the air over America flying from Tampa to New York City
August 21, 2016

From my window seat on the plane, I stare at rainbows and clouds. My heart is heavy. Saying goodbye to Mom was so very right and so very hard. She looks great, and yet . . . I don't know. It can't be the last time I see her. Not with so much loss this year. This month. My mind can't even understand all that's been lost. And I miss Dad and I miss my friends in Spain, especially the good times we all had. I even miss the guy I dated who was totally wrong for me, but felt so right for me at times. There is suddenly so much to mourn. It will take time and yet, here I am on the first leg of a flight to Brazil with my first paying freelance writing assignment in years and I can't help but be joyful about living my dream—picking up my editor's email about how she wants my contributor information written, getting clear on pitches, and contracts. And meeting so many kind people along the way. And at the same time, being so totally heartbroken. Frustrated that I couldn't finish writing Dad's story while he was alive. Feeling like a failure and at the same time feeling proud that I was blessed to share the answer to the most intriguing *why* of the story with him.

* * *

When I traveled to Brazil, I wanted to cut loose and use it as a retreat to help build my career as a travel writer. I prayed that the launch of my business would be filled with many supernatural Divine Appointments. Writing while living in the world was my dream and it began to come true. I needed to get away so I could dedicate time to my craft and hoped to find some peace in Brazil and, eventually, find a way back to writing this story.

I had to begin my writing career from scratch. I knew that. My pride wounded, discouragement tried to get the better of me. But the reality of starting over again made me doubt if I could live by my pen. A writing career seemed like a high mountain for me to climb. Around this time, I began to understand that there is always some sort of lie at the base of my fear. I would have to get better at calling those lies out to Go Big and make my dreams come true. *All things are possible*, I kept reminding myself.

So much had changed for Tatiana and I since we'd walked the Camino. As pilgrims, we enjoyed each other's company, including eating lots of pulpo (octopus) on our 500-mile trek. At one point, we'd both been so injured that we needed to walk very slowly—*Despacio Despacio,* we'd remind each other. So slowly, that we laughed about harnessing the power of the snail to get us to our ultimate goal, the tomb of St. James in Santiago.

Without Tatiana's help I wouldn't have made it. She hobbled with me to find sock liners and foot creams and in Saguine, where potentially Camino-ending blisters on the bottom of both of my feet almost sidelined me. As I walked, it felt like knives stabbed the bottom of my feet with each step I took. I'd just received a three-day bed rest order from a kind doctor at the Centro de Salud in Carrión de Los Condes, about midway through my pilgrimage. Tatiana and I were both in pain. Hers came from a small fracture in one of her feet that she didn't find out about until she returned home to Brazil.

Only a few hours after taking off for São Paulo, I realized I hadn't packed any underwear. So at the beginning of our drive out of the city and into the remote mountains, Tatiana and I stopped at a mall. This part of the journey felt all hazy, the way things do when you've flown a red-eye across the world.

We didn't have much time because Tatiana wanted to take me for a hike up to *La Pedra de São Francisco*. "The stone of St. Francis" is part of a *caminho de fe* (walk of faith), a sacred trek by Tatiana's home which rewards with jaw-dropping views of the Mantiqueira mountain range from the top of a giant stone. Since life hadn't given me much time for *caminhos* in the months before, I longed for the kind of *caminho* my soul and spirit needed. Desperate to walk, I wanted to hug nature and breathe the cool Brazilian mountain air.

In no time, I found a great lingerie store in the mall. I loved their fabrics and designs but had no clue when it came to speaking Portuguese, similar to Spanish, a language I speak. The languages even share common words. Sadly, none of them were ones I needed to use to find the right size and color of panties. Tatiana gave me lots of help.

"These are perfect. Get some of these," she said, draping some butt enhancers (garments with big pads augmenting a lady's butt cheeks) over her butt and wiggling around.

"Perfect!" I said. I'd never seen anything like them before. Brazil was full of surprises.

We both burst out laughing.

After making my selections (sans butt enhancers), the sales woman handed me my bag. I thanked her with my first Portuguese word, "Obrigado."

I held up the tiny, red-ribboned white bag gilded with the word "HOPE" and smiled.

I turned to Tatiana, and said, "I have a little bag of hope."

She gave me a hug and pointed at the store's marquee. I hadn't noticed that the name of the store was HOPE. (The jet lag, pain from a lingering digestion malady, and the general sense of rushing, combined to make me a little loopy.)

"It's great energy," Tatiana said with a big smile. Afterward, we caught up over a tasty Brazilian coffee, then tucked my little bag of hope into my friend's large Land Rover and hit the road for our journey into the mountains.

I love how the Holy Spirit gives us signs and messages. And how God works through our desires and longings. Sometimes, he's found in the perfect song at the perfect time, in the words of a friend. At other times, He arrives in the form of intuition, through whispered messages on gentle breezes. But I'd never received a red-ribboned, gilded message of hope written in English in a Portuguese-speaking country before.

Tatiana knew I needed care and some time to rest. I was meant to unwind at her hotelito (little hotel), write, walk, and relax. Nothing more. The property was breathtaking, nestled among the mountains with stunning panoramic views, where her home, restaurant, and five little chalets dotted the hillside on the path to the restaurant. Each chalet was beautifully crafted and filled with playful, sophisticated artwork that Tatiana curated.

I spent my visit in a guest room in her home at the top of the hill. The bathroom floor was made up of smooth rocks with occasional stepping stones. The loft was Daliesque where a huge steel cricket eternally crawled among the supernatural steel grass adorned with large red glass flowers and green steel leaves. The decorations were happy and adventurous. Like Tatiana's smile. That she's inspired by Dalí is no surprise. She is in love with Spain, and at that time, with a Spaniard who lived in Barcelona, very close to one of Dalí's homes in Girona.

I had the pleasure of calling Tatiana's part-house, part-art gallery home for one month. The house incorporated the boulders of the mountain into its interior. I loved the charming message of inclusion and acceptance that the architectural detail gave. The boulders were quite beautiful. They had *great energy*, as Tatiana would say. It still inspires me to know that Tatiana owns such a beautiful home and hotelito. How her sensibility is all over its design and smallest details. Her artwork intrigued and inspired me to one day live in a home that reflects my unique sensibilities too.

Our days together began in the kitchen of her restaurant, where Tatiana would make us wonderful breakfasts filled with incredible tropical fruit—mangos in cream and granola; sweet pineapple dripping in honey; avocado blended into vanilla ice cream.

"All fruits have great energy from the earth," Tatitana said. "It's best for your body to begin your day eating them."

I hadn't really given a thought to the energy in fruit. But eating fruit seemed to have a healing effect on me. I meditated on the blessing the food was to my body and realized that I had gotten out of the habit of blessing food before I ate. From that moment on I would say grace at every meal. I got back to the basics. Soon after I arrived, I washed my clothes by hand. I enjoyed the meditative state of hand washing my clothes as a pilgrim on the Camino. What a joy it was to get back to the feeling of that kind of simplicity again.

"Are you accustomed to washing your clothes this way?" Marlizza, one of Tatiana's friends on staff asked as I wrung out some of my pants.

"I am a pilgrim," I said.

She smiled. Then Marlizza and Maris, another kind woman who worked at the posada, helped me set up my washing station.

During the afternoon I helped Tatiana shop for supplies at the village market and worked a tiny bit in the kitchen, eating, mostly. Pedro, the chef, is a carioca (someone born in Rio de Janeiro). His special brand of joy flavored his delicious food. His easy way in the kitchen led him to teach me all kinds of things. One night, Pedro taught me the samba as he cooked for the guests. His all-smiles nature and laughing eyes were a tonic. Soon everyone in the kitchen joined in. It reminded me of Baba and I singing and dancing in Bandung.

In the evenings, Tatiana and I had all kinds of fun making preparations for the guests. For couples on a romantic getaway, we added special touches, like carefully arranging rose petals in the shape of a heart on their bed then trailing the petals all the way to a Japanese hot tub where we put champagne on ice. Other times, we set up wine tastings for two with tasty food pairings in her bodega. Or set a table for a private, magical candlelit dinner for two on the veranda adjacent to the restaurant, overlooking the mountains.

I was constantly amazed that the couple who created this little gem of a posada—an incredible sanctuary of love that soothed the spirit while attending to guests' every need—had fallen out of love despite making the dream of their hotelito come true. Her ex seemed like such an interesting, sweet person and they were very civil to each other. But, there was no going back for them. Working two weeks on and two weeks off helped them maintain their dream and their distance.

At night, I usually sat in the lounge area in the restaurant and wrote while I watched Tatiana, Pedro, Maria, and some of the other staff mingle with the guests. As light jazz music played, muffled laughs and sparks from the firelight provided great entertainment. Witnessing the transformation of the restaurant from a beautiful, empty little open-air dining room into a buzzing scene of adventurous eating, warmed my heart. An amazing feeling of love, healing, and peace was constantly in the air at the pousada. All the ingredients of home.

After the last guest left, we would sit in the dining room and enjoy our dinner together, often with some cava. Usually we sat outside on the deck of the restaurant where the red sun had supernaturally sunk into the purple mountains, lighting up the sky in different shades of rose. We spoke about Spain, love, and the mysteries of life, while geckos crawled on the wall. And the sounds of the busy restaurant gave over to *natureleza* (nature)—a crescendo of frogs' croaks, at times sounding like an alien spaceship.

When Tatiana was free from managing the pousada, we had fun visiting some wonderful outdoor cafes and specialty stores in the little village of San Francisco Xavier. The town was the one-time home to the Brazilian literary great Monteiro Lobato who penned the Brazilian classic *Sítio do Picapau Amarelo* which literally translates to "The Yellow Woodpecker Farm," a series of 23 novels written from 1920-1940. The books were written in response to his censorship and incarceration under the Vargas regime. The children's stories are the Brazilian equivalent of *The Wizard of Oz* or *The Chronicles of Narnia*. The town is filled with the dolls from the story, whose main character, Emilia, is as popular as Mickey Mouse in the United States.

During my visit to see Tatiana, I had only expected to hang out at the posada and the village. But then Tatiana told me she had arranged a surprise excursion for us. Soon we packed up and visited the enchanting village of Paraty on our way to Rio de Janeiro to see the Paralympics (another story for another day). Since we had met as pilgrims, it should be no surprise that we were drawn to a wonderful trek when we arrived in Rio. Corcovado called. It only took a few hours for us to climb to the statue of Christ.

Tatiana and me after our hike to Corcovado September, 2016.

I stood at Corcovado that afternoon during the Paralympics, with all of Rio at my feet. With the beaches of Ipanema below and Sugarloaf in the distance, Corcovado's gigantic arms stretched above me and over Rio. The moment more than breathtaking, more than life-affirming. We ate some ice cream to celebrate. The cool treat helped beat the heat of the day. As I finished my cone, I realized that just nine months before, I'd carefully cut out and pasted a picture of Corcovado on my vision board. Something I create yearly to inspire my work. With so much that had transpired that year, I had almost forgotten the moment of intention that began 2016.

Vision Board 2016.

"What great energy!" Tatiana said with a smile when I told her that she'd unwittingly helped to make one of my dreams come true.

It was then that our experience of the trip began the turn from the exotic to the sacred. Soon, machine-gun wielding Brazilian militia encircled us in military helicopters, machine guns drawn, pointing at us. They flew around Corcovado. Through the sights of my cell phone camera these machines of war seemed like errant flies swarming the statue of peace. Around and around they went in a kind of dance. Good and evil. War and peace. My dream had just come true one minute and we were being threatened by violence the next.

It took time to find out why we were being circled by three armed military helicopters. But we eventually heard that a security breach by a private helicopter in the closed air space around the landmark triggered the swarm. Grateful to have an explanation that wasn't more serious, I began the even more serious business of hunting for the right Corcovado souvenir in every cheesy tourist store on the top of the mountain.

"Did you find something?" Tatiana asked after I'd spent way too long in the shops.

I shook my head. Most were disturbingly awkward. Mass-made faces of Jesus that looked kind of strange. All the proportions of Corcovado seemed off. But, I wanted to remember what I felt at Corcovado. The helicopter swarm that made my heart race. *I don't believe in hazard.* The joy of having a dream come true. The excitement of life unfolding in ways one never expects. The adventure of life. The good stuff. How my heart had filled with peace the same moment my breath had been taken away by circling helicopters.

After coming up empty at the tourist shops, Tatiana and I skipped the hike down and took the train to the bottom. While there, I decided to check out one more tourist-trap to see if I could find something (a kind of Ebenezer)—anything worthwhile—to remember the experience. Instead of stones on the side of the River Jordan, mine would be a cheesy statue of Corcovado.

On my hunt, I heard a small voice ask, "Are you American?"

I turned around and came toe-to-toe with beautiful ballerinas from Missouri. Happy to run into a fellow countrywoman, they invited Tatiana and I to their performance the next evening in Rio. They were sweet, well-spoken, and as you can imagine very, very thin. Even though Tatiana and I couldn't make the performance that night because of our travel plans, I was curious and wanted to make some polite conversation.

"What are you dancing?" I asked.

"*The Screwtape Letters*,"[92] one of the ballerinas said with a smile.

Really. How do you dance to that? I thought.

---

92   The Screwtape Letters https://www.cslewis.com/the-devil-and-mr-lewis/

I'd only known the novel by C. S. Lewis because an acquaintance referenced the book once earlier that summer. In addition to being the famous author of the beloved childhood series, *The Chronicles of Narnia*, C.S. Lewis had also converted from atheism to Christianity on a walk he took with J. R. R. Tolkien at Oxford.

Lewis was a prolific writer about Christianity. His book, *The Screwtape Letters*, was based on the premise that a senior demon wanted to communicate to his minions a set of instructions on how to trap humans into making life-ending or life-altering bad choices. It is a cautionary tale about the power of choice, and a statement on the criteria humans use to make them. Basically, these southern American girls were dancing for Jesus. Evangelizing through ballet in a troupe called *Ballet Magnificat!*[93]

This, I had to see. So we made plans to attend their performance in Campinas, a suburb of São Paulo that was more convenient for us. At the performance, the ballet even served up some yummy popcorn, my absolute favorite snack. The troupe danced beautifully. One of the most enchanting moments of the ballet portrayed a demon of doubt inviting a beautiful girl to dance.

Their enthralling, passionate dance[94] showed how a woman ignored doubt, then danced willingly with it. When she wanted to break free she tried to escape, but in the swirls and spins, the woman totally lost her will to get out of doubt's clutches. The dance left me enthralled, disturbed and convicted. I thought about all of my needless dances with doubt. How I was still in its clutches. Horrified, while watching the ballerina give over to doubt totally, I realized that I never wanted to be bewitched like that ever again. The wisdom and insight of the ballet had a peaceful, powerful message for me—our greatest power

---

93   http://www.balletmagnificat.com/
94   https://youtu.be/JapnsQTLOkk

is the power to choose. To dance another way. To refuse the invitation. That night God gave me strength for my journey. He was "making all things new."[95]

During the performance, Tatiana whispered that she had been a professional ballerina. The performance brought back memories she hadn't had in years. What a joy it was to get to know my dear friend in a new way that I never had before. All because we lingered in the cheesy gift shop at Corcovado. I continually marvel at God's humorous, playful, extravagant ways. He got my attention . . . again. It was time to stop doubting. It was time to trust myself, my abilities, and my choices. It was time to write Dad's story no matter how unqualified I felt to write it.

After a week of working at the pousada, we were off on another unexpected adventure—flying in a small commercial plane over the jungles of Brazil to "the cataratas" (waterfalls). When we arrived at Iguaçu, I told Tatiana about Dad's photo. She didn't know anything about my connection to Iguaçu before we arrived. She just wanted to show me the falls, so she made arrangements for us to stay at the beautiful Hotel das Cataratas. The unique, luxurious property right by the waterfalls felt less like a hotel than a kind of nature palace.

---

95   "Therefore, if anyone is in Christ. he is a new creation; old things have passed away; behold, all things have become new." — 2 Corinthians 5:17 (NKJV)

Tatiana at Iguaçu.

We enjoyed incredible, long walks among the falls and took a very wet boat ride to experience the force of the cataratas in new ways. When I let Tatiana know that Dad had done some consulting work at Itaipú (which was, at the time, the world's largest hydroelectric power plant) we made a short side trip to check that out too. Another story, for another day.

Since Dad went home to be with the Lord a little over a month before, I'd felt God with me more closely than ever. He began showing up in new, exciting and even playful ways. Hotel das Cataratas would be the first place where I worked remotely to conduct an interview and write an article for a new online travel magazine. My dream of writing in the world and living by my pen became a reality during our visit.

One of the most unique and intimate moments in all of my travels happened early one morning on the day we were to return to São Paulo. There was a specialness about this last walk among the cataratas. This would be my last time to feel their energy. But, that still, small voice assured me I would return one day.

When I stepped out for my early morning walk, the park wasn't due to open to the public for another hour. Staying at the only hotel within the park, just across from the waterfalls, granted hotel guests this kind of special access. Something I only took advantage of on my last day. I didn't encounter any other hotel guests at that time, so it felt like the cataratas were all mine.

As I walked deep into the falls, I took a minute to survey the stunning view of the largest waterfall system in the world—so large it spans the frontier borders of Brazil and Argentina. Rainbows danced around the falls as I reflected on the happy accident that led me there. During the days Tatiana and I walked around the falls together, I saw many spots from where Dad could have taken his photo. *Maybe, I had literally walked where he had walked.*

At one spot, I stopped to take in the view of the massive, constantly flowing, booming and beautiful cataratas and took a deep breath. In these last moments of saying goodbye to Iguaçu, a massive double-rainbow arched over the entire width of the canyon, over hundreds of waterfalls. The jaw-dropping sight brought tears to my eyes. I lined up the shot with my cell phone.

As I took the photo, I heard a whisper from that still, small voice inside, "This is just the beginning."

"Hi, Dad," I said, with a huge smile.

I was somewhere over the rainbow, and so was Dad. I cried, awash in so much beauty and how the Lord constantly amazes me.

Iguaçu, September 15, 2016, final goodbye to Dad.

Hotel Cataratas Pool
Iguaçu, September 15, 2016

I have had the most blessed, amazing time here at Iguaçu Falls. And this morning the Lord showed me how much he loves me by speaking to me again in my favorite language of rainbows. As I was praying, he blessed me with being all alone on the trails when a beautiful complete double rainbow appeared. I was awestruck at the sight. He said that this is just the beginning and I am truly humbled by all the blessings he's given me. It seems as soon as I think something is beautiful and a great gift, the Lord makes the experience even more beautiful. Like double rainbows and having the trail to myself. It's like God wants me to feel worthy of all the riches in the world. He cherishes me and wants me to know how special he thinks I am and how much he loves me. It's amazing to feel loved. I've felt Dad so close here—in the hibiscus, the music, the hundreds of yellow butterflies and at Itaipu. For the first time I believe I'm worthy of His blessings and I promise to stop dancing with doubt.

There are some people—like the Javanese with their pocongs—who believe a soul wanders the Earth after they die. During that time, they visit significant places from their life as well as their grave. On the fortieth day, their soul finally departs from this world. I believe Dad's soul visited one of the spots in the world that he held most dear and left this world when those incredible rainbows graced the waterfalls. And like some pocongs do, Dad gave me a message . . . *this is only the beginning.*

When honoring Dad at his celebration of life service, I talked about all the waterfalls in his life, the ones he designed and others he photographed. I compared his life to a waterfall—the joy it brings, the simplicity of its beauty, and its sheer force of nature. In Brazil, I not only saw incredible waterfalls, but swam in many of them too. And in the viewing and the bathing—a kind of baptism—God whispered, "*Get back to Gamelan*" (The original title I gave this story when I first started writing it.) During our final evening together in Iguaçu, Tatiana and I dined in our Brazilian bikinis, ate mango shrimp, and drank champagne.

IGUAÇU
SEPTEMBER 18, 2016

Today I awoke to the song of the waterfalls
to toucan calls
to a misted mountainside
to orchids growing on trees
to a fresh papaya and avocado breakfast
to yellow butterflies on wing
to hand washing my clothes
and giving thanks
for the ability to feel, even if it is painful

for the ability to see, even if I sometimes don't see clearly

for the constant, amazing love of God

especially when I didn't believe I deserve it.

When discouragement and despair knock, I remember the little bag of hope, the dance with doubt, and the double rainbow over Iguaçu. I remember the Lord's whispers. And I listen. This was just the beginning. Free of doubt, I headed into my very uncharted future.

COMING HOME

After Brazil, I traveled to Indonesia and Australia (another story, for another day). Then I returned to Santa Cruz, CA, to spend time with my daughters for Christmas. I rented another AirBnB close to Seascape Beach, seemingly pulled magnetically to the spot where I learned of Dad's death only five months earlier. My thoughts soon went to finding a place to rent in the area so I could spend more time with my daughters.

At that time, I had stored all of my possessions (including my car) and was a citizen of the world, free to travel wherever I needed to go. And as wonderful as my experience was, not having a place to call my own left me feeling adrift. Most of the time I would stop by my storage area, visit my stuff, swap out clothes, and drop off souvenirs (read: books). But the process of deep diving into the chaos of storage clutter eventually felt too overwhelming. Even though I'd gotten rid of many of my things and organized them well, the small storage space made it difficult to find what I needed to live and create. I longed to live in a place where I could access all my books and research easily so I could finish writing this story.

I wanted a place to land, maybe a home base. An actual home seemed far off back then. Especially since I had no idea where I wanted to live. Home had meant a beautiful, safe place built with love, filled with happy memories, and would be a comfort as I got older. But that idea of home disappeared after the divorce. Now what would "home" mean? What would "home" look like? In the aftermath of losing my home, it took me a long time to feel comfortable with the idea of committing to living in one place. I'd been searching for a different way to live. To discover my new normal. No one was more surprised than me when a new home found me.

On a rare, sunny afternoon that stormy winter of early 2017, my daughter Candice and I tasted some wine in the storybook seaside town of Capitola. When we took a stroll along Soquel Creek, we spotted some rentals on the riverbank. I took a flier that had been left at one of the rentals with the hopes that I might find something I could afford. After quickly giving the paper a glance, I put the flier in my pocket. As an inspiration, I kept it by my computer in the room I'd rented, just down the beach from Capitola.

A few days later, while I was in the middle of writing an article about Paris for a publication, the flier winked at me. It was a horribly dark, rainy afternoon and I needed a little break. So I called the real estate company listed on the flier about a rental. Their offerings were all furnished and fetching high rates. Even in the off-season I couldn't afford any of them.

When I asked who might rent unfurnished places in the area, the kind lady on the phone referred me to another company and wished me luck. When I checked out that website I found a photo of a home that spoke to me. There was just a small photo of a brown house with a gate in front, but the place intrigued me. I literally had no idea where it was but had the thought, *I could live there*. Surprised at my reaction, I read more about the home and noticed that an open house was scheduled in twenty minutes.

I got dressed for the downpour outside, then Amy and I went looking for the house. I named my car Amy. She was a gorgeous, used convertible Porsche painted Amaranth Red that I bought after the divorce settlement. I loved her.

When Amy and I went searching for the address, I quickly ran out of road. The ocean churned below the deadend street. Waves nearly crashed onto the asphalt. I got out of the car and stared at the spectacle. It looked like the surf had swallowed some wooden stairs. The way the waves crashed at high tide that afternoon it seemed there would never be a beach below. As I stood in the driving rain and listened to the booming sound of the surf, I smiled.

Wow, what an amazing place to live, I thought as I climbed back into Amy and found a place to park. Only the pointy top of the brown house was visible as I entered the property through a wooden gate. A charming courtyard garden greeted me, filled with brilliant red canna lillies. While admiring the flowers, the rest of the house came into view. Wood shingle siding added to its storybook feel.

When I opened the red-orange front door, the place was packed with young techies from San Francisco, all dressed in black, looking to get out of the city. This was the first time I really felt my age. I wasn't that old, but was definitely the oldest person in the house besides the listing agent. I took a breath and smiled at the pleasant agent who invited me to step inside and take a look. With her encouragement, I shouldered my way through the small kitchen and upstairs where I met the young woman moving out, whose name was also Laura.

The house seemed perfect. It felt like home in so many ways. The upstairs loft would be an ideal writer's retreat. I imagined the views of the Monterey Bay keeping me company as I wrote. I peered through a sliding glass door and spotted a small wooden deck, imagining summer sunshine, gorgeous views of the bay and vivid sunsets. A fireplace downstairs felt like the cherry on top. One thing I longed for was a fireplace, especially in the cold, maritime climate of a Santa Cruz winter.

But, it surely wouldn't be anything I could afford, I thought. I sighed.

It was good to see what was on the market. But, it was time to get back and finish my article. On my way out of the house, the listing agent walked up to me in the crowded kitchen and held out an application. She asked me to fill it out and get it in by Friday. The landlord would be deciding on the next tenant over the weekend. The moment felt dreamlike. I looked into the lady's kind eyes and instinctively took the application out of politeness, not intending to actually fill it out since I thought it would be pointless.

As I drove back to my AirBnB, the deliberate way the listing agent handed the application to me made me think that I should apply. So I filled out the form, trusting in my future as a writer. In the end, the selection process came down to me and three other couples. When the landlord eventually selected me, I couldn't believe it. It felt like I had won the lottery. I couldn't wait to tell my girls that I had a home.

That first night in my beach home my bench and a sofa I'd bought on sale that same day were my only furnishings. I dubbed it the "salmon sofa" (after its color) imagining all the wonderful chats I'd have with friends and family upon it. It felt liberating to leave the world of storage lockers behind. For dinner, I bought some food from a wonderful bakery in town and relished in the silence and the freedom of having a place to create. Before I went to sleep, I opened a few windows. The sound of the surf comforted me as I laid my head down and fell into a deep sleep on the sofa.

When I woke up in the morning, I made my own cup of coffee the way I used to when I had a home. I heated water in a kettle on the stove and poured it over coffee, brewing the perfect cup. The whole experience of waking up in a place that was mine felt so foreign and familiar, strange and satisfying. Those first days in the beach house I only had the things I could pack into Amy. Movers brought the rest up from LA about a week later, including my first art acquisition, a teak sculpture that weighs one-hundred pounds and looks like it's blowing in the wind. It's named "Turn to the Right." When I look at it, the statue reminds me to continue my walk to the west.

I bought the sculpture in Bali about a year and a half earlier, on an ill-fated bike ride with two Dutch fast friends I'd made who teased me about my habit of almost getting killed by falling coconuts (yeah, it's a thing). We called ourselves the Cocos Locos. The adventure of purchasing the sculpture, shipping it to the U.S., and how it had to be restored after the movers broke it is another story. How I had it repaired was a miracle and yet, another story.

I didn't ship the sculpture after I bought it because I couldn't figure out where to send it, since I didn't really live anywhere. For a while, I thought I might live in Europe and dreamed of one day owning my own "woman cave," thinking I could buy a cave home in Spain (a fixer) and live there. But it was so very far away from my daughters and I didn't think I knew enough Spanish to manage a cave renovation. But I loved my time in Spain and felt at home there.

While I was in Australia, right before I'd returned to celebrate Christmas with my daughters, I decided to ship the sculpture to Los Angeles, and store it until I found a place to live. In the two months after the sculpture set sail from Surabaya, Indonesia, and arrived in the port of San Pedro, California, I discovered the beach house and signed the lease for my new home. As the sculpture sailed the Pacific, my home on the Pacific found me. I enjoyed having "my things about me" as Mary Kate Danaher says in the movie *The Quiet Man*, one of my Mom's favorites.

Having a home again is a gift. A home I had surely stumbled into. *But, did I?* It felt more like a Divine Appointment. The Lord had answered my prayer, yet again. He had brought me to the people I needed and to the people who needed me. I found the beach house of my dreams just eight months after Dad died, up the shore from the beach where Dad and I said our final goodbyes. My house is also located a couple blocks from a windmill. Once a candy shop, it is now a charming, health-conscious café. It's located in a neighborhood where I walk to a fabulous farmer's market every Sunday, with an adorable French bakery that features the most scrumptious authentic French delicacies. Dad loved windmills and chocolate and fresh produce from the garden. I got chills when I remembered that I had also pasted windmills on my vision board a few years back. I'd come home.

FAITHFULLY YOURS

In September, 2019, three years after Dad's death, my husband, Jerry, and I got married on his boat, *Blue Moon*, at anchor in Eastsound, Orcas Island, in the Salish Sea off the coast of Washington state. Boating has been our happy place for a handful of years now. Each summer, for about two months, we cruise on our boat, *Blue Moon*, among the San Juan and Gulf Islands just off the coast of Washington State and Canada. We call this precious time "Summer Camp." It usually begins with a Fourth of July celebration at Roche Harbor. Then we simply let the tides and our whims take us where they will. I love writing at sea. Our life on the water there has been an incredible source of inspiration.

It is a second marriage for both of us and the intimacy and spontaneity of simply stating our vows on the stern of *Blue Moon* during a spectacular late-night sunset in one of our happy places felt perfect—especially with our little Havanese, Lucy, officiating. We enjoyed wine from Church & State, a gorgeous vineyard we'd discovered in Victoria, Canada, and ate a crusty baguette with beautiful bowls of fresh clam chowder that I had made from clams we had dug up in Westcott Bay. It's been fun having two anniversaries, one that evening in Eastsound, and the other about a month later at the Santa Cruz courthouse where my girls celebrated with us. We have five children and four grandchildren between us.

My ability to take pleasure in cooking came back to life in the years Jerry and I have been together. I remember provisioning for our first voyage on *Blue Moon* and how foreign it felt to grocery shop again. But shopping at new stores in new ways, and preparing food in the galley of *Blue Moon* acted as a chef whisperer. We have enjoyed cooking together ever since. Coincidentally, Jerry owned and operated The Harbor Café in Santa Cruz for many years, which is still going strong. We were both foodies.

The sea provides the kind of peace and tranquility that feeds my creativity. After a few years of supporting myself with my pen through travel writing, and ghostwriting books, speeches, and screenplays, it was time to make room for my own writing. I rededicated myself to trying to write this story over the summer of 2019. The discoveries I made aboard *Blue Moon* that summer regarding the technology and science behind this story refueled my belief that I could write this book even if I wasn't a scientist or expert in nuclear technology. I decided that I was an expert about my experience and where my research led. That was good enough.

On our way back home to California, Jerry and I visited my Uncle Reinier and cousin David in Seattle. David was in the midst of helping my uncle downsize from a home he'd lived in for decades. My cousin struggled with the compassionate task at hand—what to do with a lifetime of precious possessions. He confessed as we walked onto his houseboat on Lake Union, that he'd soon be throwing away my grandfather's writings because there were so many, all written in German, and filled with minutia. I didn't know these writings existed.

When I asked David if he might send them to me instead, he kindly said yes. I thanked him very much for honoring my request, especially at such a tumultuous time fraught with plenty to do, and tough decisions to make.

When the box of writings arrived on my doorstep, a few days after we returned home to Santa Cruz, I stored it for months, too busy with work and life to tackle what I believed would be the monumental task of translating a mountain of German writings. But, one day, over the holiday season, my husband kindly reminded me about the package. I'd nearly forgotten about it.

As I cut open the packaging tape, I remember thinking *why in the world would I want volumes of journals and diaries written in a language I don't understand? What could I possibly do with them? Wouldn't their interpretation and translation just extend the timeline to finish the writing of the book (which seemed never-ending already)?* When I finally opened the box, a repurposed carton of *The Northwest's Finest Cherries*, I wondered what I would find.

I expected to see a bunch of random mounds of handwritten papers, but instead discovered Grandpa's bound, meticulously written diaries and journals. In those journals, I found some indications to corroborate my research. However, in glancing over his entries, I realized that I might never have all the answers.

Questions about aspects of this story will undoubtedly continue. In reading Grandpa's journals and hearing his voice through his handwritten words on the page, I felt okay with not having to be the one to answer all of my questions. I would simply reveal what I could, one of many chapters of history, instead of feeling the burden of trying to figure out the science behind the work Grandpa did for the Japanese. I also released myself of the burden of whether the type of work Grandpa did for the Japanese army meant that the Japanese atomic program was much further along than anyone had imagined.

I received two great surprises as I read over the vast amount of information contained in that cherry box at the decade's end in 2019. Grandpa not only wrote in German but also in English. The second, more fascinating surprise, came from what had been omitted, or more accurately, carefully cut out. Sections of many pages had been cut with an Exacto knife. Other pages had been ripped out entirely, leaving only jagged edges of journal paper on the spine—uncharacteristically gaping wounds of omission in an otherwise careful and thoughtful accounting of thoughts, ideas, and letter writing. Can we tell more about what is left out of a story than what appears on its pages? My heart sank. *What information had he carefully removed and what had he seemingly just ripped out of his journals? Why had he kept such detailed accounts of his everyday life? Did someone else rip out the missing pages and meticulously cut parts of pages? If so, why?*

Reading on, I noted that my grandfather signed most letters "faithfully yours." This stuck with me as I read correspondence that spanned the years of 1951-1964. A treasure trove of drafts of letters he sent, running the gamut from a request to work as a radio engineer in Australia; thank you notes; requests for everything, such as more of the fountain pens he loved to shoes he particularly enjoyed; a letter to my newly engaged mother's family for being so gracious and hospitable to Dad who had recently immigrated to America; a letter marked with a crimson silk ribbon sending condolences to my mother's parents on the sudden, untimely death of their son, my uncle Ron; congratulatory letters to my parents on the birth of their daughter, Laura; scientific notes on the hydrogen bomb dated January 31, 1955, including a chart on possible hydrogen fusion reactions which concluded that "*the titanium-deuterium reaction not only yields the greatest energy but requires the briefest instant of time, an important consideration in the design of a hydrogen bomb."*

I couldn't help but feel that Grandpa had been writing to encourage me. *Faithfully yours.* Have faith. Keep telling the story. The symbolism of the cherries on the box in which the letters arrived wasn't lost on me. Throughout Japan, the cherry, or 'sakura' tree is representative of good fortune, new beginnings, and revival. This would be a new beginning, yet another rededication to the story.

I'll never fully comprehend the kind of fortitude, endurance, courage, and grace my family needed to cultivate in order to survive an experience that would kill most people or at least crush their souls. But Dad didn't just survive. He thrived. And from reading Grandpa's journals and Grandma's letters previously, it seemed they learned how to thrive too. All of them had an unshakable faith in the Lord. It was time for me to have that same kind of faith.

Mom & The Home Front

Along with many families who lost their loved ones during the pandemic, my family waited years to celebrate Mom's life. The crushing experience of not being able to properly say goodbye when Mom died is something I can't put into words. Especially since she hosted the celebrations and planned so many of our family memorials over the years. And yet, along with its horrors, the pandemic granted unexpected blessings.

At the end of September 2020, my sister called to let me know that it would be a good idea to come see Mom sooner rather than later. So, right after Summer Camp, as newlyweds, my husband and I took a cross-country road trip with our dog Lucy. On October 16, 2020, we drove our trailer nearly 3000 miles from Santa Cruz, CA, to Largo, FL, to visit Mom. We cherished the adventure, even as our hearts were heavy that Mom wasn't well. Skirting two hurricanes proved challenging—one on the way into and the other on the way out of Florida.

We had traveled during the most active Atlantic hurricane season on record. Zeta, a category 3 storm, made landfall in Louisiana on the night of October 28th. And Eta, a category 4 storm, swept over

Northern Florida in early November as we headed west. (Ironically, we visited only a few months after historic hurricane Laura, a category 4 storm and one of the strongest hurricanes on record to make landfall in Louisiana). The storms caused us to put the pedal to the metal much quicker than our spontaneous plan allowed. It's really hard to outrun hurricanes while towing a Lance 16' trailer behind a GMC Yukon. Another story, for another day.

About a year and a half earlier, in February, 2019, Mom and most of my family in Florida met Jerry for the first time, about two years after Dad died. Unfortunately, Dad never met Jerry. But Jerry has met Dad through my stories. He's championed Dad and me by providing so much love and support as I finished writing this book. When we visited Mom and my family in Florida for the first time, I was working on an assignment for *LA Parent* magazine and my editor was gracious enough to fly me out a bit earlier than needed so I could arrange a visit with Mom.

She looked radiant when Jerry and I visited her in her new apartment. It felt like a huge weight had lifted. I'll never forget how Mom had gotten her nails painted with sparkly clear nail polish for our visit. I'd never seen her fingernails painted before. Her manicure was so pretty that I took a picture of her hands and treasure that photo. Our day together was filled with laughter and great stories just like old times.

Mom loved meeting Jerry and was all smiles as she shared in our happiness at finding each other. We told her about our adventures and how we met while sailing my boat, *Tessa*, a 1968 Trintella designed by Van Der Stadt. I'd once read about a boat similar to *Tessa* described as 'a Ferrari for the eyes' and that's exactly how I saw her. My sailing dream came true when Captain Joseph Rodgers asked me to be his boat partner. He was an old friend of Jerry's and an experienced captain who'd sailed all the world's oceans but the Atlantic. Another story, for another day.

Mom and Dad had given me a love of boating on their beautiful wooden power boat *Undine*. I have a picture on my refrigerator of our whole family sitting on the dock by *Undine* when I was six, with Dad wearing a captain's hat. My love of boating grew into a love of sailing with my high school friends when I joined the American Field Service. Sailing was a great way to bond with the exchange students that came to our high school. I spent many summers sailing on Lake Geneva in Wisconsin and getting to know the handful of exchange students that came our way from New Zealand, Germany, and Italy. However, sailing had faded from my life until I captained *Tessa*.

Mom, Suzy, and me—my last picture with Mom.

When Jerry and I visited Florida in 2020, my sister smuggled Mom out of her independent living facility so we could visit with her in a parking lot in Largo's Central Park. It was great to spend some time with Mom, even masked, from six feet away standing outside of Suzy's car. We talked to each other through Mom's open passenger seat window. She looked beautiful and didn't wear a mask so I could see she was all smiles. Her hair had been done to perfection, as usual, and had gone gray for the first time ever in her ninety-two years. The world had drastically changed in the year since we'd seen Mom and it took a terrible toll on her. Her ashen face eclipsed her gorgeous smile and her once healthy frame had become thin and fragile.

The next day, Suzy and I took Mom to an MRI appointment in the hopes her doctors would be able to diagnose the terrible back pain she'd suffered for months. Medication no longer eased her discomfort and the pandemic made its timely diagnosis difficult. She'd gotten up at 3 a.m. that morning because she was so nervous about the MRI. At 9 a.m. she'd gotten her hair done and looked beautiful when we picked her up for the long drive to the only open MRI in the area.

But when we arrived at the MRI office, a gale force blew just as Mom got out of the car. She was discouraged as she used her walker to make the short walk from Suzy's car to the building, saying she shouldn't have bothered with a hair appointment that day. But after we brushed her hair a bit, every strand fell back into place and made her feel better.

I could tell how much pain Mom was in when I helped her sit down in a chair in the lobby of the medical building while we waited for Suzy to park the car. She winced as she sat in the seat and told me again how she wished she'd already gone home to meet Dad in heaven. She missed Dad beyond measure and the loneliness of the pandemic made her sadness even worse. Her words broke my heart. And I knew there was nothing I could say or do to make that go away. All I could do was listen and tell her I understood.

While waiting for the procedure, Mom and I talked about how much we loved each other. As I lightly rubbed her back, she turned and looked up at me with her big, beautiful brown eyes and said, "I'm so happy you came."

I melted upon hearing her words. "Of course, Mom. There's no place in the world I'd rather be than right here with you. I love you so very much," I said.

Soon Suzy came with a wheelchair. We took Mom's pearls off and I held them and her purse in my hands. I watched Suzy wheel Mom out of sight. Only one person was allowed to accompany Mom due to COVID. It was the first time I held Mom's purse without her. She always kept it with her. I carefully tucked her pearls into the purse's inside pocket for safekeeping and spotted her familiar red Parker pen and Franklin planner neatly stowed away.

While staring into Mom's purse as I never had before, a small voice whispered that this might be the last time I would see Mom alive. I shivered at the thought and took a long look at all the precious possessions she'd tucked away in her purse. I remembered how she'd reached into her purse when I was a little girl to give us kids the cherry and lemon candies that we loved on our long road trips to Florida in the family station wagon. Or how she'd have me reach into her purse to find her eyeglass case to help her exchange her glasses for sunglasses while she drove.

Before long, Suzy wheeled Mom back into the lobby. She later told me that Mom was so exhausted, she slept like a baby during the MRI. Afterward, we made the very windy drive to take her back home.

I remember how delicate she looked using her walker as she entered her building all by herself at the Royal Palms of Largo. I prayed that she would be steady enough to walk to her apartment without falling. We weren't allowed to go inside with her as we normally did due to the pandemic.

Days later, Jerry and I drove back to Santa Cruz. We decided to cut our stay short in St. Augustine because of a sleepless night. Powerful winds, early bands of Eta, had battered our trailer. Then Suzy called to let me know that Mom had fallen in her apartment. As Tampa and even St. Augustine were already in the crosshairs of hurricane Eta by then, it would have been too dangerous for us to drive back. It was heartbreaking to keep on driving. We had to get to safety in Mississippi.

In the meantime, Mom underwent a successful surgery to repair her hip, but in rehab she suffered serious complications due to pneumonia. Suzy fought tooth and nail to gain access to Mom. But she wasn't allowed to see her due to a COVID outbreak at the facility. Mercifully, the rehab center allowed Suzy to be with Mom during her last moments, so she didn't die alone. Suzy held the phone up so I could talk to Mom. But since Mom couldn't speak, I couldn't talk with her. So I sent one of Mom's favorite songs from one of her favorite movies to Suzy so she could play it for her—"Amen", by Sydney Poitier from the movie *Lilies of the Field*. We all listened to it together. Suzy said hearing it brought Mom peace. She had played it just before Mom passed away. By the time Jerry and I reached Austin, Texas, Mom had died. No one would ever call me *Darlin'* ever again. She had always called me Darlin'.

We were camping along the Colorado River just outside of Austin when Suzy called to tell me the news. Time stood still. I sat on a lounge chair just outside of our trailer and stared at the river. I couldn't move.

Some time later that day we got back on the road. Our reservation for the campsite was over and we had to get back to California before Thanksgiving, so we needed to get moving even though I had a hard time doing anything that day. On our way through Texas we made a stop just outside the charming town of Fredericksburg. We'd camped there on our way to Florida, so we knew the Hill Country. My niece had told me about a beautiful vineyard and we decided to make a stop.

Jerry and I honored Mom's memory with a gorgeous lunch on the vineyard's beautiful veranda. Mom would have loved it. She so enjoyed going to lunch and visiting over a meal. As Jerry and I raised our glasses to Mom, we sensed she was accompanying us on our return trip home. What a blessing it was to see Mom before she passed away. My shock of losing Mom just days after seeing her was tempered by the blessing that God had answered her prayers. She and Dad were finally together again.

A few years later, in 2022, as I prepared a movie of Mom's life for her celebration service, I read a story she'd authored decades earlier. While helping to write Dad's family history, she also wrote the story about her family. In it, she warned of revisionist history. She had graduated from middle school just after Pearl Harbor, in late January 1942. In high school she was awarded a Good Citizenship Award medal by the Daughters of the American Revolution. As Dad was in prison a world away, Mom was caught up in WWII on the home front in the United States.

"I do not have much recollection of my high school years, they were war years for the nation, so even we young people had to step into the war effort. We cleaned the house and began dinner, washed clothes, scrubbed floors, ironed, and helped in every way we could so that our moms could go to work to help in the nation's war production factories. There was definitely

a cloud over the nation in those days—especially in 1942 and 1943, when the nation was mobilizing an incredible national effort, and news from the European and Pacific theaters of war was so very bleak.

Even I had an after-school, part-time job in the Production Control Department of American Phenolic Corporation[96] in Cicero, Illinois, (which I reached on the elevated train) from September 1944, and was working there in May 1945, on V-E Day (Victory in Europe Day). We all closed down the department and went down to Chicago to celebrate the end of the War in Europe—what a celebration!

Of course, we weren't quite finished yet, and we and the nation returned to "mop up" the Japanese in the Pacific. But things didn't look so rosy, and we were very sure that once an invasion of the Japanese homeland began, our American fighting men would suffer incredibly high casualties. This belief was reinforced by the February 1945, invasion of the tiny Japanese island of Iwo Jima, during which 20,000 American fighting men, mostly Marines, lost their lives capturing the island. Therefore, in August 1945, when the first atomic bombs were dropped on Hiroshima and Nagasaki, and the Japanese surrendered, our nation was euphoric—at last the war was over, and no more of our American fighting men would die. All of the husbands, fathers, and sons and brothers would return to their families.

Once again, we all headed for Chicago to be in on the big celebration which engulfed our entire country. It was an ecstatic and glorious time. You cannot imagine the euphoria!!!!

I have lived long enough to witness that in the interests of "Political Correctness" some have made an attempt to rewrite history to condemn our generation for the dropping of the atomic bomb. Dear reader, make no mistake—we U.S. citizens, young and old, were all united in putting an end to the war the Japanese had so ignominiously begun, and we were all

---

96   http://waywiser.fas.harvard.edu/people/1467/american-phenolic-corporation

thankful that our country had developed the atomic bomb to drop on our enemy to accomplish the goal without losing one more American life than absolutely necessary!!!!!!!!!!!!!!!!

That was war—not an exercise or a game—U.S. blood was being spilled.

During a visit to Japan in 1985, we went to Hiroshima. We saw the museum which the Japanese have erected to the memory of those who died there as a result of the atomic bomb attack. No mention was made of the fact that they, the Japanese, began the war with a cowardly sneak attack on Pearl Harbor, causing the deaths of innocent U.S. civilians. We spoke to a young Japanese student who, unbelievably, did not know that their government attacked the U.S at Pearl Harbor, thereby beginning the U.S. involvement in WWII. Madness!!

* * *

Mom had two cousins in the U.S. Army who fought the Japanese. Her cousins, Edward and Miles Huml, made headlines because Miles flew to New Guinea (the largest island in The Dutch East Indies) to see his brother, Edward, for his birthday. How rare it was for two servicemen to visit each other during the war. Through the work of a dear relative that collects our family's stories, I was made aware of this story and another about a member of the WAC (Women's Army Corps) who also was sent to New Guinea. I think it's important to note the stories of Mom's cousins (Dad's soon-to-be relatives) as well as a WAC they never knew, who all fought and worked hard to liberate the Dutch East Indies while Dad and the family were imprisoned. These stories add to the context of the war in the Pacific. All the while the Dutch engineers and their families were prisoners, there were throngs of brave men and women fighting for their freedom. This is the newspaper article that appeared in the scrapbook of Miles Jr.'s mother along with several photos of the reunion—

Sgt. Edward Huml and Pvt. Miles Huml, Jr., New Guinea,
(February, 1945 approx.).

"Looking for a novel way of celebrating your birthday? From New Guinea comes the following suggestion: have a brother or friend who is overseas, fly home to see you. For in spite of restrictions on transportation, Pvt. Miles Huml, Jr., who knew that his brother was stationed in New Guinea, looked up Sgt. Edward Huml's A.P.O [Army Post Office] number and platoon, boarded a "bully beef bomber"[97]

---

97   "The 6th Airlift Squadron is the oldest airlift squadron in the U.S. Air Force having served with distinction since 1 October 1933. The squadron made airlift history during World War II when, in October 1942, it was transferred to Port Moresby, New Guinea. Then flying C-47s . . . the 6th became the first personnel transport squadron to fly in the Pacific. It was during this assignment that the squadron earned the nickname *"Bully Beef Express"*, as it carried tons of boiled beef to allied combat troops in Australia and New Guinea." https://www.squadronposters.com/product/c-17-bully-beef-80th-anniversary/?srslti-d=AfmBOooRi66svaawjDN2_jbxzG1EHUBHt30Ji_3j4We_KIt6kvgpAalW

somewhere in Shangri-La, and paid a surprise birthday visit to his brother. Pvt. Miles is with the Army Signal Air Corps[98] in the Dutch Indies, and the trip he undertook was his first holiday since leaving for service 18 months ago.

The brothers had not seen each other for two years, for Sgt. Edward, or "Doc" as he is known to his service company, has been in the Army's 108th engineers corps for the past three and a half years. He was stationed in the Hawaiian Islands for one year, and was shipped to New Guinea about four months ago. Private Miles Huml has the distinction of having had 15 different addresses in his 18 months of service; he has been sending souvenirs to his parents . . . since he received an overseas assignment and the most recent additions to his collection are a Japanese box and a Jap bayonet.

While together the brothers sent a letter to their mother relating the good times they had in "talking shop" and comparing meals. Pvt. Miles met Sgt. Edward's best buddy M/Sgt. Paul Bales of Chaleston, Ill., who has been with the sergeant during their past three and a half years of service. They've become such fast friends that the Huml family has adopted Bales as a pen pal. The three servicemen were able to be together for three days before Pvt. Huml had to board a plane back to his camp.

Says Mrs. Miles Huml, their mother, "I only wish that more mothers could experience the thrill of having their sons meet overseas. I can tell by the change in their last letters how much good the reunion has done for each of my sons."

---

98   https://www.army.mil/article/236799/signal_corps_in_world_war_ii

Sergeant Edward Huml, M/Sgt. Paul Bales, and Private Miles Huml, somewhere in New Guinea, February, 1945 (approx.).

A separate article from the *Berwyn Beacon* has this headline, "Letters In Same Envelope Proves The Reunion Of Bros." The article says that Sergeant Edward Huml had spent four birthdays away from home in the armed forces, since April 21, 1941. It also talks about their uncle and another cousin being in the same war zone.

* * *

The story from one of my relatives tells of his recent meeting in March, 2025 with a ninety-nine-year-old WAC that speaks to the conditions in New Guinea and in the Philippines:

"About 3 weeks ago a few of us from our VFW post went over to Bethlehem Woods assisted living home to have lunch with veterans who live there. We got there early and while waiting, the veterans who live there came into the dining hall and sat down with us. One of them was a woman. When she sat down, Pete Zika leaned over to me and whispered that somebody should tell her this was only for veterans. Well, she heard that and said she is a veteran. This now gets interesting. She is 99 years old and was a WAC from WWII. As a young lady, she volunteered for the Army, volunteered for overseas duty and was sent to New Guinea. Now as I am sure you know where that is but today, very, very few people had even heard of New Guinea.[99]

She told me how miserable it was there as it rained like crazy and the temperature was often above 100 degrees. She was a typist and served there for almost a year. Then, when MacArthur invaded the Philippines she was sent up to Manila. She told me how the city had been destroyed and she had been sent to St. Thomas University to help process our POW's. Can you believe that?

She told me how Japs were still in Manila when she was there and she could hear gunfire as our troops went out to rid the city of Japs. I ate lunch with her that day and sat mesmerized. She is living history and let's face it, at the age of 99 she is one of the few left who can attest to what happened in the Philippines back then. I told the parade committee about her and they all seemed interested in having me submit her name for Grand Marshall. By then, she will be 100, God willing, and I think the town would love to hear her talk about her experiences. We live in interesting times. Regrettably, the WWII veterans are quickly passing on and with them we lose learning from them.

Today, in history books, you can read brief passages about that period of time but to think that we actually have a few people who lived that history still alive. One of the stories she related to me is when she arrived in New Guinea. She and other American WACs boarded a truck after disembarking from a ship. They started off on a dirt road

---

99 A lot of people hadn't heard of Pearl Harbor before its bombing too. So they didn't know where the attack had occurred.

only to suddenly have these American soldiers step out from the jungle with their camouflage and "sticks and branches sticking out from their helmets" and began chasing after their truck. She said they were throwing coconuts with their names on them into the truck. Many of them were reaching out to try and touch them when they caught up to their truck. She said she was so scared and didn't recognize them as American soldiers with their face paint and camouflage. When she related that to me, I could imagine how she felt."

* * *

After Mom's death, I shuddered at the thought that I might never finish this book. Not only because I wanted to honor the promise I made to Dad to tell his story, but also because of the dangers of revisionist history. The fullness of time has ways of overlooking, omitting, and sometimes trying to redefine facts. Just as recently as March, 2025, the WAC's story put Dad's story into greater context. She talked of the destruction of Manila. After reading her account, I realized that when Dad and the family had been flown to Manila to heal at a hospital there, they were healing among devastation, in the middle of what was one of its biggest battlegrounds.

Primary witnesses, documentation, and corroborated facts are the only way we can truly know the truth of our past which informs our present and charts our future. And sadly, most of those who lived through WWII have died, lost along with their stories. Individuals and governments destroyed primary documents during the war, either intentionally or inadvertently. Duty called. I had a responsibility to write where my research led. But there was one more mystery to solve before my research would be complete.

THE SCROLL

In 2000, on one of Dad's visits to our family home in Dos Vientos, he brought his Japanese scroll. It surprised me that Dad brought it all the way from Chicago. It had hung on the wall of his study for as long as I could remember. As Candice and Margaux sat around the dining room table on that visit, Dad rolled out the four-foot-long scroll to reveal a golden, tall skinny man with unusually large ears floating on a puffy white cloud. Two other golden, short men hovered below on their own clouds in front of him. One of those attendants held his hands in prayer, and the other carried an object with dangling colorful beads that flew in the breeze. All of them had downcast eyes. A halo crowned the tall man, who also has a pinkish stone embedded in his hair.

The girls were probably around eleven and fourteen years old and they sat long enough for Dad to tell a few stories about the war. They looked over the scroll politely, but then were quickly on their way. Dad wanted that moment with his granddaughters and his scroll.

After the girls left, Dad and I had a discussion I'll never forget.

"Would you like the scroll?" he asked.

Dad wants to give it away? To me?

I didn't know how to reply, except to say, "Yes."

This was something I hadn't expected. The time had come for him to let it go.

"Well, I can't just give it to you," Dad said.

"Oh, um . . . how much do you want for it?"

He weighed an amount in his mind for a bit.

"One hundred dollars," he said, nonplussed.

I got up out of my chair, left the room to fetch the money, then handed him a one-hundred dollar bill. Dad put the money in his wallet, rolled up the scroll, then handed it to me. At that moment, something much greater passed between us. The look in his eye told me as much. I would be the keeper of the scroll.

The Japanese word for scroll is *kakemono*. A scroll can be made from papyrus, silk, parchment, or rice paper and is usually mounted, like Dad's, on quality silk brocade with wooden dowels (over time, a portion of the bottom dowel on Dad's scroll had broken off). I felt the weight of the wood and rolled-up canvas in my hands. I'd never held Dad's scroll before. Rolling up its beautiful image seemed wrong somehow. The surprising transaction fueled my already burning curiosity about Dad's past.

"How did you get this scroll?" I asked. It occurred to me how strange it was that I knew so little about something I'd admired my whole life. I suppose my lack of curiosity about the scroll and what it meant to Dad speaks to things that become too familiar, and simply fade into the background. Dad loved the scroll. I never knew or questioned why. Not until then, and again very recently.

"I stole it," he said.

What? Stealing wasn't in Dad's nature. He was a pillar of society, and a founding member of our local church. He led a Bible study called the Nehemiah ministry, an outreach to business leaders who wanted to keep the teachings of Jesus front and center in the workplace. The man I knew wasn't capable of stealing anything, let alone what appeared to be an ancient scroll.

"Why?" I said, stunned.

"When they took us to the Kotakuji temple as prisoners, they'd taken so much from us. I wanted something in return. So, I took it off the wall." He never spoke about it again.

He *stole it*. He didn't *take it*. Later, I hung the scroll on the wall in the foyer of my home. I remember how majestic it looked hanging there because the golden color of the wall set off the golden paint of the figures on the scroll.

When the time was right, I intended to research the scroll's history, and especially the meaning of the golden men painted on it. But my desire fell victim to the many unfulfilled good intentions of a busy life. The scroll sat in deep storage while some of the most difficult and simultaneously glorious years of my life unfolded. During that time, I would think back to that conversation with Dad. I wondered if I should own something that didn't really belong to either of us. Over the decades, the thought occurred to me of possibly reaching out and returning the scroll to the temple. But something always stopped me.

Raising the girls and seeing them through college, my divorce, and finding my new way in the world, left me precious little time to research the scroll's story and consider what, if anything I should do about its return. When I had the means, I lacked the time and inclination. When I didn't have the means, more pressing matters demanded my attention.

Once I had settled into my new life as a single woman, as I continued to unravel the mystery of Dad's story, the memory of that afternoon in Dos Vientos haunted me. On one hand, our discussion that long-ago afternoon was like the dozens of times Dad and I had talked about his past. And yet, it was unlike any other discussion we'd had before. He had never asked for me to pay for anything else he handed down to me. Perhaps, the scroll simply had too much value for him to simply give it away.

I wonder what he thought about every time he admired the scroll. Did it symbolize freedom? Justice? Retribution? Revenge? Did its significance change over the years? He had stolen it as a young man dying of starvation; a young man who had everything taken away from him, stripped of his life and home. He hadn't known if he'd live or die. Perhaps the scroll was a promise of the future. Perhaps as he struggled to survive, he imagined a future home where it would hang. Had he perhaps envisioned it hanging in his daughter's home one day?

SOLVING THE MYSTERY
OF THE SCROLL

Renting the perfect beach house in Santa Cruz gave me goosebumps in early 2017. It's just one of many examples when the Lord graciously, playfully, and outrageously blessed me over the years. Giving me a supernatural kind of encouragement by providing a sanctuary for me to rest and write this story. It feels like Dad, Mom, and the rest of the family are smiling down on me here.

As they began to feel closer than ever, I stared at the scroll hanging in my hallway. The energy of the scroll passed to me. But what kind of energy had Dad let go of and what kind of energy had I inherited? I needed to know more about the meaning of the scroll. Who were these men I'd been living with all these years? What did they represent? Perhaps the discovery would also shine some light on the reason why the families were taken to Kotakuji for safety and would help me with my decision about its return. Maybe there was some kind of hidden clue in the scroll that Dad wanted me to find. Maybe there was more to the story that Dad wanted me to know.

Finding out the meaning behind the scroll began with a familiar search for answers to some basic questions. For example, I wanted to know what *Kotakuji* meant in English. Ironically, the word means "lottery." And while the word lottery has several definitions, one of them took my breath away, *"a process or thing whose success or outcome is governed by chance."* A chilling, yet accurate description of the five Dutch families' fate.

My thirst for knowing more about the temple and the time the families spent imprisoned there increased even more when my cousin, David, Uncle Reinier's son, shared a memory with me a few years back. About thirty years ago, he was a high school exchange student in the 1980s in Nagoya and he visited the temple. During his visit, an old Japanese woman called out, "Are you Hans's son?"

Shocked, David said, "No, why? Why did you use that name?"

She said that David looked exactly like my dad, Hans, who she knew very well. She didn't go into how, and David didn't have much time to find out more, but the haunting memory stuck with him, and the long arm of history connected the dots of the family experience even then.

Dad said there were seven different scrolls hanging at the temple. Of all the scrolls, why did he choose to steal the one hanging on my wall? Sadly, I never thought to ask Dad while he was alive. Motivations are difficult to suppose. After Dad's death, there were so many mysteries I had to uncover on my own.

During my time in Santa Cruz, I'd contacted a few scholars over the years from prestigious local universities like Stanford and University of California Santa Cruz. I thought if I sent them a photo of the image on the scroll, they might be able to tell me about its meaning. When I didn't hear back from any of them, I got discouraged and didn't really know how to keep researching. I wondered how I could ever find out the meaning of the imagery on the scroll by myself as I'm no expert in ancient Japanese scrolls.

A few more busy years went by.

I finally decided to research the meaning behind the images on the scroll myself a few years ago. While reading the English version of Ineke's book, *The Temple with the Chrysanthemums*, I learned that the Dutch families saw many red *torii* gates outside of temples as they sailed along the Inland Passage of Japan on their voyage from Indonesia. When I investigated the meaning of the red gates, I discovered that they are considered a barrier between the ordinary world and the sacred and spiritual realms. It's customary for one to bow before walking through them—anywhere but in the center, a space reserved only for deities. Once a person enters the temple they are on holy ground. How could such a sacred place be used as a prison? The idea seemed unthinkable.

In the process of researching, I got curious about the religion practiced at Kotakuji and believed those details might help unravel the meaning of the painting on the scroll. The scroll's Buddhist imagery sent me on a quest that soon led to the Myoshinji branch of the Rinzai school of Zen Buddhism. Buddhism appeared in Japan in the sixth century, and much later, Zen was introduced from China. Rinzai Zen Buddhism had a unique feature—"The koan, illogical questioning, participates in the teaching of the Rinzai masters. Example: A buffalo goes through a window. Its head, body, and all four legs have entered. Why doesn't its tail go through?"[100]

As I dug deeper, I discovered that followers of the Myoshinji branch of the Rinzai school of Buddhism worshiped the Amida Noryai

---

100 https://www.japan-experience.com/plan-your-trip/to-know/understanding-japan/zen

Buddha. It didn't take me long to realize that the Amida Noryai Buddha had been the one painted on the scroll and been my lifelong companion, one who also represented asking questions to reach insight or gain enlightenment.

According to Webster, the koan was "used to train Zen Buddhist monks to abandon ultimate dependence on reason and to force them into gaining sudden intuitive enlightenment," in other words to go beyond conditioned thinking and explore higher states of awareness and understanding. Had that been an unintended result of my quest? Had that been what the Lord wanted me to do in my life while endeavouring to understand my family's fate?

Reason seemed to have little to do with how I arrived at so many of my answers to the questions that created this story. Perhaps, Amida Buddah had been helping me to trust my intuition from the many walls where he hung, encouraging the telling and writing of this story. And yet, he had been such a riddle. Once I finally met my nearly constant companion after so many years, I wanted to learn more about him.

"Pure Land worship centered on the Amida Buddha (Sanskrit: Sukhāvatī), also known as the Buddha of Immeasurable Light and Buddha of Limitless Life. Amida presided over a heavenly paradise and promised salvation and rebirth in his paradise for all worshippers. Works of art were essential to the Pure Land doctrine and its next-world emphasis on rebirth and salvation.

Until the twelfth century, Amida Buddha was usually represented seated on a lotus flower; however, during the Heian period (794–1185) and Kamakura period (1185–1333) the concept of Raigō (welcoming descent) flourished and Amida Buddha was often represented in a standing pose descending from the heavens to fetch his devotees and personally transport them back to his blissful paradise."[101]

The Amida Buddha on Dad's scroll descends from the heavens with his devotees and he displays one of nine different mudra (hand gestures) which determine the nine possible paths for the dying to enter paradise. The gesture on Dad's scroll, jōbon geshō (bottom level of the first class), is one of the best-known gestures in Japanese Buddhist imagery.

"Other distinguishing features of the Amida Buddha are the extended lobe on top of his head to accommodate his advanced understanding of the truth, his large ears that allow him to hear all people in need, the rose-coloured crystal among his curly hair that emits rays of light displaying his supreme knowledge . . . "—Wayne Crothers, Curator, Asian Art, National Gallery of Victoria[102]

"Amida appears with great frequency in Japanese religious painting and statuary, and is often accompanied by two main attendants in artwork called the Amida Sanzon 阿弥陀三尊 (lit. = Amida Triad) which depicts the three descending from above to welcome the souls of the dying into Amida's pure land.[103]

I had been living with the symbol of Life in the Beyond, Immeasurable Light, Limitless Life, Heavenly Paradise, Promised Salvation, Rebirth, Meditations, Prayers, Sutras, Advanced Understanding of The Truth, Hearing All People in Need, Supreme Knowledge, Love, Affection for Humanity, Compassion For All People, The Life To Come,

---

101 Jōdo Shū: Pure Land Buddhism National Gallery of Victoria.
102 Crothers, Wayne. *Japanese Amida Buddha*. Jan 30, 2013. https://www.ngv.vic.gov.au/essay/japanese-amida-buddha. Accessed December, 2022.
103 Amida Buddha. Buddha of Infinite Light and Life. Lord of the Beyond and the Afterlife. Lord of Gokuraku, the Land of Ultimate Bliss. Savior of Japan's Pure Land Sects. *A to Z Photo Dictionary Japanese Buddhist Statuary* https://www.onmarkproductions.com/html/amida.shtml. Accessed December, 2022

Ruler of the Western Paradise of Ultimate Bliss. It was as if Amida had been a message of constant comfort all these years.

Shortly after I discovered Amida, I became inspired to email an art appraiser through The Art Appraisers Association of America, one who specialized in Asian art. The work is priceless to me, so I wasn't interested in selling it. I just hoped that I might glean some additional information about it from an expert in the field and verify if I had correctly interpreted the scene it depicted.

It only took a few hours for the appraiser, a very generous man named Dan Herskee, to offer a free consultation if I sent him some good photographs of the scroll. The next day, he got back to me and affirmed where my research led.

> *Dear Laura,*
>
> *Thank you for sending these images.*
>
> *This appears to depict what's called a Raigo painting.*
>
> *I have no doubt your scroll is old (Edo period perhaps?) and I find it completely plausible that it came from the collection of a well-known temple in Japan.*
>
> *Best wishes,*
>
> *Dan*

The Tokugawa shogunate ruled Japan from the city of Edo (modern-day Tokyo) during 1603 to 1868, a time of relative stability and peace, known for its flourishing culture, art, and literature, the development of the samurai class—those granted the right to wear two swords and have first and last names—and the growth of cities and urbanization in Japan.[104]

Dan concurred with my research. The thrill of finally knowing who had been my constant companion all these years set in. All along my journey, I mistakenly considered myself unqualified to know how to uncover the answers to the most intriguing questions of this story—be it in the worlds of art or science, or within the gaps of Dad's memory. As I sat in my Santa Cruz home during a very rainy day in December 2022 (the beginning of what would be 12 atmospheric rivers that would pummel our seaside haven), I had a moment of clarity. Curiosity is a way God inspires us. Through that inspiration, our intuition works miracles to help point us in the right direction. His still, small voice gives us wisdom beyond our own comprehension. I didn't need to be an expert in WWII history or ancient Asian art, I simply needed to go where God led.

The story of the scroll was a small detail in the epic story, yet finding out the meaning of the painting felt so momentous. In my excitement, I almost rushed to answer my next questions without taking a pause to acknowledge the profundity of my discovery. Because of my search, I finally knew so much more about Kotakuji. Jerry and I sat by the fire that night and had a glass of champagne, toasting Amica and our journey together.

With Dan's verification that I had discovered the correct meaning of the scroll, I could concentrate on the next piece of the puzzle, the actual location of the temple. A task that should have been easy in this age of Google was anything but. When I finally sleuthed the location of the temple where Dad had been imprisoned (how unbelievable that sentence truly is), I felt like I'd won the lottery. As it turned out,

---

104 https://www.history.com/topics/asian-history/meiji-restoration

many temples in Japan bear the name Kotakuji. Drowning in a sea of Kotakujis, I got my cousin David in on the hunt. He had no idea of the address or even the town where it was located as he'd been there so many years ago as a teenager. So, I tried texting certain plausible temple websites to him to see if we could whack-a-mole the location.

Each time, his reply was the same, "Nope!"

David told me it was such a small, unassuming temple compared to the others he'd toured in Japan that it probably didn't even have a website. Just as it seemed I'd hit a dead end, I decided to email Ineke, who very graciously took the time to send me a few new pieces of the puzzle—a short YouTube video that one of the Italian prisoners' descendants made with their family to chronicle their pilgrimage to the temple; and a link to a documentary one of the Italian families made about their prison experience, *Haiku on the Plum Tree*. As it had been years since the film's release, it wasn't available to stream anywhere.

I watched the YouTube video immediately, and at the end, the family included a satellite image of the temple. I pieced that together with the name of the train station where the family had disembarked in order to take a car and drive to the temple. When I located the train station on Google maps, I had enough information to begin my long-distance search. I knew the temple was close to a narrow spot in a river, but I didn't know which spot on which river. A few landmarks on the satellite image from the video (which included a high school that is now next to the temple) were things I could try to use to recognize the location of the temple on a satellite map.

As I searched the satellite imagery, my instinct told me to follow the Yahagi river. I dragged the image through my browser window, winding upriver from the train station into the hills. The river became very wide in spots, and I had my doubts that this little exercise would lead anywhere. But I kept going. Something told me that I would find it there. An otherworldly encouragement silenced my doubts. And then, I spotted the temple. It had all the same distinguishing landmarks as the one on the YouTube video.

I just stared at the word *Kotakuji* on the map for a while. *Could it be?* Then, I made the satellite image bigger and clicked on the precious few photographs that were included on the satellite map. For the first time in my life I saw the temple with my own eyes. The only physical building still standing of the six prisons where Dad had been held— "Camp Pasar Andir, Bandoeng on September, 28, 1942; Palace Hotel Bandoeng, on October 10, 1942; Baros, Tijmahi, on July 7, 1943; Tjiboenoet, Bandoeng on December 17, 1943; [Chilean Embassy] Tokio, Japan January 17, 1944; [Kotakuji] Nagoya, Japan on April 15, 1945 (note: this date is should have been May 15, 1945)."[105]

I met Kotakuji on Google. I even knew its physical address: Japan, 〒470-0307 Aichi, Toyota, Higashihirosecho, Gokuraku–13 (〒470-0307 愛知県豊田市東広瀬町極楽13). The moment felt as gratifying as it did alarming. Sitting in my loft overlooking the calm Pacific, almost a world away, I looked upon the temple's pictures. The setting of some of the stories Dad told, and many more he wasn't willing or able to tell. I'd have to read about those in Ineke's book, and learn of them from the documentary. (Eventually, filmmaker Mujah Maraini-Melehi granted me access to view the film.)

Here is the description of *The Haiku on the Plum Tree* in creator Mujah Maraini-Melehi's own words. "The film explores the legacy of the Maraini family's experience in a Japanese war camp during WWII. Interviews, animation, and Basil twist's Dogugaeshi (Japanese theater

---

105 Netherlands Indies Government: Netherlands Indies Welfare Organization For Evacuees For Queensland (N.I.W.O.E.) dated November 1945. Misspelling of Tokio left since it was referenced this way.

of screens) take us on a voyage back in time, while we also prepare an actual journey back to the sites of the two camps as they are today. My mother, poet and historian Toni Maraini, and my aunt, acclaimed Italian author Dacia Maraini, were only 2 and 7 years old when they entered the first camp in 1943 with their parents, anthropologist Fosco Maraini and Topazia Alliata."[106]

After a screening of the film at NYU, Toni Maraini called the Japanese soldiers sadistic. She said they used to eat lavishly on a balcony on the temple grounds and laughed as they threw their scraps, usually fish heads and bits of potato, down to the starving children who fought for them. But, like Dad, Toni didn't hate the Japanese people. She talked about sneaking out of the prison, an act that could have gotten her killed, to glean food from neighboring farms. The Japanese farmers never reported her because they didn't agree with what was going on. She knew they were good people.

There was so much more to the story than I ever imagined. As there were many more things I wanted to discover upon learning of these resources, I thought it best to celebrate this next big accomplishment of finding the temple and quickly shared my good news with Ineke. David was also pleased I had found the temple. Since he was an exchange student when he toured the temple, I wondered which high school he'd attended as an exchange student.

"[I went to] Aichi High School in Nagoya," he said in a text. "Complete random high school as they were somehow affiliated with my high school Japanese teacher's wife back in Olympia, Washington. Finding Kotakuji was only due to a host family relative who was part of that sect and could figure out where the temple was. A lot of low probability events lined up to make that visit possible!"

---

106 https://www.kickstarter.com/projects/haikus-maraini-doc/haikus-on-a-plum-tree

So many random events led to David's encounter with the old woman who knew Dad by name. After discovering so much rich new material about the temple, more about the story of other prisoners who had suffered there, and its whereabouts, I wondered why I didn't do this kind of research with Dad while he was alive. I guess we were so busy sorting out his history and chronicling his stories, I wanted to focus my time on those memories, thinking the actual settings of the story would be easy pieces of the puzzle to put in place.

Once I encountered the right Kotakuji, I did some more research and found out that it is part of the Japanese Buddhist movement called Shinshu Otani-ha, which follows the Pure Land teachings of the Amida Buddha and belongs to Jōdo Shinshū, also known as Shin Buddhism. So, everything lined up nicely in my research and gave me some peace.

* * *

I have returned to Seascape beach many times over the years to enjoy long walks and picnics, sometimes when I need to be close to Mom and Dad, or want to spend time with God, or just have fun with my husband and our sweet dog Lucy. That beach has and will always be a place where I find true peace and joy. With the questions about what to do with the scroll in my heart, I made my usual pilgrimage there. I stopped at a quaint little grocery store and bought some food for a picnic to take down to the sand. I decided to walk the beach on a May day, 78 years after the families were brought to the prison at Kotakuji, and coincidentally a day before my milestone birthday.

When I sat down in the cold sand, I crossed my legs, and closed my eyes. Dad had turned twenty-one in February of 1945 and so he'd lost nearly four of the most magical years of life as a POW. He was imprisoned when most teenagers exercised their independence and freed when most twenty-one-year-olds in America would be celebrating their first legal drink. How much is time worth? What could possibly pay Dad back for nearly four lost years and the endless painful things that were inflicted on him—things which his trauma would never allow him to share? How much Dad wanted to make things right in the way a twenty-one-year-old could. He took the scroll and called it even.

Now that I knew the story behind the scroll, what did it mean to me? What did Dad's spirit want me to do with it? While alive, Dad wanted and needed to have the scroll as a type of compensation for so much suffering. Would the Amida Buddha, the Buddha of Immeasurable Light and Buddha of Limitless Life, be my constant companion? Was the scroll a metaphor for Dad's own Pure Land? The representation of a slice of heaven he could only dare dream about during his imprisonment and the death and destruction of war?

THE QUEST

JAKARTA, JAVA, INDONESIA
NOVEMBER, 1945

After my family's rescue by the U.S. Marines off a beach in Japan and a month of healing in a hospital in Manila, the Philippines, they were airlifted as refugees to Camp Columbia in Brisbane, Australia[107], where the Netherlands established a government in exile in preparation for its return to Indonesia. Only a few months later, in October of 1945, Grandpa went back to work for the PTT in Indonesia to support the family and secure his pension.

Happenstance and coincidence seemed to rule Grandpa's life in ways logic never could—a German married to a Dutch woman; an Iron Cross decorated WWI soldier who was an outcast in the Dutch East Indies; a POW and scientist. His life of contradiction took its toll. He returned to Java the same way he and his pregnant wife had arrived over twenty years prior—unexpectedly and in desperate need of a job.

---

107 The Dutch prepare for the liberation of Netherlands East Indies https://campcolumbia. com.au/heritage-park-camp-columbia/dutch-take-over-camp-columbia-1944-1947/

However, the Indonesian Archipelago had fallen into total chaos after the war. Two days after Emperor Hirohito surrendered, Sukarno and Mohammad Hatta proclaimed Indonesia's independence, triggering a revolution and four years of bloody conflict[108]. Everything had changed—the names of people, streets, and towns. Overnight, Batavia had been renamed Jakarta, which means *Complete Victory* in Indonesian.

While working in Jakarta, Grandpa's job was to inventory abandoned radio equipment that had once belonged to the Dutch and put it back in service. The tedious, methodical work gave him time to try and process all he had been through. In his years as a POW during the war and months as a refugee afterward, something had switched over inside of him. He felt an overwhelming need to make sense of the madness he'd endured and embarked on a seemingly impossible quest.

When his workday ended, the quest took over totally. With every step he took along Jakarta's shop houses, he searched for the one thing he might find among the ruins. A discovery that could, perhaps, bring him some peace. Everywhere he walked, he saw in his mind's eye an Indonesia that no longer existed, the Batavia he chose to remember—a place of elegance, beauty, and refinement.

As Grandpa ambled along, taking special care to keep track of the shops where inventories had changed, his eyes darted among the piles of things never sold before the Japanese Occupation—a curious rubble of orphaned artifacts and extinguished lives. There, just outside the wooden doorway of the last shop he visited that fateful day, Grandpa stood as broken as the porcelain inside.

He paused at the threshold, as if to read a phantom Chinese scroll advertising the store's menu of prices. After the war it was forbidden

---

108 Indonesian Political Timeline https://www.pbs.org/wgbh/commandingheights/lo/countries/id/id_political.html

to display the once requisite listings that had been written with elegant black brush strokes on rice paper. Only the Indonesian language was permitted, written, or spoken. As Grandpa walked over the threshold into the shop, he remembered taking Grandma into his arms and carrying her over the threshold of their bamboo hut in the jungle of Java only months after their first child, my Aunt Aletta, had been born.

Grandpa walked from his spot at the entrance with determined steps, not only to find what he was searching for, but to try to walk away from haunting memory and closer to his future, however foggy. He imagined his once grand villa in Bandung among the banana and Banyan trees. And heard in his mind's eye the monkeys, kalas, and tokeh lizards among the lovely garden and ponds of his home on the edge of the jungle. The lizards had been named after their evening calls, *to–keh*. Legend has it that a person who hears the tokeh call seven times may make a wish and it would be granted. The tokeh usually stopped at six.

On a stroll through the shop, Grandpa imagined the fate of his villa after the Japanese had taken the family as prisoners. Looted and deserted in the heat and the rain. The servants long gone. No one was left to fill the small kerosene cans placed under the legs of the pantry cupboards, a last defense against bugs. No one would fill the home with music; or sing or cook or laugh or run. The tropics would have silently taken his empty house back, engulfing its walls and shuttering its doors. He couldn't imagine that kind of silence, though. The world had been too loud for too long.

As Grandpa put one foot in front of the other, he spotted a silver glimmer among the splintered ruins of chopped up wood. His pulse quickened. *Perhaps. Might it be?* Among teak, scrolls, and oil paintings, in the stench of looted memory, surrounded by broken pieces of fine china and a few intact Victrolas; the remains of a piano sat in the corner.

He had seen a few chopped up pianos in other shops before and almost passed this one by, but the glint of silver among the ruins drew him closer. He froze at the sight of piano keys strewn about like so many toy soldiers. As he picked his way through shattered piano legs, piano hammers, and music wires, he caught sight of the silver nameplate he'd etched a lifetime ago.

It was still fastened to a piece of the shiny, black lacquered mahogany bearing the name, Steinway. He traced some of the letters on the nameplate with his finger, as if that simple act might bring the piano back to life. And in that instant Bach's *Prelude in C Major* played in his mind. He had played Bach on his piano every Sunday in those days.

He took out his handkerchief, spat on it, then bent down low so his eyes were even with the silver plate. This caused a great deal of pain in his back where he'd grown truly old, older than his years. And the act of bending, as hurtful as it was, gave him great joy. He ran his handkerchief over the etching making it his mission to rid the silver of every speck of dust and muck that had accumulated in the great heat and humidity of Java.

"What are you doing to my piano?" The shopkeeper said in Indonesian.

"This isn't your piano," Grandpa said in Dutch with a German accent, as he broadened his polishing to the cracked ebony and ivory pieces just below his name.

The shopkeeper raised an eyebrow upon hearing Dutch, and said, "Like hell it isn't. This is mine!"

Grandpa slowly stood upright. There was no need to hurry. There would be no more shop houses to scour. No more broken things to sift through. His quest had come to an end. A small victory. He swallowed hard and picked up the splintered piece of shiny, black lacquered mahogany with his nameplate. He held it up and said, "My name is Alexander Von Hasenstab, and this is my piano."

Grandpa pointed to the silver plate still as solidly screwed into the wood as the day he'd fastened it in the bamboo hut his family called home. He took pride in his handiwork, an echo of the life he'd lived before.

The shopkeeper pulled out his glasses to verify. Then he bowed to Grandpa and half-spoke, half-whispered, this time in Dutch, "Indeed it is," with a glance, only two men stripped of their identities could share. The city wasn't the only place to have its name changed. Chinese inhabitants had to change their names too. Some said this was just as good as killing them.

Grandpa smiled and thanked the shopkeeper, then tucked his handkerchief back in his pocket and placed the splintered wood with the nameplate under his arm. Then a kind of terror sliced through him. Like it had when he stared down the barrel of a Japanese gun for the first time. The terror of something going horribly wrong.

He walked out the door, into the muggy heat of Jakarta. At high tea, as was his custom, he sipped ginger tea in celebration of his successful quest to recapture a piece of his stolen past. With each sip, he basked in his quiet victory as his first experiences on the island of Java flooded his memory. He recalled the very first time he'd heard Malay. The very first word. How many a boy looking for fortune had jumped aboard ships leaving Europe sailing the Na-yang for Java. The Southern Sea. Long ago, one trip was all it took. In one trip, a boy could make a fortune, enough to last a lifetime if he survived. Grandpa hadn't been one of the fortune seekers. Java had simply insisted upon him. Soon, his thoughts settled on his next quest, my Aunt Aletta.

Grandpa's instincts told him his daughter must be alive. But there had been no word yet. Aletta had been at the wrong place at the wrong time a few too many times in her life. This tendency had landed her half a world away in London when the world went mad. Six years earlier, in September, 1939, Grandpa had missed the launch of her ship the day she sailed for England. Aletta had been bitterly disappointed at not being able to say goodbye to her father. In a desperate attempt to make amends and say goodbye, he had raced his baby blue Chrysler convertible on a dirt road to catch up to her, nearly driving it into the Java Sea. Aletta spotted the car from the deck of the ship and knew it was her father. When he ran out of land, he got out of his car and stood at the edge of the island. They watched each other disappear over the horizon.

* * *

Dear Laura,

After the war when Paps got the offer in Hollandia to re-establish radio on Java, the first thing he did was to search for his piano. He hunted and hunted for it and found it in a Chinese shop, the keys all broken and the piano in a sorry state. Father said to the Chinaman, 'That's my piano.' And the Chinaman said, 'No it's not, it's mine!' My father pointed to the silver plaque he had fastened to the piano before the war and said, "My name is Alexander Von Hasenstab and this is my piano." The Chinaman relented and agreed it was my father's. But, afterward, my father just turned around and walked out of the shop with the slivered piece of wood that still held his nameplate. It wasn't about reclaiming the piano. It was about finding out what had happened to it. This surprised the Chinaman."

Love Daddy

HOLLANDIA

DUTCH NEW GUINEA

After the war in 1945, when Grandpa was 53 years old, the Dutch Government got an offer to inspect a U.S. supply dump in Hollandia, Dutch New Guinea, established to supply the invasion of Japan which was no longer needed. Grandpa was asked to accompany the inspection team to see if there was any radio equipment worth salvaging for reestablishing communications in Batavia (Jakarta) with Holland. When Grandpa arrived at Hollandia, he found that the deserted supply depot did, indeed, contain many items that could be used to immediately establish radio communication with Holland. Dad said that Grandpa was alone when he had the opportunity to inspect what was once General Douglas MacArthur's house on the island. While there, Grandpa took the opportunity to sit at MacArthur's desk.

Dear Laura,

While Paps was in Hollandia, the Dutch tried to reestablish their presence in Batavia. Events were very confusing. There was nobody in charge in Indonesia. It took the years of 1946 to 1949 as the Dutch tried to regain Indonesia. There was bitter fighting, but in 1949, under the United Nations Negotiations, the Dutch agreed to grant Indonesia its independence from the Netherlands, except for Dutch New Guinea. There were conferences between the Dutch and the Indonesians about the terms of the Independence Agreement. One of our relatives, Dick Van Der Meulen, participated in the negotiations. He was the previous Dutch Ambassador to Saudi Arabia, and he worked for better treatment of the Indonesian pilgrims to Mecca, pilgrims who carried Dutch passports. Because of his work in Saudi Arabia, many Indonesian Muslims were friendly to him. The sticking point was the Indonesian Treasury, which was kept in Holland. Under the terms of the Independence Agreement, all Dutch Colonial Government Employees could return to Holland and receive retirement and medical benefits for the rest of their lives, and a portion of the Indonesian Treasury was kept in Holland for that purpose. These terms benefited Paps, who could now go to Sydney and live in the house that I built in Wahroonga, a suburb of Sydney. Alex came to Wahroonga after I had left to go to the United States in August, 1951, when he was 60 years old. He later returned to Holland sometime after Mams passed away in 1961.

Love, Daddy

* * *

After arriving at the deserted base on a still intact landing strip on the stunningly beautiful island, Grandpa walked up to the rumored "million-dollar mansion" of Douglas MacArthur, nothing but three prefabricated engineer huts at the top of a rise on Hollandia with panoramic views of the Pacific. As Grandpa got closer to the storied "home" (MacArthur actually only occupied a handful of days on his way to battle), he took time to admire Lake Sentani and the Cyclops mountains behind, with a waterfall descending a thousand feet through clouds that wreathed the summit. The architects of war had fiercely fought for that land, then constructed a place to live and plan the end of the war in its utter paradise.

Grandpa took a deep breath as he turned the knob, opened the door and stepped into the hallowed, deserted building. He had great reverence for the man who brought peace to the world. And, as he walked through the interior, Grandpa discovered a huge desk that overlooked the lake and took a seat.

Blue Moon

Uncle Reinier and I had many calls over the summer of 2021 to talk about his memories, Dad's life, and about the writing of this book. That September, I caught up with him as my husband and I were making our road trip back to California after Summer Camp. Jerry and I treasured our months together on *Blue Moon*. That was our fourth year of Summer Camp. After our time at sea, even during the pandemic, we usually met up in person with our families before traveling home—a step-daughter, son-in-law and grandkids; my cousin and his family; and Reinier. But time didn't allow for any visits that year. So we caught up with Reinier on a call as we drove through Seattle.

He was preparing to camp at La Push, a nearby beach, with David, and his grandson Alexander that weekend. As he talked about his upcoming trip, he mentioned that he had scattered Grandma and Grandpa's ashes at a small beach close by called Hole in the Wall.

"They go around the world twice in a century," Reinier said.

It was a detail about the story I'd never heard before. The revelation of knowing about their final resting place gave me solace and joy. Even though why isn't a spiritual question, I found myself asking it a lot during the writing of this book. I wondered why I made so much progress relatively recently. So many of the stories had happened at sea, in the Pacific. Perhaps the ocean has a kind of memory. I like to think that Grandma and Grandpa visited us during Summer Camp while we moored on the Salish Sea and helped me put the last of the puzzle pieces together on their eternal journey around the world.

I type these last words from my beach house in Santa Cruz, over-looking the Pacific ten days after the 100th year celebration of Malabar. The book began on my oldest daughter's first birthday and I typed "The End" on my birthday. My present is a promise kept to Dad—to tell his story, the kind that only happens once in a blue moon.

Blue Moon anchored in Eastsound, Orcas Island.

Epilogue
80 Years After The War

As Dad grew older, he was as I expected him to be for many, many years. But then, as he got closer to leaving this world, he became present in a different way. His love for us was heightened, and he became more childlike. As his time came near, he'd sleep most of the day. I'm not sure when he crossed the threshold of being in this world. But, a time came when our work of telling his story was done, and it was time to say goodbye.

So much came to light during and after Dad's death. About life, about this story. One of the things I learned is to appreciate (and not take for granted) the person we know. Because a time may come when they can no longer be with us in the way we are accustomed. We can lose them so much sooner than we realize. So much sooner than we are ready for. I wish Mom and Dad were here to talk to again. To sing to me. I wish for one last tea. One more chocolate chip cookie. One more itinerary. I wish for so many things that will never be. And yet, in death, Mom and Dad are somehow closer to me than ever before.

Sometimes, when I care for my infant grandson, Reinier, I'll look out the window and see Dad in my imagination. He and his three-year-old great-grandson, Algernon, hunch over six nails and five pieces of wood. Dad steadies the planks so he can help Algernon hammer the nails into the wood. Then Algernon climbs on the bench they've made together, takes his seat, and swings his feet with a big smile. His blonde curls reflect the warm sunlight.

A songbird lands on the bench beside Algernon and his eyes light up.

"Pa-pa!" Algernon squeals, pointing at the bird, now in flight. "Caw, caw!"

Dad picks Algernon up as they watch the bird fly to the top of a fence.

"He's my old friend. Now, he'll watch over you, too," Dad says. "Remember, my darling boy, birds always sing after a storm."

* * *

After receiving his degree in Civil Engineering in Australia, Dad immigrated to the United States to the city of Chicago where he met his bride, June, in the church choir. They had hot chocolate on their first date. He took Mom to the Taj Mahal and everywhere she wanted to go. She squeezed fresh orange juice each morning and brought it to Dad in bed when he woke up every day of their 62-year marriage. When we were young, every Saturday morning, Dad made bacon, and all of us kids made pancakes while Mom slept in. We always drenched our pancakes in pure Canadian maple syrup (nothing but the best). One of Mom and Dad's passions was ballroom dancing, which they enjoyed all over the Chicagoland area, especially at the Aragon ballroom. They were born four years apart and died four years apart. In

2016, Dad died of heart failure on the left side of his heart. Mom died of heart failure on the right side of hers. They both lived until they were 92 and had their first ballroom dance in heaven after Mom's death in November, 2020.

I stand at your gate and the song that I sing is of moonlight.
I stand and I wait for the touch of your hand in the June night.
The roses are sighing a moonlight serenade.
The stars are aglow and tonight how their light sets me dreaming.
My love, do you know that your eyes are like stars brightly beaming?
I bring you and sing you a moonlight serenade.
Let us stray till break of day
In love's valley of dreams.
Just you and I, a summer sky,
A heavenly breeze kissing the trees.
So don't let me wait, come to me tenderly in the June night.
I stand at your gate, and I sing you a song in the moonlight,
A love song, my darling, a moonlight serenade.

—*Moonlight Serenade*, a song by Glenn Miller and His Orchestra[109]

109 "Moonlight Serenade" Written by Glenn Miller and Mitchell Parish © 1939 (Renewed) Sony/ATV Music Publishing Used by permission. All rights reserved.

Mom and Dad at their engagement dinner in 1952,
seven years after Dad's rescue.

ABOUT THE AUTHOR

Laura, in 2024, in her garden in Santa Cruz, CA,
sitting on the last "concentration camp" bench she made with her Dad.

As a teenager, Laura's love for story began in the Amazon where she water-skied with piranha while learning about headhunters. She is a *USA Today*, Kirkus-star reviewed, and *Wall Street Journal* bestselling ghostwriter of award-winning books, specializing in biography, memoir, historical non-fiction, business, and leadership.

An award-winning screenwriter, Laura specializes in telling stories about true survival, crime, war, and journeys of the heart. She earned her chops at E! Entertainment Television working on shows like *E! True Hollywood Story*, which gave Laura an appetite for finding the story behind the story. She further developed her skills at the *Los Angeles Times*, where she told interactive stories reporting on features, entertainment, crime, hard news, politics, and investigative journalism. Her experience writing feature films, documentaries, and limited series shapes her cinematic writing style. She's contributed scores of travel and lifestyle articles to outlets such as the *Los Angeles Times*, *World Travel Magazine*, *LA Parent Magazine*, as well as other regional newspapers and magazines.

She is a member of the International Screenwriters' Association and the Association of Ghostwriters. Her search for the truth, wherever it leads, continues to call her on many adventures. Some have come in heartbeats and others in decades. Learn more about Laura at Laurasmagicday.com.

RESOURCES

JAPAN'S ATOMIC BOMB PROGRAM

In order to understand the science behind the project Grandpa and the other engineers most likely worked on, I did the best I could to piece together what is known about the Japanese atomic bomb program. This certainly was an ambitious goal for someone like me, completely outside of the field of atomic science or history. However, I wanted to gain a better understanding of the stakes involved and learn about what kind of projects Grandpa might have worked on for the Sumitomo corporation during our family's captivity as Japanese POWs. The Dutch families had been forced to work for the Japanese Army for a reason, and that reason is believed to be the development of a remote detonation device for a nuclear weapon. So, I reasoned that the weapon must have existed in some capacity. Admittedly, what follows is not an academic discussion of this topic, but my own understanding as I pieced the information together during my research. Much of the information that I used to understand the Japanese atomic bomb program is taken from Robert Wilcox's book *Japan's Secret War: Japan's*

Race Against Time To Build Its Own Atomic Bomb. Interestingly, new information is being discovered all the time and has come from sources as recently as 2023.

* * *

"If we'd built the bomb first, of course, we would have used it. I'm glad, in some ways, that our facilities were destroyed."[110] Chieko Takeuchi, widow of Masa Takeuchi, recalled her husband's words in an interview in 2015. Masa Takeuchi played a central role in researching thermal diffusion under the Nigo Research project, headed by Yoshio Nishina, head of the Nigo Research project, a physicist at the Riken Institute in Tokyo during WWII.

"On December 8, 1941, Japan entered World War II with the attack on Pearl Harbor. In April of the same year, the Japanese army's air force had requested Masatoshi Okochi to begin a project to build an atomic bomb. Yoshio Nishina's lab, RIKEN, the Mecca of nuclear physics in Japan, was entrusted with the enrichment of uranium for the project. But American air raids in April 1945 destroyed two-thirds of RIKEN's buildings and facilities, including Nishina's apparatus for enriching uranium, putting an end to the project.

On August 15, 1945, the war in Japan ended. In September 1945, the U.S. forces started investigating Japan's atomic bomb program and decided to destroy the two cyclotrons Nishina had spent 10 years building and to dump them into Tokyo bay."[111] Nishina, said in the 1960s that Japanese researchers had completed a thermal diffusion device that would have allowed extraction of uranium 235 as early as 1944, but U.S. bombings destroyed their secret facilities.

---

110 https://www.latimes.com/world/asia/la-fg-japan-bomb-20150805-story.html
111 https://www.riken.jp/en/about/history/story/

Efforts in Japan by individuals and groups of scientists to develop an atomic bomb began as early as 1937. Scientists formed a Colloquium to press both the Army and the Navy for funding to develop such weapons long before Pearl Harbor in 1941. During much of World War II there were two Japanese teams working in isolation to create an atomic bomb. In 1944, these teams were amalgamated to rationalize their efforts. This gave rise to many postwar claims that the Japanese Army's project under Yoshio Nishina was abandoned. It did in fact cease, however its efforts were resumed by a succeeding project.

The Imperial Japanese Navy (IJN) and the Imperial Japanese Army (IJA) were fierce rivals who viewed each other with contempt and suspicion. Co-operation was non-existent between the two armed forces. As a result, they duplicated everything. For example, each had an air force operating aircraft which shared no engines, or components in common. Even machine guns used different calibers, so that neither branch of the military could use the other's material. Into this bizarre situation was injected an ambition by each service to out-do the other in obtaining nuclear weapons.

Japan's Navy was intoxicated by its early success in the Pacific and at first did not believe Japan would need the advantage of atomic weapons, but reversals in the Battle of Coral Sea and the Battle of Midway began to change the Navy's thinking. As a nation, except for one small mine at Ishikawa, Fukushima prefecture in the Home islands, Japan lacked Uranium deposits, thus relied upon finding deposits within the vast territory conquered early in 1942. Of primary importance to the Army NI Project were alluvial Monazite sands in the rivers of Burma. Monazite is composed of Phosphorus, Thorium and Uranium. Recovery of these sands was one of the driving purposes behind Japan building the railway from Thailand to Burma. At least 5,000 tons of Uranium oxide from Burma reached Tokyo early in 1943.[112]

Even from the very start the Japanese Navy set up a secret scientific advisory committee distinct from the Physics Colloquium. It was from the advice of this group that the navy withdrew support for the Nishina Project in March 1943 to find a better approach. The Navy's parallel, but stubbornly different nuclear project code named F-Go was led by Professor Bunsaku Arakatsu, a former pupil of Albert Einstein, at Kyoto University. The Imperial Japanese Navy project is claimed to have commenced in 1943, but informally began on June 14, 1941, with Arakatsu building his cyclotron at Kyoto University. Cyclotrons were particle accelerators used to bombard atoms. With these devices, aspects of nuclear reactions could be tested and measured on a laboratory scale laying the theoretical groundwork for nuclear weapons.

The F-Go project differed from the Army's NI-Go Project especially in their approach to Uranium enrichment. F-Go emphasized development of gaseous Uranium centrifuges. Little detail of the Navy's project has ever been declassified. Much of what we know today comes from Arakatsu's disclosures in interviews for postwar magazine articles. This itself was after many years of silence had been imposed by strict Allied post war censorship. By contrast, the postwar U.S. Government laid bare details of Nishina's far less successful Thermal Diffusion Enrichment facility at Tokyo's Riken Institute with declassification of wartime archives. Archives relating to the F-Go project have remained classified.

---

112   Wilcox, Robert K. Japan's Secret War: Japan's Race Against Time to Build Its Own Atomic Bomb, Morrow Publishing, NY 1985

F-GO NAVY PROJECT

The Imperial Japanese Navy (IJN) decided to create its own atomic bomb project in 1943. Known informally as the Kyoto Group, IJN funded a team around the maverick scientist Prof Arakatsu with 600,000 yen in March 1943.

The Imperial Japanese Navy (IJN) project to enrich Uranium 235 was led by rear Admiral Nitta Shigeru. Nitta worked closely during early stages of the project from 1942 to 1944 on isotope separation with Sakae Shimizu. Dr. Shimizu who developed F-Go's gaseous Uranium centrifuges. IJN's centrifuges were developed by a company specializing in precision ship gyros, Hokushin Electric Company with assistance from Tokyo Keik Electric Co. These were built under contract by heavy engineering firm Sumitomo. [113]

This was an impressive speed since even today the best centrifuges only operate at about 50,000 RPM. The measure of efficiency for any centrifuge at enriching Uranium depends upon the speed at which the centrifuge spins. It has been claimed that these centrifuges were never built, but the revolution could not be known without testing of an actual prototype machine. The biggest hurdles for any centrifuge are in creating bearings and rotor drums able to withstand the enormous forces involved. The earliest rotors were made of aluminum. Subsequently steel construction allowed even higher speeds, but the Japanese used alloys with Rare Earth metals to create exceptionally strong rotor drums. The Nazis developed carbon fiber brushes and may have shared these concepts with Japan.

Leading nuclear theorists for the Naval A-bomb were Professor Arakatsu Bunsuku, Dr. Sugimoto Asao, Dr. Yukawa and Dr. Kobayashi. Heavy water was harvested by two heavy water plants, one in Kyushu

---

113 Ibid.

and another at Noguchi's JNFC-Nitchisu Fertiliser factory in Korea. Heavy water was harvested as a by-product of Ammonia Production for explosives. Noguchi is now a company known by the name Shoji Kamata. Heavy water was used by F-Go in a nuclear reactor project about which there is little publicly available evidence, except post war claims by Prof. Arakatsu.[114]

URANIUM ACQUISITION

From March to May 1944 Uranium procurement for F-Go was taken over by Lt. Cmdr. Ishiwatari Miroshi. Kyoto University geologist Takubo Jitsutaro was employed by Japan Nitrogen Fertilizer Company (JNFC, also called by its Japanese name, Nitchitsu) to survey Manchuria and Korea looking for Uranium Ores. The Imperial Japanese Navy found Uranium Ores in the hills above Konan, present day Hungnam, North Korea. Ores were assayed under direction of Kyoto University's Physicist Dr Kumura Kiichi. Between 1915-1916 the RIKEN[115] was set up by the Japanese Government to exploit private investment in public owned research facilities. Private companies were encouraged to back specific scientists to create specialist laboratories and in return could reap private rewards.

"Before the war JNFC-Nitchitsu had created a major plant to export fertilizer to the Soviet Union. This plant also had the industrial capacity to meet Japan's need for nitrates used in wartime for explosives. JNFC-Nitchitsu therefore leveraged its huge supply of industrial hydroelectric power and ability to produce Heavy Water in its Hungnam fertilizer plant, by funding another vital wartime project.

114 Ibid.
115 https://www.riken.jp/en

JNFC-Nitchitsu recruited massed laborers, both Japanese, Korean and Manchurian nationals to conduct mineral sample surveys. Japanese authorities lined up thousands of Korean workers to walk, side by side, over Korean hills in search for outcrops of mineral ores which might bear radioactive elements. Even the smallest deposits were dug out, by hand if necessary. Likely findings were spirited away to JNFC-Nichitsu for analysis. Ten significant sites bearing Fergusonite were located producing in excess of 500,000 tons of radioactive ores. These ores were shipped to Wonsan in Korea for refining to oxide and then to Konan for reduction to metal. The entire project was conducted on the same scale as Manhattan's Oak Ridge facility."[116]

In June 1944, 308,483 Yen in funding was released via the Army Aviation Bureau for development of a nuclear weapon for the purpose of aerial attack against the USA. It was given the cover name for funding purposes Kokudoryoku Keikaku (Project Aeropower). This project appears to have been the founding of F-NZ. Later on 6 December 1944 a further One Million Yen was released for this project. It is this project which seems to have amalgamated with efforts by the Japanese Navy.

F-NZ, or "ENNUZETTO," was a secret joint services project led by Admiral Hasagawa Hideo. Captain Mitsui was also involved with the ultra secretive F-NZ laboratory at Konan.[117] F-NZ was said to be a joint forces amalgamation of efforts by the previous Nishina Project and the Kyoto project. It has also been associated with General Kawashima and the 8th Imperial Army Laboratory in Korea. The relationships between these organizations remains unclear.

---

116 King, Byron. Article: North Korea's Nukes: Of Nukes and Ammonium Nitrate, Feb 2005, Pub. Whiskey & Gunpowder.

117 Snell, David, "Japan Developed Atom Bomb; Russia Grabbed Scientists," *Atlanta Constitution*, 2nd October 1946.

"The history of F-NZ is less clear and only came to light from the escape from North Korea of Chemical Engineer Otogoro Natsume in October 1946. This forced U.S. Army Intelligence to re-open investigation of the Japanese Atomic bomb project. Earlier in August 1945 the OSS had parachuted into Korea just one day after the formal signing of a peace agreement aboard USS Missouri.

This had led to a clash with the Manhattan Committee which wanted to keep the Japanese Atomic bomb project secret. Part of this desire appears founded on a secret agreement with the Japanese for the USA to acquire all research details from Unit 731 and from Japanese nuclear projects. This was highlighted in 2002 when documents about the Japanese A-bomb project were returned to the Japanese Government, which refuses to make them public. Immediately following Japan's surrender to the American military government in Japan, SCAP [Supreme Commander of the Allied Powers] exercised draconian powers of censorship to silence Japan's scientists about their wartime activities.

Konan was captured quite suddenly and unexpectedly by Soviet paratroop assault 24 August 1945. In October 1946 a chemical engineer Otogoro Natsume stole a fishing boat and escaped to reach American lines in South Korea where he was interrogated. Otogoro Natsume corroborated Snell's account of a nuclear test blast and asserted that scientists working for F-NZ who were captured by the Soviets, and included Oishi Takeo, Wakabayashi Tadashiro, Takahashi Rikizo, Sato Sei, Fukuda Koken and Tsuchida Meiro, none were physicists and all were under the command of Admiral Hasegawa Hideo."[118]

When the Soviets took over they continued the operation of a Thorium refinery at Konan and a secret facility on a hillside above

---

118 Report Interrogation of Otogoro Natsume by Dr H Kelly, October 31 1946, NA, RG
      224, Box 3.

Konan which Otogoro Natsume said was ringed with barbed wire fences. This appears to have surrounded the entrance to an underground facility. The Soviets continued whatever the operation was there until the Korean War began in 1950, removing thorium in small wooden boxes loaded into submarines. The Thorium thus removed was taken back to Russia via Vladivostok where it was to be used to harvest Uranium 233. The strategic significance of Konan prompted Andrei Gromeko, in December 1948, to approve the building of a special railway line to connect Konan to Russia's own rail network.

Albert Speer in his memoirs wrote of a Ju-390 flight from Bardufoss Norway to Tokyo via the "Polar Route" in 1945, flown by civilian test pilots. Two wartime test pilots who flew the giant Ju-390 Junkers also referred after the war to the Ju-390's Polar flight to Japan.

Conventional cyclotrons are extremely heavy equipment and unsuited to long range flights because of the extreme weight of their magnets. The German particle accelerator device for production of Uranium 233 described by Dr Rolf Wideroe however appears from descriptions to have been lighter than a conventional Cyclotron and more like a centrifugal synchrotron.

Any Synchrotron would also require extremely high voltage power supply from a Marx Generator. One clue to this is these particle accelerators were termed Betatrons by the Germans. The Americans however called the same concept a Caultron. During November 1945 after Japan's surrender, half a dozen of these so-called Caultrons were gathered by U.S. occupation forces and dumped from a small vessel off Yokohama. These would be the type of artificial radiation sources required to transmute Thorium 232 into Uranium. Japanese scientists protested that they were not used for constructing atomic bombs, however the Allied Government was clearly spooked by information to the contrary to take such action.

Photo-fission can be utilized to bombard Thorium 232 and convert it to Uranium 233, or alternately to bombard Uranium 238 and convert it to Plutonium 239. This breeding process could therefore have provided an Atomic weapon with its fissile core.

It may be therefore that the Uranium centrifuges developed by F-Go made a contribution to Japan's A-bomb. Arakatsu continued to research photo fusion during the war and wrote further papers on the topic. It could be inferred from this that perhaps photo-fusion was the path taken by Arakatsu and that F-NZ was created after F-Go to explore an entirely different approach to nuclear weapons.[119]

JAPAN'S INTENDED USE OF THE ATOMIC BOMB

Japan's biggest problem in 1945 was delivery systems. Twelve V-2 rockets had been imported by U-boat before the collapse of Nazi Germany. The correct beach in Kyushu had been identified for the intended Allied invasion in 1946. It seems conceivable that underground launch silos would have been prepared to fire these V-2 rockets at the Allied beachhead and the fleet offshore. Had these been nuclear tipped, an invasion of Japan could have been carnage.

Bomber missions to mainland USA were a goal but as the war dragged into its closing sequences this became less important. Japan was slow to grasp strategic bombing. The distances involved were immense. Honshu Island to Los Angeles was 4,720 nautical miles one way. Seattle was approximately 4,100 nautical miles. On the outbound trip a heavily laden bomber would have to climb to 30,000 ft. to hitch

---

119   Wilcox, Robert K. Japan's Secret War: Japan's Race Against Time to Build Its Own Atomic Bomb, Morrow Publishing, NY 1985.

a ride on Jetstreams and take advantage of higher ground speeds at altitude. The return journey however was against prevailing winds. The shortest possible route was from Paramushiro in the northern Kuril Group. During WW2 the island had four air bases, most with 4,000 ft. runways. Had these heavily laden aircraft been able to take off from such runways then the distance to attack Seattle was an acceptable 3,040 nautical miles.

It is rumored amongst Nazi veterans that the third Ju-390 prototype was not destroyed but rather completed and flown to Japan. The claim is completely unverifiable, but possible and such an aircraft would have permitted raids on cities along the western USA seaboard. Such an aircraft would have looked something like this:

Japan of course produced its own bomber aircraft but strategic bombers came too late. One was the G8N Renzan (RITA)[120] four-engined bomber which was made from steel, as aluminium was in short supply. It was comparable in performance to the B-17 and could never reach the USA. Only four prototypes were built but one was later flown to the USA after the war for evaluation.

Another prospect which might have managed a one-way trip that would be ditched into the sea or possibly a two-way trip by returning to the Paramishiro islands in the North Pacific was the four engined Kawasaki Ki-91. It could carry an 8,800 lb bomb load with a total range of 6,214 sm (10,000 km). The factory tooled up to build these aircraft was destroyed by B-29 raids in February 1945.

The I-400 class submarine, also known as STO class, were very large vessels capable of extremely long range with large watertight hangers for three Aichi M6ASeiran float plane bombers with foldable wings. These aircraft could be launched from catapults on the forward

120 Jake Leigh-Howarth, G8N Renzan – Japan's Long-Range Colossus, https://planehistoria. com/g8n-renzan/. January 16, 2023.

decks of the submarines. The first such submarine, I-401 was intended to undertake a mission with fellow float planes carrying submarines I-13 and I-14 against the Gatun locks of the Panama Canal in April 1945. Their mission with six aircraft was recalled however, possibly so aircraft could be equipped with small tactical nuclear weapons for an attack on the massed U.S. Fleet at Ulithi Atoll. Such an attack hardly makes any sense without nuclear weapons as these aircraft could barely pin-prick such a large force with conventional weapons.

Mainland USA was not the only conceivable target for a Japanese nuclear weapon. The U.S. fleet at anchor inside Ulithi Atoll[121] was a high priority target.

NEW EVIDENCE OF JAPAN'S EFFORT TO BUILD ATOM BOMB AT THE END OF WWII[122]

By Jake Adelstein

August 5, 2015 3 AM PT

In August 1945, the U.S. dropped atom bombs on Hiroshima and Nagasaki. Now, as Japan and the rest of the world prepare to mark seven decades since the end of World War II in the Pacific, new evidence has emerged about the Japanese military's own secret program to build a nuclear weapon.

A retired professor at the state-run Kyoto University recently discovered a blueprint at the school's former Radioisotope Research lab, Japan's Sankei newspaper and other local media reported recently.

121　Ulithi Atoll: The Tiny Speck of Land that Became the Largest Navy Base of World War II https://veteransbreakfastclub.org/ulithi-atoll/. 2020.

122　https://www.latimes.com/world/asia/la-fg-japan-bomb-20150805-story.html. Reprinted with the permission of the author.

The notebooks were related to research work by Bunsaku Arakatsu, a professor at the university whom Sankei said was asked by the Japanese navy to develop an atomic bomb during the war.

Also found were drawings of a turbine-based centrifuge apparently to be used for the study of uranium enrichment. It was dated March 1945. Another blueprint was found of a centrifuge that a Japanese company, Tokyo Keiki, was producing, with a notation indicating the device was scheduled to be completed Aug. 19, 1945 — four days after Japan announced that it was surrendering.

Experts say the material buttresses information contained in U.S. archives and casts light on the direction the research was headed.

For some, the documents also have contemporary resonance, and are a painful reminder that Japan was headed toward developing the same kind of intensely destructive weapons the United States had.

The disclosures come as Japan is in the midst of national debates on nuclear activities and on the use of soldiers.

Japanese parliament members are weighing whether to reinterpret the constitution to allow Japan's Self-Defense Forces to fight abroad with strategic allies such as the United States. Meanwhile, the country is considering whether to restart its nuclear power plants, idled since a meltdown at Fukushima after the devastating 2011 earthquake and tsunami.

"These drawings are more confirmation of the Japanese atomic bomb effort, something many in Japan do not want to admit," said Robert K. Wilcox, the L.A. based-author of "Japan's Secret War: Japan's Race Against Time to Build Its Own Atomic Bomb."

Wilcox, who has been researching the program for decades, said Japan's problem was not a lack of know-how.

"They knew the physics needed for creating the bomb and the engineering needed to build it," he said. "It was lack of element resources like uranium that was the real problem for them."

Such supplies were not readily available in Japan so its leaders looked toward occupied territories.

"In 1945, the Japanese navy alone spent a fortune to gather uranium," Wilcox said. "They needed a win-the-war weapon and an atomic bomb was seen as one of those."

The Japanese government burned thousands of documents as the war was ending. Researchers believe many documents related to Japan's atomic bomb program were destroyed. U.S. occupation forces confiscated almost anything that remained.

So the documents discovered in Japan have drawn intense interest.

"We can say the blueprint is a monument to the elementary levels the research reached at the early stages," Masakatsu Yamazaki, an expert on nuclear development history and an emeritus professor at Tokyo Kogyo University told the Sankei. "It's historically meaningful and it's amazing that it remained."

After the American bombings, there was little public discussion about Japan's attempts to develop an atomic bomb. But Wilcox and Japanese scholars who have since studied the matter say there were two programs to produce a nuclear weapon.

The first plan was commissioned by the Japanese navy and code-named F Research, which involved Arakatsu, the professor. The Japanese army carried out the other program, known as the Nigo Research project, headed by Yoshio Nishina, a physicist at the Riken Institute in Tokyo.

Some scholars believe Japan would have made a nuclear bomb if it had succeeded in acquiring uranium and been able to enrich it. Two major setbacks delayed progress, researchers and those involved in the programs have said.

Masa Takeuchi, who had played a central role in researching thermal diffusion under Nishina, said in the 1960s that Japanese researchers had completed a thermal diffusion device that would have allowed extraction of uranium 235 as early as 1944, but U.S. bombings destroyed their secret facilities.

The other problem was that Japan couldn't get enough uranium to move forward, another researcher, Kunihiko Higoshi of Gakushuin University, said in 2013.

"Nishina told us that a U-boat from Germany would bring us the uranium. It never arrived," Higoshi said.

On May 19, 1945, a Nazi submarine was captured and discovered to be delivering 1,200 pounds of uranium oxide to the Japanese military. The vessel was dispatched for Japan shortly after Adolf Hitler committed suicide, a time when the Germans wanted to dispose of their large amounts of uranium. Two Japanese officers were aboard the submarine; both committed suicide upon being captured.

In an article published in October 1946, the *Atlanta Constitution* cited an unidentified Japanese officer as saying that U.S. air raids on Japan forced the military to move its bomb plant to Japanese-occupied territory in what is now North Korea, delaying Tokyo's bomb development schedule by three months.

Most experts believe that Japan did not have the capability to build a nuclear weapon before the U.S. bombings.

Takeuchi told the Yomiuri newspaper that when he heard that 'a new type of bomb" had been dropped on Hiroshima, he thought to himself, 'How the hell did the U.S. come up with an atomic bomb!'

"It was overwhelmingly regrettable and frustrating," he said.

When Japan surrendered, the occupying U.S. forces discovered just five cyclotrons, devices that speed up atoms in order to separate isotopes that can then be used for a bomb. U.S. atomic facilities in New Mexico, by comparison, contained hundreds of separators operating day and night to produce just four bombs.

"I don't think Japan's nuclear program was very advanced or that it played a role in the decision to bomb Hiroshima and Nagasaki," said Jeff Kingston, director of Asian Studies at Temple University's Japan Campus, and author of "Contemporary Japan."

The uranium seized from the German submarine ended up in the American atom bombs, John Lansdale Jr., head of security for the Manhattan Project, said in a 1995 New York Times interview.

Chieko Takeuchi, widow of the atomic scientist, recalled her husband saying, "If we'd built the bomb first, of course we would have used it. I'm glad, in some ways, that our facilities were destroyed."

What If, in World War II, Japan Got the Atomic Bomb First?

A controversial book about Japan's race to build an atomic weapon in 1945 is published there for the first time. It also raises questions about how North Korea finally got a bomb.

Jake Adelstein and Mari Yamamoto Published Aug. 6 2019 5:16 AM EDT

Universal History Archive/Getty.

TOKYO—What if Japan had been the first to use the atomic bomb in World War II—and what if its top-secret research provided the backbone for the nuclear threat the world now faces from North Korea?

These are some of the tough questions asked in Robert K. Wilcox's book, Japan's Secret War, first published in the United States in 1995, but appearing now for the first time in Japan as the world marks the 74th anniversary of the bombing of Hiroshima and Nagasaki.

The book, bound to be controversial here, has been updated extensively, and the subtitle has been changed. Formerly it was "Japan's Race Against Time to Build Its Own Atomic Bomb." Now it's "How

Japan's Race To Build Its Own Atomic Bomb Provided The Groundwork For North Korea's Nuclear Program."

Its Japanese translator views it as a nuclear deterrent in itself.

Wilcox has written a number of books examining historical mysteries and conspiracy theories, from the Shroud of Turin to the Kennedy assassination, which may put some readers off. But over the next nearly 24 years since the first publication of Japan's Secret War he has continued to research this country's WWII atomic program, building on his already extensive research as he gathered first-hand interviews with Japanese scientists who worked on the project, talked to U.S. officials, gathered classified and declassified documents from many countries, and put together a compelling narrative of Japan's attempts to acquire the ultimate weapon. (Ironically, this third edition of his book is being published in Japan <u>before it will be published in the United States</u>; it won't be available in America until January.)

While it is known that Japan was developing an atomic bomb, the scale and intent has been sharply debated. Wilcox notes that U.S. officials, out of political expediency, helped Japan cover up some horrendous war-crimes, including cruel biological experiments on prisoners of war. He argues that in the same vein the U.S. government may also have kept secret much of what it knew about Japan's nuclear program.

"Make no mistake," he writes, "Japan would have used the bomb without hesitation or compunction" had it successfully produced one. The Japanese leaders and their scientists "were committed to creating such a device" at a moment when they and other nations "raced against each other and time to make history's first nuclear weapon. They failed but they were closer to success than history has given them credit for."

Wilcox makes a case that Japan successfully detonated an atomic device close to what was then called Konan, Korea, on or about August 12, 1945, which is to say six days after Hiroshima was bombed on August 6, killing over 90,000 civilians, and three days after the Nagasaki bomb that killed at least 40,000 people on August 9. Japan's decision to accept unconditional surrender on August 15, according to Wilcox, came after its own test and, perhaps, the realization that it was too late to respond in kind.

In 1991, William Chapman, a former Washington Post Tokyo Bureau Chief, in his book, Inventing Japan, noted that post-war education here ensured that most people knew little about the suffering of others under Japanese rule.

"For the average Japanese, Japanese atrocities were the rumors of war . . . . The atomic bombings of Hiroshima and Nagasaki, the incendiary raids on [Japanese] cities, these were indisputable . . . . The war made sense only if Japan were a victim, and that is how a great many people remembered it."

Those observations are even more true now. The current administration of Prime Minister Shinzo Abe, backed by a strong Shinto cult and right-wing lobby, Nippon Kaigi, has made tremendous efforts to erase memories of Japanese war crimes, or flatly deny them. (This desire to hide the past is likely the driving force behind the current trade war with Korea, which comes after Korea's Supreme Court ordered Japanese firms to pay added compensation to former Korean slave laborers.)

There are many here who still have no idea Japan was building its own atomic bomb—and almost succeeded—but was too late. The United States was almost too late learning that fact as well.

The U.S. likely became aware that Japan was attempting to develop an atomic weapon by early 1945, and was caught off guard.

In February 1945, the OSS (the predecessor to the CIA) circulated a report about "stories" of "an atomic discharge to be used against [Allied] aircraft."

A few months later, allied intelligence sources filed a report about a scientist rising to speak to the Japanese House of Peers [the parliament of Japan at the time] and announcing "he is succeeding in his research for a thing so powerful that it would require very little potential energy to destroy an enemy fleet within a few moments." It was clear to those who knew about such things, that the scientist must have been speaking of an atomic bomb. So, when a large Nazi submarine was captured in May of 1945 that was supposed to be carrying a half a ton of uranium to Japan, the U.S. was greatly alarmed.

After the war ended, intelligence officials learned that the Japanese military, just prior to their surrender, had actually developed and successfully test-fired an atomic device. The project had been housed in or near Konan (the Japanese name for Hungnam), on the coast in the northern part of the peninsula.

To make matters worse, by the end of 1945 the Soviets—who did not yet have an atomic bomb—had occupied much of Korea north of the 38th parallel and the plant where the Japanese atom bomb had been developed was under their control.

In the summer of 1946, David Snell, an agent with the 24th Criminal Investigation Detachment in Korea, who had been discharged from service, wrote about it publicly in the *Atlanta Constitution*. He had interviewed a Japanese officer on his way home from Korea who said he had been in charge of security for the atom bomb project. The name used for the source was an alias. You can read the original dispatch and related dispatches here. Snell wrote:

Japan developed and successfully tested an atomic bomb three days prior to the end of the war . . . . .She destroyed unfinished atomic bombs, secret papers and her atomic bomb plans only hours before the advance units of the Russian Army moved into Konan, Korea, site of the project.

Japanese scientists who developed the bomb are now in Moscow, prisoners of the Russians. They were tortured by their captors seeking atomic "know-how." The Korean project was staffed by about 40,000 Japanese workers, of whom approximately 25,000 were trained engineers and scientists. The organization of the plant was set up so that the workers were restricted to their areas. The inner sanctum of the plant was deep in a cave. Here only 400 specialists worked.

The article summarizes the tactical and strategic goals of the project:

When task forces and invasion spearheads brought the war ever closer to the Japanese mainland, the Japanese Navy undertook the production of the atomic bomb as defense against amphibious operations. Atomic bombs were to be flown against Allied ships in Kamikaze suicide planes.

Since the Soviets did not explode their own device until 1949, it is unclear how much they knew about the Japanese research efforts, in fact, and how useful the intelligence was, or was not. David Holloway, in his scholarly tome Stalin and the Bomb, does not mention the

Japanese nuclear program. Much of the Russian research was based on information stolen from the Manhattan Project in the United States.

But in his book, Wilcox sets out to substantiate much of the 1946 scoop and add much more detail.

Japan had been considering an atomic bomb from early in the war and research had taken place in the late 1930s. The original plan was to detonate an atomic bomb in the continental United States. Circa late 1942 or early 1943, Premier Hideki Tojo called Minister of War Gen. Toranosuke Kawashima to his office. He told him, "The atomic bomb projects of the U.S. and Germany are progressing. If we are behind, we will lose the war. You start to make it."

Japanese scientists had a good knowledge of atomic theory, and they knew they needed massive amounts of uranium. The plan to make an atomic bomb began in earnest, and scientists all across the Japanese empire began working on the project, especially at the Korean complex, where there was a wealth of hydroelectric power and possibly uranium deposits. The Korean site became the Los Alamos of Japan's Manhattan Project as Japan began searching for uranium all over its empire before, finally, turning to its Nazi allies. They had a source for it in Czechoslovakia.

There are moments of dark comedy in the book as it describes Japan's attempts to get enough uranium from its German allies. Yasukazu Kigoshi, technical specialist and embassy attaché with the Japanese contingent in Berlin, said at first the German Ministry of Economics was uncooperative.

In his interview with Wilcox, Kigoshi recalled, "So because of my nature, I got very angry and I sent a telegram to the German government by myself. I told them, 'The reason we need pitchblende [uranium ore] is for the development of atomic power. We are now under the Tripartite Pact [the Axis agreement] and we are both fighting against America and England. So what is going on here that you don't want to cooperate?' Either my telegram was good or Oshima [the official] talked to Hitler directly . . . . They answered that they would give us two tons."

Toward the end of the war, as Nazi Germany fell apart, a German submarine was dispatched to Japan with two Japanese officers on board and 1,234.59 pounds of uranium oxide for the Japanese military—which if successfully enriched would be enough to make one atom bomb. During the expedition, Germany was defeated and Hitler committed suicide. Less than a week later the ship surrendered to Allied forces on May 14, 1945, roughly 500 miles from Cape Race, Newfoundland. The discovery of the uranium sent off shock-waves.

J. Robert Oppenheimer, the father of the American atomic bomb, is said to have personally come to inspect the cargo. It was requisitioned for the Manhattan Project.

Wilcox notes the "irony" is that uranium bound for Japan's atomic bombs may have "helped bring atomic devastation to Japan" with the bombing of Hiroshima and Nagasaki in August that same year.

Yoshiaki Yano, who translated the Wilcox book, was formerly a major general in Japan's Self-Defense Forces and is a noted expert on nuclear deterrents, explains the reasons are more complex.

"The first and second editions were both deemed possibly fabricated for lack of evidence," Yano told The Daily Beast. "That made things easier for the scientists involved in the development, the industry, and the allies . . . for Japan to position itself as a nation that was just a victim of nuclear weapons and incapable of possessing these powers itself. The Japanese, especially in the academic world, the media and the education industry took it upon themselves to follow through on this and collectively worked to conceal this part of history and ignore the facts presented in this book."

Yano also is convinced that the work left behind by Japanese scientists helped create North Korea's nuclear program as detailed in the book. He is also of the opinion that Japan should have its own nuclear weapons for defense.

"It's clear that the United States, the Soviet Union, North Korea and China and the Chinese Nationalist Party all must have known the truth about Japan's nuclear weapons, but have hidden it through and through along with the fact that they have intercepted Japan's work in the past. The father of North Korea's nuclear program is very closely connected to Japan. The irony is that Japan is now being threatened by China, Russia and North Korea's nuclear powers."

Yano sees the publication of the book as a positive thing.

"The Japanese people and especially the people running this nation should know that Japan has a high potential ability to possess nuclear arms and that [we] do not need to be scared of the nuclear threats."

He adds, "Japan possesses an independent power of nuclear deterrence. It should strive towards independence in its national defense while actively sharing the management and stabilization of international society."

In the end, the takeaway from *Japan's Secret War* isn't that the bombing of Hiroshima was justified because the Japanese would have bombed the United States first if they had been faster. The real lesson is that Japan was one more nation that came very close to creating a viable nuclear weapons program, and like Dr. Frankenstein, may have helped create its own monster.

Wilcox calls for further study of Japan's atomic bomb history and into the reasons the U.S. government still keeps many of the materials classified. The Japanese destroyed much of the research related to their weapons programs at the close of the war, but new evidence continues to be found. Certainly, more study would be merited.

There are lessons to be learned from the tragedies of war, but in order to learn them you have to accept history as it is, not as you would like it to be. And in modern Japan revisionist leaders like Prime Minister Shinzo Abe are more concerned about rewriting history than learning from it. That is also tragic.[123]

---

123 https://www.thedailybeast.com/in-world-war-ii-what-if-japan-got-the-atomic-bomb-first/. Copyrighted 2019. The Daily Beast Company LLC.

USS LARDNER

During a visit with Dad in 2006, he gave me a small red photo album my Uncle Reinier had sent him a few years earlier. He thought I should have Reinier's letter and the photos inside. In reading the letter, I learned that Reinier had searched for the captain and crew of the USS *Lardner* so that he could thank them personally.

> *"Jim Meadow's name, address, and phone number were found on the Internet by Annie, a daughter of his old friend and colleague, David Whitener, when she searched for any information on the USS Lardner, the only name I could remember. When I called Mr. Meadows and told him that I wanted to personally thank Captain James Boyd, he mentioned the upcoming reunion in St. Louis 15-17 Sept 2003. I asked whether I could attend. He replied that I could not attend but that I would be ordered by the captain to do so and be made an honorary member of the USS Lardner crew for the duration of the reunion. I also told him that as a 91/2 year old, I had taken some of the captain's service ribbons from his cabin, and that I would like, in return, to give the only one I earned as an airman in the U.S. Air Force in 1959, a Good Conduct Medal. Mr. Meadows suggested that I should find and give the captain a Naval Good Conduct Medal and Ribbon which only an enlisted person can earn. So Captain Boyd is the only U.S. Naval Officer to be given a Good Conduct Medal by an Ex USAF enlisted man.*
>
> *In my first conversation with Captain Boyd, in March 2003, I thanked him for rescuing our family. I also thanked him for graciously providing his personal cabin for my mother and me, he replied, "It was an honor to help bring you home."*

Captain Boyd and his family founded California Agriboard[124] in 1996 to manufacture a new product, medium density fibre-board, made from waste rice straw. He and his daughter help manage this enterprise in Willows, California in partnership with the Sumitomo Corporation of Japan.

Ironically, Sumitomo was responsible in 1943 for our captivity with four other Dutch Radio engineer families in Tokyo. Sumitomo also kept us alive. During the firebombing of Tokyo, we were evacuated to a small Buddhist temple Kotakuji, near Nagoya, guarded by Kempeitai, the Japanese secret police. After the Japanese Surrender, U.S. Marines rescued us from Nagoya and took us by landing craft to a U.S. Naval Hospital ship and from there to the USS Lardner for the voyage to Tokyo. General George MacArthur ordered all surviving POWs be brought to Tokyo to be present at the signing of the Japanese Unconditional Surrender aboard the U.S. Navy Battleship USS Missouri. We arrived after the signing ceremonies and saw the USS Missouri in full dress regalia, with all flags flying.

Mr. Lawrence R. Hendricks, Chief Commissary Steward remembered personally lifting the rescued Dutch Children onboard the USS Lardner.

This history of captive, captor, liberator, and universal human kindness is indelibly remembered.

—Reiner G. Hasenstab, Seattle Washington, USA, December 2003

My uncle gave each crew member a blue envelope with a personal note of thanks and appreciation, and also enclosed a folded origami

---

124 https://onlinelibrary.wiley.com/doi/pdf/10.1162/108819803323059497

peace crane. Ron Hosmer, son of crew member Felix Hosmer, gave Reinier the USS *Lardner* Reunion Memorial Plaque as he was made an honorary crew member. Ron had each one made in honor of each attending crew member.

Reinier mentioned the following attending captain and crew: Captain James Boyd; Jim Meadows, Torpedo Officer; Lawrence Hendricks, Chief Commissary Steward (in charge of all food preparation on the *Lardner*; Kevin Hendricks, son of Lawrence, who compiled a comprehensive written and illustrated history of the USS Lardner, which included his father's detailed memoirs of his service onboard from 1942-1946; Felix Hosmer; Ron Hosmer (son of Felix; Executive Officer, 1st Lieutenant Mike Wanty.

Some of the crew of the *USS Lardner*.
(Captain Boyd seated center, bottom row)

Books and Links

Books

Hans Hasen. Davis' Handbook of Applied Hydraulics, 4th Edition, McGraw-Hill, Inc., 1993 Co-Editor;

Hans Hasen. "Guri Power Complex-Design", Co-Author, American Power Conference, Apr. 1979;

Hans Hasen. "Raising Guri Dam", Co-Author, International Commission on Large Dams, 1997;

Hans Hasen. "Lopez Angostura Power Tunnel", Co-Author, American Society of Civil Engineers, 1987.

LINKS

The writers walk, Sydney, Australia
https://monumentaustralia.org.au/themes/culture/community/
display/94161-sydney-writers-walk-

How Many People Died in Hiroshima and Nagasaki? :
https://www.newsweek.com/how-many-people-died-hiroshima-naga-
saki-japan-second-world-war-1522276

The bombings:
https://atomicbombmuseum.org/2_manhattan.shtml

Java Occupation and Bersiap
https://www.indischekamparchieven.nl/en/occupation-and-bersiap/
by-region/java

"The more than 30,000 Dutch, Indo-European, Australian, British and American POWs in West Java were initially assembled in large
camps in Tasikmalaja, Leles, Garut, Sukabumi, Bandung, Tjimahi, and
Batavia.

The assembly camp in Sukabumi, centrally situated in West Java,
was gradually evacuated to camps in Tjimahi in May and June 1942.
The POWs in the assembly camps in Garut, Leles, and Tasikmalaja, all
located in the eastern part of West Java, were transferred to Tjimahi,
Bandung, Batavia, and Surabaya in July 1942. In the course of 1942
and 1943 POWs from Central and East Java were also brought to
Tjimahi, Bandung and Batavia.

The large POW camps in Tjimahi were the military barracks of the 4th and 9th Battalion Infantry, Mountain Artillery, the 6th Depot Battalion and the Train camp. In addition, in the area surrounding Tjima two labour camps were established on farms in Leuwigadjah and Tjimindi. In Bandung the prisoners were concentrated in the encampments of the 15th Infantry Battalion, the 1st Depot Battalion, and the Anti-aircraft Artillery."
https://en.wikipedia.org/wiki/Netherlands_in_World_War_II#/media/File:73-Japanse_kampen_in_Nederlands-Indi%C3%AB.jpg

The NSB rally in Amsterdam where Seyss-Inquart and Mussert spoke about the necessity of invading the Soviet Union, 27 June 1941 (Photo): https://en.wikipedia.org/wiki/Netherlands_in_World_War_II#/media/File:Demonstratie_Mussert_en_Seyss-Inquart_-_Fotodienst_der_NSB_-_NIOD_-_76333.jpeg

Kotakuji Temple:
https://www.google.com/maps/place/Kotakuji/@35.1540569,137.2267731,88m/data=!3m1!1e3!4m6!3m5!1s0x600359105e725ff1:0x90f0030187648 1ad!8m2!3d35.1538359!4c137.2271261!16s%2Fg%2F11rxqd_7pg

Haiku on a Plum Tree (2016) trailer:
https://vimeo.com/189303626

Mujah Maraini-Melehi, filmmaker:
https://www.haikuonaplumtree.com/

Raigo Painting:

https://en.wikipedia.org/wiki/Raig%C5%8D#:~:text=The%20 belief%20of%20the%20Western,person%20who%20is%20near%20 death.

https://www.metmuseum.org/art/collection/search/45249

Edo Period:

https://www.history.com/topics/asian-history/meiji-restoration

Malabar's 100 anniversary celebration May 5, 1923:

https://radioclublimburg.nl/mk/

A picture of the wires strung by my Grandpa at Malabar.

Krytron information:

https://en.wikipedia.org/wiki/Krytron

Excerpted:

Krytrons and their variations are manufactured by Perkin-Elmer Components and used in a variety of industrial and military devices. They are best known for their use in igniting exploding-bridgewire and slapper detonators in nuclear weapons, their original application, either directly (sprytrons are usually used for this) or by triggering higher-power spark gap switches. They are also used to trigger thyratrons, large flashlamps in photocopiers, lasers and scientific apparatus, and for firing ignitors for industrial explosives.

Because of their potential for use as triggers of nuclear weapons, the export of krytrons is tightly regulated in the United States. A number of cases involving the smuggling or attempted smuggling of krytrons have been reported, as countries seeking to develop nuclear weapons have attempted to procure supplies of krytrons for igniting their weapons. One prominent case was that of Richard Kelly Smyth, who allegedly helped Arnon Milchan smuggle 15 orders of 810 krytrons total to Israel in the early 1980s. 469 of these were returned to the United States, with Israel claiming the remaining 341 were "destroyed in testing." Krytrons and sprytrons handling voltages of 2,500 V and above, currents of 100 A and above, and switching delays of under 10 microseconds are typically suitable for nuclear weapon triggers.

New Evidence of Japan's effort to build atom bomb at the end of WWII
https://www.latimes.com/world/asia/la-fg-japan-bomb-20150805-story.html

What if, in WWII, Japan got the atomic bomb first?
https://www.thedailybeast.com/in-world-war-ii-what-if-japan-got-the-atomic-bomb-first/

ACKNOWLEDGEMENTS

Many people all over the world supported Dad and I while writing *Dear Laura*. The long list of everyone who touched our hearts and changed our lives would be a book in itself. I'll attempt to list as many here as space allows. Dad and I have treasured and I still treasure everyone's love and encouragement. I thank God every day for the incredible walk we take together. I thank Dad for answering my questions and Mom for her constant joy. I thank the stranger who gave me the powerful prayer, I wish I knew her name. I also thank my gracious family, and extended family who gave Dad and I the time and space to create this story the way Dad wanted, while also honoring my creative process.

To my precious daughters Candice and Margaux. Thank you for the patience you had with me during these years to research and find my answers in the world. I know it wasn't easy on you and I love you for your grace and support. Thank you for all the fun times we've had around the world and at home. What a blessing it is to see you grow and thrive and live life to the full. To my grandchildren, Algernon and Reinier, your pure joy and hugs light up my life in ways I never knew possible. I love our time together. To my son-in-law, David, for wanting to go to Japan with me some day to visit the temple. Thank you,

Candice, for reading a draft of this book, and giving me your amazing feedback, and wanting to go to Japan with me too. Here's to many more years of spontaneous fun in the sun and in the snow.

Suzy, your unwavering love, support, and laughter is one of the biggest blessings of my life. Rachel, Emily June, and Katie thank you for being such bright lights and for all the good times we've shared. Mike, thanks for helping me ask the first question that started this adventure. Susie, thank you for your kind words of encouragement when I needed them most. Alex and Maidea, your love is a joy to behold. Mark, no matter what was going on you gave me wisdom and lots of laughs when I needed them most. Suzy, Mike, and Mark thank you for all the fun over the years, especially the birthday surprises. Thank you to Vincent Huml and Sue Viders for your encouragement and advice.

To Reinier and David for being supportive and patient with my questions. Reinier, thank you for the time we shared during our conversations about Dad and the family over the years, particularly while I was at sea on *Blue Moon*. David, your perspectives have encouraged me, especially your help in locating the site of the temple. To Trevina, Alex, and Sasha for all the fun get togethers. To Michael for your understanding and for generously offering your home in Sonoma for me to seek solace and have fun at a time when I needed it the most. To MaryAnn and the boys for all your hospitality.

To Ineke Van Der Wal and Seline Hofker for your wonderful books and for your pivotal help in getting to the heart of Dad's story and my own.

To all my friends who became like family along the way—especially the Cocos Locos, Bill Van Eck, Lucy, Helena, Bernard, Derek, Hannah, Tim, Sukio, Saiopel, Ru, Kathy and the Global Dental Relief team in Kathmandu. The strangers who pulled me out of the ditch after my bike accident in Bali. My hairdresser in Los Angeles and his wife and for her wonderful family who so graciously hosted me in Bandung. Special thanks to Adeline, Christophé, Valentín, Camille, Joëlle, and François for the good times in Belgium that helped to heal my heart. To Tatiana and everyone at her pousada who gave me a home and watched over me in the months after Dad's death, allowing me to concentrate on writing, waterfalls, food, wine, and dancing the salsa. For the incredible trip to Brazil, especially to Iguaçu where Dad said his final goodbye in double rainbows.

To my supportive friends who helped me remember how to laugh and got me through—especially Katherine, Ronni, Marsha, and their mother Shirley (may she Rest In Peace); Edna and her family (Mark, Kai, and Luke), Dee and Micheal and their sweet family, Mary Jane and Steven, Stephanie and her family for watching over Amy and all the good times. Karen, Lizzy, and Laurel for all the good times (and hanging through the bad times) from high school until now. Everyone at Calvary Community Church in Thousand Oaks, CA, especially the women in the amazing Bible studies there, Pastor Shawn, Sharon, Laura, and MaryKay; and the members of Church of The Epiphany in Agoura Hills, CA. To Michelle Telfer for her inspirational sermons and for the wonderful afternoon spent in Agoura where she told me the story about the mud puddle. To all my friends from Twin Lakes Church in Aptos, especially Pastor René, Val, the incredible worship team, the 2017 Jordan mission team, and especially Miller, Jennifer, Jackie, Sherri, and Rachel for praying over me constantly. All the light workers in my life—especially Elena, LeAndra, Wayang, and the holy man.

To all my teachers and my teachers' teachers.

The kind people at the d'Omah in Yogyakarta. The town of Ubud, Bali, and everyone at the Ubud Writers and Readers Festival for providing the setting where I would connect the most important dots of Dad's story and for years of writing inspiration. Mpho Tutu and her father Desmond for writing *The Book of Forgiving* which helped me learn how to forgive and how forgiveness is a journey; and Desmond Tutu and the Dalai Lama for writing *The Book of Joy* which helped me heal from heartbreak. To John Eldgredge for writing *Beautiful Outlaw* which changed my life and taught me so much about the playful, extravagant, and outrageous nature of Jesus and what it means to truly follow Him. To the Holy Spirit's gentle nature and the special surprises that have and continue to take my breath away.

To my friends at the harbor and the boatyard, especially dearly departed Captain Joseph Rogers. Thanks for believing in this story. We told each other so many wonderful tales on the sea as we sailed *Tessa*. Thanks for reminding me to "always keep on smiling."

To my mentor, Tony, at Art Center College of Design and all my classmates there for helping me learn how to believe in myself again and for teaching me the true meaning of enthusiasm. To my mentor Glenn Benest who helped me learn the art of writing screenplays which helped give a structure to this story before I traveled the world. To Ashley, Makena, Kelly, and Emily at Merack Publishing for all the great work they have done in publishing this book and for their support, encouragement, and belief in this story. To Bradley Clark for his gorgeous illustrations. To Linda Langton for her gracious support and wisdom that helped to shape this book. To Marcia, my editor, thank you for wanting me to go deeper. To Mary Morrisey and her team at the Brave Thinking Institute for helping me to think bravely and act boldly. To Jake Adelstein and Richard Wilcox for their articles and books that have helped to fuel my quest when I was discouraged and for their graciousness in allowing me to use some of their material in this book.

Thank you to the U.S. Marines who saved my family and the American people who welcomed Dad as an immigrant to the United

States so that he could lead a wonderful life here making important contributions to better the lives of others as a citizen, hydroelectric engineer, civic leader, husband, father, and a man of faith.

To my husband, Jerry, who has been my champion and cherished me in ways I never knew possible. Thanks for all the adventures! Here's to many, many more. I love the way you always ask me, "What's next?" And to our sweet little Lucy, the best little girl in the whole wide world, who snuggled every word onto the page and will forever be waiting at the top of the stairs.

A SPECIAL NOTE:

The holy man and I met up again a year later, in 2015, on my second trip to Bali. I wanted to let him know that I had found happiness and thought I was on my way to finding my path. I also wanted him to know that he and Wayang would and will always have a special place in my heart. He and his wife were happy for me. It was good to see them again. But, after our reunion, he shared the sad news that Wayang had died in a traffic accident since I had last visited.

I stood in stunned silence trying to absorb the news. I asked about his wife and family. Wayang had young children. Being with the holy man without Wayang felt strange. The hollow feeling made me realize again how fleeting life is. How important it is to protect and cherish those precious people we love. I understood in new ways how doing anything less with those we love is unconscionable. Doing anything less is not love. Memories of my time spent with the holy man and Wayang became even more treasured. If I'd waited to visit Bali I might never have met Wayang. *What would my life have been like without their kindness, wisdom, and graciousness?*

www.ingramcontent.com/pod-product-compliance
Lightning Source LLC
Chambersburg PA
CBHW061129120626
46546CB00005B/1715